Multiple Identities

MULTIPLE IDENTITIES

MIGRANTS, ETHNICITY, AND MEMBERSHIP

EDITED BY PAUL SPICKARD

INDIANA UNIVERSITY PRESS   *Bloomington & Indianapolis*

This book is a publication of

INDIANA UNIVERSITY PRESS
Office of Scholarly Publishing
Herman B Wells Library 350
1320 East 10th Street
Bloomington, Indiana 47405 USA

iupress.indiana.edu

Telephone orders 800-842-6796
Fax orders 812-855-7931

Manufactured in the
United States of America

Library of Congress
Cataloging-in-Publication Data

Multiple identities : migrants,
ethnicity, and membership / edited
by Paul Spickard.
   p. cm.
   Includes bibliographical references
and index.
   ISBN 978-0-253-00804-6 (cloth : alk.
paper) – ISBN 978-0-253-00807-7 (pbk. :
alk. paper) – ISBN 978-0-253-00811-4
(electronic book) 1. Group identity
– Europe – Case studies. 2. Immigrants –
Europe – Case studies. 3. Minorities –
Europe – Case studies. I. Spickard,
Paul R., [date]
   HN373.5.M85 2013
   305.80094 – dc23

                                    2012046667

1 2 3 4 5 18 17 16 15 14 13

FOR JIM AND JEAN MORISHIMA

Contents

Acknowledgments

FIRST THANKS ARE DUE TO THE AUTHORS OF THE VARIOUS chapters that follow, for the excellence of their work, their patience as I have done the editing, and their suggestions for my chapters and the shape of the volume. Several of the chapters originated as contributions to a conference, "Generations in Flux," sponsored by the Finnish Society for the Study of Ethnic Relations and International Migration and the Finnish Youth Research Society, held at the University of Helsinki in October 2008. Heidi Villikka was the organizer of the conference. Viggo Vestel, Anna Martinez, Maia Nukari, Perpetual Crentsil, and Tiina Likki all took part with us in that conference and shared many good ideas.

At the time of that conference, I was teaching and doing research at the Westfälische Wilhelms-Universität Münster, in Germany. I am grateful to several people there who helped make this project successful, among them Marie-Theres Brands-Schwabe, who gave generous academic support, insight, and unfailing good humor; Carmen Fleischmann, who helped me with living arrangements; Judith Prinz and Lisa Schwabe, who were kind and efficient research assistants; and Mark Stein, who, as director of the Englisches Seminar, was my host and a genial intellectual companion. Special thanks go to Maria Diedrich for making it possible for me to be in Germany and for giving me a constant example of what a professor and colleague should be. She, as founding president, and our many smart and generous colleagues in the Collegium for African American Research started me down the road toward this project some fifteen years ago, for which inspiration I am grateful. I am also grateful to the Deutsche-Amerikanische Fulbright Kommission for financial support during my time in Germany.

Compiling and editing were largely accomplished at my home institution, the University of California, Santa Barbara. I am grateful for a timely sabbatical and an especially salubrious work environment in the UCSB History Department, as well as to colleagues in the university's three ethnic studies departments. Ken Hough gave unstintingly of his time and intelligence as a research assistant. UCSB's Identities Research Group and its leader, Cynthia Kaplan, encouraged my work on this subject and listened courteously to my ideas. Several UCSB history colleagues shared ideas and books with me, among them Harold Marcuse, John Lee, Adrienne Edgar, and Beth DePalma Digeser.

It will surprise no one who has worked with Bob Sloan at Indiana University Press that he was a model editor from start to finish: knowledgeable, incisive, enthusiastic, and patient; Bob, Angela Burton, Mary Lou Bertucci, and their colleagues made bringing this book into being an unusual pleasure. Jim Spickard, now as on several earlier projects, gave me ideas for avenues of research to chase down. Tuomas Martikainen sent frequent emails filled with leads. Taoufik Djebali and Patrick Miller have made innumerable contributions to my thinking about matters of race, ethnicity, migration, and membership, in Europe and elsewhere, over many years. Anna Martinez has served nearly all the functions listed above and, in addition, gave me all the other things that my life once lacked.

PART ONE

Orientations

ONE

Many Multiplicities: Identity in an Age of Movement

PAUL SPICKARD

THE FACE OF EUROPE IS CHANGING. PEOPLE WHO ARE NOT supposed to be there are there in abundance. Each nation of Europe has its own story, but each imagines itself as a naturally ethnically homogeneous place. Yet each contains large numbers of people who do not fit that ethnic self-definition. Some are migrants (see Table 1.1), some domestic minorities of long standing. Despite the fond wishes of some members of the dominant ethnic group in each country, the migrants are not going back where they came from. In many cases, they are already two or three generations resident in their European host country. The degree to which they have succeeded in making places for themselves in their host societies – and, conversely, the amount of discrimination they experience – varies widely.

Over the past several years, the peoples of most European nations and their leaders have engaged in sharp debates about migrants, less so about domestic minorities. Such discussions have focused on migrants as social problems, as people with deficits that need to be measured and remediated, and, all too often, as people who ought to go away. The discussions have in most cases missed who the migrants and minorities are, how they live their lives, and what the content of their identities may be. Simply put, policy makers and the educated public in Europe need to know more about migrants and minorities, how they conceive of themselves, and how they actually live their lives.

The scholars who wrote this book are all students of the lived experiences of migrants and minorities in Europe. It turns out that migrants and minority group members have complex identities, often multiple identities at one time, and that those identities shift and change over the course of time and changing circumstance. This book is about how those migrants and minorities experience their lives and manage their multiple identities. It addresses the situations of migrants and minorities in some powerful European nations like Germany and the United Kingdom and also in Finland, Sweden, Poland, Italy, Switzerland, and Kazakhstan. It looks at minorities who have received a lot of attention, like Turkish Germans, and also at some who have received little notice, such as Kashubians and Tatars in Poland and Chinese in Switzerland. It explores the lives and social locations of children, young adults, and mature people. It examines international adoption and cross-cultural love. Finally, it describes a few situations that may provide models for multicultural success.

MIGRANTS AND MINORITIES:

A PROBLEM FOR EUROPEANS

Every modern European nation is founded on an idea of ethnic homogeneity that is thought to reach deep into its past. The idea can be summed easily in this equation:

One Nation = One Ethnic Group
= One Religion
= One Language
= One Territory
= One Government

This is the way it is supposed to be. For most Europeans, as for scholars who study nationalism, it is taken for granted that each nation is founded on a single ethnic group – a specific people from a specific place, with a shared history, language, and ancestry.[1] For many such people, like the Czech philosopher Ernest Gellner, multiethnic states are conceptually incoherent and inherently unstable. Such people see an intimate connection between the formation of particular ethnic groups and particular nations. In the words of the British sociologist Anthony D. Smith, "modern nations – a fusion of premodern ethnic identities and modern 'civic' elements – require the symbols, myths and memories of

Table 1.1. Immigrants as Percentage of 2010 Population, Europe

Luxembourg	35.2
Switzerland	23.2
Ireland	19.6
Croatia	15.9
Austria	15.6
Latvia	15.0
Spain	14.1
Sweden	14.1
Estonia	13.6
Ukraine	11.6
Iceland	11.3
France	10.7
Netherlands	10.5
United Kingdom	10.4
Greece	10.1
Norway	10.0
Belgium	9.1
Denmark	8.8
Russia	8.7
Portugal	8.6
Slovenia	8.1
Italy	7.4
Montenegro	6.8
Serbia	5.3
Czech Republic	4.4
Finland	4.2
Lithuania	4.0
Hungary	3.7
Slovakia	2.4
Poland	2.2

Sources: United Nations, Department of Economic and Social Affairs, "Trends in International Migrant Stock: Migrants by Age and Sex," country profiles, http://esa.un.org/MigAge/p2k0data.asp, retrieved October 21, 2011. See also United Nations, Department of Economic and Social Affairs, Population Division, "International Migration 2006" (March 2006); Apolonija Oblak Flander, "Immigration to EU Member States down by 6% and emigration up by 13% in 2008," Eurostat: Statistics in Focus. Population and Social Conditions, 1/2011, http://epp.eurostat.ec.europa.eu/cache/ITY_OFFPUB/KS-SF-11-001/EN/KS-SF-11-001-EN.PDF, last accessed October 21, 2011; Katya Vasileva, "Foreigners living in the EU are diverse and largely younger than the nationals of the EU Member States," Eurostat: Statistics in Focus. Population and Social Conditions, 45/2010, http://epp.eurostat.ec.europa.eu/cache/ITY_OFFPUB/KS-SF-10-045/EN/KS-SF-10-045-EN.PDF, retrieved October 21, 2011; and "Migration and migrant population statistics," Eurostat: Statistics Explained, http://epp.eurostat.ec.europa.eu/statistics_explained/index.php/Migration_and_migrant_population_statistics, last accessed October 21, 2011.

ethnic cores if they are to generate a sense of solidarity and purpose. ... there is ... [an] inner 'antiquity' of many modern nations." The essence of nationalism is the assumption of the existence of a founding race.[2]

These are powerful ideas. They have attended the making of every modern nation, and they lie at the root of many ethnic groups' yearnings for nation-states of their own.[3] For Germans, the racial or ethnic foundation of the nation is an idea – which can be found in the writings

of J. G. Herder, J. G. Fichte, Friedrich Nietzsche, and Arthur Schopenhauer, as well as in the soaring imagination of Richard Wagner – that
the German *Volk* were a mystical entity that existed in germ form many
centuries prior to the predestined establishment of a German state. In
this construction, all people who speak some language that may be called
Germanic are necessarily Germans (no matter that they live in the Czech
Republic or Ukraine), and all people who stand outside that historical,
spiritual (dare one say biological?) essence are not true Germans and
cannot become Germans. Never mind that a state called *Germany* did
not exist throughout most of human history, nor that a very substantial
portion of the supposedly Germanic peoples have never been part of
that polity, nor indeed that the population of German territory always
included many non-Germanic peoples. The Germanic-speaking peoples
are supposed to be its grounding, and wherever they are, they are natural
Germans, while others are not, even if they live within German borders
and carry German passports.[4]

We can see the artificial (though undeniably powerful) quality of
nationalism alive in the history of every modern state. Throughout the
Middle Ages, there was, of course, a political entity called *France,* but the
affiliation of people in outlying provinces like Aquitaine or Burgundy
was often nominal at best. Then, at the dawn of the modern era, Kings
Henry IV and Louis XIII unified the state, centralized control with a
modern bureaucracy loyal to the king rather than the nobility, drew a
corps of bureaucrats from the rising middle class, built a large standing
army that was loyal to its king rather than to feudal lords, imposed the
Parisian dialect (more or less) on the rest of the country, and created a
unified (and largely fictional) ethnic history for modern France. The
rhetoric of French citizenship changed radically with the revolution, but
the idea of the ethnic origin of France never wavered.[5]

In Turkey, in the wake of World War I and the decline of the Ottoman Empire, an Ottoman elite defined by class and religion shaped
themselves and the people around them into a nation defined by a mostly
fictional ethnicity they created: the Turks. They imposed a centralized
language and created a fictional history that told a tale of long-standing
ethnic and national unity for the Turkish people in Anatolia, as one of
the grounds for their nation-building enterprise.[6]

Among the Kurds of modern Iraq and Turkey, it is widely assumed that they, who have never in modern history had a state of their own, are ethnically qualified – in fact, destined – to govern themselves in an ethnically homogeneous Kurdish state. Similar claims have been made in recent decades by Basques in Spain and France, by Hawaiians, Timorese, Biafrans, Kosovars, Sikhs, and many others.[7]

So ethnic commonality is widely assumed to be the ground upon which the modern nation-state is built. Yet every European country is today in fact home to a variety of peoples who are not part of that unifying imagined history. In Germany, France, and Denmark today, about 20 percent of the people are either immigrants or their children. In Sweden and Ireland, immigrants and their children make up a quarter of the population. In Austria and Switzerland, the percentage tops 30.[8] This is largely due to the increasing scope and velocity of late twentieth- and early twenty-first-century people movements. But the reader should not suppose that international migration is a new thing, or that it was until recently directed only to places like Australia, Canada, and the United States. Since the dawn of the industrial age, workers have been moving all over the northwestern quarter of the Eurasian land mass: from Ireland and Scotland to England and then beyond; from southern Italy to the industrial North, and some then on to France and Germany, others to the Americas; from Poland into Germany and Russia; back and forth throughout the Austro-Hungarian Empire, and then on to other points in Europe and the Americas; and so on.[9]

Every European country faces a deep demographic dilemma that strikes at the core of its national identity. I do not know if demography is destiny, but you could make a good case that it may be so in Europe these days. The problem is that Europeans are insufficiently fecund. In order to maintain a stable population without taking in immigrants, each country must average 2.1 children born per woman. Every European nation falls below that replacement level. France has the highest fertility rate in Europe at 1.98; Italy and Spain stand at 1.31; the Czech Republic is lowest at 1.24. Recognizing this problem, several European governments have offered incentives to their citizens who give birth – sometimes in the form of extended, paid maternity leave and sometimes as a grant (ranging as high as $4,000 in Spain) for each child born. But even such extreme inducements have failed to nudge the birthrate upwards significantly.[10]

The bottom line is that every European nation must take in immigrants, most of them quite different racially and culturally from the current citizenry, in order for its economy to survive, now and as far into the future as anyone can see. The problem is that no European country has developed a language to talk about, or institutions to accommodate, this phenomenon.[11] Several countries have taken up the issue over the past decade, but none has yet met success in the attempt to understand this manifest multiplicity.

The European response to the election of Barack Obama to the United States presidency provided a snapshot of the problem of integrating multiple peoples into supposedly homogeneous nations. Europeans were wildly enthusiastic in the wake of the 2008 American election.[12] Witness these headlines that covered the front pages of European newspapers on November 6: *Die Welt* said, "Obama schreibt Geschichte" – Obama writes history. *Neue Ruhr Zeitung* added, "Willkommen, neues Amerika!" (Welcome, new America!). *The Guardian* of England echoed, "Obama's new America." *De Volkskrant* of the Netherlands declared, "With Obama cynicism is past." *Bild* chanted, "YES, WE CAN Freunde sein!" (Yes we can be friends!). *Berliner Kurier* simply showed a picture of Barack Obama, tall, thin, and agile against a black background, with the legend "Daddy Cool!" The weekly newsmagazines also were in love with Obama: *Paris Match* devoted forty pages of pictures to its cover story: "Historique Barack Obama au sommet du monde" (historic Obama stands atop the world). *Der Spiegel,* also in a cover story, declared Obama "Der Weltpräsident" (the president of the world).

Only the *International Herald Tribune,* an American newspaper published abroad, sounded a note of caution, in the form of a comparative question. The week following the election, on November 12, its headline read, "Can Europe produce an Obama?" The paper did not mean a brilliant leader, a charismatic man with good judgment and broad vision, with intellect, a feel for the common people, and an uncanny knack for building coalitions – nor even a phenomenally lucky politician.[13] It meant someone Black, a member of a racialized minority. They asked: Could any European nation elect a member of a minority group as its top official? Can a member of a racialized minority be a full member of any European society at the highest level?

The answer seems to be "no." Italy had a blithely racist prime minister in Silvio Berlusconi, and he remains insanely popular despite failures and corruptions on many fronts. There is only one Black member in the Italian Parliament. Italy has only about 4.5 million immigrants (about 7 percent of the population, a low figure compared to other countries in Europe), and one of the lowest birthrates on the Continent – hence, the great need for immigrants. And some Italian towns and businesses have welcomed them.[14]

But most have not. In recent years, tens of thousands of Balkan and African migrants have tried to enter Italy, but they have not been received warmly. Italian authorities have pushed boats of immigrants back into the sea and deported those who reached shore. Muslims are regularly discriminated against on the job, in stores, and on the streets of Italian cities.[15] There is a good deal of overt race-mongering in Italian politics, particularly on the part of the Northern League, one of Berlusconi's coalition partners.[16] Various localities have tried to close kebab shops, banned burqas, and forced noncitizens to sit in segregated sections on buses. The Italian government has singled out Gypsies for deportation. African-descended people suffer regular abuse and even murder on Italian streets. Northern Italians direct racialized rhetoric against even their Neapolitan and Sicilian fellow Italians and threaten to secede from the country.[17]

Of all the European nations, Britain has done the most to integrate multiple peoples into its citizenry, most often under a banner that might read, "the Empire has come home." Chicken tikka masala is the national dish and can be found on the menu of nearly every pub across the archipelago. Most Britons do not have a serious problem with Sikh men wearing turbans on London streets, nor with Muslim girls wearing headscarves in classrooms. But politics is another matter: there are barely over a dozen people of color out of 646 members in the House of Commons. And in an era devastated by a troubled economy, White, non-Muslim, native-born Britons have begun to express doubt and fear about immigrants generally, and Middle Eastern–descended Britons especially.[18]

In 2005, in the wake of bombings on London streets and subways, British police saw a brown man walk out of his apartment building. They chased him into the subway, knocked him down, put a gun to the back of his neck, and shot him several times. It turned out that he was a Brazilian electrician, Jean Charles de Menezes, not the Muslim terrorist they imagined him to be, but they did not take the time to find out. A court absolved the officers of any wrongdoing, and no one pointed to the racial nature of their selection of him for execution.[19]

Germany has an all-White, almost all-ethnic German Bundestag, despite the fact that one in five German residents lives in an immigrant household. Cem Özdemir, the best-known Turkish German politician, was born in Swabia, serves as a legislator in the European Union parliament, flaunts his idiomatic Swabian dialect, and has sometimes been called "the German Obama." In 2008, he was named cohead of the Green Party, yet he could not get on the Green Party ballot for a Bundestag seat. According to Turkish German writer Mely Kiyak, Germans love Obama, "but we don't have minorities anywhere, not in media, in politics, in the executive or the judiciary." The conservative government of the Christian Democratic Union (CDU) tried to make history in 2010 by appointing a Hamburg-born Turkish German, Aygül Özkan, to a minor ministerial post in Lower Saxony. Within days, she had provoked howls of protests from other CDU politicians and the Right-leaning press.[20]

Germany only grudgingly and recently allowed a tortured pathway to citizenship for German-born descendants of Turkish immigrants. At the same time, anyone who can claim a vague ancestral connection to a mythical Greater Germany can obtain German citizenship easily. This has included, for instance, Volga Germans, whose ancestors moved to the Ukraine centuries before there was a German state and who may not have originated within the boundaries of modern Germany at all.[21] It was even easier for Chris Kaman, an American professional basketball player who was granted German citizenship and a spot on the 2008 German Olympic team, without speaking any German or ever having gone to Germany.[22]

In a sharp break with a monoethnic past, Germany's 2010 World Cup team was made up nearly half by players who were immigrants themselves or the sons of at least one immigrant parent. Some among the German public celebrated that diversity, but there was also a right-wing reaction. The web site *Deutscher Standpunkt* complained, "The squad is not a German national team and those people with dark complexions are the Federal Republic of Germany, but they are not Germany. Not tall and blond, but black, brown, puny and Muslim. . . . These new Federal Republic citizens are and will remain foreigners."[23]

In 2004, the people of Ireland, alarmed over large numbers of Polish and Chinese immigrants in their midst, voted to amend their constitution's citizenship clause. Henceforth, Ireland would reckon citizenship primarily by *jus sanguinis* rather than *jus soli,* and one could become naturalized only if one married an Irish citizen or was descended from one.[24]

France initially went crazy for Obama. Yet the government of Nicolas Sarkozy offered only token inclusion for French citizens of Arab or African descent. Many of my Gallic French friends say that there is no racism in France, outside of fringe groups like Jean-Marie le Pen's Front National, because French citizens are all equal.[25] Nonsense. The unemployment rate in the mostly North African *banlieues* around Paris does not *just happen* to be several times higher than for the general population. Race is a major factor. Muslims and Africans face bias in the workplace. Elite schools discriminate against them. Studies show bias and racial profiling on the part of Paris police directed against Arabs and Blacks. Although Muslims make up 10 percent of the French population, they are more than half the country's prison inmates.[26]

Public discourse targets immigrants as irrevocably un-French. In 2006, the National Assembly passed a bill clamping down on immigration by unskilled workers. A year later, it passed another bill, authorizing compulsory DNA testing for would-be immigrants. The center-right government of President Nicolas Sarkozy sought to expel immigrants and force them to take French language and culture tests.[27] Most French citizens oppose letting Muslim women wear headgear appropriate to their faith. In 2004, the government forbade Muslim schoolgirls to wear headscarves. In 2010, it passed a ban on the burqa, or full-body covering, anywhere in public within France's borders.[28] The Sarkozy government that same year launched a deportation campaign that sent hundreds of Roma – European Union citizens all – out of the country, until the EU forced it to desist.[29] This last was hardly an isolated incident. Roma are probably the most despised, segregated, impoverished, and abused segment of the population in countries throughout Europe.[30]

Sometimes, violence is the result. Vandals desecrated the graves of hundreds of Muslim French soldiers in 2008, and someone repeated the indignity two years later. The first French prefect who was both foreign born and a Muslim, Aissa Dermouche, survived three sophisticated bomb attacks in 2003 and 2004.[31] During the Sarkozy campaign to ban the burqa, a retired schoolteacher attacked a veiled Muslim tourist in a Paris shop, biting, punching, and scratching her.[32] In fall 2005, weeks of rioting took place in slum suburbs of Paris, where North African immigrants and their French-born children live and where a quarter of the men were without work. The French government (and even some Muslim citizens) said that race was not the issue. When more riots broke out in 2007, Sarkozy said, "What happened in Villiers-le-Bel [and other riot spots] has nothing to do with social crisis and everything to do with thugocracy."[33]

Yazid Sabeg, who was born in France to Algerian parents, saw the matter differently. In 2008, he wrote a manifesto that called for affirmative action policies and an end to France's policy of pretending to race blindness. The manifesto was endorsed by Carla Bruni-Sarkozy, the French president's second wife. Said Fouad Douai, a leader of Strasbourg's Muslim community, "There's great hypocrisy in French politics. People don't name things as they are. Every time they see a swarthy skin or a Muslim name, you're oppressed."[34]

IS RACE THE ISSUE?

I believe it is.[35] Many of my ethnic German friends, nice people all and smart to boot, seem to believe that there is little or no racism in Germany because they are nice people and the word *race* is more or less banned from public discussions. Their brown-skinned Muslim neighbors, in my interviews in recent years, completely disagree.[36] I recognize that Germany has an especially troubled history with race, and I respect the fact that German public discourse – government statements, school curricula, and polite society – has since the late 1940s dealt forthrightly with past problems in that area. I can understand how, given that background, they might be reluctant to bring out the R word again. But that does not mean that race is not an issue in Germany.

In 2009, I attended a conference at the University of Bielefeld that included some of the smartest, most thoughtful, and most interpersonally sensitive people I have met. There I laid out the ideas that appear in chapter 12 of this book. Along the way, I made the observation that a lot of Germans who come from immigrant families – especially those whose parents came from Turkey, West Africa, North Africa, or Asia – experience discrimination and humiliation frequently in German daily life. One of my listeners, a kind man who seemed genuinely surprised and hurt by my observation, said, "You're accusing us of being racists, of being the Ku Klux Klan."

I was not. But most ethnic Germans simply do not see immigrants as part of Germany; they do not perceive the German-born children of immigrants as Germans, either; and they are not aware of the daily slights that such people experience. Racialized discrimination is infinitely worse for those from Africa, Asia, or the Middle East who are pigment rich than for those whose German-style bodies disguise their foreignness. I was not accusing my listener of being like a Klansman, any more than I would say that I am a Klansman. But I, as a White American, am implicated to some degree in the racial politics of my homeland, and not completely disconnected from its more extreme expressions, despite my personal stance in opposition to them. I am a part of the society that created and nurtures KKK extremism, although I am not personally an extremist; I benefit from White privilege whether I want to do so or not. Just so, to the extent that racialized discrimination takes place in Germany, every ethnic German is to some degree implicated in that discrimination, no matter what her or his personal political position or social engagements may be.[37]

So it is elsewhere in Europe. Racialized issues abound in every European country today, and for a long time, most Europeans have tried resolutely not to talk about them.[38] Of course, race has been the issue in many European conflict situations. By this, I do not mean race in the long-discredited, biologistic sense espoused by Arthur Comte de Gobineau, Madison Grant, Lothrop Stoddard, and the eugenicists; nor even in the slightly more genteel versions promoted by Richard Herrnstein, Charles Murray, and the sociobiologists.[39]

I refer rather to the process of *racialization,* of imputing fundamental characteristics to people – writing those character qualities onto their bodies, into their genes and their essential nature – based on their membership in an ethnic group.[40] It is a racialized perception for a Gallic Parisian to assume that a particular person is like this or like that, simply because she was born in North Africa. The same is true for an ethnic German when he assumes certain things about his Turkish-descended neighbor or for Flemish Amsterdammers when they speak disparagingly about Muslims in their midst. It is a racialized situation when a quarter of the people in Paris suburbs populated mainly by North Africans are unemployed or when Swiss voters ban minarets. In this sense – of seeing people from disadvantaged groups as essentially different from oneself in their core character, based on the fact that they belong in a particular group, and in acting institutionally against them – racialized relationships are everywhere in Europe (as in Asia, in Africa, and indeed around the world).[41]

I know lots of people in Europe who are eager to talk about race. They read and write books about race. They attend conferences and give lectures on race. But by and large, they conceive race as something that does not exist where they live. Race, for these knowledgeable, smart people of goodwill and Left politics, is something that happens at a safe distance – usually between Black and White in the United States, safely between the covers of books. When I start to talk about race, they ask me to use instead *ethnicity, culture,* or *ethnic group* – for, they say, race is a discredited concept that polite people do not use any more.

Yet racialized relationships exist, no matter what one calls them. Moreover, as the critic Vijay Prashad said,

> The problem of the twenty-first century is the problem of the color-blind. This problem is simple: it believes that, to redress racism, we need to *not* consider race in social practice, notably in the sphere of governmental action. The state, we are told, must be *above* race. It must not actively discriminate against people on the basis of race in its actions. At the dawn of a new millennium, there is widespread satisfaction of the progress on the "race problem." . . . That is, we are led to believe that racism is a prejudicial behavior of one party against another rather than the coagulation of socioeconomic injustice against groups. . . . Color-blind

justice privatizes inequality and racism, and it removes itself from the project
of redistributive and anti-racist justice. This is the genteel racism of our new
millennium.[42]

Prashad was writing about the United States, but the observation applies
to Europe as well. As Alessandro Portelli wrote in response to Prashad,

> This fits Italy perfectly. They [Italians] are not a race, and racism has nothing
> to do with it. These are the main props of the Italian discourse on race in which
> denial plays an essential role. Italians believe themselves to be immune from
> racism because they do not see themselves as "White" but rather as "normal," as
> human by default. . . . Thus, jokes and songs from the colonial period never op-
> pose a White and a Black person, but always an *Italian* and a Black. I always have
> to remind my students that they, too, are *White*, and that Protestants are also
> Christians. . . . there may be no open or conscious hostility or denigration, but
> the line of difference between what is marked and what is unmarked is always
> drawn. We are *us* and they are *the other.*[43]

We identify our privilege by what we do not want to talk about. I
had a friend who taught courses about race at Brown University. At the
beginning of each term, she would ask each student to identify him- or
herself, without giving any other instructions. One person might say she
was a Black single mother, and right away you got an idea of who she was.
Another person would say, "I'm a woman," and you did not need to look;
you knew she was White. A third person might say, "I'm a citizen," or
"I'm an American," or "I'm a human being" – that was inevitably a White
male. And none of the students identified him- or herself as a student at
a hyperprivileged Ivy League university.

In recent years, reluctantly and without much skill, every European
nation has begun to engage in a national conversation about race and
membership, sometimes civilly and sometimes not.[44] Denmark has one
of the smaller immigrant populations in Europe (see Table 1.1). Nonetheless, the governing coalition from 2001 to 2011 was racially nationalist
and angry at residents who were not ethnic Danes. The coalition's vital
minority member was the Danish People's Party (DPP), which, together
with its somewhat more genteel partners, rammed through legislation
that drastically reduced the right of asylum and sharply cut social benefits for refugees, changing one of Europe's most welcoming societies for
immigrants into one of the most hostile. The DPP's platform proclaimed,
"Denmark belongs to the Danes and its citizens must be able to live in

a secure community . . . developing along the lines of Danish culture."
New laws wound a tight web of restraints against any Danes who married
non-Danes, which drove many hundreds of couples into exile in Sweden
(though some of the Danish spouses commuted back to their jobs in
Copenhagen). This prompted Pia Kjaersgaard, the DPP head, to respond:
"If they [Swedes] want to turn Stockholm, Gothenburg or Malmoe into
a Scandinavian Beirut, with clan wars, honour killings and gang rapes,
let them do it. We can always put a barrier on the Oeresund Bridge." In
2010, Karsten Lauritzen, integration spokesman for the main coalition
partner Venstre, proposed that the minimum wage for immigrants be
set at half that for Danish natives. Finally, in 2011, Denmark reinstituted
border controls, in violation of the Shengen Agreement on passport-free
travel throughout Europe. In September 2011 elections, the nationalist
coalition was narrowly defeated by a more liberal coalition that promised
to roll back some of these measures.[45]

Austria has more than double Denmark's immigrant percentage,
and there the debate has proceeded differently. On one hand, discrimination against Muslim and African immigrants is common, and the extreme Right has steadily risen in national politics, based largely on its
opposition to immigration. Two parties made up of disciples of the late,
charismatic racial populist Jörg Haider were the big winners in 2008's
provincial elections. Yet they have failed so far to translate their rising
popularity into control of national political institutions.[46]

Germany in 2008 installed a new examination for would-be citizens,
testing them on German history, culture, and political institutions.[47] This
was part of a developing national discussion over what should constitute the grounds for membership in German society. In 2000, Germany
reformed its citizenship laws to allow nonethnic Germans to apply for
naturalization after eight years' residence. At that time, the original plan
had been to allow immigrants' children born in Germany automatically
to become German citizens, but that feature was deleted due to conservatives' protests. The German-born generation could apply for citizenship
at age eighteen, but they did not become citizens simply by virtue of their
place of birth, as in France or the United Kingdom. The 2008 test was designed to add a barrier of German literacy and cultural knowledge to the
existing naturalization requirements. It was much mocked by German

news media outlets and by politicians on the Left. The multiple-choice questions were simple; some examples: How many states are there in Germany? (Answer: sixteen). What is the capital of Nordrhein-Westfalen? (Düsseldorf). Publishers quickly put out study booklets, and immigrant organizations developed citizenship courses, so the ability of those immigrants who were fluent in written German to become citizens was not impaired significantly. But there surely was a class bias built in, for those without education were significantly hampered.[48]

The German debate took a more extreme, racialized turn in 2010. Conservative politician Peter Trapp demanded IQ tests for all immigrants, but that idea did not initially gain traction in the national debate. Then Thilo Sarrazin, a functionary in the center-left Social Democratic Party, shook the nation with *Deutschland schafft sich ab* (German Abolishes Itself), a racist screed couched in pseudoscientific language à la Richard Herrnstein and Charles Murray's *Bell Curve*. Sarrazin's runaway best-seller (it sold more than a million hardback copies in the first three months) contended that Germany's education and welfare systems encouraged a fecund horde of low-IQ Muslim immigrants to make Germany their home. These migrants were outbreeding Christian-descended ethnic Germans and dumbing down the population. Together, the education system, the welfare system, and the immigrants were destroying the German economy and social system.[49]

Sometimes, as with Sarrazin, the conversation uses religious labels rather than racial ones. There the talk is of "Dutch culture" or "German culture" (perhaps even "European culture" or "Western culture") versus "Muslim culture," but the people who use this language are, in fact, making racialized distinctions.[50] That is, they are asserting differences between groups of people, differences that they mark as essential, as immutably part of the core of one's being, not simply as matters of intellectual choice or voluntary affiliation.[51]

No country in Europe has seen a more pointed public dialogue about race, culture, and immigrant status than the Netherlands. A series of outspoken politicians and commenters, from Pym Fortuyn to Theo Van Gogh to Ayaan Hirsi Ali to Geert Wilders, have fanned the flames of anti-immigrant, anti-Muslim sentiments.[52] This is not to argue that their objections to aspects of fundamentalist Islam are without merit, nor to sympathize with the murderers of Fortuyn and Van Gogh.[53] It is only to note that these and other critics have tended toward what one might call Serial Whole-and-Part Fallacy Syndrome. In the rendering of Wilders, who may be the most extreme in this crew (and who in 2010 led his Freedom Party to a second-place finish in fractured national elections), the fallacy runs like this:

· The Netherlands has a severe crime problem [that contention may be debated, but I will grant it for the purpose of illustrating his style of argument].
· Some of those who commit crimes are immigrants.
· Therefore, immigration should be banned or severely restricted.

Even if there may be a crime problem, are immigrants the cause of that crime, and will keeping them out solve the problem? These questions are highly debatable, yet Wilders treats the whole set of ideas as a truism because he is interested only in the conclusion: the immigrants must go. Wilders performs similar sleight of hand on another theme and reaches a similar conclusion:

· Some immigrants are Muslims.
· Some Muslims (immigrants and citizens) do not share common Dutch liberal attitudes toward women's rights, gay rights, access to recreational drugs, and other issues.
· Therefore, immigration of Muslims especially should be banned or restricted. In addition, the Qur'an should be banned.

Even granted that there exist Muslims who do not share the liberal views of a lot of Dutch people on these issues, it does not follow that all or even a majority of Muslims in the Netherlands share the extreme fundamentalist position Wilders attributes to them all. And there are other people besides Muslims who, on these issues, stand close to the position that Wilders assigns to all Muslims – Christian fundamentalists, for example. Yet Wilders does not call for a ban on Christian immigration, nor for the Bible to be banned.[54] His conclusion: "There is a tremendous danger looming, and it is very difficult to be optimistic. We might be in the final stages of the Islamization of Europe. This is not only a clear and present danger to the future of Europe itself, it is a threat to America and the sheer survival of the West."[55] This is quite a rhetorical leap. The Dutch conversation over race, religion, immigration, and national membership has only just begun.

Nearly a quarter of Swiss residents came from outside the country, and the Swiss economy is dependent on their presence. Yet a discussion of whether, and if so how, to incorporate these people into the citizenry is just beginning; it does not look favorable for at least certain categories of immigrants. As in Germany (and unlike Britain and France), birth on Swiss soil does not automatically confer the right of citizenship. In 2004, the Swiss electorate rejected a referendum that would have made it easier for the children and grandchildren of immigrants to gain Swiss citizenship. The anti-immigrant forces were led by the Swiss People's Party (SPP), a partner in the governing coalition, and its leader, billionaire industrialist Christoph Blocher. Among other tactics, the SPP's anti-immigrant campaign featured pictures of Osama Bin Laden, and of Black hands trying to grab a Swiss passport. On the other side of the debate, the rapper Stress chanted, "My Switzerland sees its future in multiculturalism. My Switzerland doesn't see mosques and minarets as a threat. My Switzerland is open, pro-European, and she doesn't make a fuss about granting citizenship to foreigners."[56]

The debate took an especially charged religio-racial turn in 2009. The bulk of Switzerland's immigrant population is from Western Europe, with substantial numbers of workers also having come from the countries of the former Eastern Bloc. Yet in that year, Muslims from Turkey, the Middle East, and North Africa became the main object of the immigration debate. In a popular initiative, the Swiss voted to ban the building of any new minarets in the country. Most existing minarets were smaller than typical church steeples; some were symbolic structures only a dozen or so feet tall. But a majority of the electorate found them threatening and forbade any more to be constructed.[57]

Such issues came terrifyingly into focus on July 22, 2011, when mild-mannered Anders Behring Breivik, by his own later declaration, blew up a government building in Oslo and murdered scores of young people at a camp near the city. A 1,518-page online manuscript that Breivik posted hours earlier made clear that he was seeking to combat what he viewed as the Islamization of Europe and the corruption of European values.

He saw this, like Samuel Huntington and Geert Wilders, as one stage in a millennium-long clash of civilizations between "The Islamic World and The West." He felt called, he said, to kill European politicians and future politicians who were opening the door to an evil Islamic empire. All his language treated Islam in a racialized way, and his account was sprinkled with explicitly racial rants. It may surprise some readers to learn that there are, in fact, very few Muslims in Norway. Norway ranks nineteenth out of twenty-eight European nations in the percentage of immigrants in its population, and two-thirds of those immigrants come from Europe. Far less than 1 percent of Norway's population were Muslims, but to Anders Breivik they represented an existential threat of desperate proportions.[58]

No European nation yet has achieved an understanding of itself as a nation made up of immigrants, but that is surely Europe's future.[59] Lots of people in every European country are uncertain about their future as immigrant-receiving nations, and some of them are angry at the thought that their nation and culture may have to change as a result of changing population dynamics. What few seem to recognize is that the change has already taken place. Every country in Europe is already a nation made up of many different kinds of people, many of them people from immigrant backgrounds and from outside Europe.

The question is not whether immigrants will come – they are already there. The relevant questions are how they will be incorporated and whether Europeans will face up to the racialized relationships between peoples that have already developed in their midst. It is a big problem, and it is time to talk about it. That is what my coauthors and I propose to do in this book. We are not at the point of proposing solutions, for these problems are not easy to solve, but we do hope to contribute to the growing discussion. Specifically, we want to ask, more elementally, this question: Leaving aside all the misguided public rhetoric, how do migrants and minorities actually experience their lives and their identities?[60]

THE SHAPE OF THIS VOLUME

In the past several pages, I have described a lot of negativity and some terrible violence that have clouded public discussions of migrants, minorities, and race in Europe. It may be inevitable that the public discourse should concentrate on immigration as a *problem;* after all, political institutions are mainly set up for the purpose of solving problems. But immigrants are not, in fact, problems, contrary to the tone of the public discussion throughout Europe. They are people living their lives – sometimes successfully, sometimes in difficult circumstances. Their life experiences are much closer to the gentle, cross-cultural engagement portrayed in the 2003 French movie *Monsieur Ibrahim* than to the crime and culture clash one finds in Fatih Akin's 2004 German film *Gegen die Wand*.[61]

The focus of this volume is not on the public policy debates that are taking place, but rather on the lived experience of migrants in complex societies, all but one of them located in Europe (the other is not far away, in Kazakhstan). In an era when people move about the globe with unprecedented velocity and in multiple directions, the question of multiple memberships and complex identities has come to the fore as never before. Take just one example among millions of possibilities: Christine, Susan, and Benta Wauna are sisters who work as nannies in Rome, far from their native Kenya. They send money back to the family at home and have put their personal lives on hold in order to do so. Benta came first and then paid for the others to follow. Their work in Italy helps support the family in Kenya.

Are they Kenyans or Italians? After more than a decade in Rome, it is hard to tell where their identities lie.[62] Migrants like the Wauna sisters may prefer to identify with the place of their origin, with the place where they end up living, or both. On the other hand, their choice may be circumscribed by governments, by hostile local people, or by the pull of people back home.[63] Nations across the developed world have received large numbers of migrants in the past decade. Their models for incorporation are historically various, and now many of those models are under challenge.

This book explores the multiple ways that identities are experienced by people from migrant backgrounds in several European nations and in Kazakhstan, one of the former republics of the Soviet Union. We are interested in people who cross borders, such as Turks in Germany or North Africans in Italy, and the struggles they may have with identity issues. We are interested also in the even more complex identity situations their German- or Italian-born children may encounter, born in Europe but possessing also an identity that some Europeans regard as alien. And we are interested in the identity situations of people with multiple ethnic heritages, such as Muslim and Christian, Swedish and African, Asian and European, and so on. We are interested in the ways people conceive, seek to preserve, or transform their identities, and the networks through which such identities are mediated.

These essays are arranged in four sections: *Orientations, The Complexities of Identities, Family Matters,* and *Modes of Multicultural Success?* I wrote earlier in this chapter that I believe race to be a central issue in the status, life experiences, and prospects of immigrants throughout Europe. In chapter 2, my esteemed colleague Anna Rastas takes a different approach. In addition to being a scholar, she is an antiracist activist, and in her chapter, she makes clear that race is indeed central to the lives of her subjects. But she argues that sometimes laying aside concrete and perhaps overused terms such as *race* and *identity* and choosing instead other rhetorical and analytical points of entry may make it possible to explore with more subtlety the ways that people negotiate their multiple identities and the complicated ways that race and racism work in their daily lives. Professor Rastas presents a subtle, humane meditation on such ideas as race, ethnicity, and identity, grounded in her ethnographic study of young Finns who possess complex international family backgrounds. Rastas finds that a simple discourse of race or ethnicity does not express exactly the social positionings that her young subjects inhabit, in part because racism, while it surely exists, has been so little discussed in Finnish society. Her subjects' lives embody multiplicity and contingency of connections, not only in Finland but also in places abroad to which they owe part of their roots. She proposes the term *transnational subjectivities* as a more fruitful way to conceptualize the experiences of the people she studies, and chapter 2 explores the ways that term may better describe the way Finnish young people (and others) with multiple backgrounds live their lives.

The four essays that follow in Part 2 show just how complex identities may be. In chapter 3, Saara Pellander of the University of Helsinki reports on her interviews with several young women who have grown up in Finland but who have origins in South or Southeast Asia. Some of them are Finland-born children of immigrants; others were adopted by ethnic Finnish families and came to the country when they were very young. Pellander delicately traces the subtle and complex ways by which those women construct and understand their identities as Finns, and sometimes as something else.

Serine Gunnarsson of Uppsala University, in chapter 4, explores the negotiations of autonomy, identity, and cultural affiliation of young women of Middle Eastern descent in Sweden, both Christians and Muslims. She finds their cultural choices to be individual, complex, and not dependent on parental mandates, Swedish cultural imperatives, or their religious background. Thus, her findings are likely to surprise followers of the daily press and of political discussions about Islam and gender in Europe. She portrays her subjects as "strategically dis-identifying," both with their Middle Eastern parental cultural imperatives and with Swedish cultural norms, in their pursuit of autonomous selves.

Katarzyna Warmińska takes rather another tack in chapter 5, "To Be or Not to Be a Minority Group?" She lays out the complex identity negotiations for two minorities in Poland: Kashubians and Tatars. The Polish Tatars, descendants of Mongol Empire soldiers, number only a few thousand and do not inhabit a particular territory or speak a distinctive language any longer, although they do make up the largest single element in Poland's Muslim population. Despite their small size and lack of a distinctive language, they are recognized by the Polish government as an official ethnic minority, on the grounds of their consciousness of distinct historical origins and their family traditions and, especially, because they are identified with Islam. By contrast, the Kashubians make up a large part of the population of the Pomeranian provinces in northwestern Poland and they maintain a distinctive language, yet they are regarded by the government as a regional, rather than an ethnic or national group. Individuals in both groups make a variety of strategic identity choices – some hyphenated Tatar-Poles or Kashubian-Poles, and some simply Poles – within (and sometimes in resistance to) the limits placed by the homogenizing national discourse of Polishness.

In the final essay of Part 2, Marylène Lieber and Florence Lévy take issue with one of the grand assumptions of modern history and migration studies: that there is such a thing as a Chinese diaspora.[64] They examine the various sorts of people who are marked and who mark themselves as Chinese in Switzerland and who organize what they call "Chinese language schools" for their children. Lieber and Lévy explore whether such people, in fact, constitute a discrete population or a meaningful group and whether there may be such a thing as an essential Chineseness. They say "no." Teasing nuance out of many interviews, Lieber and Lévy uncover a much more complicated web of identities, connections, and nonconnections. They argue that, in the instance of people called Chinese in Switzerland, "language is constitutive of identity" but that the language and the identity are not fixed things; rather, they are complex and shifting negotiations.

Part 3 is devoted to family matters. Saija Westerlund-Cook, in chapter 7, takes a position on international and transracial adoption that some social workers would not support. Most of the social work profession in the United Kingdom clings to the principle of racial matching of parentless children and adoptive parents. Westerlund-Cook explains the provenance and reasoning behind that policy but challenges its racial presumptions. Contrasting the U.K. policy with the race-blind policies in Finland (for which she also has a trenchant critique), Westerlund-Cook injects a humane voice into what has often been a politically and racially charged policy discussion. Ultimately, the lives and identities of the children are at stake.

Enzo Colombo and Paola Rebughini, veteran sociologists from the University of Milan, assay the life situations of teenage children of immigrants in Italy in chapter 8. Contrary to the assumptions of politicians and pundits, they find these people do not see themselves as stigmatized or caught between cultures. Rather, they embrace complex identities – Chinese and Italian, Italian and Egyptian, and so forth – and use these as tools of belonging in Italian society. Some might call this mere "symbolic ethnicity,"[65] the vestigial remnant of their parents' cultures. But Colombo and Rebughini believe it to be "instrumental ethnicity," something more powerful, purposeful, and perhaps enduring.

Gaia Peruzzi explores international romance and marriage in Italy in chapter 9, "Possible Love: New Cross-cultural Couples in Italy." Her analysis, built carefully on statistical data and a wealth of personal interviews, leads us deep into the social patterns and personal choices that frame these most intimate of intercultural encounters. That she examines international marriage for Italians is a particularly welcome move, since most studies of intermarriage have dealt with the United States, the U.K., or Latin America. Very few studies heretofore have explored this rapidly growing phenomenon in the Italian context.

In Part 4, the authors describe ethnic situations in Germany and in Kazakhstan that might promise hope for the achievement of harmonious, integrated, multicultural societies. Mira Foster explores the lived experiences of Polish-German *Aussiedler* in chapter 10. She draws attention to the voices of Polish people with some German ancestry who have migrated to Germany since the 1970s. She weaves individual microhistories into the larger context of Germany's macrohistory of immigration. Using oral histories, this chapter outlines the process by which the Polish immigrants transformed their identities under the influence of their new German environment. It concludes that their individual stories allow us to see the variety of ways in which people coped with and reacted to their situation as Polish resettlers in Germany and managed their emerging identities as Germans.

In chapter 11, "The Politics of Multiple Identities in Kazakhstan," Karina Mukazhanova shows a relatively new nation grappling with how to construct a national identity among manifest ethnic complexity. Kazakhstan, the largest of the former Soviet republics in West Central Asia, has a heterogeneous population made up of 130 different ethnic groups (or "nationalities" in Soviet parlance). The ethnic Kazakh plurality was long subordinated to imperial Soviet impositions of Russian language and culture, and some older Kazakhs are today nostalgic for the Soviet era. The government of Nursaltan Nazarbayev, to the contrary, has adopted a strategy of trying to build its national identity on the nation's very multiplicity. Language and cultural policies stress diversity, tolerance, and accommodation among the various ethnic communities, as well as encouragement of previously suppressed languages and cultures (especially the Kazakh). The attempt is to make national unity out of the very embrace of ethnic, cultural, and linguistic multiplicity. How well it will glue together Kazakhstan society will be an interesting matter to witness in the years ahead.

Finally, in chapter 12, I lay out what I take to be similarities in the historical trajectories of two racialized groups in different countries: Chinese immigrants and their descendants in the United States and Turkish immigrants and their children in Germany. Both Chinese Americans in the latter nineteenth century and Turkish Germans in the latter twentieth were recruited to do dangerous, low-paid body work, with the expectation that they would not become part of the host society but that they would return to their homeland. Both were subjected to considerable discrimination and to negative stereotypes surrounding allegations of criminality, violence, and patriarchy. In the Chinese case, an American-born generation grew up that confounded those stereotypes and overcame that discrimination to earn a place in United States society. In the Turkish case, a very similar German-born generation has now come of age and is embarked on similar social tasks. This bodes well for the future of Turkish Germans, so long as non-Turkish Germans can let go of their stereotypes and deal with the actual Turkish Germans in their midst.

In each of these countries, from Britain to Kazakhstan and from Finland to Italy, there exist multiple peoples within a single polity. Some like Polish Tatars have lived long in the land; others, the majority, are recently migrant peoples. Each of these nations is engaged in a process that is common throughout Europe: debating and figuring out what are and ought to be the grounds of identity and the limits of citizenship. And each of these migrant and minority peoples is engaged in the process of working out its multiple and changing identities in an evolving social context.

Are there things we can say in general about the life experiences and identity fashionings of migrant and minority peoples across Europe? Surely, there are a few that will be common in the chapters to come. In almost every nation across Europe, there live today more migrants and minority group members than most nonmigrant, nonminority people acknowledge, and they are not going away. They are part of the fabric out of which each nation is fashioning its future, whether or not their divergent backgrounds are accepted or their manifest involvement in local society is acknowledged. Among the migrants – as the Norwegian case shows most vividly, but as is true throughout Europe – fewer are Muslims than most White, Christian-descended Europeans imagine. As we will witness in the chapters ahead, the Muslims who are present do not constitute a threat to the local society, whether in Germany or Sweden or Finland or elsewhere, contrary to the tone of public debate. They are simply people trying to make their lives in the local context. Most migrants and members of domestic minorities experience complicated, hybrid, layered identities, maintaining ties to ancestral identities even as those are constantly being reshaped, and alongside them experiencing emerging identities as citizens of their European homes. The ins and outs of how the members of these various migrant and minority groups, in various countries across Europe, manage their multiple and mutating identities we will discover in the chapters ahead.

NOTES

1. The monoreligious vector in nationalism took a blow with the Reformation.

2. Ernest Gellner, *Nations and Nationalism* (Ithaca, NY: Cornell University Press, 1983); Anthony D. Smith, *The Ethnic Origins of Nations* (Oxford: Blackwell, 1986); Anthony D. Smith, *Nationalism and Modernism* (London: Routledge, 1998). See also E. J. Hobsbawm, *Nations and Nationalism since 1780* (Cambridge: Cambridge University Press, 1990).

3. Some may argue that nations like the United States and Australia are exceptions to the general rule of an ethnic-origin-to-nation formation. For my argument against that understanding of the United States, see my book *Almost All Aliens: Immigration, Race, and Colonialism in American History and Identity* (New York: Routledge, 2007); see also Roger Daniels, *Guarding the Golden Door: American Immigration Policy and Immigrants since 1882* (New York: Hill and Wang, 2004); Nell Irvin Painter, *The History of White People* (New York: Norton, 2010). On Australia, see James Jupp, *From White Australia to Woomera*, 2d ed. (Cambridge: Cambridge University Press, 2007); Gwenda Tavan, *The Long, Slow*

Death of White Australia (Carlton North, AU: Scribe Publications, 2005); Catriona Elder, *Dreams and Nightmares of a White Australia: Representing Aboriginal Assimilation in the Mid-Twentieth Century* (New York: Peter Lang, 2009); Jane Carey and Claire McLisky, eds., *Creating White Australia* (Sydney: Sydney University Press, 2009); Margaret D. Jacobs, *White Mother to a Dark Race: Colonialism, Maternalism, and the Removal of Indigenous Children in the American West and Australia, 1880–1940* (Lincoln: University of Nebraska Press, 2009); John Docker and Gerhard Fischer, eds., *Race, Colour, and Identity in Australia and New Zealand* (Sydney: University of New South Wales Press, 2000).

4. Patrick J. Geary, *The Myth of Nations: The Medieval Origins of Europe* (Princeton, NJ: Princeton University Press, 2003); Rogers Brubaker, *Citizenship and Nationhood in France and Germany* (Cambridge, MA: Harvard University Press, 1992); William A. Barbieri Jr., *The Ethics of Citizenship: Immigration and Group Rights in Germany* (Durham, NC: Duke University Press, 1998). For Johann Gottfried von Herder, places to begin are the *Über den Ursprung der Sprache*

[Treatise on the Origin of Language, 1772] (Berlin: Akademie-Verlag, 1959) and *Von deutscher Art und Kunst* [Of German Character and Art; written with J. W. Goethe, 1773] (München: A. Langen, 1940). See also Johann Gottfried von Herder, *J. G. Herder und die deutsche Volkwerdung* [J. G. Herder and the Development of the German People], ed. Kurt Hoffmann (Berlin: Langenscheidt, 1934). Johann Gottlieb Fichte can be read in *Addresses to the German People*, ed. and trans. Gregory Moore (Cambridge: Cambridge University Press, 2009). There are many editions in English of the works of Arthur Schopenhauer and Friedrich Nietzsche. For insights into the constructed nature of these processes, see Benedict Anderson, *Imagined Communities: Reflections on the Origin and Spread of Nationalism*, rev. ed. (London: Verso, 1991).

5. David A. Bell, *The Cult of the Nation in France: Inventing Nationalism, 1680–1800* (Cambridge, MA: Harvard University Press, 2003); Brubaker, *Citizenship and Nationhood in France and Germany*. For similar developments in England, see Linda Colley, *Britons: Forging the Nation, 1707–1837*, 2d ed. (New Haven, CT: Yale University Press, 2005); Catherine Hall, *Civilising Subjects: Metropole and Colony in the English Imagination, 1830–1867* (Chicago: University of Chicago Press, 2002).

6. Howard Eissenstat, "Metaphors of Race and Discourse of Nation: Racial Theory and State Nationalism in the First Decades of the Turkish Republic," in *Race and Nation: Ethnic Systems in the Modern World*, ed. Paul Spickard (New York: Routledge, 2005), 239–56; Sibel Bozdogan and Resat Kasaba, eds., *Rethinking Modernity and National Identity in Turkey* (Seattle: University of Washington Press, 2000); Erik J. Zurcher, *The Young Turk Legacy and Nation Building: From the Ottoman Empire to Ataturk's Turkey* (London: I.B. Tauris, 2010); Carter Vaughn Findlay, *Turkey, Islam, Nationalism, and Modernity*

(New Haven, CT: Yale University Press, 2010); Christopher de Bellaigue, *Rebel Land: Unraveling the Riddle of History in a Turkish Town* (New York: Penguin, 2010). Bassam Tibi addresses related issues for the Arab peoples in *Arab Nationalism: Between Islam and the Nation-State*, 3d ed. (New York: Palgrave Macmillan, 1997).

7. Mustafa Al Karadaghi, "The Kurdish Nation Has the Inalienable Right of Self-Determination," *Kurdistan Times*, 1.2 (Summer 1992); Joost Hiltermann, "Waiting for Baghdad," *New York Review of Books*, May 12, 2011, 55–56; Marianne Heiberg, *The Making of the Basque Nation* (Cambridge: Cambridge University Press, 2007); Mark Kurlansky, *The Basque History of the World: The Story of a Nation* (New York: Penguin, 2001); Haunani-Kay Trask, *From a Native Daughter: Colonialism and Sovereignty in Hawai'i* (Monroe, ME: Common Courage Press, 1993); J. Kehaulani Kauanui, *Hawaiian Blood: Colonialism and the Politics of Sovereignty and Indigeneity* (Durham, NC: Duke University Press, 2008); Damien Kingsbury and Michael Leach, eds., *East Timor: Beyond Independence* (Clayton, AU: Monash University Press, 2007); Arthur Agwuncha Nwankwo and Samuel Udochukwu Ifejika, *Biafra: The Making of a Nation* (New York: Praeger, 1969); Henry H. Perritt Jr., *The Road to Independence for Kosovo* (Cambridge: Cambridge University Press, 2009); Darshan Tatla, "A Race Apart? The Paradox of Sikh Ethnicity and Nationalism," in *Race and Nation*, ed. Spickard, 299–318; Giorgio Shani, *Sikh Nationalism and Identity in a Global Age* (New York: Routledge, 2007); Darshan Singh Tatla, *The Sikh Diaspora: The Search for Statehood* (London: UCL Press, 1999).

8. Anna Reimann, "German Immigration Report Card: Immigration Fairytale Fails to Spread from Football Field to Society," Spiegel Online, July 7, 2010, http://www.spiegel.de/international

/germany/german-immigration-report
-card-integration-fairytale-fails-to-spread-
from-football-field-to-society-a-705237
.html, accessed July 24, 2012 (all further
URLs for Spiegel Online in this chapter
were accessed on the same date); Wikipedia, "List of Countries by Foreign-born
Population in 2005," http://en.wikipedia
.org/wiki/List_of_countries_by_
immigrant_population, retrieved July 24,
2012. Wikipedia's numbers are taken from
the United Nations report, *World Population Policies 2005* (New York: United Nations, Department of Economic and Social
Affairs, March 2006).

9. Dirk Hoerder, *Cultures in Contact:
World Migrations in the Second Millennium*
(Durham, NC: Duke University Press,
2002); Donna Gabaccia, *Italy's Many Dia-
sporas* (Seattle: University of Washington
Press, 2000); Walter F. Willcox, ed., *In-
ternational Migrations*, 2 vols. (New York:
Gordon and Breach, 1969).

10. Jason Bremner, Ashley Frost, Carl
Haub, Mark Mather, Karin Ringheim,
and Eric Zuehlke, *World Population
Highlights: Key Findings from PRB's 2010
World Population Data Sheet,* vol. 65.2 of
Population Reference Bureau, *Population
Bulletin* (July 2010), http://www.prb.org/
Publications/PopulationBulletins/2010/
worldpopulationhighlights2010.aspx;
United Nations, *World Population Policies
2007,* http://www.un.org/esa/popula-
tion/publications/wpp2007/wpp2007
.htm, retrieved July 24, 2012; U.S. Cen-
tral Intelligence Agency, *The World Fact
Book,* "Country Comparison: Total
Fertility Rate," https://www.cia.gov/
library/publications/the-world-factbook/
rankorder/2127rank.html, retrieved
July 24, 2012; "Sexual Politics: Making
Babies Is Patriotic," *Seattle Times,* June
26, 2004; Elizabeth Bryant, "European
Countries Offer Incentives for Having
Kids," *San Francisco Chronicle,* August 10,
2008; Leigh Phillips, "Europe's Popula-

tion Would Decline without Migrants,"
Eurozone, September 24, 2008, http://
euobserver.com/851/26799, retrieved
July 24, 2012.

11. The United Kingdom has made
more progress toward creating a language
of inclusion and effective institutions to
manage multiplicity than has any other
European nation. I should point out that
the discussion has begun to take on a
supranational aspect, as the European
Union has taken up migration as a region-
wide issue. In that case, the discussion has
begun to move beyond strictly nationalist
concerns, though, as we shall see, those
nationalist impulses remain very strong.

12. That President Obama has not
retained his popularity in Europe (or the
United States) is the subject of another
paper entirely. I presented some of the
ideas for the following paragraphs at a
conference – "Minorities and Power in the
English Speaking World" – hosted by the
University of Caen in November 2008. I
am grateful to Taoufik Djebali for inviting
me, and to several conference participants,
among them Salah Oueslati, Lanouar Ben
Hafsa, Pierre Guerlain, and Steve Whit-
field, for their critiques.

13. Nor did it mean, as some in the Tea
Party would have it, a Kenyan-Indonesian-
Muslim-Nazi-Socialist, charlatan, and
failure as president.

14. Rachel Donadio, "Albanians in
Italy: Some Fit Right In," *International
Herald Tribune,* September 6, 2008; Juliane
von Mittelstaedt, "'City of the Future': Ital-
ian Villages Welcome Refugees with Open
Arms," Spiegel Online, February 4, 2010,
http://forum-international.spiegel.de/
showthread.php?t=632; Tracy Wilkinson,
"Slave in the Lap of Luxury," *Los Angeles
Times,* February 20, 2008.

15. Jason Horowitz, "Italy Bangs the
Door Shut on the Castaways from Africa,"
New York Times, July 23, 2004; Jason Horo-
witz, "Survivors Rescued on Boat Smug-

gling Africans to Italy," *New York Times*, August 9, 2004; Tracy Wilkinson, "Italy Deporting Illegal Migrants as They Pour In," *Los Angeles Times*, October 6, 2004; Sebastian Rotella, "Human Wave Hits Italian Isle," *Los Angeles Times*, March 23, 2009; Peter Popham, "Hundreds Feared Dead as Migrant Boats Sink Off Libya," *The Independent*, April 1, 2009; Elisabetta Povoledo, "Italy Returns Migrants to Libya," *International Herald Tribune*, May 8, 2009; "Affirming Policy, Italy Sends More Migrants Back to Libya," *International Herald Tribune*, May 11, 2009; Guy Dinmore, "UN Urges Italy to Take Back Asylum Seekers," *Financial Times*, May 13, 2009; Elisabeth Rosenthal, "A Poor Fit for an Immigrant: After 20 Years of Hard Work in Italy, Still Not Italian," *New York Times*, January 1, 2006.

16. Jason Horowitz, "A Small Northern Party Has a Sizable Presence in Italian Politics," *New York Times*, December 29, 2003; Paul Bompard, "Italy's Northern League Seeks to Block New Mosques," *Financial Times*, August 25, 2008; "Italian Politician Resigns after Singing Racist Chant," *International Herald Tribune*, July 9, 2009.

17. Tracy Wilkinson, "Italian Mayor Sees Veiled Threat," *New York Times*, September 22, 2004; Elisabetta Povoledo, "In Italy, Sign of Defiance in a Kebab and a Coke," *New York Times*, April 24, 2009; Tracy Wilkinson, "Angry about Crime, Italy Zeroes In on Foreigners," *Los Angeles Times*, November 9, 2007; Tracy Wilkinson, "Italy Is Rebuked for Step against Gypsies," *Los Angeles Times*, July 11, 2008; Rachel Donadio, "Italy Feeling Racial Tension: Attacks on Immigrants Include Killings," *International Herald Tribune*, October 13, 2008; Alessandro Portelli, "The Problem of the Color-Blind: Notes on the Discourse of Race in Italy," in *Race and Nation*, ed. Spickard, 355–63.

18. "Different Skies: In Words and Pictures, Four Young Refugees Explain How London Is Becoming Their Home," *Financial Times*, October 5, 2008; Tom Mills, Tom Griffin, and David Miller, "The Cold War on British Muslims," Spinwatch, August 2, 2011, http://www.thecordoba foundation.com/attach/SpinwatchReport _ColdWar12.pdf, accessed July 24, 2012; "Britain Begins Issuing ID Cards for Foreigners," *International Herald Tribune*, November 26, 2008; Rebecca Wood, "Two Thirds of Newspaper Stories Say British Muslims Are 'a Threat' or 'Problem,'" Institute of Race Relations web site, September 9, 2008, www.irr.org.uk/2008/September/ bw000009.html, accessed July 24, 2012; "Racial Slurs Earn Rebuke for Britain's Prince Harry," *International Herald Tribune*, January 20, 2009; Patrick Wintour, Martin Wainwright, and Allegra Stratton, "Foreign Works Dispute: Refinery Strike Is Over – But Jobs Fight Goes On," *The Guardian*, February 5, 2009; Nicola Piper, *Racism, Nationalism, and Citizenship: Ethnic Minorities in Britain and Germany* (Aldershot, UK: Ashgate, 1998).

19. Sebastian Rotella, "London Police Kill Suspect in Subway," *Los Angeles Times*, July 23, 2005; Sebastian Rotella and John Daniszewski, "Police Concede Slain Suspect Not a Bomber," *Los Angeles Times*, July 24, 2005; Alan Cowell and Don Van Natta Jr., "Britain Says Man Killed by Police Had No Tie to Bombings," *New York Times*, July 24, 2005; "No Charges for Police Who Shot Brazilian," *International Herald Tribune*, February 14–15, 2009.

20. Lisa Erdmann, "Integration Boost: German State Appoints First Minister of Turkish Origin," Spiegel Online, April 20, 2010, http://www.spiegel.de/internatio- nal/germany/integration-boost-german- state-appoints-first-minister-of-turkish- origin-a-690036.html; "CDU Turkish Minister Appointment 'Flops,'" Spiegel Online, April 27, 2010, http://www .spiegel.de/international/germany/the -world-from-berlin-cdu-turkish-minister

-appointment-flops-a-691562.html. On Özdemir, see Cem Özdemir, *Ich bin Inländer: Ein anatolischer Schwabe im Bundestag* (Munich: Deutscher Taschenbuch Verlag, 1997); Cem Özdemir, *Currywurst und Döner: Integration in Deutschland* (Bergisch Gladbach: G. Lübeck, 1999). For immigration and membership issues in Germany, begin with Deniz Göktürk, David Gramling, and Anton Kaes, eds., *Germany in Transit: Nation and Migration, 1955–2005* (Berkeley: University of California Press, 2007); Richard Alba, Peter Schmidt, and Martine Wasmer, eds., *Germans or Foreigners? Attitudes toward Ethnic Minorities in Post-reunification Germany* (New York: Palgrave, 2003); Betigül Ercan Argun, *Turkey in Germany: The Transnational Sphere of Deutschkei* (New York: Routledge, 2003); Wesley D. Chapin, *Germany for the Germans? The Political Effects of International Migration* (Westport, CT: Greenwood, 1997); Thomas Faist, *Social Citizenship for Whom? Young Turks in Germany and Mexican Americans in the United States* (Aldershot, UK: Avebury, 1995); Norbert Finzsch and Dietmar Schirmer, eds., *Identity and Intolerance: Nationalism, Racism, and Xenophobia in Germany and the United States* (Cambridge: Cambridge University Press, 1998); Simon Green, *The Politics of Exclusion: Institutions and Immigration Policy in Contemporary Germany* (Manchester: Manchester University Press, 2004); David Horrocks and Eva Kolinsky, eds., *Turkish Culture in Germany Today* (Providence, RI: Berghahn, 1996); Mark Terkessidis, *Migranten* (Hamburg: Rotbuch, 2000); Uli Bielefeld, *Das Eigene und das Fremde: Neuer Rassismus in der Alten Welt?* (Hamburg: Junius, 1991); Faruk Sen and Andreas Goldberg, *Türken in Deutschland: Leben zwischen zwei Kulturen* (Munich: Beck, 1994); Faruk Sen and Hayrettin Aydim, *Islam in Deutschland* (Munich: Beck, 2002).

21. Abraham Friesen, *In Defense of Privilege: Russian Mennonites and the State Before and During World War I* (Winnipeg: Kindred Productions, 2006); Hans Werner, *Imagined Homes: Soviet Immigrants in Two Cities* (Winnipeg: University of Manitoba Press, 2007); Renate Bridenthal, "Germans from Russia: The Political Network of a Double Diaspora," in *The Heimat Abroad: The Boundaries of Germanness,* ed. Krista O'Donnell, Renate Bridenthal, and Nancy Reagin (Ann Arbor: University of Michigan Press, 2005), 187–218; Pieter Judson, "When Is a Diaspora Not a Diaspora? Rethinking Nation-Centered Narratives about Germans in Habsburg East Central Europe," in *Heimat Abroad,* ed. O'Donnell et al., 219–47; Nancy R. Reagin, "German *Brigadoon*? Domesticity and Metropolitan Perceptions of *Auslandsdeutschen* in Southwest Africa and Eastern Europe," in *Heimat Abroad,* ed. O'Donnell et al., 248–66.

22. Apparently, Kaman's great-grandparents were German citizens; Chris Hine, "Germany's Newest Citizen: Center Chris Kaman," *Los Angeles Times,* July 4, 2008.

23. Siobhán Dowling, "Right Wing Rejection: Neo-Nazis Spurn Germany's Diverse New National Team," Spiegel Online, July 2, 2010, http://www.spiegel .de/international/zeitgeist/right-wing-rejection-neo-nazis-spurn-germany-s -diverse-new-national-team-a-704362 .html; Borzou Daragahi, "A More Diverse Germany Heads toward Cup Greatness," *Los Angeles Times,* July 7, 2010.

24. "Ireland Votes to End Birth Right," *BBC Home* (UK version), June 13, 2004, http://news.bbc.co.uk/1/hi/world/europe /3801839.stm, accessed July 24, 2012; *Referendum on Irish Citizenship* (Dublin: The Referendum Commission, 2004), http:// www.refcom.ie/en/Past-Referendums/ Irish-citizenship/Refcom-information -booklet-on-Referendum-on-Irish -Citizenship/, accessed July 24, 2012.

25. On French citizenship, see Brubaker, *Citizenship and Nationhood in France and Germany*; Pierre Birnbaum, *The Idea of France* (New York: Hill and Wang, 1998); Miriam Feldblum, *Reconstructing Citizenship: The Politics of Nationality Reform and Immigration in Contemporary France* (Albany, NY: SUNY Press, 1999); Adrian Favell, *Philosophies of Integration: Immigration and the Idea of Citizenship in France and Britain*, 2d ed. (New York: Palgrave Macmillan, 2001); Craig S. Smith, "What Makes Someone French?" *New York Times*, November 11, 2005. On le Pen and the Front National, see Peter Davies, *The Extreme Right in France, 1789 to the Present: From de Maistre to Le Pen* (New York: Routledge, 2002); J. G. Shields, *The Extreme Right in France: From Pétain to Le Pen* (New York: Routledge, 2007); Jonathan Marcus, *The National Front and French Politics: The Resistible Rise of Jean-Marie Le Pen* (New York: NYU Press, 1995).

26. Thomas Fuller, "In France, Worker Bias Has a Name," *International Herald Tribune*, November 24, 2004; "French Muslims Face Job Discrimination," BBC News Online, November 5, 2005, http://news.bbc.co.uk/2/hi/europe/4399748.stm, accessed July 24, 2012; Craig S. Smith, "Elite French Schools Block the Poor's Path to Power," *New York Times*, December 18, 2005; Steven Erlanger, "Study Says Blacks and Arabs Face Bias From Paris Police," *New York Times*, June 30, 2009; "Study Shows French Muslims Hit by Religious Bias," *Associated Press*, March 26, 2010; Craig S. Smith, "Growing Muslim Prison Population Poses Huge Risks," *International Herald Tribune*, December 9, 2004.

27. "French Reform Targets Immigrants," *International Herald Tribune*, May 18, 2006; Elaine Sciolino, "Plan to Test Immigrants' DNA Divides France," *International Herald Tribune*, October 12, 2007; "Pseudoscientific Bigotry in France," *International Herald Tribune*, October 22, 2007; Elizabeth Bryant, "Immigration Stirs France: President Bids to Enforce Expulsion Rules as Lawmakers Debate Culture, Language Tests," *San Francisco Chronicle*, September 21, 2007; Devorah Lauter, "As the French Debate Their Identity, Some Recoil," *Los Angeles Times*, December 14, 2009.

28. Devorah Lauter, "Muslims in France Feel Sting of Bias," *Los Angeles Times*, July 22, 2010; Elaine Sciolino, "Ban Religious Attire in School, French Panel Says," *New York Times*, December 12, 2003; Elaine Ganley, "Muslims Protest French Plan to Ban Veils," *Oregonian*, January 18, 2004; Elaine Ganley, "French Lawmakers Pass Law to Ban Islamic Head Scarves," *Oregonian*, March 4, 2004; Elaine Sciolino, "France Vows to Enforce Scarf Ban despite Threat," *New York Times*, August 30, 2004; Sebastian Rotella, "Most Muslim Girls Comply with France's New Head Scarf Ban," *Los Angeles Times*, September 3, 2004; "Banning the 'Burqa': France's Quest to Maintain its Secular Identity," Spiegel Online, January 27, 2010, http://www.spiegel.de/international/europe/banning-the-burqa-france-s-quest-to-maintain-its-secular-identity-a-674390.html; Devorah Lauter, "France Considers Burka Ban," *Los Angeles Times*, January 27, 2010; Stefan Simons, "France's Controversial Immigration Minister: The Man Who Launched the Burqa Debate," Spiegel Online, February 1, 2010, http://www.spiegel.de/international/europe/france-s-controversial-immigration-minister-the-man-who-launched-the-burqa-debate-a-675164.html; "Don't Ban the Burka," *Los Angeles Times*, February 3, 2010; Alexandra Sandels, "France Denies Citizenship over Burka," *Los Angeles Times*, February 5, 2010; "France's Veil Threat," *Los Angeles Times*, May 24, 2010; "The Burqa Debate": Are Women's Rights Really the Issue?" Spiegel Online, June 24, 2010, http://www.spiegel.de/international/europe/the

-burqa-debate-are-women-s-rights-really
-the-issue-a-702668.html; "France's Veil
Threat: Basically, the Measure Is Simply
Religious Discrimination against Muslims"
(editorial), *Los Angeles Times,* May 24, 2010;
"Justice Minister Pushes Burka Ban," *Los
Angeles Times,* July 7, 2010; Alison Culli-
ford, "French National Assembly Approves
Ban on Face Veils," *Los Angeles Times,* July
14, 2010; Gregory Rodriguez, "Behind
France's Veil Ploy," *Los Angeles Times,* July
19, 2010; Pew Global Attitudes Project,
"Widespread Support for Banning Full
Islamic Veil in Western Europe" (survey
report, Pew Research Center, Washington,
DC, July 8, 2010), http://www.pewglobal
.org/2010/07/08/widespread-support-for
-banning-full-islamic-veil-in-western
-europe/, accessed July 24, 2012; Henry
Samuel, "French Women Cause a Stir in
Niqab and Hot Pants in Anti-Burka Ban
Protest," *Daily Telegraph,* October 1, 2010.
For an interpretation of the head-scarf is-
sue that differs from my own, see Elaine R.
Thomas, "Keeping Identity at a Distance:
Explaining France's New Legal Restric-
tions on the Islamic Headscarf," *Ethnic and
Racial Studies* 29.2 (2006): 237–59.

29. Devorah Lauter, "France Cracks
Down on Roma Migrants," *Los Angeles
Times,* August 13, 2010; Stefan Simons,
"Sarkozy Finds a Scapegoat," Spiegel Online, August 19, 2010, http://www.spiegel
.de/international/europe/sarkozy-finds
-a-scapegoat-france-begins-controversial
-roma-deportations-a-712701.html; Devorah Lauter, "Deportations Fray Catholic
Tie to Sarkozy," *Los Angeles Times,* August
25, 2010; Jan Puhl, "Unwanted in France,
Unloved in Romania: A Desperate Home-
coming for Deported Roma," Spiegel Online, August 31, 2010, http://www.spiegel
.de/international/europe/unwanted
-in-france-unloved-in-romania-a-desperate
-homecoming-for-deported-roma-a
-714649.html; "The Roma Are EU Citizens
– Everywhere in the European Union,"

Spiegel Online, September 6, 2010, http://
www.spiegel.de/international/europe/
the-world-from-berlin-the-roma-are-eu
-citizens-everywhere-in-the-european
-union-a-715900.html; "'A Disgrace': EU
Rebukes France over Roma Expulsions,"
Spiegel Online, September 14, 2010,
http://www.spiegel.de/international/
europe/a-disgrace-eu-rebukes-france
-over-roma-expulsions-a-717496.html;
Ullrich Fichtner, "Driving out the Unwanted: Sarkozy's War against the Roma,"
Spiegel Online, September 15, 2010, http://
www.spiegel.de/international/europe/
driving-out-the-unwanted-sarkozy-s-war
-against-the-roma-a-717324.html; "France
Has Acted Systematically against an Entire People," Spiegel Online, September 15,
2010, http://www.spiegel.de/interna
tional/germany/the-world-from-berlin-
france-has-acted-systematically-against-
an-entire-people-a-717643.html; Hans-
Jürgen Schlamp, "Paris vs. Brussels: Roma
Row Dominates EU Summit," Spiegel Online, September 17, 2010, http://www
.spiegel.de/international/europe/paris
-vs-brussels-roma-row-dominates
-eu-summit-a-717976.html; "Roma Ulti-
matum: Frances Pledges to Comply With
EU Migration Rules," Spiegel Online,
October 14, 2010, http://www.spiegel.de/
international/europe/roma-ultimatum
-france-pledges-to-comply-with-eu
-migration-rules-a-723087.html.

30. On Roma in Europe, see Isabel
Fonseca, *Bury Me Standing: The Gypsies
and Their Journey* (New York: Vintage,
1996); Ian Hancock, *We Are the Romani
People* (Hatfield, UK: University of
Hertfordshire Press, 2002); Jan Yoors, *The
Gypsies* (1967) (New York: Simon
and Schuster, 1983); Angus Fraser, *The
Gypsies,* 2d ed. (Oxford: Wiley-Blackwell,
1995).

31. "500 Muslim Soldiers' Tombs Desecrated in France," Huffington Post, December 8, 2008, http://www.huffington

post.com/2008/12/08/500-muslim-soldiers-tombs_n_149267.html, accessed July 24, 2012; "Muslim Soldiers' Graves Desecrated in France," *Agence France Presse,* May 6, 2010; Craig S. Smith, "Third Bomb Attack Directed at France's First Muslim Prefect," *New York Times,* January 30, 2004.

32. "Veil Assault Case Goes to Trial," *Los Angeles Times,* October 15, 2010.

33. Craig S. Smith, "Immigrant Rioting Flares in France for Ninth Night," *New York Times,* November 5, 2005; "French Riots Rage for 9th Night," *Los Angeles Times,* November 5, 2005; Sebastian Rotella, "On the 10th Day, Violence Spills across France," *Los Angeles Times,* November 6, 2005; Craig S. Smith, "As Riots Continue in France, Chirac Vows to Restore Order," *New York Times,* November 7, 2005; Richard Bernstein, "Officials Cautious on Violence in Germany and Belgium," *New York Times,* November 7, 2005; Sebastian Rotella, "Rioting Youths See 'No Future,'" *Los Angeles Times,* November 8, 2005; Richard Bernstein, "Despite Minor Incidents, Chance of Large-Scale Riots Elsewhere in Europe Is Seen as Small," *New York Times,* November 8, 2005; Olivier Roy, "Get French or Die Trying," *New York Times,* November 9, 2005; Katrin Bennhold, "French Riots Expose Handicaps Faced by Immigrants' Children," *International Herald Tribune,* November 10, 2005; Katrin Bennhold, "French Cabinet to Ask for Extension to Emergency Powers," *International Herald Tribune,* November 14, 2005; Craig S. Smith, "French Unrest Subsides, but Violence Persists in Lyon," *New York Times,* November 14, 2005; Craig S. Smith, "Chirac to Ask for Extension of Crisis Rules to Combat Riots," *New York Times,* November 15, 2005; Sebastian Rotella, "Chirac to Fight Civil Unrest on Two Fronts," *Los Angeles Times,* November 15, 2005; Molly Moore, "Sarkozy Says Riots Were 'Thugocracy,' Not a Social Crisis," *Washington Post,* November 30, 2007.

34. Steven Erlanger, "Alsace Debates Support for a Mosque," *International Herald Tribune,* October 7, 2008; "Muslim Soldiers' Tombs Desecrated in France," *International Herald Tribune,* October 23, 2008; Steven Erlanger, "Youth Gangs Turn Violent in a District in Paris," *International Herald Tribune,* September 25, 2008; "Sarkozy Acts to Aid Ethnic Minorities," *International Herald Tribune,* December 18, 2008.

35. For others who share this general perspective (although we have quite disparate takes on many particulars), see Rita Chin, Heide Fehrenbach, Geoff Eley, and Atina Grossmann, eds., *After the Nazi Racial State: Difference and Democracy in Germany and Europe* (Ann Arbor: University of Michigan Press, 2009), esp. Geoff Eley, "The Trouble with 'Race': Migrancy, Cultural Difference, and the Remaking of Europe," 137–81; Allan Pred, *Even in Sweden: Racisms, Racialized Spaces, and the Popular Geographical Imagination* (Berkeley: University of California Press, 2000); Rita Chin, *The Guest Worker Question in Postwar Germany* (Cambridge: Cambridge University Press, 2007); Paul A. Silverstein, *Algeria in France: Transpolitics, Race, and Nation* (Bloomington: Indiana University Press, 2004); Sue Peabody and Tyler Stovall, eds., *The Color of Liberty: Histories of Race in France* (Durham, NC: Duke University Press, 2003); Paul Gilroy, "One Nation under a Groove: The Cultural Politics of 'Race' and Racism in Britain," in *Anatomy of Racism,* ed. David Theo Goldberg (Minneapolis: University of Minnesota Press, 1990), 263–82; Jeffrey M. Peck, "Rac(e)ing the Nation: Is There a German 'Home'?" *New Formations* 17 (1992): 75–84; Herrick Chapman and Laura L. Frader, eds., *Race in France: Interdisciplinary Perspectives on the Politics of Difference* (New York: Berghahn, 2004); Trica Danielle Keaton, *Muslim Girls and the Other France: Race, Identity Politics,*

and *Social Exclusion* (Bloomington: In-
diana University Press, 2006); Kathleen
Paul, *Whitewashing Britain: Race and
Citizenship in the Postwar Era* (Ithaca,
NY: Cornell University Press, 1997);
Michèle Lamont, Ann Morning, and Mar-
garita Mooney, "Particular Universalisms:
North African Immigrants Respond to
French Racism," *Ethnic and Racial Studies*
25.3 (2002): 390–414; Piper, *Racism, Na-
tionalism, and Citizenship*.

36. See chapter 12, "Chinese Americans, Turkish Germans: Parallels in Two
Racial Systems," for some of the perspectives I gained by interviewing fifty adult
children of immigrants in Germany. I am
currently at work on a book based partly on
those interviews, which bears the working
title *Growing Up Ethnic in Germany*.

37. For a fuller discussion of this issue
in the U.S. context, see Tim Wise, *White
like Me: Reflections on Race from a Privileged
Son* (Brooklyn, NY: Soft Skull Press, 2005).

38. Racialized relationships occur in
every part of the world – for example, in
Russia (see Maxim Kireev, "National-
ists Calling for 'Clean Moscow': Planned
Mosque Sparks Controversy in Russia,"
Spiegel Online, October 19, 2010, http://
www.spiegel.de/international/world/
nationalists-calling-for-clean-moscow
-planned-mosque-sparks-controversy-in
-russia-a-723799.html; Matthias Schepp,
"Anarchy in Dagestan: Islamists Gain Up-
per Hand in Russian Republic," Spiegel
Online, July 30, 2010, http://www.spiegel
.de/international/world/anarchy-in
-dagestan-islamists-gain-upper-hand
-in-russian-republic-a-709176.html),
and in Israel ("Israel's Cabinet Approves
Controversial Loyalty Oath," *Los Angeles
Times*, October 11, 2010; Edmund Sand-
ers, "Israel to Deport Children of Some
Migrant Workers," *Los Angeles Times*, August 2, 2010). For a start on the subject of
racialized hierarchies in many countries in
different parts of the world, see Spickard,

Race and Nation, especially the bibliogra-
phy, 365–82.

39. Arthur Comte de Gobineau, *The
Inequality of Human Races* (1853–55) (New
York: Fertig, 1999); Madison Grant, *The
Passing of the Great Race, or, The Racial
Basis of European History* (New York:
Scribner's, 1916); Lothrop Stoddard, *The
Rising Tide of Color against White World-
Supremacy* (New York: Scribner's, 1923);
Edwin Black, *War against the Weak: Eu-
genics and America's Campaign to Create
a Master Race* (New York: Four Walls /
Eight Windows, 2003); Daniel J. Kevles,
*In the Name of Eugenics: Genetics and the
Uses of Human Heredity* (Cambridge, MA:
Harvard University Press, 1985); Nancy
Ordover, *American Eugenics: Race, Queer
Anatomy, and the Science of Nationalism*
(Minneapolis: University of Minnesota
Press, 2003); Gregory Michael Dorr, *Seg-
regation's Science: Eugenics and Society in
Virginia* (Charlottesville: University of
Virginia Press, 2008); Alexandra Stern,
*Eugenic Nation: Faults and Frontiers of Bet-
ter Breeding in Modern America* (Berkeley:
University of California Press, 2005);
Richard J. Herrnstein and Charles Mur-
ray, *The Bell Curve: Intelligence and Class
Structure in American Life* (New York:
Free Press, 1994); Steven Fraser, ed., *The
Bell Curve Wars: Race, Intelligence, and the
Future of America* (New York: Basic Books,
1995); Edward O. Wilson, *Sociobiology: The
New Synthesis* (Cambridge, MA: Harvard
University Press, 1975); Pierre L. Van den
Berghe, *The Ethnic Phenomenon* (New
York: Elsevier, 1981); J. Philippe Rushton,
Race, Evolution, and Behavior (New Bruns-
wick, NJ: Transaction Publishers, 1997);
John Alcock, *The Triumph of Sociobiology*
(New York: Oxford, 2003); Richard Lynn,
*Race Differences in Intelligence: An Evolu-
tionary Analysis* (Augusta, GA: Washing-
ton Summit Publishers, 2006).

For tracings of the history of these ideas,
see Spickard, *Almost All Aliens*, 262–73;

Bruce Baum, *The Rise and Fall of the Cau-
casian Race: A Political History of Racial
Identity* (New York: NYU Press, 2006);
Stephen Jay Gould, *The Mismeasure of Man,*
rev. ed. (New York: Norton, 1996); Joseph
L. Graves Jr., *The Emperor's New Clothes:
Biological Theories of Race at the Millennium*
(New Brunswick, NJ: Rutgers University
Press, 2001); William H. Tucker, *The Sci-
ence and Politics of Racial Research* (Urba-
na: University of Illinois Press, 1994); Paul
Spickard, "The Return of Pseudoscientific
Racism? DNA Testing, Race, and the New
Eugenics Movement" (manuscript in
submission).

40. I lay this concept out in more detail
in "Race and Nation, Identity and Power:
Thinking Comparatively about Ethnic
Systems," in *Race and Nation,* ed. Spick-
ard, 1–29, especially 11–13. See also Yehudi
O. Webster, *The Racialization of America*
(New York: St. Martin's, 1992); Robert
Miles, *Racism after 'Race Relations'* (New
York: Routledge, 1993); Michael Omi and
Howard Winant, *Racial Formation in the
United States,* 2d ed. (New York: Rout-
ledge, 1994); Steve Martinot, *The Rule of
Racialization: Class, Identity, Governance*
(Philadelphia: Temple University Press,
2003); Tania Das Gupta et al., eds., *Race
and Racialization: Essential Readings* (Ed-
inburgh: Canongate Books, 2007).

41. For an examination of racial sys-
tems in seventeen countries, see Spick-
ard, *Race and Nation.* For Asia, see also
Frank Dikötter, *The Discourse of Race in
Modern China* (Stanford, CA: Stanford
University Press, 1992); Frank Dikötter,
ed., *The Construction of Racial Identities in
China and Japan* (Honolulu: University
of Hawai'i Press, 1997); Adrienne Lynn
Edgar, *Tribal Nation: The Making of Soviet
Turkmenistan* (Princeton, NJ: Princeton
University Press, 2004). A place to begin
on the voluminous literature on race in
Latin America is Henry Goldschmidt and
Elizabeth McAlister, eds., *Race, Nation,*
and Religion in the Americas (New York:
Oxford, 2004).

42. Vijay Prashad, *Everybody Was Kung
Fu Fighting: Afro-Asian Connections and
the Myth of Cultural Purity* (Boston: Beacon, 2002), 38.

43. Portelli, "Problem of the Color-
Blind," 355–56.

44. The Balkan nations may be the
exception, in that there the conversation
seems not to have begun. In fact, the
widespread interethnic mixing that was
officially encouraged in the days of the Yu-
goslav federation has come to be denied,
replaced by fictions of national ethnic
homogeneity. See, for example, Jasminka
Dedic, Vlasta Jalusic, and Jelka Zorn,
*The Erased: Organized Innocence and the
Politics of Exclusion* (Ljubliana: Mirovni
Institut, 2003).

45. Peter Finn, "Fear of Muslims Ben-
efits Europe's Rightists," *International
Herald Tribune,* March 30–31, 2002; Jef-
frey Fleishman, "'Love's Refugees' Feel
Betrayed by Denmark," *Los Angeles Times,*
September 6, 2004; "Denmark's Immigra-
tion Issue," BBC News, February 19, 2005;
Jeffrey Fleishman, "A Mutual Suspicion
Grows in Denmark," *Los Angeles Times,*
November 12, 2005; Jeffrey Fleishman,
"Muslim Lawmaker Assimilated and
Berated," *Los Angeles Times,* October 8,
2006; John Tagliabue, "Denmark's Un-
abashed Lightning Rod on Immigration,"
New York Times, November 10, 2007;
Anna Reimann, "Integration through
Penury? Denmark Debates a Lower Minimum Wage for Immigrants," Spiegel Online, July 15, 2010, http://www.spiegel
.de/international/europe/integration-
through-penury-denmark-debates
-a-lower-minimum-wage-for-immigrants
-a-706762.html; "Denmark to Reintro-
duce Border Controls on Tuesday," Spiegel Online, July 1, 2011, http://www
.spiegel.de/international/europe/
corrosion-of-the-freedom-to-travel

-denmark-to-reintroduce-border-controls
-on-tuesday-a-771888.html; Christopher
Schult, "The Saboteurs among Us: Danish
Border Controls Shake EU Foundations,"
Spiegel Online, July 5, 2011, http://www
.spiegel.de/international/europe/the-
saboteurs-among-us-danish-border
-controls-shake-eu-foundations-a-772517
.html; "Border Barbs: Danish Populists
Have Harsh Words for German Critics,"
Spiegel Online, July 12, 2011, http://www
.spiegel.de/international/europe/border-
barbs-danish-populists-have-harsh
-words-for-german-critics-a-773731.html.

46. Mark Landler, "Immigrant Girl's
Plight Draws Debate in Austria," *Interna-
tional Herald Tribune*, October 18, 2007;
Rod Nordland, "Charging to the Right,"
Newsweek, October 4, 2008; Nicholas
Kulish and Eugen Freund, "Austrian
Far-Rightist is Killed in Car Crash: Jörg
Haider Changed Nation's Politics," *Inter-
national Herald Tribune*, October 13, 2008;
"Austrian Anti-Muslim Video Game:
'We'd Rather have Sarrazin than a Muez-
zin,'" Spiegel Online, September 2, 2010,
http://www.spiegel.de/international/
zeitgeist/austrian-anti-muslim-video
-game-we-d-rather-have-sarrazin-than
-a-muezzin-a-715278.html.

47. Partly this seems to have been a
response to a 2006 move by the conservative state of Baden-Württemburg to use
a test to discourage orthodox Muslims
from applying for citizenship there; David
Sells, "German Citizenship Test Causes
Uproar," *Los Angeles Times*, February 17,
2006.

48. "Citizenship Tests to Become
Compulsory across Germany in Fall,"
Deutsche Welle-World, June 11, 2008;
"New German Citizenship Questions
Flunk Cultural Sensitivity Test," *Deutsche
Welle-World*, July 8, 2008; "Objections to
Citizenship Test Continue to Mount,"
Deutsche Welle-World, July 10, 2008; "Ger-
man Citizenship Test Goes into Effect,"

The Local, September 1, 2008, http://www
.thelocal.de/national/20080901-14041
.html; "Turkish, Jewish Groups Slam
German Citizenship Test," *Jewish World*,
October 7, 2008, http://www.ynetnews
.com/articles/0,7340,L-3566733,00.html.
An example of the test preparation books
is *Einbürgerungstest* (Wuppertal: Spinbooks, 2008). Spiegel Online has sample
test questions for English speakers at
http://www1.spiegel.de/active/quiztool/
fcgi/quiztool.fcgi?id=32516 (I got a perfect
score; but then, I have a PhD in history).

49. Trapp said, "We have to establish
criteria for immigration that really benefit our country. In addition to adequate
education and job qualifications, one
benchmark should be intelligence. I am in
favor of intelligence tests for immigrants";
"Germany's Immigration Debate: Politician Demands IQ Tests for Would-Be Immigrants," Spiegel Online, June 28, 2010,
http://www.spiegel.de/international/
germany/germany-s-immigration-debate
-politician-demands-iq-tests-for-would
-be-immigrants-a-703328.html. On Sarrazin, see Thilo Sarrazin, *Deutschland schafft
sich ab: Wie wir unser Land auf Spiel setzen*
(Berlin: Deutsche Verlags-anstalt, 2010);
Institut für Staatspolitik, *Der Fall Sarrazin*
(Albersroda: Rittergut Schnellroda, 2010);
Deutschlandstiftung Integration, *Sarrazin: Eine deutsche Debatte* (Munich: Piper
Verlag, 2010); Herrnstein and Murray, *Bell
Curve*.

50. David Charter, "Banned Dutch MP
Geert Wilders Hits Out at 'Cowards' after
Being Sent Back," *Times of London*, Febru-
ary 13, 2009.

51. An extreme – and extremely popular – version of this kind of racialization
of religion is Samuel P. Huntington, *The
Clash of Civilizations and the Remaking
of World Order* (New York: Simon and
Schuster, 1998). On the racialization of
religion, see Goldsmith and McAlister,
eds., *Race, Nation, and Religion in the*

Americas; Warren J. Blumenfeld, Khyati Joshi, and Ellen E. Fairchild, eds., *Investigating Christian Privilege and Religious Oppression in the United States* (Rotterdam: Sense Publishers, 2008); Kevin M. Dunn, Natascha Klocker, and Natanya Salabay, "Contemporary Racism and Islamophobia in Australia," *Ethnicities* 7.4 (2007): 564–89; Khyati M. Joshi, *New Roots in America's Sacred Ground: Religion, Race, and Ethnicity in Indian America* (New Brunswick, NJ: Rutgers University Press, 2006); Paul Spickard, *Almost All Aliens,* 288–89, 423–28, 452–56; Tariq Modood, *Multicultural Politics: Racism, Ethnicity and Muslims in Britain* (Edinburgh: Edinburgh University Press, 2005).

52. On these figures and the Dutch racial-religious-nationality debate, see Sebastian Rotella, "Maverick Dutch Politician Is Slain before Elections," *Los Angeles Times,* May 7, 2002; Marlise Simons, "2 Dutch Deputies on the Run, from Jihad Death Threats," *New York Times,* March 4, 2005; Christopher Caldwell, "Daughter of the Enlightenment," *New York Times,* April 3, 2005; Andrés Martinez, "The Borders Are Closing," *Los Angeles Times,* June 1, 2005; Ian Buruma, *Murder in Amsterdam: Liberal Europe, Islam, and the Limits of Tolerance* (New York: Penguin, 2006); Ayaan Hirsi Ali, *The Caged Virgin: An Emancipation Proclamation for Women and Islam* (New York: Free Press, 2006); Timothy Garton Ash, "Islam in Europe," *New York Review of Books,* October 5, 2006; Arthur Max, "Durch Coalition Aims to Ban Burqas," *Seattle Times,* November 18, 2006; Paul Sniderman and Louk Hagendoorn, *When Ways of Life Collide: Multiculturalism and Its Discontents in the Netherlands* (Princeton, NJ: Princeton University Press, 2007); Ayaan Hirsi Ali, *Infidel* (New York: Free Press, 2007); Ron Eyerman, *The Assassination of Theo Van Gogh: From Social Drama to Cultural Trauma* (Durham, NC: Duke University Press, 2008); John

Vinocur, "On Dutch Left, a Retreat from 'Tolerance' of Old," *International Herald Tribune,* December 30, 2008.

53. Both assassins were Dutch citizens, but one was from an immigrant family, and both seem to have acted from political motives.

54. This information came from Wilders's web page: http://www.geert wilders.nl/, accessed July 24, 2012. See also John F. Burns, "Britain Deports Dutch 'Provocateur'," *International Herald Tribune,* February 2, 2009; Juliane von Mittelstaedt, "The Netherlands' Fearmonger: Geert Wilders' One-Man Crusade against Islam," Spiegel Online, November 12, 2009, http://www.spiegel.de/international/ europe/the-netherlands-fearmonger -geert-wilders-one-man-crusade-against -islam-a-660649.html; Folkert Jensma, "Hatred Trial in Amsterdam: Has Geert Wilders Broken the Law?" Spiegel Online, January 20, 2010, http://www.spiegel .de/international/europe/hatred-trial -in-amsterdam-has-geert-wilders-broken -the-law-a-672925.html; Mirjam Hecking, "The Hunt for Moderate Voters: Will Geert Wilders Move toward the Center? Spiegel Online, March 10, 2010, http://www .spiegel.de/international/europe/the -hunt-for-moderate-voters-will-geert -wilders-move-toward-the-center-a -682788.html; "Geert Wilders' Success: Anti-Muslim Populists Make Big Gains in Dutch Vote," Spiegel Online, June 10, 2010, http://www.spiegel.de/international/ europe/geert-wilders-success-anti -muslim-populists-make-big-gains-in -dutch-vote-a-699862.html; Mike Corder, "Anti-Islam Lawmaker not Part of Dutch Government," *Associated Press,* July 30, 2010; Jurjen van de Pol and Maud van Gaal, "Wilders's Anti-Islamic Party Holds Key in Dutch Government Deal," *Bloomberg News Service,* August 2, 2010; "Another EU Country May Ban Burka," *Los Angeles Times,* October 1, 2010.

55. Ian Buruma, "Parade's End: Dutch Liberals Get Tough," *New Yorker,* December 7, 2009, 36–41. Lest one imagine that this is dispassionate analysis, note this view by Frits Bolkestein, a leading Dutch politician and former European commissioner (and critic of immigration): "One must never underestimate the degree of hatred that Dutch people feel for Moroccan and Turkish immigrants"; Garton Ash, "Islam in Europe."

56. Clare Nullis, "Nationalist's Election to Swiss Cabinet Stirs Strong Views," *Oregonian,* December 11, 2003; "Swiss Reject Easing of Citizenship Rules," *Los Angeles Times,* September 27, 2004; Tom Wright, "Swiss Vote to Join Europe Plan to End Some Passport Controls," *New York Times,* June 6, 2005; Tom Wright, "Easing Foreign Workers' Way in Switzerland," *New York Times,* September 26, 2005; "Swiss People's Party Rejoins Government," *International Herald Tribune,* December 11, 2008; Michael Kimmelman, "Swiss Culture War Has Genteel Spin," *International Herald Tribune,* May 28, 2009; Marc Hujer, "The 'National Conservatives': An Urbane Publisher Becomes the Populist Voice of Switzerland," Spiegel Online, March 18, 2010, http://www .spiegel.de/international/europe/the -national-conservatives-an-urbane -publisher-becomes-the-populist-voice -of-switzerland-a-684220.html.

57. Michael Soukup, "Anger over Anti-Islamic Poster: Why the Swiss Are Afraid of Minarets," Spiegel Online, October 13, 2009, http://www.spiegel.de/ international/europe/anger-over-anti-is-lamic-poster-why-the-swiss-are-afraid-of-minarets-a-654963.html; Deborah Lauter, "Swiss Ban on Minarets Stirs Debate in Europe," *Los Angeles Times,* December 1, 2009; Christopher Hawthorne, "Minaret Ban Built on Mistrust," *Los Angeles Times,* December 2, 2009; Jean-François Mayer, "Analysis: A Majority of Swiss Voters

Decide to Ban the Building of New Minarets," *Religioscope,* http://religion.info/ english/articles/article_455.shtml, accessed July 24, 2012.

58. Anders Behring Breivik, "2083 – A European Declaration of Independence," posted online July 22, 2011 (available immediately at several net locations, including http://thepiratebay.org/torrent/ 6569021/Anders_Behring_Breivik_Oslo _Bomber_Manifesto); Thomas Hegghammer, "The Rise of the Macro-Nationalists," *New York Times,* July 30, 2011; "The Trail of Evil: Can Europe's Populists Be Blamed for Anders Breivik's Crusade?" Spiegel Online, August 1, 2011, http:// www.spiegel.de/international/europe/ the-trail-of-evil-can-europe-s-populists -be-blamed-for-anders-breivik-s-crusade -a-777710.html. For a more dispassionate analysis of the state of Islam in the Nordic region, see Göran Larsson, ed., *Islam in the Nordic and Baltic Countries* (London: Routledge, 2009).

59. Europe is not alone in this. It is also true of Japan, South Korea, and Singapore among industrialized nations, and Japan, at least, is beginning to talk about it. On Japan, see Paul Spickard, "Managing Multiculturalism: America's Identity, Japan's Task?" *Civilizations* 11–12 (2007): 23–32; Michael Weiner, ed., *Japan's Minorities: The Illusion of Homogeneity,* 2d ed. (New York: Routledge, 2008); John Lie, *Multiethnic Japan* (Cambridge, MA: Harvard University Press, 2004).

60. For a start toward solutions, see *Muslims in Europe: A Report on 11 EU Cities* (New York, London, Budapest: Open Society Institute, 2010). Two dozen Open Society Institute social scientists conducted surveys and focus groups among Muslims, immigrant and native born, in Belgium, Denmark, France, Germany, the Netherlands, Sweden, and the United Kingdom. Their conclusions about the state of prejudice and discrimination mirror those laid

out in this chapter so far. They also go on to make a number of constructive recommendations for local governments and majority populations.

61. François Dupeyron, *Monsieur Ibrahim* (ARP and France 3 Cinema Production, 2003); Fatih Akin, *Gegen die Wand* (Bavaria Film International and Strand Releasing, 2004).

62. Tracy Wilkinson, "A Sister's Sacrifice," *Los Angeles Times*, April 22, 2006. Cf. Tracy Wilkinson, "Muslims' Slice of Italy's Life: He's Egyptian, She's Tunisian, and Their Kids Are Roman," *Los Angeles Times*, October 28, 2005; Tracy Wilkinson, "Italy's Migrants Moving Up to Front Office," *Los Angeles Times*, November 7, 2004; Rhacel Salazar Parreñas, *Servants of Globalization: Women, Migration, and Domestic Work* (Stanford, CA: Stanford University Press, 2001).

63. Craig S. Smith, "French-Born Arabs, Perpetually Foreign, Grow Bitter,"

New York Times, December 26, 2003; Sebastian Rotella, "In the Projects, Emerging Culture: Arab, African and Muslim Roots Are Part of France's Next Generation," *Los Angeles Times*, September 27, 2005 – note that this hopeful note was struck just before the riots broke out.

64. Cf. Lynn Pan, *Sons of the Yellow Emperor: A History of the Chinese Diaspora* (Tokyo: Kodansha, 1994); Philip A. Kuhn, *Chinese among Others: Emigration in Modern Times* (Lanham, MD: Rowman and Littlefield, 2008); Ien Ang, *On Not Speaking Chinese: Living between Asia and the West* (London: Routledge, 2001); Adam McKeown, *Chinese Migrant Networks and Cultural Change: Peru, Chicago, Hawaii, 1900–1918* (Chicago: University of Chicago Press, 2001).

65. Herbert Gans, "Symbolic Ethnicity: The Future of Ethnic Groups and Cultures in America," *Ethnic and Racial Studies* 2.1 (1979): 1–20.

TWO

Ethnic Identities and
Transnational Subjectivities

ANNA RASTAS

THE NUMBER OF NEW ETHNIC MINORITY COMMUNITIES AND the numbers of people belonging to these minorities have grown in many Western societies due to migration. Because of the rapid increases in the diversity of the population, there are also more people, especially children and young people, who are often categorized as immigrants and as members of ethnic or racial minorities but who themselves are not comfortable with these categorizations. This essay discusses problems related to the ethnicity paradigm and identity talk in studies of young people and their positionings in multiethnic societies. I will start with a story about Mika, a fourteen-year-old boy from Finland, which will illustrate that, during a single day or fifteen minutes in a schoolyard, there can be so much variation in subject positions offered for some young people, and in their means to negotiate their positionings, that to name their experiences and their means to negotiate them as ethnic identities is difficult. To talk about changing, fragmented, and contradictory social and cultural identities is nearer the truth, but what is the explanatory power of descriptions of complex and ever-changing identities?

FIFTEEN MINUTES IN A SCHOOLYARD

It is nine o'clock in the morning. Mika is talking with his classmates in the schoolyard. They all look hip-hop with their loose hoodies and jeans with chains. Girls in his class always say that Mika looks even more hip-hop than the other guys because he is Black. The other guys (they are all White) envy him a little because of that, but they are also pleased to have a Black guy in their posse. They have their iPods, and during the school day, they listen only to rap, even though Mika likes different kinds of music. In the evenings at home, he also plays heavy metal, but to be a dedicated fan of heavy metal would be difficult for him. He has never seen Black men in heavy-metal bands. That makes him a little bit sad. It has affected his possibilities to stay friends with some of his old friends, those guys who now wear tight, black jeans and have long, straight hair (he could never make his Afro hair look like that). They have their own group now, their own band, and different music in their iPods. Some of them are still his friends, but not all of them, like the guy who shouts "Rastaman!" every time they meet each other. Mika hates it, as if he should like reggae and stuff just because he looks African. He also hates strange people who call him *brother* when he goes downtown with his friends. His White friends are never called *brothers.*

Anyway, Mika has got friends at school. Now they talk and laugh at each others' jokes. Suddenly, one of them starts to talk about his neighbors who are "refugees from somewhere." Mika remembers how he has been called *pakolainen,* a Finnish word for refugee, many times before, even though he was born in Finland. He feels uncomfortable because of his memories of being bullied and because some of those words that his friend is using when he talks about his neighbors have been used against Mika so many times. He knows that he cannot talk about this with his White friends. He would not be one of them anymore if he started to question the way they talk about other people. At school, he has been able to talk about this name-calling thing only with Valtteri, who once came to him and said, "You are the only one who does not call me 'mustalainen' all the time." *Mustalainen* is a Finnish word, with a lot of negative connotations, referring to people who belong to the Finnish Roma minority.[1] Valtteri, who is two years older than Mika, even told him that if he ever has problems with other guys, name-calling or anything, he can always go to Valtteri who knows how to fight. Mika likes Valtteri, but they are not close friends. Valtteri has a different culture, this Roma culture, which Mika sometimes finds a little bit strange and annoying.

Mika forgets Valtteri when the others start to talk about sports. He likes the topic. He enjoys watching sports on TV since there are many good Black sportsmen and everybody knows that. Mika is a good runner himself, too, not because of his blood or genes, even though everybody seems to think so, but because he has learned how to run fast.

Then the school bell rings. One of the boys says, "History again. Boring." Mika feels a sharp pain in his stomach when he remembers the topic of the day: colonialism and slavery. "Not again," he thinks. He knows that every time they talk about Africa, or slavery, everybody will start to stare at him. He has thought about these things a lot and could talk about these issues with some people, but not with his teacher who is so eager to back Mika's "multicultural identity" in front of all his classmates, most of whom, according to the teacher, "cannot have such an interesting identity." Mika does not want to talk about how he feels about the history of Africans, or about his own "multicultural identity" with his classmates either, because he knows that they are not really interested. When Mika gets to the classroom with the others, he tries to become as invisible as possible.

CHILDREN WITH TRANSNATIONAL ROOTS
CHALLENGING ETHNIC BOUNDARIES

In the above-described fifteen minutes, "ethnicity" and "race" did matter, but not in a way that would make it easy to define the main character's ethnic identity. Some of the questions related to his (potential) identifications and ties to different local, transnational, and diasporic communities and cultures cannot be defined merely as aspects of his racial identity either, like the many meanings of relatives "who are not here." He also has feelings of solidarity with White Finns with an immigrant background, whose "belonging here" is also sometimes questioned by other Finns. For fourteen-year-old Mika, questions related to his ethnic identity are something he probably finds uncomfortable not only because they may remind him of his experiences of exclusion but also because finding definitions that would satisfy both the others and himself would be difficult or even impossible. Even though many current theorizations of ethnicity emphasize the idea that all ethnic identities are negotiated and dynamic, in everyday discussions, questions of ethnicity are still articulated and understood within old nationalistic and racializing discourses[2] that do not allow us freely to choose our ethnic identifications.

Fourteen-year-old Mika in the story above is a fictional character based on what I learned from young people during my ethnographic study about racism in the everyday life of children and young people in Finland. Every detail in the story can be found in the data that I gathered and constructed during my fieldwork between 2000 and 2007. This data comprised over fifty interviews, email correspondence with dozens of people, participatory observation in various locations where children and young people live their everyday lives (kindergartens, schools, hobbies), and a "mother's diary" in which I documented events from my own family life as a mother of two children (now teenagers) adopted from Ethiopia.[3] During those years, I also organized and participated in dozens of events and antiracism activities where children's experiences of racism were discussed.

In the case of immigrants and many ethnic minorities, questions of racism and many other inequalities are often articulated as or turned to questions of cultural differences. To show that also in Finland many phenomena have to be seen as expressions of or as consequences of racism (instead of, for example, some people's deficiency in cultural competence), I wanted to study people whose particularity and experiences cannot be explained by cultural differences or by their status as noncitizens. Thus, I decided to choose informants for my study from among two groups: those Finns who have one Finnish-born parent and one parent with an immigrant or foreign background and those who have been adopted from other countries by Finnish families. Since the majority of immigrants have moved to Finland during and after the 1990s, I had to choose children and young people as my focus group. Focusing on young people's experiences was easy to justify also because, not only in Finland but in general, children have been notably absent in studies on racism.[4]

All those young people who participated in my study were grown-up, and many of them were born in Finland, but altogether they had ties to more than thirty different countries in Africa, Asia, Europe, the Middle East, and South America. Most of them, like the young boy Mika in my story, were visibly different from the majority Finns, but among my informants there were also people who, because of their blond hair or blue eyes, can pass as Finns until other people hear their "foreign" name or get to know something about their background. Since all my informants identified themselves as Finns, or as Finns together with something else, to call their ethnicities something other than Finnish was difficult; in my opinion, it also could have been a racializing act.[5] My starting point was that both open racism and racializing discourses can be identified by studying everyday encounters in which my informants' difference was constructed.[6] By choosing individuals' (or their parents') multiple ties to different countries and nations as the criteria for my research subjects, instead of some alleged and predefined ethnic or racialized identities, I was able to avoid racializing and ethnicizing young people, and I could focus on the processes in which racism, some ideas of ethnicities, and nationalist discourses affect their everyday life and those processes in which their identities are constructed.

Both my informants' Finnishness (as an ethnicity) and their other possible ethnic identifications were often questioned by the surrounding society and also by themselves. Our ideas of ethnicity owe much to the work of anthropologists. Traditionally in anthropological literature, as indicated by Fredric Barth, ethnicity has designated "a population which 1) is largely biologically self-perpetuating, 2) shares fundamental cultural values, realized in overt unity in cultural forms, 3) makes up a field of communication and interaction, 4) has a membership which identifies itself, and is identified by others, as constituting a category distinguishable for other categories of the same order."[7] Barth himself wanted to question traditional understandings of the meanings and workings of ethnicity. According to Barth, ethnicity should be understood as social processes of boundary maintenance, which are often based on political and other strategic reasoning rather than on biology and cultural continuances within particular groups.[8] Whatever our definitions of *ethnicity* and *race,* ethnic and racializing systems of categorization are related and intertwined in many ways. Still, they also refer to distinct aspects of social life and may "operate under completely distinct relations of social and economic power."[9]

Since my study was about racism, I had to make a distinction between ethnic and racial(ized) identities, at least on a theoretical and analytical level. However, to categorize my informants according to their "race" was not any easier than talking about them in terms of their eth-

nicities.[10] In the Finnish language, at the time of my study, there were
no good terms for the descriptions of how my research subjects could be
positioned in racialized relations. In Finland, neither "racial" nor ethnic
categorizations are used in official statistics, and the word *race* is avoided
because of its historical burden.[11] Most ethnic minorities and racialized
groups in Finland are so new and so fragmented that it was difficult
to find established expressions of collective racialized identities, like
"Black" in some other societies.[12] The most appropriate word referring to
"people of color" in Finnish is *tummaihoinen* (dark-skinned), but among
my informants who had experienced racism, there were also some people
who themselves did not identify with that category (who were never
categorized as "dark-skinned" by other people), for example, children of
Russian background.[13] Also, even those who themselves described their
skin color as "dark" or "brown" (usually small children) or "non-White"
could not use those, or any other words, as terms referring to collective racialized identities in Finnish society. Finding words to describe
individuals' positionings in racialized relations would have been easier
if I had studied adults, but since, in Finnish, most color terms, as well as
other words referring to racialized groups, have negative connotations,
using those words to describe my young informants was also ethically
debatable. During my research, I was lost in translation while trying
to apply words from theoretical discussions, mostly in English, to my
analyses of Finnish children's experiences in a society in which proper
words for the descriptions of racialized relations are missing, because,
thus far, there has been so little discussion on racism.

Now, years after my fieldwork, the word *musta* (black) has become
more popular in Finland, both in public discourses and also among "people of color." Compared to the situation in the beginning of 2000, there
are now more young adults, including many media celebrities, who talk
about their racialized difference in public. Some of them have started to
use the word *musta* when they talk about themselves and other racialized groups in Finland. This has created possibilities also for other young
people to use this word as a political collective identity with positive connotations. Nevertheless, being Black in the Finnish language still means
risk taking, and many young Finns avoid using *musta*, even though they
may use the word *Black* as a self-definition when they speak in English.[14]

It took me quite a long time to find words, a kind of a category, to describe my focus groups, since I wanted it to underline both my informants' Finnishness, their right to belong to Finland and their roots here, and also their ties to other countries, nations, and cultures. I finally decided to call my focus group "children with transnational roots." "Transnational roots" is a metaphor, and it has its problems, as do all metaphors. Both in everyday discussions and in research, the roots metaphor strongly refers to ideas of blood or genes, to ideas of how our belonging (to a family, to an ethnic group, to a nation) is based on so-called biological ties.[15] Contesting these ideas has been a central project in studies of racism. However, even though there are risks for an antiracist researcher to use these roots metaphors, roots can also be thought about differently. In plural form, the term *transnational roots* challenges the idea that we have ties only to one place, one nation, and one culture. Even if we only refer to genes when we talk about roots, we cannot ignore the fact that every individual has two (four, eight, etc.) different sources from which his or her genes come. We can also question the nature of our roots. There is always the biological, material dimension of being a human being, but it does not mean that we should place all our questions there. Our task as social scientists is to explore the social and cultural meanings of roots and their consequences in our everyday life.

Transnationalism has become such a central concept in studies of migration and multiethnic societies that some scholars talk about a transnational turn in migration research.[16] In anthropology, the shift toward a study of transnational communities as a consequence of an epistemic move away from methodological nationalism has resulted in what Andreas Wimmer and Nina Glick Schiller call the "dissing" of previous paradigms.[17] In light of the demographic changes in Europe, caused by the increased mobility of people, this shift is inevitable especially in research on children and young people. The notion of transnationality is useful here because it refers to individuals' and groups' multiple ties and relations across the borders of nation-states and to ideas that our relations to different places and nations, at the same time, are significant. We can, of course, question the usability of this metaphor by saying that every individual in this world has transnational roots. However, in everyday social interaction, subject positions, or identities, offered for some people are different from subject positions available for those who are seen, and who identify themselves, as members of only one nation or one ethnic group. The meanings of some people's roots arise especially when their belonging "here" is questioned by other people, in encounters in which also some people's difference is constructed. When some people's transnational roots matter – meaning when these processes, individuals' negotiations of their personal relations to several nations and cultures at the same time, including global diasporic collectives and cultures, become an important part of their lived subjectivity – we can talk about transnational subjectivities.[18]

People who are categorized as members of and who themselves identify with particular ethnic minorities are, without dispute, most often potential victims of racism in many societies. Focusing on people whose ethnic identities are not clearly defined was a choice embedded in my research design due to some special characteristics of Finnish society. However, it made me realize that, even in other countries, we cannot focus only on ethnic minorities, or individuals' ethnicities, if we want to identify racism in contemporary Western societies. Even if we ignore discussions on the many problems related to the ethnicity paradigm in studies of racism and the requests to make a distinction between ethnic and racial categorizations and ethnic and racialized identities,[19] defining research subjects in terms of their ethnic identities, or in terms of their race, has become difficult, especially in the case of younger population groups in Europe. There are differences between different countries in how ethnicity and "race" is, or is not, used as a variable in national censuses[20]; therefore, giving exact numbers, as well as making comparisons between countries, is difficult. However, demographic statistics in many countries reveal rapid increases in population diversity. For example, in Britain, around 85 percent of individuals described themselves as White British in a study based on labor-force household data between 2004 and 2008. Yet, according to the same study, one in five children under sixteen were from minority groups, and almost one in ten were living in families that contained mixed or multiple heritages.[21] In Sweden, already twenty-five percent of children were either themselves born or have at least one parent born outside Sweden.[22] In the United States, the majority of the population has always been of immigrant background.[23]

Today, every fifth child in the United States has, or her parents have, an immigrant background.[24]

In Finland, the numbers of children and young people are higher in many immigrant groups than the numbers of children and young people on the national average. Among immigrants' children, there will always be people who do not necessarily identify themselves with their parents' ethnic groups. Also, even though the rapid increase of the number of individuals with differently racialized parentage in Europe is difficult to prove by statistics, it can be seen in most day-care centers and schools. Young people of differently racialized parentage, as well as transnational adoptees, have become visible groups in many countries also through their own activities and their attempts to have a voice in this world. These groups run their local and global networks on the Internet; autobiographies, anthologies, and other texts written by people who belong to these groups have become a growing genre in literature in many countries. Their existence can also be seen in popular youth cultural representations in the "hot EA (ethnic ambiguity)" discourses.[25]

SOME DIMENSIONS OF TRANSNATIONAL SUBJECTIVITIES

During the interviews I conducted with children and young people, in addition to their experiences of racism, other themes were discussed, such as their ideas of belonging to Finland on the one hand and to the other country or nation or culture on the other. I also asked questions related to their ideas toward different minorities and minority issues, as well as questions related to multiculturalism in Finland. Even though my intention was to focus on their experiences of racism,[26] many other meanings of their ties to different countries and nations and cultures arose during our discussions. Both stories of encounters with other people and expressions of their inner negotiations of their transnational roots cannot totally be separated from phenomena that can be articulated as questions of ethnicity and/or racism. However, I could not ignore my young informants' attempts to explain how frustrated they were with other people's categorizations referring to "their ethnic or 'racial' identities." Even though they could not provide me with any alternative vocabularies of belonging, I realized that, to understand the processes in which their multiple identities are constructed and negotiated, I should find alternative ways to conceptualize these questions. Therefore, to avoid preconceived categorizations and to make visible the various identificatory possibilities, I decided to approach some questions as aspects of their transnational subjectivities, or, as indicated by Floya Anthias, "translocational positionalities,"[27] rather than as their ethnic (or any other particular) identities.

Let us go back to my story of Mika. We do not know anything about his personal history. I did not include those things in my story on purpose. I wonder how many people can read the story without starting to speculate about the reasons behind his particularity as a non-White child in the Finnish schoolyard where most children are White. While the other children in his class are regarded as just Finnish children, even when Mika's Finnishness is accepted, he is always a person with a particular history that other people start to inquire about. Children like Mika are used to questions like "Where are you from?" "Where are your parents from?" "Are you adopted?" "Are you half-Finnish?" "Are you really 100 percent Finnish?"

The need to explain things about your (or your parents') personal history, even to strangers, becomes a central aspect of some people's subjectivities. Even in societies like the United States or Britain or France, where at least in some locations White people may be in the minority, some people's "being from here" is considered as something natural,[28] while some other people always have to be prepared to explain their roots and their reasons for their being here. Mika in my story probably wants to be above all just a Finnish boy, like most of his friends, but questions about his roots elsewhere, or about his multicultural identity, construct and constantly remind him of his nonbelonging. In Finland, where the majority of people with an immigrant background come from Estonia and Russia, it can be very difficult to be "just a Finn" also for a White child whose name is, for example, Aleksandr or Jekaterina. While forcing young people to negotiate and articulate their belongings, even to places and people and cultures that may be strange to them, these seemingly innocent questions and assumptions become part of the processes in which some people's transnational subjectivities are constructed.

Some of my informants had lived also outside Finland, in the other parent's country, and they had real, existing ties to that country and culture. For those young people, it was much easier to make a list of the different meanings of their roots: "I can speak two languages properly"; "I have a place where I can go if I don't want to live in Finland"; "I know two different cultures, and I know what cultural differences are about." Some of these young people underlined their Finnishness; others said that they enjoy being able to choose things from both of these different cultures. Most of them seemed to be quite happy with their double or hybrid identities. In spite of their experiences of racism, and momentary feelings of exclusion both in Finland and in that other place, they were able to benefit from their roots. However, among my informants, there were also many people who were forced to negotiate and explain their relations to particular places and people and cultures even when there were no real ties and even when the truth of their own roots was not known. In the case of many adoptees, nothing is known about their biological parents, and many transnational adoptees do not have any memories of their birth country. For many of them, issues of separation and loss, of belonging and difference, are central aspects of their subjectivities throughout their lives, but especially in their childhood and youth.[29] Among my informants, there were also people whose mother is a Finn but who did not know their (biological) father's ethnic background, not even his nationality with certainty. Not being White is a heavy burden for Mika, especially because, in his class at school, he, like many Finnish children of African descent, is the only one who looks African. Bibi Bakare-Yusuf writes that, while examining the lived experience of diasporicity, we need to understand more deeply "how on a physical and psychic level the effects of uprooting, rooting and re-rooting can be experienced with mixed emotions and responses."[30] Mika often thinks how much easier life would be if he were White. But being treated as White by his White color-blind friends is not necessarily nice either: in their "White club," racial and ethnic slurs are not disapproved of, even though these words hurt our boy. To be able to speak about his experiences and share his feelings of exclusion, he needs other people who, like himself, are not categorized as White, or as Finns. If he were from an immigrant family, he probably would have some contacts with people like him, but he could also be one of those adoptees who do not know anything about their biological parents' ethnic background or one of those people who cannot be sure about the truth of the stories they have heard about their biological fathers. So, there is no particular nationality (other than Finnish) or ethnic group he could identify himself with. To think about himself as an African is also difficult. Things related to Africa and Africanness are often related to him by other people, even though he does not have any definite social or cultural ties to Africa or Africanness. In Finland, as in every Western society, most things related to Africa or Africanness, for example, in the media or in the teaching at school, are somehow negative: racist representations,[31] histories of oppression, images of war and poor people who are seen only as objects of humanitarian aid.[32] For many young people, the international Black diaspora is a more likely source of identification than the African cultures they are unfamiliar with. However, in countries like Finland, especially outside the bigger cities, being able to learn about and identify with the global Black culture(s) can also be difficult, even impossible, for some young people.

By being hip-hop, Mika is able to benefit from being Black or non-White. Positive representations of particular cultures and discourses of commercialized ethnicity may offer extra social and cultural capital, even extra opportunities for some young people.[33] Among my interviewees, there were some young adults whose fathers were from Japan. Most of them had memories of bullying at school in the 1990s. Other children had called them "Nips." Unlike in their childhood, Japan (especially phenomena like *anime* and *cosplay*) is now cool among Finnish children. According to my informants, it makes things much easier for Finnish-Japanese children today. Many young Finnish-Japanese are nowadays active participants not only in activities related to Japanese popular culture but also, for example, in the hip-hop genre. For teenagers and young adults, crossing racial boundaries through youth cultural consumption[34] is easier than for children, whose world on the level of everyday interaction can be more prejudiced and to whom challenging other people's ideas and opinions can be more difficult. Still, there are limits in how young people are able to "turn the new celebratory discourses into empowering identity recourses."[35] The accessibility to those fashion worlds is defined in discourses in which gender, prevailing beauty ideals, commercial trends, and old images of different cultures, races, and nationalities intertwine, allowing only some young people to celebrate.

A young woman who was born in Africa but had lived in Finland most of her life told me how she had taken off her headscarf in a reggae club because "Everybody said that my [White] friend's scarf looked really good. They admired her dreadlocks and her scarf, but for me they said that I look like an immigrant with my scarf." In a predominantly White society, non-White people are often categorized as immigrants and seen through negative ideas that are related to immigrants. Many immigrant groups are seen as people who lack language skills and cultural competence, as beneficiaries of social welfare (wasting good taxpayers' money), potential criminals, and so on. For many young people, being positioned as a noncitizen or as a less-than-full citizen in local social hierarchies, in addition to being labeled with the negative ideas associated with many immigrant groups, means that they are forced to negotiate not just the ethnicities that they may identify with but also all those other positionings imposed on anyone who is not considered as one of "Us." Transnational subjectivites are constructed not only out of individuals' real identifications with particular people, places, and cultures but also out of their negotiations of all those representations and images associated with them by other people. This sometimes creates pressure for some children to distance themselves from a particular or all other ethnic and racialized minorities and things related to those cultures. Still, being associated with other "Others" and knowing that there are some connective bonds like experiences of racism may also create solidarities and imaginative ties between people, also across ethnic and racial boundaries.

Mika in my story does not identify himself with any particular ethnic minority in Finland, but there are momentary solidarities between him and immigrants and between him and those Finns who belong to different ethnic and racialized minorities. These solidarities are constructed in encounters in which Mika knows that they know, and they know that Mika also knows, that their everyday life can be as complicated as his life. Having mixed emotions and feelings toward some people just because they "look like him," being able to identify with particular groups of subordinated people because of his own experiences of racism and other forms of exclusion, and at the same time not being able to share many things with these people, including some people categorized as Black, make Mika's inner negotiations of belonging and not belonging to various others an integral – and, at the same time, a complex and often confusing – part of his growing up.

OPPRESSIVE IDENTITY TALK

Children's right to learn what some regard as "their own culture" is emphasized in discussions of multiculturalism and ethnic minorities. This "own culture" usually refers to particular aspects of children's parents' ethnicities rather than those various cultural fields where children and young people negotiate their belonging. However, if we view children as subjects of their own lives, as active agents, a child's own culture is made of her everyday negotiations of belonging and not-belonging to here and there, to various constructions of Us and various Them, to real and imagined diaspora communities and cultures, popular youth cultures, and other cultures transmitted among peers. To be able to join and belong to those communities, whether real or imagined, that may welcome an individual and that may feel like "home"[36] means not just maintaining but also creating ties to other people and places and cultures.

The meanings of our ties and roots to different places and people and cultures are situational. They depend on time and place, age and gender, and people and cultural representations with which we may or may not identify and which we are or are not forced to negotiate. Therefore, ideas of fixed ethnic or racialized or whatever identities do not necessarily help us understand transnational subjectivities or social relations and all those processes of cultural production that take place in multiethnic and multicultural societies. Ethnicity and identity are useful and valuable theoretical concepts that we still need when we study ethnic relations, racism, and questions related to migration. Ethnicity is a good concept for many purposes, but it has become either too broad and vague or too restrictive for descriptions of the particularities of some people's lives and of the complexity of social relations in contemporary societies. The idea of transnational subjectivities, instead of ethnic identities, may help us see the complexity of the everyday life of many children and young people.

The problem with the notion of identity is that, even though researchers see identities as complex and contradictory and changing, in everyday discussions ideas of identities as fixed still dominate.[37] In the field, I often felt that talking about identities is for many of my informants really frustrating. I did not use the word *identity* in my questions to them, but still I remember many discussions in which my informants started to talk about their difficulties in defining their identities. Identity was something they felt they are expected to talk about, especially with strangers. Any identity that differentiates them from other Finns seemed to be something they should reach for, whether it was a stable ethnic identity or a particular kind of political or mixed or whatever identity; at the same time, it was something that most of them saw as difficult to reach and too complex to describe. Therefore, I have chosen transnational subjectivities, instead of (ethnic or racial or any other) identities, as a starting point for my analyses (of young people's multiple identities!). It helps me keep some of my thinking on a theoretical level and allows more critical examination of pregiven vocabularies of belonging. It also makes me think harder before I start to write descriptions of some people's identities and helps me avoid labeling people who do not want to be labeled all the time.

In "A Bill of Rights for Racially Mixed People," Maria P. P. Root writes, "I have the right to identify myself differently than strangers expect me to identify . . . differently than how my parents identify me, . . . to change my identity over my lifetime – and more than once, to have loyalties and identify with more than one group of people, to freely choose whom I befriend and love."[38]

Identity talk still seems to be very much about our being able or not being able to achieve some kind of a feeling of completeness, after we have settled in social relations by making choices between those people and places and cultures we are somehow related to or with which we are associated by other people. This kind of identity talk seems to be more about marking boundaries (between me and the world around me, between us and others) than about crossing borders. With the story of Mika and some other accounts of my research on racism in the everyday life of

Finnish children, I have tried to illustrate how, in multiethnic societies, individuals' negotiations of their relations to various groups of people, to various cultures and various places, may be even more significant than their relations to and identifications with their parents' ethnic groups. For young people with transnational roots and differently racialized parentage, there are borders that make their lives complex and difficult, but that is not the whole story: their everyday life is also about crossing various borders and boundaries.

The fact that some young people's subjectivities are constructed out of many different complex and contradictory elements forces them but also gives them an ability to imagine the world differently. The ability to imagine ourselves elsewhere, among other people, is one important aspect or dimension of transnational subjectivities. Even though it is often racism, and other forms of exclusion, that make some people think about their possibilities to belong somewhere else, it is not only because of racism they have experienced but also because they have feelings toward and imaginary bonds with other people: people who look like me; people who are not from here but who might welcome me if I ever meet them; people whom I can imagine as my relatives; people who are not my relatives and who are not from here but who, anyway, may see the world, or at least some things, the way I do; people whom I do not know and will probably never meet but to whom I am somehow connected. That is something many young people have learned to value, even when these ties, whether real or imagined, may sometimes confuse them. The power to imagine is important, since we all have to imagine our futures, and the way we can do it also affects our agency, what we actually do, how we meet the world and other people.

Some people's identities seem to be more interesting than others'. It is true that the notion of identity is still a valuable analytical concept when we attempt to make sense of individuals' translocal positionalities, the various meanings of their (many) roots, and the complex social relations in multiethnic societies. There are many reasons to be interested in the multiple identities of people whose transnational roots matter. However, if everything we talk and write about *some* young people and if everything that affects their lives are always articulated as questions of "their (ethnic or racial) identities," there is the danger that we, as researchers, may become oppressors in projects in which some people are forced to choose and to perform identities which they themselves know are not 100 percent true or not always true. In contemporary multiethnic societies, we need to focus on the various aspects of individuals' transnational subjectivities, including those that sometimes make young people contest some of the subject positions offered for them. Otherwise, all this identity talk, created and reproduced by us researchers, may turn against some people in their everyday struggles of being and belonging.

NOTES

1. The most usual English translation for the word *mustalainen* is "Gypsy." Even though *mustalainen* is often considered as an ethnic label, it should be understood also as a racializing categorization (in Finnish language, *musta* is "black") and a pejorative label with a lot of negative connotations. The word *mustalainen* is sometimes used among the Finnish Roma themselves, but their organizations recommend the use of *romani* (Roma) instead of *mustalainen*. On how the word *mustalainen* is used among Finnish children, see Anna Rastas, "Racializing Categorization among Young People in Finland," *Young* 13 (May 2005): 156, 160. On the Roma and their position in Finland, see, e.g., *Finland's Romani People*, Brochures of the Ministry of Social Affairs and Health 2004:2 (Helsinki, 2004), http://www.stm.fi/c/document_library/get_file?folderId=28707&name=DLFE-3777.pdf&title=Finland_s_Romani_People_Finitiko_Romaseele_en.pdf, accessed July 30, 2012.

2. See, e.g., Liisa Malkki, "National Geographic: The Rooting of Peoples and the Territorialization of National Identity among Scholars and Refugees," *Cultural Anthropology* 7 (February 1992): 24–44.

3. My dissertation, Anna Rastas, "Rasismi lasten ja nuorten arjessa. Trans-

nationaalit juuret ja monikulttuuristuva Suomi" [Racism in the everyday life of children and young people. Transnational roots and multicultural Finland in the making] (University of Tampere, 2007), was published in Finnish. In English, see, e.g., Anna Rastas, "Racism in the Everyday Life of Finnish Children with Transnational Roots," *Barn* 27 (April 2009): 29–43.

4. E.g., Mani Maniam, Vijay Patel, Satnam Singh, and Chris Robinson, "Race and Ethnicity," in *Doing Research with Children and Young People*, ed. Sandy Fraser et al. (London: Sage, 2004), 232.

5. The idea of Finnishness as an ethnicity is still common in everyday discussions in Finland. It was interrelated with the formation of the nation-state, and it can be identified also in "the ethnographic imagining of Finnishness" in ethnological and folkloristic studies focusing on the ideas of relationship between language and people, even though the place of the Finno-Ugric culture "could not be bounded by political borders"; see Jukka Siikala, "The Ethnography of Finland," *Annual Review of Anthropology* 35 (October 2006): 157, 161.

6. See Sara Ahmed, *Strange Encounters: Embodied Others in Post-Coloniality* (London: Routledge, 2000).

7. Fredrik Barth, "Introduction," in *Ethnic Groups and Boundaries: The Social Organization of Cultural Difference*, ed. Fredric Barth (Oslo: Universitetsforlaget, 1969), 10–11. Cf. Richard Jenkins's summary of "the basic social anthropological model of ethnicity" in Richard Jenkins, *Rethinking Ethnicity: Arguments and Explorations* (London: Sage, 1997), 13.

8. Barth, "Introduction," 11–38.

9. Vilna Bashi, "Racial Categories Matter because Racial Hierarchies Matter: A Commentary," *Ethnic and Racial Studies* 21 (September 1998): 964.

10. See Rastas, "Racializing Categorization among Young People in Finland."

11. Avoiding the word *race* in public discourses and especially in official contexts is common also in other Scandinavian countries; on Norway, see, e.g., Marianne Gullestad, "Blind Slaves of Our Prejudices: Debating 'Culture' and 'Race' in Norway," *Ethnos* 69 (June 2004): 193; on Sweden, see, e.g., Lena S. Sawyer, "Black and Swedish: Racialization and the Cultural Politics of Belonging in Stockholm, Sweden" (PhD diss., University of California, Santa Cruz, 2000).

12. E.g., Darlene Clark Hine, Trica Danielle Keaton, and Stephen Small, eds., *Black Europe and the African Diaspora* (Urbana: University of Illinois Press, 2009); Marta Sofía López, ed., *Afroeurope@ns: Cultures and Identities* (Newcastle on Tyne, U.K.: Cambridge Scholars Publishing, 2008); Nadia Joanne Britton, "Racialized Identity and the Term 'Black,'" in *Practising Identities: Power and Resistance*, ed. Sasha Roseneil and Julie Seymour (London: Macmillan, 1999), 134–54.

13. In Finland, the largest immigrant group is people from Russia and from other parts of the former Soviet Union. See "The Population of Finland in 2008," Statistics Finland, March 27, 2009, http://www.stat.fi/til/vaerak/2008/vaerak_2008_2009-03-27_tie_001_en.html, accessed July 30, 2012.

14. The use of the word *musta/black* has become common also in Finnish media, e.g., in news about Barack Obama. The fact that most people in Finland, including Finnish politicians, openly sympathized with Obama and considered him as the best candidate in the presidential election in the United States, has had it impacts on images of Black people in general, and it has given new, positive connotations to *musta/black* in Finland.

15. See, e.g., Malkki, "National Geographic"; Paul Gilroy, *Against Race: Imagining Political Culture beyond the Color Line* (Cambridge, MA: Harvard University Press, 2001), 111.

16. E.g., Thomas Faist, "The Transnational Turn in Migration Research: Perspectives for the Study of Politics and Polity," in *Transnational Spaces: Disciplinary Perspectives*, ed. Maja Povrzanovic Frykman (Malmö: Malmö University, IMER 2004), 11. See also, e.g., Aihwa Ong, *Flexible Citizenship: The Cultural Logics of Transnationality* (Durham, NC: Duke University Press, 1999); Steven Vertovec, *Transnationalism* (London: Routledge, 2009).

17. Andreas Wimmer and Nina Glick Schiller, "Methodological Nationalism and Beyond: Nation-state Building, Migration and the Social Sciences," *Global Networks* 2 (2002): 301–34.

18. This idea of transnational subjectivities was first presented in "With Near and Distant Kin: Growing Up in Transnational Families," a paper coauthored by Ulla Vuorela and Anna Rastas, presented at the EASA (European Association of Social Anthropologists) Conference, August 26–30, 2008, Ljubljana, Slovenia.

19. See, e.g., Bashi, "Racial Categories Matter," 963.

20. See, e.g., David I. Kertzer and Dominique Arel, eds., *Census and Identity: The*

Politics of Race, Ethnicity, and Language in National Censuses (Cambridge: Cambridge University Press, 2002); Jayne Ifekwu-nigwe, ed., *'Mixed Race' Studies: A Reader* (London: Routledge, 2004).

21. Lucinda Platt, *Ethnicity and Family: Relationships within and between Groups: An Analysis Using the Labour Force Survey* (Institute for Social and Economic Research, University of Essex, 2009), 4. These changes could have been seen also in earlier population statistics in Britain; see, e.g., Charlie Owen, "'Mixed Race' in Official Statistics," in *Rethinking "Mixed Race,"* ed. David Parker and Miri Song (London: Pluto Press, 2001), 150.

22. Camilla Hällgren, "'Working Harder to Be the Same': Everyday Racism among Young Men and Women in Sweden," *Race, Ethnicity and Education* 8 (September 2005): 320.

23. Paul Spickard, *Almost All Aliens: Immigration, Race, and Colonialism in American History and Identity* (New York: Routledge, 2007).

24. Peggy Levitt and Mary C. Waters, "Introduction," in *The Changing Face of Home: The Transnational Lives of the Second Generation*, ed. Peggy Levitt and Mary C. Waters (New York: Russell Sage Foundation, 2002), 1.

25. Jin Haritaworn, "'Caucasian and Thai Make a Good Mix': Gender, Ambivalence and the 'Mixed-Race' Body," *European Journal of Cultural Studies* 12 (February 2009): 59–78.

26. In the scope of this essay, I am not able to deal with all my informants' experiences of racism or with racism in Finland in general. I have dealt with these questions, e.g., in Rastas, "Racializing Categorization"; Rastas, "Racism in the Everyday Life of Finnish Children"; and Anna Rastas, "Am I Still 'White'? Dealing with the Colour Trouble," *Balayi: Culture, Law and Colonialism* 6 (2004): 94–106.

27. Floya Anthias, "Translocational Belonging, Identity and Generation: Questions and Problems in Migration and Ethnic Studies," *Finnish Journal of Ethnicity and Migration* 4.1 (April 2009): 12, http://www.etmu.fi/fjem/pdf/FJEM_1_2009.pdf, accessed July 30, 2012; see also Floya Anthias, "Where Do I Belong? Narrating Collective Identity and Translocational Positionality," *Ethnicities* 2 (2002): 491–515.

28. E.g., see Spickard, *Almost All Aliens*, 416.

29. E.g., see Perlita Harris, ed., *In Search of Belonging: Reflections by Transracially Adopted People* (London: BAAF, 2006); Barbara Yngvesson, "Going 'Home': Adoption, Loss of Bearings, and the Mythology of Roots," in *Cultures of Transnational Adoption*, ed. Toby Volkman (Durham, NC: Duke University Press, 2005), 25–48.

30. Bibi Bakare-Yusuf, "Rethinking Diasporicity: Embodiment, Emotion, and the Displaced Origin," *African and Black Diaspora* 1 (July 2008): 147–48.

31. See, e.g., Stuart Hall, "The Spectacle of the 'Other'," in *Representation: Cultural Representations and Signifying Practises*, ed. Stuart Hall (London: Sage and Open University, 1997), 223–90.

32. See Anna Rastas, "Writing Our Future History Together: Applying Participatory Methods in Research on African Diaspora in Finland," in *Afroeurope@n Configurations: Readings and Projects*, ed. Sabrina Brancato (Newcastle upon Tyne, U.K.: Cambridge Scholars Publishing, 2011), 98–120.

33. See, e.g., Sunaira Maira, "Henna and Hip Hop: The Politics of Cultural Production and the Work of Cultural Studies," *Journal of Asian American Studies* 3 (October 2000): 329–69; Haritaworn, "Caucasian and Thai."

34. See Maira, "Henna and Hip Hop," 331.

35. Haritaworn, "Caucasian and Thai," 60.

36. On home as a world in which race does *not* matter, see Toni Morrison, "Home," in *The House That Race Built,* ed. Wahneema Lubiano (New York: Vintage, 1998), 3–12.

37. See also Anthias, "Transnational Belonging," 9–10.

38. Maria P. P. Root, "A Bill of Rights for Racially Mixed People," in *Race Critical Theories,* ed. Philomena Essed and Theo Goldberg (Oxford: Blackwell, 2002), 359.

The Complexities of Identities

PART TWO

The Early exiles of ...

THREE

Between Difference and Assimilation: Young Women with South and Southeast Asian Family Background Living in Finland

SAARA PELLANDER

SHE WALKS ALONG THE STREET AND HEARS SOMEONE SHOUT, "Go home, nigger!" She pretends not to hear and keeps walking.[1] She is out with her friends, hears someone ask how much she charges for the night, and tries to ignore it. When asked where she is from, she says she is a normal Finn. When no one is asking questions, she proudly emphasizes her difference.

Due to the fact that immigration and transnational adoption are relatively new in Finland, adults who do not look like the Finnish majority but speak fluent Finnish are still fairly rare.[2] They are mostly treated as foreigners by people who do not know them, spoken to in English instead of Finnish on the street, at the grocery store, and even at their workplace. Being mistaken for foreigners is, however, only one way in which young adults who were brought up or even born in Finland are treated as "Others." Most of them have experienced various forms of racism: yelling on the street, bullying at school, and the questioning of their abilities at work. In this article, I consider questions of gendered forms of racial discrimination in Finland as experienced by women with a South or Southeast Asian family background who are either adoptees who came to Finland at a very young age or who were born in Finland to one or two parents of South or Southeast Asian descent. In particular, I focus on the question of how these young women evaluate questions of their national identity. They grew up at a time when immigration and transnational adoption were very marginal phenomena in Finland, which is why they have had to struggle for their place in a society that reminds them daily of their difference.[3] The experiences and situations

of these women do not fit the public perception of immigrants in Finland. Public debates about immigration and integration focus mainly
on asylum seekers, and most other issues, such as family migration or
transnational adoption, do not receive as much public attention.[4] Studying the way different groups make sense of experiences of exclusion and
difference seems even more relevant in light of the growing public debate on inclusions and exclusions of people with migratory backgrounds
and the recent rise of populist anti-immigration parties in both Finland
and many other European countries.

The article is based on nine interviews with eight women.[5] The interviews were analyzed by a combination of various discourse analytical
approaches and coding using a program for qualitative text analysis.[6] The
article consists of two parts. First, I discuss the notion of being Finnish
and the various definitions the interviewees relate to it. In the second
part, I explore the question of identity and identification in general and
consider what identity options these women see for themselves, whether
national identity plays an important role in their lives, and how other
people's questioning of their identity affects their feeling of belonging.

CONSTRUCTING AND QUESTIONING FINNISHNESS

Notions and Conditions of Being Finnish

Most of the young women interviewed for this study identify themselves
as Finnish. It thus seems relevant to investigate how they construct Finnishness, and what inclusions and exclusions are related to this construction. While the interviewees see themselves as Finnish, they are often
excluded from being Finnish by others, and they at times even want to
distance themselves from Finnishness. When analyzing the meanings
that the interviewees give to the concept of being Finnish, my aim is
not to unravel a presumed truth about the very nature of Finnishness.
I take a constructionist approach to what Finnishness means and base
this analysis on the presumption that no traits or characteristics can be
seen as Finnish by definition.[7] According to this view, Finnishness is
a concept that is produced by ascribing certain attributes as "Finnish"
and others not. Stereotypical notions that have been ascribed as being

Finnish throughout Finland's history include negative attributes such as backwardness, rawness of manners, extensive use of alcohol, shyness, and quietness. Other, more positive traits include being family-oriented, diligent, and humble.[8]

Matti Peltonen differentiates between three levels on which the concept of being Finnish is constructed. The first is that of a Finnish identity, which he defines as a unity conveyed through well-known and often-repeated experiences, symbols, and rituals. Second, Peltonen speaks of being Finnish as a mentality that is passed on from one generation to the next. The third level of being Finnish is built of national stereotypes and national self-perceptions.[9]

The majority of the interviewees define Finnish identity as being conveyed through experiences, which falls under Peltonen's first identity category. I will introduce Dyani as an example of this first category. One interviewee – Jonina – bases her definition of Finnishness on a concept of a mentality that is passed on from one generation to the next, so her case will be introduced as an example of Peltonen's second category. Marja, the third interviewee I will introduce here, has a stereotypical notion of what Finnishness means to her, so her definition of Finnishness will be examined as an example of Peltonen's last category.

Twenty-nine-year-old Dyani's father is from Sri Lanka, and her mother is Finnish. She was born in Finland and works as a journalist for Finnish broadcast radio and television. Dyani is pregnant at the time of the interview and ponders quite a lot about questions related to her background and her identity, wondering how her child will experience these questions and how her identity affects her abilities as a parent. She has experienced a lot of Othering by being stared at and expresses in the interview that she sometimes longs to be "invisible" and not be seen as a foreigner by others. She gives many examples of everyday encounters that display various forms of racialized exclusions. For her, these exclusions prevent her from being Finnish – in her definition, to be Finnish is to be treated as a Finn. Toward the end of the interview, Dyani wonders whether a dark-skinned person in Finland would ever be able really to become Finnish, and she concludes that this is probably impossible. Becoming Finnish is, in her understanding, strongly linked to other people's recognition of one's national belonging:[10] "It is really difficult, then, to

feel kinda fully Finnish because this society reminds me all the time that
I'm different."

Peltonen's second level at which being Finnish is constructed – passage from one generation to the next – is only shared by one of the interviewees – twenty-one-year-old Jonina, who is also among the youngest of
the women I interviewed. She was adopted from India at the age of two
months and brought up in a small town in the middle of Finland. Jonina
shows strong feelings of belonging in relation to that town, as will be
shown later in this chapter. A perky and optimistic person, Jonina tries
throughout the interview to downplay her experiences of racism and
emphasizes how she has been able to defend herself verbally in situations
in which her dark skin tone led to problematic encounters. Her definition
of Finnishness is strongly related to her upbringing in a Finnish family:

> Um, well, maybe that all your relatives are Finnish and that the family is Finnish
> and all the schools that you have attended. It would be different if the family
> would, for example, be Indian and one would attend a Finnish school. Then one
> would still be a little Indian, still behave a little differently.

The third of Peltonen's levels of Finnishness as displayed through
stereotypes is referred to only by thirty-year-old Marja, who has never
met her biological father from Bangladesh and was born in Finland to a
Finnish mother. Marja has been active in municipal politics but was the
victim of a racist campaign of a right-wing politician, which led Marja
to quit her position in the local council of a town in southwest Finland.
To Marja, being Finnish means individualism, introversion, and a preference to spending time with one's family instead of other people – criteria that meet the aforementioned stereotypical notion of the family-
oriented Finn.

It is not surprising that most of the interviewed women see Finnishness as something that is constructed in their own life situations and
biographies.[11] What is more striking is that, despite the fact that most of
the interviewed women refer to their skin color as the most prominent
marker of exclusion that prevents them from being treated as a Finn,
none of the interviewees explicitly refers to Finnishness as a racial process or something that is related to Whiteness.

Tuula Gordon and Elina Lahelma have analyzed the perceptions of
Finnishness of teachers and pupils at Finnish schools. Some associations

of both teachers and pupils were exclusionary, meaning that Finnishness was restricted to those meeting certain demanding requirements, such as purely Finnish ancestry or white skin color. Other definitions were more inclusive, being open to a larger group of people, such that being Finnish means living in Finland or applies to all the people in Finland.[12]

Most of the interviewees set the standards for being Finnish in a narrow and exclusionary way. They seem to take their own experiences – such as, for example, upbringing in a Finnish family – as a basis for their definitions of what kind of a person can be Finnish and, at the same time, exclude people whose family background and life experiences differ from this definition. They stress the difference between themselves and, for example, immigrants who obtain Finnish citizenship and were brought up by non-Finnish parents. By doing so, they do what identity building is, to a great degree, about – differentiation between oneself and others.

Negative Perceptions

The women interviewed for this research speak negatively about being Finnish in regard to tolerance, discrimination, and other people's reaction to their family background.[13] In her research on second-generation immigrants and young adoptees, Anna Rastas states that "when speaking about other Finns' attitudes and evaluating them, young people who otherwise identify themselves as Finns need to speak about racism from above or outside of being Finnish."[14]

That the attributes related to being Finnish are negative when speaking about racist experiences is not surprising. There are, however, other negative perceptions of being Finnish as well. These could be considered part of a phenomenon that Peltonen calls the underestimated self-perception of Finns.[15] Satu Apo has also researched Finnish self-perception and finds that linking negative attributes to the concept of being Finnish derives from the beginning of the nineteenth century, a period of Finnish nation building.[16] The central negative perception of Finns in her findings relates to excessive use of alcohol.[17]

In my own interviews, alcohol is mentioned only by twenty-four-year-old Laura, when she criticizes the kind of Finnishness from which she would like to distance herself.[18] Laura was born in Bangladesh. She was adopted and brought up by one Swedish-speaking, and one Finnish-speaking parent in Helsinki. Laura used to work in a bank but had to quit because she could not bear the constant questions and doubts by customers who questioned her language skills, asked intruding questions about her background, and implied that she was not proficient at her job. She found the questioning of her Finnishness disturbing in her work life. Yet this does not mean that she would not at other times actively distance herself from the label of "being Finnish":

> Laura: Often, abroad, when we have flown with Finnair or some Aurinkomatka [chartered] vacation, we pretended to be Swedish; we didn't even want to be Finnish
>
> Saara: Why?
>
> Laura: Well, it is on vacation there, when you see Finns on vacation who stumble around drunk, then we don't want to be that Finnish. So it is positive that people abroad don't know what country I am from.

Laura and her family say they do not want to be "that" Finnish. The way Finns are believed to behave when drinking is one defining aspect of Finnishness for Laura. To her, being Finnish is something that can be obtained to a lesser or fuller degree. Her reference to being "that" Finnish suggests that it is also possible to be less Finnish. She clearly makes a difference between herself and the prevailing image of Finns who do not behave themselves as tourists. The fact that she and her family do not fit this stigmatized stereotype of the drunken Finn does not lead her to criticize the accuracy of the stereotype, but rather to deny being part of the category to which the stigma is attached. Instead of changing the generalization that all Finns drink to excess and misbehave when they are abroad, she uses her physical difference as a defense mechanism. Because she is not perceived as a Finn due to her appearance, she avoids the negative stereotypes about Finns. Her skin color thus works two ways – it evokes stigmatization by other Finns, and, at the same time, it works to defend against some stigmas related to being Finnish.[19]

Normal Yet Different

The interviewed women feel that their family background gives them the possibility to negotiate the terms on which they fit into the category of

Finnish. By doing so, they navigate between normality and difference. Most of the interviewees stress that they like to be Finnish in a different way. Twenty-five-year-old Ranja is an adoptee with biological roots in India and works as a primary school teacher in southern Finland. She states that "it is nice to be a slightly different Finn, so that one doesn't know where I am from." She seems to enjoy the fact that she is not recognized as a Finn by others. This affords her the self-granted status of a "different Finn"; "normal Finns," in contrast, seem to be more easily recognizable.[20]

Identity is negotiation between difference and similarity,[21] and the interviewees conduct these negotiations in relation to their own Finnish identity. Another adoptee, Shila, is twenty-four and was born in India, just like Jonina and Ranja. She has many friends with a foreign background and compares her experiences of racism and Othering with theirs. Like most of the interviewed women, she has experienced sexualized forms of racism, such as getting sexual offers and more attention from men than their White friends, and she even has been mistaken for a prostitute. She still finds that her male friend with an African background has harsher racist experiences than she has. She feels that she would be discriminated against more if she were a man, an opinion that the majority of the interviewees seemed to share. The prevailing perception among the interviewed women seems to be that men experience more violent forms of racism, which they perceive as more severe than their own racist experiences of sexualization and exoticization.

When speaking about her Finnish identity, Shila describes her Finnishness as somehow different from that of others, stating that she is not part of the general public in Finland: "Well, I do feel like a Finn, but I do not see myself... how do you put this, um, well, in some way, I have this feeling that I am not like the average people or that I am kind of outside, although I am not but these [are the] kind of feelings you get."

She then argues that her different Finnishness and feelings of exclusion have to do with the fact that she has traveled a great deal and spent some time abroad. Thus, she does not see her family background to be what makes her feel "kind of outside" from the average Finnish person. Instead, she ascribes this feeling to her international experiences she gained from living and traveling abroad. The feeling of difference and how the interviewees relate to it depends on the context in which it is presented and the person who is presenting it. Mostly, this seems to relate to the question of stigmas and the associations related to them.[22] When they speak about negative associations with being Finnish, the interviewees want to stress that they are different from other Finns. When their being Finnish is being questioned and they are stigmatized as "immigrants," they stress that they are just normal Finns.

Olli Löytty has found a normality rhetoric prevalent in mainstream discussions about Finnishness, within which the women I interviewed are also operating.[23] Laura states, "I am nonetheless just a normal Finn." Ranja, when speaking about her experiences as a teacher, says one of "the first questions the children have is always, 'What is your nationality? What country are you from?' It never is the assumption that I am just from here and normal just the same as they are." When the pupils ask where she is from, she responds by saying that she is a Finn and has always lived in Finland; she thus actively participates in shifting racialized notions of what a "normal Finn" is supposed to look like.

The normality rhetoric of the interviewees can be seen as fulfilling two functions. It firstly matches up to Löytty's proposal that normality is part of being Finnish in general and can thus be seen as a way to stress their being Finnish. The normality that all Finns are supposed to be sharing, at least in representations of Finnishness, is not, however, automatically shared by the interviewees. It has to be produced verbally by repeating their own normal way of being Finnish.[24] By speaking about their own normality regarding their Finnishness, they also suggest, however, that there may be abnormal ways of being Finnish. The normality rhetoric can thus also be considered a strategy to set aside possible differences and the meanings these differences are given.[25] Though the interviewees experience themselves to be normal Finns, they are still not perceived as normal parts of Finnish society. Every one of them reports having been asked the innocent-sounding question, "Where are you from?"

Where Are You from? Questioning Nationality

Finland is perceived as a very homogeneous nation. Although Finland has been throughout its history a place where people with different religious and cultural backgrounds have lived together, within the public debate as well as within academia, it is often taken for granted that Finland has been an isolated and monocultural country and has begun to internationalize only since the beginning of the 1990s.[26] This perception includes the presumption that those who differ visually from what is seen to be the average Finn must be immigrants. The interviewees in this study – although they were either born in Finland or have been brought up in Finland from a very early age – are often confronted with questions about where they have come from.[27] The public rhetoric and concepts and representations of being Finnish described above leave very little space to negotiate what is and is not Finnish. Within a standardized norm of Finnishness, anyone differing from that standard is confronted with being questioned about her or his background.[28]

Dhooleka Sarhadi Raj argues that the question about the true origin of a person always defines that person's identity as being foreign and other. Although some scholars have found that the question "Where are you from?" is felt to be exclusionary and even racist,[29] the interviewees did not attach only negative meanings to being questioned about their origin. Their attitudes toward other people's questions can be divided into four groups, each attitude being shared by two interviewees. Two of the interviewees find the questions to be positive and say they enjoy speaking about their own background. Two others, however, experience the questions as intrusive and feel that their belonging in Finland is being questioned. Another two stress their willingness to understand the motives of the person asking about their background; they find the questions sometimes annoying but less annoying at other times. The last two interviewees mention foremost that they have gotten used to the questions; while they do not particularly enjoy such inquiries, they no longer find them particularly bothersome.

Ranja is one of the interviewees who displays a positive attitude toward other people's questions. She emphasizes at different stages of the interview that she enjoys telling people about her origin and background, especially in her work as a primary school teacher:

> I find it great that someone dares to ask. . . . I like the fact that people ask me. . . . It is great that one more person knows that someone looking like me can speak Finnish and be a Finn. . . . I like the fact that I have the chance to make a difference and give these small children the example of an adult who can be of

a different skin color but just the same otherwise and make them notice that the skin color can be just a normal person.

Ranja does not take a passive role as the target of these questions but transforms the fact that people ask about her background into an active process in which she changes other people's perceptions.

While Ranja does not find questions about her origin problematic, Dyani seems to suffer under the burden of having to respond to questions about her background. Among all the interviewees, she feels most disturbed by other people's questions and ponders the gap between her own feelings and the questioning of her national belonging:

> I just said to my husband that I probably won't ever feel fully Finnish, that I just kinda can't, but that is an okay thing, that that isn't a problem, that I have just accepted that. But I cannot, I won't ever be, well, I kinda . . . that that comes on a weekly basis when I call 'cause my name is so different on the phone . . . that evokes so many questions about backgrounds and so how do you speak Finnish so well [they ask].

Dyani was born in Finland, has a Finnish mother, and Finnish is her mother tongue. Yet she will never be able to feel fully Finnish. She needs outer acceptance of her Finnishness; for her, people's questions and her national identity are strongly linked to each other. Due to her unusual surname, she encounters weekly situations where, in her work as a journalist, she must reassure contacts over the phone that she really is a Finnish journalist working for Finnish television and that she does speak Finnish.[30] While other interviewees try to understand the motives of people who ask them about their background or interpret the questions as mere curiosity, Dyani finds herself pitying such people and is disappointed in them. Pitying and lowering another in one's esteem, which at the same time allows one to position oneself above the other person, seem to be a common strategy when dealing with experiences of exclusion and racism.[31]

According to Stuart Hall, all immigrants are faced with the question of why they are in the country they are in. Yet the reasons for a person's migration can be very personal; in Hall's case, he moved abroad in order to get away from his mother.[32] As innocent as the questions "Where are you from?" and "Why are you here?" might sound, they imply two things. First of all, they imply that the presence of the person addressed by the questions requires further explanation; thus, the assumption is that the person is not where he or she is supposed to be but has a true home elsewhere and a reason why that home was left behind. The second implication is that details of one's assumed home country are public information that does not contain anything problematic or delicate. The questioner assumes that he or she has a right to have his or her curiosity about one's origins satisfied.

NAVIGATING IDENTITY

The Importance of Identities

When speaking of identities, I have referred mainly to national identities, although the nation is only one of many possible identity categories.[33] Each of the interviewees has a Finnish passport. This juridical status does not, however, say a lot about her perception of what having a Finnish passport means in her own understanding of belonging. As Sara Ahmed puts it, "The individual, who encounters others in daily life, comes to identify as not only *having* but *being* a nationality" [italics in original].[34] When investigating national identity, it is thus necessary to collect information on how or whether the individual constructs her sense of her nationality in her daily life.

I will in the following section investigate, first, what role national identification plays in the interviewed women's conceptions of themselves and whether they consider this form of identification important to their lives. Next, I will present findings that show a link between national identity and the geographical nation space – in this case, Finnish identity and Finland – in the interviewees' perceptions. I will then examine whether the way other people behave toward the interviewees seems to influence their national identity. Because identity categories are not limited to national belonging, I will also discuss other identity options that arise from the interviews. Lastly, I will explore how their ethnic background offers identity options based on difference, which the interviewees see as a positive part of their identity construction.

The interviewees have a variety of understandings of the definition and role of identity. Dyani sees identity as being connected to one's mental stability: "When one's identity is somehow intact and in order, that means that that person does well." She speaks of identity as being "intact and in order," which implies that one's identity could also be broken or disturbed. This is a similar rhetoric as the often-used expression of the need to find one's identity. Identity is, in that understanding, something existing that can be found, broken, or lost.

According to Emma, identity is mostly influenced by other people and one's surroundings. To her, identity is "how you feel yourself in relation to others and in which surrounding you feel at home and what you see as your own thing, what ideas you support, and what you think of things." Emma's relating identity to others resembles Hall's conception that identity construction is not positive, as identity is always in relation to what it is not.[35]

Shila does not find national identity the most relevant identity category. She sees identity in general as being produced in everyday habits. Identity, in this case, is something that is lived by the individual and in which there is space to change and question one's choices.

When asked whether they find having a national identity important, almost all the women stated that it is important to feel some sort of belonging. The feeling of belonging seemed to be more relevant than the content of that national identity.

"It is good for me here" – Identity as a Place

> As important as *when* identities are performed is *where* performing them takes place. It is about the stage of national identity, where identities are dramatized, transmitted, adopted and renewed.[36]

This understanding draws attention to the connection between identity and place. For my interviewees, Finland is not only the stage for their various identity performances, but their willingness to live in Finland seems to be the content of how they define their Finnish identity. The majority of the interviewees repeatedly convey their willingness to live in Finland. When talking about her friend's negative experiences with racism in public places, Emma adds, "but it is good to live here for me; I don't want to go away." When asked later in the interview whether she would identify herself as being Finnish, she says "yes" and adds quickly,

"I have never wanted to move away, so it is good for me here." Emphasizing the point, when she says that she enjoys traveling a little later, she repeats, "but that still doesn't mean that I want to move away." She was at no point asked whether she likes living in Finland or wants to move away from Finland.

In the interview situation, I did not understand immediately that her stating that she enjoys living in Finland is at the same time her answer to the question about her national identity. When asked again later whether she sees herself as a Finn, she repeats that she does not want to leave Finland. Finland, as a geographical place in which to live, is not merely the stage of her identity, but also, in one sense, the substance of her identity.

Another interviewee, Laura, compares her own willingness to live in Finland to that of others when she says, "It is just as difficult for me to move somewhere else as for someone completely Finnish." She makes a distinction between completely Finnish people and herself, implying that she is not completely a Finn. When trying to distance herself from the parts of Finnishness of which she does not approve, she again refers to wanting or not wanting to live in Finland – for example, she says that the Finnish way of using alcohol is the only reason that she could imagine moving elsewhere. She even sees her willingness to live in Finland as possibly being threatened by becoming drawn to Bangladesh, the country from which her biological parents came. She does not want to travel there because she is worried that she would not want to live in Finland anymore. She does not speak about her Finnish identity as such being threatened but about her will to live in Finland. Indeed, Finnish identity and the will to live in Finland seem for her to be much the same thing.

"It ain't where you're from, it's where you're at."[37] This quote by Paul Gilroy captures the relevance of space for identity formation in quite a similar fashion to the way the interviewed women describe their Finnish identity. While acknowledging the growing scholarly recognition of transnational belongings and shifting identities, Elizabeth H. Jones asks whether the destabilization of national boundaries and culturally homogeneous space really means that identities are not spatially grounded. She argues that, in the formation of identities, places and spaces have not lost relevance but are of growing importance: "In fact, it seems that one of the most significant results of transformations in the experience of contemporary space is the growing prevalence of an urgent search for home space and cultural belonging."[38] Nadia Lovell points out how a highly spatial belonging might actually work to counterbalance possible feelings of dislocation and displacement.[39]

The Other in the Mirror

Identifying is based in part on our understanding of how similar or different we see ourselves in relation to other people.[40] This difference or similarity is not only created in our own understanding but reflected or contested by the reactions of other people. When talking about their self-perceptions, the interviewees mention other people's ways of reacting to them. According to Marja, the way other people perceive and categorize us affects and reflects how similar or different we feel. She finds that "we are finally just mirrors to our own self." The theme of a mirror repeats itself in many of the interviews. The interviewees forget their own skin color until they look into the mirror and are only reminded of their visual otherness when people approach them in English instead of Finnish. Jonina explains, "That is in that way funny that I think, 'Hey, why do they speak English to me?' But then when I look into the mirror it is difficult, it can be difficult to imagine that this one really speaks Finnish fluently." It is interesting that Jonina here objectifies her image in the mirror, referring to "this one" instead of "I." The person who does not look as if she could speak fluent Finnish is not herself but some objectified other.

The question of the relation of physical outer appearance and identity is raised by Sara Ahmed, who approaches this relation through the concept of passing for someone: "passing may function at the level of the intentional subject (the subject who seeks to pass in order to secure something otherwise unavailable to them), or it may function as a misrecognition on the part of others (one may pass for something other than one's self-identification but not seek to, or know it)."[41]

Passing for someone at the level of the intentional subject is at hand when women who have lived all their lives in Finland are, in their own perception, passing for being White and forgetting the color of their skin. Jonina continues: "One feels white skinned and does not notice because one does not look at oneself all the time in the mirror, so that 'Oh, yeah,

I am dark skinned.' And so it starts to feel like that for oneself that one starts to look at weird-colored people who are somewhere, that 'Hey, that is weird,' which is really funny." In her own perception, she is passing for a White person to such an extent that she sees other different-looking people as being "weird." The misrecognition about which Ahmed speaks is then again part of the interviewees' daily lives when they are asked where they are from or spoken to in English at the supermarket, reminding them of the fact that they are not passing for a Finn after all, but rather perceived as foreigners.

Many of the interviewees have been to the country of origin of their biological parents or of the parent that is not from Finland. There, their difference was not marked by the color of their skin or hair, but rather through a lack of language skills and their ways of dressing, gesticulating, and behaving. Shila was very disappointed when she realized that, also in India, she was different from other people:

> And then when I was in India . . . they saw right away that I have Indian features but the behavior and dressing was totally Western, so they did not take me for an Indian, and then again Finns don't take me as a Finn. Then I got the feeling that, well, what am I then, or that it is really ambiguous.

Although at another point she says that other people's behavior does not affect her Finnish identity and that she does not identify as an Indian, it is still clear that experiences of Othering in India and Finland have led her to ponder her identity when she asks "What am I then?"

Despite such momentary, situational questionings, Finnish national identity seems overall to be a stable and unshaken basis of the self-perception of the Finnish women I interviewed who have a South or Southeast Asian family background. This perception does not change, even though they do experience a lot of questioning, discrimination, and racism. The question is not whether they identify as being Finnish or not but more about what other identity categories they may choose in addition to Finnishness and how strong those other identities may be.

Adoptee, Foreigner, Finn – Multiple Identity Categories

Being Finnish is the dominating category that the interviewees use when speaking about themselves. This category proves to be insufficient, how-

ever, when they speak about their family background, as Dyani's interview illustrates:

> We moved to this really little place that had – would it have five thousand inhab-
> itants? – and we were sort of the first and only foreign family there, if it could be
> put this way, although I, of course, under no circumstances would see myself as
> being, or at least I am not foreign, because I was born in Finland and my mum is
> Finnish and all, but.... um....

Dyani does not seem to find the right words when speaking about her
family. She hesitates about the accuracy of the term "foreign" by saying
"if it could be put this way" and then wants to confirm quickly that she
does not see herself as a foreigner. She hesitates here, though, too, finally
adding "or at least I am not foreign." Her insecurity about the identity
category that she would refer to can be seen by how, at the end of the
quote, she gives proof of her Finnishness, by mentioning Finland being
her place of birth and having a Finnish mother.

Finnishness as a national identity does not, however, seem to be the
only or even the most relevant identity category available. Jonina emphasizes that she identifies strongly with her little Finnish hometown. She
feels secure when going out with her friends from that town and stresses
that youth from her hometown always stand up for each other and would
always protect her against any racist verbal attacks that youth from other
cities might address at her. Identifying with this community gives her
a stable ground for defying other people's attacks on her background:

> I don't have anything like "Who am I? Where am I from?" I have never had that.
> To me it is clear that I know who I am, and that is why it feels so stupid if some-
> one comes up to me to say something, and then I am just ha ha ha you cannot
> offend me that easily.

Laura feels that being bilingual – she speaks Swedish, one of the
official languages in Finland, as a second mother tongue – is the most
important way of identifying herself compared to other entirely Swedish-speaking populations in Finland.

Another identity option that takes a prominent position in the interviewees' accounts of identities is being an adoptee. Twenty-four-year-old
Lilia emphasizes her being an adoptee, and she replies to many questions
with "being an adoptee" or "since I am an adoptee." She is very proud of
her adoptee background and is very active in an adoption organization.

She was born in the Philippines but does not speak of the Philippines or Asia as a place with which she would identify. Lilia has been to the Philippines with her parents, and when speaking about that visit, she emphasizes how she differs from the local population: "I noticed that they were one head shorter than I am [laughs], and I am really short, but they were in my opinion clearly one head shorter and smaller in their physique. That was different. I had gotten good Finnish food, yes [laughs]."

In addition to stressing how her outer appearance is more Finnish than that of the local population in the Philippines, Lilia also actively distances herself from other women from Asia living in Finland:

> I actually recognize Asian women's way of walking. I can recognize that and, well, I really think that, if the way I walk is looked at from behind, one cannot say whether that is Asian or not, since they just have such a distinct way of walking. Of course, they also have all different kinds, but there is something, well, you just sort of notice.

Lilia here displays a stereotypical view. First of all, women from different countries are summed up as being "Asian women." In addition, she claims that they share a common way of walking that she does not share. Her identity building is done by making a difference between her as an adoptee and other so-called Asian women.

The interviewees thus have a variety of other identity options that do not relate to the country they currently live in or the country of origin of their biological parents. Identity that relates to one's family background is often spoken about as ethnic identity, especially in the U.S. context.[42] While the second or third generation with an Asian background in the United States might refer to themselves as Asian American,[43] in Finland, the category Asian-Finnish is not in use. Emma even says that she feels guilty for not wanting to identify as Asian. For Emma, Marja, and Dyani, who were the three interviewees with a nonadoption background but with one non-Finnish parent, the relation to the "other country" is more complex than for the adoptees. For most of the adoptees, the country from which they came to Finland is not of particular interest. Instead, they feel that expectations regarding this identity are thrust on them. They are expected to represent that country, although they often do not have any connection to it.

The identity options that second-generation immigrants or adoptees have are as manifold as the options of those who do not have a transnational background. What makes their life more difficult than that of the average person in Finland is that they encounter national and ethnic identities contrived for them by others in their everyday lives. They have to navigate their way between these contrived, imposed identities and their own self-perception. They are also excluded through various ways of racialized stereotyping against which they have to defend themselves and their identity conceptions.[44] Being seen as different from the majority of Finns is, on the other hand, something that at times they employ as a positive way of identification.

Defining Differences

Being seen as different is not only a means of exclusion; it is also part of these women's identity construction. Standing out as being different can be seen as something positive that has become an essential part of the self. The way difference is seen and defined changes over time. Although the number of interviews conducted here is too small to make generalizations, it can, nonetheless, be clearly seen that the oldest interviewees have the most positive approach toward standing out and being different from others. Similar findings have been made in other research.[45] There seems to be a life-course effect: getting older includes higher acceptance of one's individual traits and differences, while the opinion of others becomes less important. Marja explains how her attitude toward her background has changed as an adult:

> Now as a grown up, it's something nice. Every one of us likes at some stage that my grandmother is from Karelia or someone is from the Finnish west coast. That becomes meaningful once you grow up, and that is a nice thing. But back then were the times as a child, when you have the will to be so similar to the others, and you think, "Why am I, why can't I be and look like the most average child in the class?" and [you] just want to be like that one, so unnoticeable and so normal and don't want to explain anything to anyone. And also during puberty and also in high school, [you] want to really be that there is nothing different about me, I'm just so the same, but now that's real different.

The way the interviewees' ethnic background is seen by others is clearly gendered. They experience that their Asian features and dark skin color evoke notions of sensuality in others and can often lead to very disturbing cases of sexualized racism.[46] They all have experienced that they attract more attention than their friends who do not have any Asian family background. When they are complimented as being beautiful, they stress that the way the compliments are expressed influences how they feel about them. Laura says that she is often asked, "Where has such a beautiful girl come from" and that she likes to be addressed that way. How strongly the attention due to visual difference is linked to self-perception can be seen through Marja's example. She wonders what it would be like if she lived in India, where she would look like everybody else:

> then a part of me would be taken away. Kinda something really significantly would change. Of course, that is always this way. For example, if any healthy person would become sick, for example, lose the ability to walk, there part of the self drops out or then comes another self instead.

"[A] part of me would be taken away" is how Marja describes what it would be like if her visually perceived difference would not exist. The attention she receives due to her Bangladeshi family background is part of her everyday life and, as such, has become part of their identity construction. The role of the exotic Other has been experienced and accepted for so long that Marja is not ready to give it up, even though it also includes many negative experiences. Being treated differently has become part of the image these women have of themselves. The negotiations about the self happen on the middle ground between the way they are treated by others, their own comparison to others, and their perceptions of themselves.

The positive and negative experiences these interviewees encounter and that influence the way that they make sense of their own identity constructions can be best captured with the concept of intersectionality – it is not a single category like gender, race, nationality, or class that is at work, neither the mere addition of these categories, but the way that different categories work together in an interlocking system.[47] It is not only racial difference, not only the upbringing in a middle-class family in Finland or their gender that determines or dominates their experiences, but the way these and other categories work together in different situations at different stages of their lives.

CONCLUSION

In many ways, women with a transnational family background share concepts of Finnishness similar to those of other people in Finland. As they have lived all their lives in Finland, it is not too surprising that they share similar notions of Finnishness as other people who were brought up in Finland. They have, after all, been exposed to similar public discourses on the meanings and portrayal of the contents of Finnish national identity. A transnational family background is by no means a guarantee of a more open, inclusive, or broader understanding of national belonging. The criteria for being Finnish that are defined by the women dealt with in this paper are entirely exclusive. They set standards for Finnishness that the interviewees themselves, but not necessarily many other people, can meet. Expecting their biological roots to affect the way they understand Finnishness is a form of racialization that assumes the color of somebody's skin to influence the way that person thinks. For a researcher, there is a great risk of this racialization being applied when choosing to do research on a certain group of people defined by biological origin. In this respect, I would agree with the interviewees' plea to see them "just as normal Finns."

What differs from other common notions of Finnishness is the strong linkage the interviewees draw between Finnishness and Finland as a place to live. Their geographical surrounding is not just the stage for their Finnish identity performance but the content of it. Moving abroad and not wanting to live in Finland could thus be seen as possible threats to their Finnish identity.

Although the young women I studied find belonging in general important, it is not national belonging that is the central aspect in their lives. Especially the possible identification with the home country of their biological parent(s) is something that is rendered relevant by others rather than by themselves. Other people's questioning of their Finnishness, which happens by asking about their origin and speaking English to them instead of Finnish, is something that disturbs some interviewees more than others. In general, it does not seem to have much impact on the way they see themselves; they rather stress that looks, questions, and speaking English remind them that they look different from the average

Finn. This difference does not only lead to experiences of racism and exclusion; it is also something these women have managed to include into their own identity building as something positive. The problematic part is that they are not able to choose how important they render their biological roots in their everyday lives, as being subject to regular questioning, gazes, and even racist comments and practices keep on reminding them of being the Other. Despite an increase of immigration during the past two decades, people who differ visually from what is taken to be the average, blond, light-skinned Finn, unfortunately, still keep on being confronted with exclusionary practices in their everyday lives. Research on Otherness, inclusion, and exclusion is always also research about the balancing act between the boundaries and overlaps of difference and similarity. For this balancing act to succeed, it is important that the actors are able to define the boundaries and overlaps themselves.

> Not quite the Same, not quite the Other,
> she stands in that undetermined threshold place
> where she constantly drifts in and out.
> Undercutting the "inside/outside" opposition,
> her intervention is necessarily that of both
> a deceptive insider and a deceptive outsider.
> She is this Inappropriate Other/Same
> who moves about
> with always at least two/four gestures:
> that of affirming "I am like you"
> while persisting in her difference;
> and that of reminding "I am different"
> while unsettling every definition
> of otherness arrived at.[48]

NOTES

1. I want to thank Johanna Valenius and Elli Heikkilä for their invaluable encouragement and many important comments on the thesis on which this article is based. I am also grateful to Paul Spickard who is a pleasure to work with and who maintained such a positive spirit throughout the entire writing and editing process. I am thanking him and the two anonymous reviewers for their insightful suggestions on how to improve this chapter. I also want to thank Christina P. Saarinen and Sami Torssonen for their help improving the language of this chapter.

2. During the 1980s, 85 percent of incoming migrants were Finnish return migrants from Sweden, and it was not until the 1990s that the majority of immi-

grants in Finland were of foreign descent.
While Finland had about 26,300 foreign
residents in 1990, this number had grown
to almost 168,000 by 2010. Proportionally,
the total foreign population in Finland
is around 3 percent. Finnish Immigration Service, Statistics, Statistics Finland
2011, http://www.migri.fi, September
2011; Official Statistics of Finland (OSF),
Population Structure, Helsinki: Statistics
Finland, http://www.stat.fi/til/vaerak/
kat_en.html, accessed July 31, 2012. Anna
Rastas states that "In the light of demographic statistics, Finnish citizens who
identify themselves as Finns but can be
categorized as belonging to racial and/
or ethnic minorities are predominantly
children and young people." Anna Rastas, "Am I Still 'White'? Dealing with the
Colour Trouble," *Balayi: Culture and Colonialism* 6 (2004): 95.

3. Saara Pellander, *Aasialainen sukutausta, suomalainen elämä: Naisten kokemuksia ja tulkintoja toiseudesta* [Asian
family background, Finnish life: Women's
experiences and interpretations of Other-
ness], Web Reports Series of the Finnish
Institute of Migration, Web Report No. 27
(2007), http://www.migrationinstitute.fi/
pdf/webreports23.pdf.

4. See Saara Pellander, "Sending and
Receiving, Welcoming and Excluding:
Developments and Debates in Finland's
Migration Policy," in *Debating Migration:
Political Discourses on Labour Immigration
in Historical Perspective,* ed. Stefanie May-
er and Mikael Spång (Innsbruck: Studien
Verlag, 2009), 128–36.

5. The call for interviewees was sent
to Finnish adoption agencies and several
immigrant associations. The requirements
were that the interviewee be female, have
grown up in Finland, have one or two
parents from a South or Southeast Asian
country, speak Finnish as a native language, and be over eighteen years old. The
interviews were conducted by the author

of this paper between October 2004 and
June 2006. The interviewees' first names
(as I have used them in this chapter; these
are pseudonyms), age at the time of the
interview, country of birth, and, if not adopted but born in Finland, home country
of the non-Finnish parent are as follows:
Dyani, twenty-nine, Finland, father from
Sri Lanka; Emma, eighteen, Finland,
mother from Malaysia; Jonina, twenty-
one, India, adopted; Laura, twenty-four,
Bangladesh, adopted; Lila, twenty-four,
the Philippines, adopted; Marja, thirty,
Finland, father from Bangladesh; Shila,
twenty-four, India, adopted; Ranja, twenty-five, India, adopted.

6. The interviews were coded using
NUD-IST qualitative research software.

7. See Mikko Lehtonen, "Johdanto:
Säiliöstä suhdekimppuun" [Introduction:
From a container to a bundle of relations],
in *Suomi toisin sanoen,* ed. Mikko Leh-
tonen, Olli Löytty, and Petri Ruuska
(Tampere: Vastapaino, 2004), 10–11.

8. Satu Apo, "Suomalaisuuden stigmatisoinnin traditio" [The tradition of the
stigmatization of Finnishness], in *Elävänä
Euroopassa: Muuttuva suomalainen identiteetti,* ed Pertti Alasuutari and Petri Ruuska (Tampere: Vastapaino, 1998), 83–128.

9. Matti Peltonen, "Omakuvamme
murroskohdat: Maisema ja kieli suomalaisuuskäsitysten perusaineksina"
[Turning points of our self-perception:
Landscape and language as main elements
of concepts of Finnishness], in *Elävänä
Euroopassa,* ed. Alasuutari and Ruuska,
20–22.

10. On recognition as part of national
identity, see, for example, Sara Ahmed,
*Strange Encounters: Embodied Others in
Post-Coloniality* (London: Routledge,
2000), 96.

11. Harinen makes similar findings
among people with dual citizenship: "According to the view of people with dual
citizenship, national traits are passed on

through the environment in a concrete way.... Single persons, Finns or Indians, are influenced more by their living environment, local life style, language, and local cultural circumstances than national roots or internalized tradition." Päivi Harinen, *Valmiiseen tulleet: Tutkimus nuoruudesta, kansallisuudesta ja kansalaisuudesta* [Arrivals at the complete: A study of youth, nationality and citizenship] (Helsinki: Nuorisotutkimusseurary, 2000), 148.

12. Tuula Gordon and Elina Lahelma, "Kansalaisuus, kansallisuus ja sukupuoli" [Citizenship, nationality and gender], in *Elävänä Euroopassa*, ed. Alasuutari and Ruuska, 264–65.

13. Similar findings have been made by Heidi Virkki, "Suomalaisuuden peilissä: Kansainvälisesti adoptoitujen nuorten kokemuksia suomalaisuudesta ja erilaisuudesta" [In the mirror of Finnishness: Experiences of transnationally adopted youth on Finnishness and otherness], Master's thesis, University of Tampere, 2006, 50–51.

14. Anna Rastas, "Miksi rasismin kokemuksista on niin vaikea puhua?" [Why do young people not talk about their experiences of racism?], in *Puhua vastaan ja vaieta: Neuvottelu kulttuurisista marginaaleista*, ed. Arja Jokinen, Laura Huttunen, and Anna Kulmala (Helsinki: Gaudeamus, 2004), 50.

15. Peltonen, "Omakuvamme murroskohdat," 23.

16. Apo, "Suomalaisuuden stigmatisoinnin traditio," 86.

17. Ibid., 105–16.

18. Also, other research suggests that young people in the second generation or with an adoption background choose not to identify with Finnish drinking culture. Virkki, "Suomalaisuuden peilissä," 50–51; Veronika Honkasalo, "'Nyt mä oon suomalainen ... varmaan': Nuoret maahanmuuttajat, etnisyys ja rasismi" ["Now I am Finnish ... I guess": Young immigrants,

ethnicity and racism], Master's thesis, University of Helsinki, 2001, 61.

19. On stigmas and stereotypes, see John F. Dovidio, Brenda Major, and Jennifer Crocker, "Stigma: Introduction and Overview," in *The Social Psychology of Stigma*, ed. Todd F. Heatherton, Robert E. Kleck, Michelle R. Hebl, and Jay G. Hull (New York: Guildford Press, 2000); Monica Biernat and John F. Dovido, "Stigma and Stereotypes," in *Social Psychology of Stigma*, ed. Heatherton et al.

20. Ahmed states that "The recognition of others as being from the same nation, or as sharing a nationality, hence involves an everyday and much rehearsed distinction between who does and who does not belong within the nation space" (*Strange Encounters*, 99).

21. Stuart Hall, "The Question of Cultural Identity," in *Modernity and Its Futures*, ed. Stuart Hall, David Held, and Tony McGrew (Cambridge: Polity Press and Open University, 1992).

22. Carol T. Miller and Brenda Major, "Coping with Stigma and Prejudice," in *Social Psychology of Stigma*, ed. Heatherton et al., 243–60.

23. Olli Löytty, "Erikoisen tavallinen suomalaiuus" [Especially normal Finnishness], in *Suomi toisin sanoen*, ed. Lehtonen et al., 46–48.

24. Ibid., 53–54; see also Mikko Lehtonen, "Suomi on toistettua maata" [Finland is repeated land], in *Suomi toisin sanoen*, ed. Lehtonen et al., 142. Emphasizing Finnishness seems to correlate with Päivi Harinen et al.'s findings that "a young immigrant is more easily accepted if he/she tries to be as Finnish as possible." Päivi Harinen et al., "Membership Contests: Encountering Immigrant Youth in Finland," *Journal of Youth Studies* 8.3 (2005): 291.

25. See also Ien Ang, *On Not Speaking Chinese: Living between Asia and the West* (London: Routledge, 2001), 28.

26. Olli Löytty, "Meistä on moneksi" [Diversity is us], in *Suomi toisin sanoen*, ed. Lehtonen et al., 224, 236.

27. Petri Ruuska finds it impossible to identify a certain geographical origin where someone would belong more than anywhere else. See Petri Ruuska, "Toisen nahoissa ja vähän sanoissakin" [In the skin and sayings of the other], in *Suomi toisin sanoen*, ed. Lehtonen et al., 208–20.

28. Mikko Lehtonen and Olli Löytty, "Miksi erilaisuus?" [Why otherness?], in *Erilaisuus*, ed. Mikko Lehtonen and Olli Löytty (Tampere: Vastapaino, 2003), 9.

29. Ang, *On Not Speaking Chinese*, 144–45; Dhooleka Sarhadi Raj, *Where Are You From? Middle-class Migrants in the Modern World* (Berkeley: University of California Press, 2003), 198, 200; Kath Woodward, "Questions of Identity," in *Questioning Identity: Gender, Class, Ethnicity*, 2d ed., ed. Kath Woodward (London: Routledge, 2004), 33; see also Anna Rastas, "Racializing Categorization among Young People in Finland," *Young* 13.2 (2005): 152–53.

30. This is interesting when contrasted with the experiences of, for example, Laura, who states that her Finnish first name and Finnish surname make it possible for her to escape people's questions. She says that she feels most comfortable when she is on the phone, as then she is not questioned about her background.

31. Rastas, "Miksi rasismin kokemuksista on niin vaikea puhua?" 49; Pellander, *Aasialainen sukutausta, suomalainen elämä*.

32. Stuart Hall, "Minimal Selves," in *Identity: The Real Me*, ICA Documents 6 (London, Institute of Contemporary Arts, 1988), 44–46.

33. On definitions of identity, see, for example, Stuart Hall, "Who Needs Identity?" in *Questions of Cultural Identity*, ed. Stuart Hall and Paul du Gay (London: Sage, 1996); Chris Barker and Dariusz

Galasiński, *Cultural Studies and Discourse Analysis: A Dialogue on Language and Identity* (Thousand Oaks, CA: Sage, 2001), 42; Ang, *On Not Speaking Chinese*, 150–53. National identity means, in this case, the way in which the individual identifies with the nation and/or the state. According to Pasi Saukkonen, national identity can either refer to the state's political identity, the nation's identity, or the question of how the individual identifies with the nation and/or the state. Pasi Saukkonen, "Kansallinen identiteetti" [National identity], in *Nationalismit*, ed. Jussi Pakkasvirta and Pasi Saukkonen (Helsinki: Werner Söderström Osakeyhtiö, 2004), 90.

34. Ahmed, *Strange Encounters*, 98.

35. Hall, "Who Needs Identity?" 4–5.

36. Lehtonen, "Suomi on toistettua maata" 124–25 (italics original).

37. Paul Gilroy, "It ain't where you're from, it's where you're at: The Dialectics of Diasporic Identification," *Third Text* 13 (Winter 1991): 3–16.

38. Elizabeth H. Jones, *Spaces of Belonging: Home, Culture and Identity in Twentieth-century French Autobiography* (Amsterdam: Rodopi, 2007). On the importance of place particularly for women's identities, see Stephanie Taylor, *Narratives of Identity and Place* (London: Routledge, 2009).

39. Nadia Lovell, "Introduction," in *Locality and Belonging*, ed. Nadia Lovell (London: Routledge, 1998), 1–24.

40. On the relation of identity formation and our surrounding, see Hall, "Who Needs Identity?"

41. Ahmed, *Strange Encounters*, 126.

42. On ethnic identity, see among others Marcus Banks, *Ethnicity: Anthropological Constructions* (London: Routledge, 1996); Thomas Hylland Eriksen, *Ethnicity and Nationalism: Anthropological Perspectives*, 2d ed. (London: Pluto Press, 2002); Inga Jasinskaja-Lahti, Karmela Liebkind, and Erling Solheim, "To Identify or Not To Identify? National Disidentification as

an Alternative Reaction to Perceived Ethnic Discrimination," *Applied Psychology* 58.1 (2009): 105–28; Bandana Purkayastha, *Negotiating Ethnicity: Second-Generation South Asian Americans Traverse a Transnational World* (New Brunswick, NJ: Rutgers University Press, 2005); Miri Song, *Choosing Ethnic Identity* (Cambridge: Polity Press, 2003); Woodward, "Questions of Identity."

43. See Alejandro Portes and Rubén G. Rumbaut, *Legacies: The Story of the Immigrant Second Generation* (Berkeley: University of California Press, 2001); Song, *Choosing Ethnic Identity;* on identification as Korean American, see Nam Soon Huh and William J. Reid, "Intercountry, Transracial Adoption and Ethnic Identity: A Korean Example," *International Social Work* 43.1 (2000): 83.

44. Pellander, *Aasialainen sukutausta, suomalainen elämä,* 19–59; see also Rastas, "Racializing Categorization among Young People in Finland."

45. Portes and Rumbaut, *Legacies,* 147–91; Anna Rastas: "Katseilla merkityt, silminnähden erilaiset: lasten ja nuorten kokemuksia rodullistavista katseista" [Visibly different, marked by gazes: Children's and young people's experiences of receiving racist stares], *Nuorisotutkimus* 20.3 (2002), 13–14; Virkki, "Suomalaisuuden peilissä," 52.

46. Pellander, *Aasialainen sukutausta, suomalainen elämä,* 46–60.

47. Kimberlé W. Crenshaw, "Mapping the Margins: Intersectionality, Identity Politics, and Violence against Women of Color," *Stanford Law Review* 43.6 (1991): 1241–99; Nira Yuval-Davis, "Intersectionality, Citizenship and Contemporary Politics of Belonging," *Critical Review of International Social and Political Philosophy* 10.4 (2007): 561–74.

48. Trinh Minh-ha, *When the Moon Waxes Red* (New York: Routledge, 1991), quoted in Ang, *On Not Speaking Chinese,* 146–47.

FOUR

Doing Belonging: Young Women of Middle Eastern Backgrounds in Sweden

SERINE GUNNARSSON

We have two images of foreign girls. One of the images is that she comes here to Sweden. She learns Swedish, she studies and so on. She's a good daughter to her parents. She follows their conditions and stuff. Doesn't oppose, comes home on time, doesn't argue, doesn't quarrel with them, doesn't cause problems for herself, etc. Finally, she'll get married to someone of her parents' choice because she has lived under their supervision and conditions, for nineteen or eighteen years. She will automatically want them to decide because they know what's best for her. There we have one girl. The other, she's the total opposite. Or, she's like that for a while; later she'll be influenced by the society and by her circle of friends. She starts asking questions: "What's right and what's wrong? Are my parents right? Or should I choose my own path? Should I follow their path? Or should I choose my own path? It's my life after all! I have my own rights."

THE QUOTATION ABOVE IS NARRATED BY A YOUNG MUSLIM woman, Fatima, who was born in Iraq and immigrated to Sweden at the age of eight. Her story captures a crucial identity dilemma omnipresent in the everyday lives of the six young women – aged sixteen to eighteen – of Middle Eastern backgrounds interviewed for this chapter.[1] Fatima believes that a lot of young women of primarily Middle Eastern descent living in Sweden struggle with a contradictory life situation. The problem boils down to either respecting the rules and regulations of their parents and thus giving up personal ambitions in life or being brave enough to go against the mainstream and choose their own paths in life, a situation that can cause conflicts not only with the parents but within the extended family. Along with the rest of the interviewees, Fatima values her relationship with her parents highly. She feels obligated to respect their wishes, at least to a reasonable extent. Since her parents do not have the same experiences of integration in the Swedish society as she has, Fatima feels responsible to respect her parents' "conflicting immigrant situation," which causes a "clash of two world views," as she describes it. She continues, "The foundation of all these problems is the family, because the family has not lived in this society. They have lived in a totally different world. They have other roots, been raised by other traditions, an entirely different culture, another background."

The everyday life experiences of Fatima and the five other young women who all grew up in Sweden form the empirical basis for the present chapter.[2] The interviewees, who represent the first sample of my research project as a whole, showed interest in participating in my study after an introduction about the project at their school.[3] The criterion for participation was formulated as "young women of Middle Eastern backgrounds."

My research interest is to explore the social identity formation among these young women from a social-psychological perspective. The analysis focuses on interactions and practices of *doing belonging*[4] with regard to ethnic, gender, and religious identifications. Mainly, I use the social identity theory formulated by social psychologist Henri Tajfel. According to this theoretical approach, it is within daily social interaction on an intergroup level that social identity is shaped. A person's identity is, thus, an ongoing process underpinned by the interrelation between self- and public images.[5]

In line with a phenomenological approach and the works of sociologist Alfred Schütz, my study's objective is to attain a deeper understanding of the subjectively experienced *life-worlds* of the participants.[6] This conceptual framework concerns the relation between an individual and his or her in-group or out-group members on a variety of levels.[7] The goal of this method is to find out what meanings are attributed to the experiences of the participants' social reality. In phenomenology, this procedure is divided into two interrelated parts: (1) studying the actual statements and actions of the participants, referred to as "first-order constructs"; (2) developing an analytical understanding of those lived experiences, called "second-order constructs."[8] To quote sociologist Patrik Aspers, "Phenomenology takes the individual as the point of departure for studies, and it can be summarized as being a systematic way of studying the subjective perspective. The individual is the pole for the construction of meaning."[9]

YOUNG IMMIGRANT WOMEN IN SWEDEN
AS A STEREOTYPICAL CONCEPT

Since the beginning of the twenty-first century, an increasing number of academic studies have explored the topic of young women of immigrant backgrounds in Sweden. Some publications have been more extensive than others.[10] In one way or another, these studies have brought up the question of identity among the young women. Due in large part to intensive media coverage on a few cases of honor-related violence in Sweden,[11] there has been a focus on those immigrant groups who are associated with collectivistic and patriarchal traditions.

The media interest in immigrant women emerged in the late 1970s. Before then, only immigrant men located in the labor market had dominated the media reports on immigrants in general in Sweden.[12] Since then, the public image of immigrant women in Sweden has predominantly been stereotyped as deviant and characterized as oppressed, isolated, private, and withdrawn. This stereotype also includes a dimension of reducing these women to sexualized objects. Their bodies and clothes were paid great attention to in the articles.[13]

Compared to the portrayal of immigrant women in the late 1970s, media images of immigrant women today are more concerned with victimization and honor-related violence. This more-infected debate concentrates on a particular group of immigrant families, namely, the Muslim and Middle Eastern families who are viewed as bearers of an "honor culture."[14] In her study of Swedish news articles from the second half of the 1990s, Eva Karlsson concludes that the stereotype of young immigrant women refers to the "oriental" woman, that is, the non-White, Arabic, Muslim woman who is victimized by the collective pressure from her family.[15]

In January 2002, a young woman of Kurdish background, Fadime Sahindal, was murdered by her father who could not accept her choice of a free "Swedish" lifestyle. This incident became known as an "honor killing," and the media interest of young women of similar backgrounds reached its peak.[16]

In the aftermath of the murder of Fadime, numerous articles covered topics such as honor-related violence, arranged marriages, female genital mutilation, and the veil. Concepts like ethnicity, religion, gender, family, culture, and class were all ingredients in the attempts to explain the causes and effects of the honor killing.[17]

Furthermore, this issue has been discussed in relation to Swedish gender-equality policies. As Ann Towns notes, "At the same time as Sweden emerges as a gender-equal state in the mid-1990s . . . gender equality became a salient terrain of differentiation between people residing in Sweden, between 'immigrants' and 'Swedes.'"[18] Within this gender-equality discourse, the stereotyped category of young immigrant (Middle Eastern) women living in Sweden represents the opposite of what is perceived as the gender-equal, emancipated Swedish woman. In particular, the question of religiosity is brought to the fore and creates a wider gap between the categories. While the young immigrant women are assumed to be more or less practicing Muslims, Swedish women are presumed to be not very religious descendants of Christianity. This whole process can be interpreted as a historical continuation of making the immigrant woman the *Other* woman from a Swedish national identity point of view.[19]

From a social psychological perspective, external images, such as stereotypes of minority groups described in the news media, bear heavy importance in the identification process and life experiences of those being evaluated on the basis of a stereotypical social yardstick. Studies have shown how official stereotypes, often of derogatory nature, of immigrant youth – young men as (aggressive) perpetrators and women as (passive) victims – can motivate young people to form alternative identities as a reaction against the distorted image of them in society.[20] Social exclusion and stigmatization as a deviant in relation to the majority are not unfamiliar consequences of discriminatory behavior toward minority groups. The related question is how individuals and social groups who are subjects of stereotyping – that is, recognized as the Other – interpret their own identity in relation to external images.

Taking this context as a point of departure, my research intention is to investigate how young women of Middle Eastern backgrounds reflect on their life situations living in contemporary Sweden. The current research field on immigrant youth in general and young women in particular needs to be elaborated when it comes to bringing forward the life stories of these individuals. It is not far-fetched to claim that these young women have yet to make their voices heard in the public domain in Sweden. The findings in my research can provide new interpretations of key issues on ethnic relations in Sweden, such as social inclusion and exclusion, the effect of social stereotypes, and the treatment of Swedish-born youths of non-Swedish ethnic backgrounds.

STRATEGIES FOR DOING ETHNIC IDENTITY

Based on the interview material, I find the key issues are the identity category of ethnicity and the sense of emotional belonging to both Sweden and one's country of origin. A common experience among the participants is an ambivalent attitude toward their ethnic background and their relation to Swedish society. None of them could clearly explain how she viewed herself in ethnic terms. For the most part, these young women compare themselves to their parents when it comes to ethnic identity. In the following excerpt from an interview, Fatima tries to explain the dilemma that she believes a lot of young women like her go through. She speaks in third person, but it became clear that the story refers to her, too:

> Fatima: Yeah, but . . . then the clash comes. The parents want to, like, go this way, but the girl wants to go, like, the total opposite [way]. . . . Then they [the girl and her parents] must cooperate. The girl does have her values, her opinions that she herself has built up during her time in Sweden. And her parents . . .

Here, Fatima explains that the parents have to deal with two "different worlds" that "will clash." As a result, the young woman is caught in "a mixed world." The girl has both her feet neither in Sweden nor in her parents' home country. Rather, "She has one foot here, the other foot here [drawing a line with her hands on the table]. . . . Now she is here [in the middle]," says Fatima. Nadia, who was born in Iran to Kurdish parents, fills in: "She has a border in between. She doesn't know." Fatima concludes: "Now the big question . . . Should I, like, go over there, or should I go over there [illustrating with her hands on the table]? And who decides? Is it me? What happens then? Do I get rejected?" Fatima attempts to clarify that it is difficult for young women like the person in her story to choose a suitable strategy in life without risking a rejection from her family. Therefore, as a young woman with several value systems incorporated in her sense of identity, she must negotiate her way through everyday situations. Fatima continues to explain alternative strategies to deal with this dilemma:

> Fatima: No, but . . . now she has to think about, if she is smart, that is. She is a smart girl, of course. . . . So she thinks like this: If I want to go over to this world, which is to the Western world, let's say because it suits me perfectly, is up to my principles, values and everything. 'Cause I don't want to, like, go there. Now I'm here. This is my life. . . . They [young women of similar background as Fatima] will think like this: "In what way will I be able to get . . . my parents along to my world?" If she doesn't succeed to make them come along, [she thinks], "How am I supposed to try and . . . make them understand?" And if she's not . . . this I know. No girl can, by herself, change two, like, mother and father. She must get help.
>
> Nadia: Uncle or . . . Shortcuts! [laugh]
>
> Fatima: Yes, but it's like that. And then you have to, like, think, "How should I . . . what am I supposed to do? Should I, like, contact . . . is it through school, for example, then? Is it the social authorities? The municipality? Who is it that I should turn to?" . . . But, who is it that I should turn to? I can't go to . . . I can't go to them [the parents]. 'Cause obviously, they want to keep me there [at home]. They don't want me to stay here and . . . they don't want me to break the circle, you know?

After Fatima's outline of what she presents as the "typical" situation for young women like herself, the other girls in the group stated that they did not recognize themselves at all in Fatima's description. For instance, Sarah, born in Sweden to Iranian parents, says that it has never been a problem for her to adjust to her family's rules. She feels that it is up to her how much she can "push the limit." But Sarah has relatively more freedom compared to the other girls and, therefore, seldom comes in conflict with her parents in this matter. However, she says, "Just because I can, I don't push it" and compares her type of freedom to that of her Swedish peers. Indeed, it is repeatedly in comparison with Swedish girls and their assumed freedom that the participants talk about their own situation. It can also be added that the general perception among the interviewees is that Iranians are the most liberated ethnic group among those from the Middle East. Linda, who is a Christian Arab of Syrian heritage, says, "They [Iranians] are like, really free. Sometimes I don't even see them as Iranians at all."

In their discussions, the concepts of "Swedish freedom" versus "immigrant freedom" for young women serve as two distinct ways of life. A conceptualized ethnic identity combined with the gender aspect is seemingly pervasive in their identity claims. There are no clear-cut boundaries between the distinct categories of freedom for young women. Instead, the participants approach this subject by the use of various individual and strategic negotiations when describing their sense of belongingness – along an ethnicized scale of "freedom of movement." The following statement by Nadia can serve as an example of how to position oneself in relation to the above-described freedom categories: "That's what we cannot forget. Honestly, even if you had it, would you even want that kind of freedom? I don't want the freedom that Swedes have." She continues: "I don't want my parents to let me stay out until two in the morning . . . and go to sleep. I want my parents to think about where I am and care!"

Drawing from their discussions about freedom to stay out late and whether the parents care about them coming home late, restrictions about freedom of movement work as a marker for what is perceived as typically Swedish and non-Swedish. They agree that "freedom with responsibility" characterizes their own situation – or should at least be the goal for young women in immigrant families – whereas Swedish girls generally do not respect the freedom they have been given.[21] The participants also agree that these are generalizations, not to say prejudice, to say that all Swedish girls behave in a certain way. However, they draw conclusions from their own experiences and have firm opinions about some differences between how Swedish girls use their freedom in contrast to how girls with immigrant background use the relatively limited freedom that they do have. It can be added that the participants socialize predominantly with other female friends of similar immigrant backgrounds on a daily basis. However, they do have Swedish friends too, but perhaps they are not as close to them as to their friends of non-Swedish background. In addition, my impression is that the interview situation itself contributed to a stronger emotional attachment to their ethnic in-group members and a stronger identification with peers of similar backgrounds, rather than Swedish peers.

At the center of the participants' discussions about ethnic identifications is the concept of "becoming Swedicized." Using this concept, the participants claim that there is a "genuine" way of living in accordance with the idea of being a "respectable immigrant girl." In contrast, there is a group of immigrant girls who, in the participants' view, act in a perceivably "false" or "inauthentic" manner. What characterizes this attempt to "pass" as a Swede is, in Sarah's words, "If somebody asks where I come from and I say, 'I'm Swedish', although I'm not Swedish." Aisha of Kurdish descent adds, "But I think it's shameful, let's say, girls and boys who have another background but claim to be Swedish. Why not be proud? There are those who say like this: 'No, I'm Swedish.' But why? You are not! These people are called Swedicized, according to me." Furthermore, much of the discussion is focused on the gendered aspect of "becoming Swedicized." Often, it is an immigrant girl, not a boy, who is described as having crossed the line and become a "fraud," that is, has "become Swedicized." It seems that girls have more to lose than boys. The girls have to be more attentive to how they are perceived by others and avoid getting a bad reputation caused by "crossing the line."

Boys of similar backgrounds as the participants can more easily get away with romantic relationships with Swedish girlfriends and not be accused of "becoming Swedicized." If a girl, on the other hand, is romantically involved with a Swedish boy, her integrity and identity as an in-group member are immediately questioned by her ethnic community. She is likely to be accused of "becoming Swedicized." If a girl should marry a Swedish boy, her parents will have to deal with the extended family who might accuse them of being failed parents. The relatives living in their country of origin can put great pressure on the parents to keep better track of their daughters. In Fatima's words, "The home country calls: 'Well, so your girl [daughter] has got herself a Swedish boyfriend?'" Nadia adds, "'Yes, we [the relatives] heard that your daughter did this . . .' They [the relatives] influence the parents." It is striking that the same type of social control is not applied to the sons in the same families.[22]

Distinguishing herself from the rest of the participants, Sarah has actually been encouraged by her mother *not* to marry an immigrant. Sarah was shocked when her mother said, "You will have it much easier if you get involved with a Swede." Sarah's mother would only accept Sarah's marrying an immigrant boy if he had already adapted to the Swedish society. Here, the participants talk positively about Swedish

boys as more romantic, more attentive to a girl's needs, and more willing
to engage in domestic chores compared to immigrant boys who expect
their wives to "cook, take care of the children, and also to have a career
. . . to have three hands at the same time!" says Nadia.

Besides judging a girl's proper or improper behavior to determine
her loyalty toward her in-group, her physical appearance can either make
or break others' perception of her degree of "authenticity." For Nadia, it
is first and foremost the clothes of the immigrant girl that indicate her
"genuineness": "Those who dress a little more low-necked. That I perceive as the stereotype for Swedicized and what people call Swedicized.
Not that they call themselves Swedicized." Nadia makes an interesting
point here as she underscores that "becoming Swedicized" is a concept
externally ascribed to those acting "Swedicized." Thus, the concept is
not something used by immigrant girls to portray themselves in a positive light – otherwise, it would imply a self-ascription as sexually promiscuous in the view of the participants for whom such a self-image is
unthinkable. The concept is negatively connoted and ascribed to those
who appear as "frauds" and do not embrace their ethnic heritage. Linda
says that an immigrant will always remain an immigrant in Sweden,
but there are those who "really want to act like Swedes, those who only
hang out with Swedes all the time. They live like Swedes too. They go
out partying and stuff." The following statement by Fatima can sum up
this discussion: "Why should we become Swedicized? Absolutely not! I
don't want that because I'm proud of my roots. I will always be an Arab,
but I will at the same time be able to live in another, that is to be able to
handle another, like, ethnic group."

Departing from Schütz's conceptual framework of the life-world, I
see the experiences of the participants as divided into at least two dimensions when it comes to ethnic identifications. For Schütz, the life-world is
indeed twofold: one *directly* experienced and one *indirectly* experienced
social reality.[23] Based on a social process of categorization in which the
individual evaluates her own position in relation to others in terms of
ideal types, the social distance (be it physical, emotional, or temporal) between oneself and others will create different social relationships. Within
the directly experienced social world, we find the individual's immediate
consociates with which one can develop a face-to-face relationship or,

potentially, a "We-relationship."[24] Within the indirectly perceived social reality, the individual relates to her (1) *contemporaries*, (2) *predecessors*, and (3) *successors*. This latter experience of one's social reality involves a temporal dimension.[25] An elaborated examination of the interrelation between the three aspects of time can provide a holistic view of the experiences of the participants.

At this point, it can be said that the participants' immediate consociates, with whom they interact on a daily basis, are family members, peer groups, and schoolmates of primarily immigrant backgrounds. Their parents play a crucial role in the identity formation of these young women. The parents are present in almost every subject discussed during the interviews. As for the indirectly experienced social reality, it is interesting how the participants separate different groups of people among their contemporaries. Within this category, there are people of various ethnic backgrounds whom the participants potentially can come in contact with in their daily lives. These are imagined groups to which they feel various degrees of emotional attachments. Although they have not and never will meet all members of their ethnic group of origin, they still feel a strong emotional attachment to them. This cannot be easily said about contemporaries of Swedish background. However, the question of feeling emotionally attached to Sweden is complicated. For example, Linda states that her "mind belongs to Syria," while her "heart is here" in Sweden. She loves her country of birth (Sweden) as much as her "home country," Syria. She explains that the emotional attachment to either country increases or decreases depending on where she is and what she is doing at the moment.

Since the participants commonly feel that one should be proud of one's ethnic heritage, I would say that their predecessors are those imagined as their ethnic ancestors and their relatives from previous generations. This historical perspective, which appears to be important to them, emphasizes the non-Swedish part of their social identity. They do not relate to any Swedish predecessors, but perhaps their successors will include ethnic Swedes or even a mixture of other ethnic categories.

What can be inferred from the interview material thus far is that some form of Swedish identity is incorporated in their sense of self, but only partially. Sarah's story can work as an example:

> I can't say I'm Swedish. But I can't say I'm totally Iranian either. Because even
> if I go back to my home country Iran, I'm not . . . I'm not like them. . . . I can't
> go back. I can't imagine a life in Iran. But I can't imagine my life as a Swede.
> Because I'm not all-Swede. . . . I feel more Swedish than I feel as an Iranian. . . .
> Like, in Iran, I want to come home. Because I see Sweden as my home. That's me.

Yasmin, who was born in Sweden to Palestinian parents from Syria, explains that there is a difference between identifying with the Swedish
society on the one hand and the Arabic *culture* on the other: "I view myself
more like a Swede . . . as in an ordinary Swedish citizen. I have as many
rights as everyone else. But if you think about culture and stuff, then I
see myself more as an Arab." Overall, Yasmin's sense of belonging to
her cultural and ethnic heritage as an Arab overpowers her identification as a Swedish citizen, and thus as a Swede. It seems that the shared
feeling of belonging to a minority group in Sweden, while claiming to
be recognized as a full Swedish citizen, can be translated into a desire
to be "equal but different" – to use Tajfel's terminology – in relation to
the majority society.[26] As Yasmin, Linda, and the others describe their
life experiences as always feeling like a minority member in Sweden, I
can only conclude that there is a degree of resistance in acknowledging
a sense of Swedishness among these individuals. It is difficult for them
ever to see themselves as more than just Swedish citizens.

FEMALE SEXUALITY, RESPECTABILITY, AND RELIGIOSITY

The analysis of this part of the empirical material highlights the intersections of several identity categories, namely, ethnicity, gender, sexuality,
and religion. From the theoretical perspective of intersectionality, these
identity categories must analytically be treated as interdependent and
socially affected by the power relations in society across, for example,
ethnic and gender lines.[27] Perhaps the situation of young immigrant
women in Sweden is particularly interesting from this perspective. Applying an intersectionality approach, sociologist Mehrdad Darvishpour
describes the specific situation of this group in Sweden as "quadruply
repressed": "Many belong to the underclass, they are exposed to ethnic
discrimination, as women they are repressed by the patriarchate, and as

children and members of the younger generation they are subject to the parents' authority."[28]

For the participants, religion and religiosity are immediately connected to ethnic identifications and gender relations, but especially when female sexuality is discussed. In the following quotation, Linda and Yasmin discuss the meaning of being religious and what effects religiosity has on sexually related matters:

Linda: Listen, honestly . . . sure, they [parents] would rather not want me to have a man until I'm married. Then I think it also depends on the religion. I'm an Orthodox, and so, you are supposed to wait until you are married.

Yasmin: In most religions you are supposed to wait.

Linda: Well, yeah . . .

Yasmin: But it depends on how religious you are. [laugh]

Linda: Protestants are not like that anyway. [laugh]

In line with both of their religious beliefs, they stress the importance of sexual abstinence before marriage. Here, a common ground is outlined between Yasmin as a Muslim and Linda as an Orthodox Christian. Instead of claiming differences between these religions, they see the degree of religiosity as the main marker for difference and similarity between groups of people. Their shared perspective is that any "decent" immigrant girl should respect herself enough to wait until married before her sexual debut.[29]

For all the participants, keeping their virginity until married is an important symbol for a respectable young woman. They all strive to be seen as honorable and respectable, especially in the eyes of their collective in-groups. Ethnologist Annick Sjögren argues that the virginity of young women from collectivistic cultures – mainly referring to Mediterranean countries – is the central cultural and symbolic capital that determines a family's self-worth and, therefore, assures their integrity. The honor and reputation of the family are dependent on the respectability of the young woman in the family and her sexuality.[30] In her study on second-generation women of Moroccan descent in the Netherlands, M. W. Buitelaar explains, "It is well known that virginity is an important symbol in Muslim societies such as Morocco. The core value of virginity is part of a wider symbolic complex of which the chastity of women is the key-concept."[31]

It should be stressed that such control over young women's sexuality, based on the honor discourse, requires a small community built on close relationships between people. Another way to describe such group-oriented communities is to refer to them as cultures of *shame* – in contrast to cultures of *guilt*, that is, cultures based on individuals (not groups) as the smallest unit.[32] This should imply that group-oriented norms will be challenged in a Swedish individualistic and urban context. Not surprisingly, this is the reality for the participants. For them, sexual debut before marriage is associated with a "Swedish way of life." Overall, they have a relatively conservative approach to sexuality. Nadia strongly opposes what she believes is the Swedish norm on sexuality. She is also keen on stating her independence in this issue:

> I myself don't think that it affects me that much how people see me, because . . .
> I have my principles. Everyone knows about my principles. I don't want a boy-
> friend. I don't want to drink. I don't want to have sex. Nobody forces me to think
> that way. It's my own stuff! I want to be abstinent or conservative, or whatever it
> is called.

We may infer from the interviews that being a virgin until married can be viewed as showing independence, that is, going against the mainstream in Sweden. It is also an indication of how far along one has gone toward "becoming Swedicized." The perception of female sexuality thus becomes distinctively ethnicized and gendered. As ethnologist Åsa Andersson notes in her study on teenage girls in a multicultural city in Sweden, virginity and sexual respectability can additionally be used as a strategy to gain higher social status.[33] Furthermore, the idea of female sexuality and respectability must be understood in relation to how Swedish female peers' sexuality is perceived. Andersson points out that the young immigrant women in her study attain respectability by disregarding the assumed Swedish norms concerning free sexuality. Keeping her virginity, the young woman is strategically "dis-identifying" with Swedes.[34]

Margareta Forsberg makes a similar observation in her study on Swedish and immigrant girls' perception of female sexuality.[35] The girls in this study associated a certain type of sexuality with a particular ethnic appearance. Swedish girls were described as "sluttish blondes" and immigrant girls as "reserved brunettes."[36] Like the participants in Andersson's study, these immigrant girls dis-identified with their Swedish peers on the issue of female sexuality.

The cultural capital of virginity, therefore, becomes a useful marker for distinguishing "us" from "them." For my interviewees, sticking to an antimainstream position – being a virgin until married – differentiates them from other young people. They see themselves as unique in that respect. Most importantly, it fuels their confidence to be able to resist the social pressure that young people are subjected to. As for the Moroccan migrant families in Buitelaar's study, there is a struggle to maintain a "proper" moral code within the migrant in-group as a way to cope with "the supposedly inferior moral standards of the dominant society." Buitelaar continues: "Claiming moral superiority in which one otherwise occupies a subordinate position is a strategy to protect one's self-esteem."[37]

An indirect way to address the notion of female sexuality was through the talk about how girls dress in relation to their degree of religiosity. Even though Linda thinks that Muslims have "stricter rules" when it comes to covering the female body, she believes that a "true Christian" should not expose her body to the same extent as "normal Swedes" do. Linda describes that she would feel uncomfortable exposing her body publicly. She would never wear a bikini, for instance: "I feel uncomfortable . . . maybe with shorts or with a top." Yasmin responds to this by stating, "But that's the way we are raised. . . . You only want to show your body to your husband, and then nobody else." The religious differences between Linda and Yasmin are blurred because they share a much deeper cultural identification with a common value system on female sexuality.

In connection to the theme of religion, gender, and sexuality, the participants enthusiastically discussed the question of a young woman's reputation and that it can be "damaged" or "preserved." For the participants, a "good" or "bad" reputation is indicated by bodily symbols and the type of relationship the girl has with the opposite sex. A "bad girl," who can be called a "whore" by others, is recognized by her revealing and "sexualized" clothes. By dressing in a promiscuous way, a girl signals that she is "sexually available" and, therefore, gets a bad reputation. From the perspective of the participants, the stereotype of such a girl is ethnically identified as a Swede, since Swedish girls in general are presumed to have fewer restrictions concerning their clothes. In contrast, it is difficult for a girl wearing the veil ever to be called a whore or get a bad reputation, since she personifies "purity." The participants agree that the symbol of the veil conveys a message that the young woman is keeping her virginity until she is married.

Among the participants, it is only Fatima who wears the veil. For her, the veil is first and foremost a visible symbol of her Muslim identity, and it enhances her sense of being true to her religion. In addition, the veil serves practical purposes. Supported by the other participants, Fatima states that a girl wearing the veil "uses her clothes as a protection" from harms caused by society. Fatima experiences that boys are more "friendly" and respectful toward her compared to how they treat other, noncovered girls. She is comfortable not being seen as "girlfriend material," which is the intended consequence of wearing the veil. Independent of what the general public in Sweden thinks about Fatima's veil, she is "proud" of her veil: "I will never want to, ever, want to take it off, even if the entire society is against it." Fatima often senses negative attitudes from society toward her choice of wearing the veil. She feels that it is difficult to convince people that it was her own choice to wear the veil.[38]

The participants share experiences of being publicly regarded as "oppressed" immigrant girls from the Middle East. Throughout the interviews, they emphasized their rejection of that stereotypical description. Especially, they feel as though the media have stressed a victimizing attitude on the part of the general Swedish public toward young women like themselves. As a result, "they [the media] really give a bad image of us," says Fatima. Aisha adds, "Unfortunately, we are all judged alike. And it's really not like that." Instead, they want to be perceived as independent young women capable of making their own decisions. Unfortunately, their own choices to wear the veil, for instance, or to be a practicing religious person are often discredited by other people not in their group. For example, Fatima was told by an employer to remove her veil if she wanted to get the job. Fatima explains, "I applied for a job. . . . And they were really nice," but the employer said, "Let's be honest, and get straight to the point. If you take that thing off, you will get the job." As Aisha says, "The employer probably saw her as a victim then."

THE FEELING OF SHAME

Considering the above-described themes of religion, gender, and sexuality together, I find one particular emotion underlying the participants' arguments, namely, the feeling of shame. Many times, the experiences surrounding family relations, sexuality, maintaining self-respect, and so forth can be related to a motivation to avoid the feeling of shame. For instance, in their talks on female respectability, the young women measure their own standpoints in relation to the opinions and attitudes of the people closest to them (parents, siblings, and peer groups). They indirectly speak of a fine line between upholding a respectable image outwardly and being true to themselves by sticking to their own principles. Those principles, for instance, a more Western approach to gender relations, can sometimes conflict with the family's values.

In her doctoral thesis on shame and guilt, social psychologist Vessela Misheva outlines a number of characteristics for the feeling of shame. The underpinning principle for the experience of shame can be said to be the fear of loss of face or fear of losing one's *self*.[39] In my material, this can be related to the fear of losing self-respect as an honorable and respectable young, unmarried woman. What makes shame so interesting in this context is that "Shame as a *self-conscious emotion* is considered to be an experience that involves the self as a whole."[40] For my phenomenological approach, the experience of shame in everyday life is highly relevant, especially as the analysis shows that the feeling of shame can be a navigating factor in the identity construction among the participants. For instance, if the young woman experiences discomfort and hesitation to pursue an individual goal in life that contradicts the values of the family, perhaps the risk of feeling ashamed in front of the parents stands in the way of that pursuit.

Shame can also be related to the risk of getting a bad reputation, to disappointing one's parents, or to losing one's respectability. One of the fundamental characteristics of the feeling of shame is that it "points to a particular relation of dependency upon 'the other.'"[41] Shame, as understood by Misheva, appears to be "an obstacle to the attainment of *freedom* and even *subjectivity*," since shame "is always shame before someone."[42] There are some social groups on whom the participants are especially dependent and before whom they are at higher risk of losing face. Such a social in-group is, of course, the family, particularly the parents. But the parents' restrictions on freedom of movement, for example, are not always respected entirely. The young women in my research have different views on how to stretch these restrictions; they argue instead for "freedom with responsibility." Depending on the situation, the young women come up with creative strategies to negotiate their freedom of acting space. They are determined to make sure that people around them perceive them as *independent subjects* who have the rights to make their own decisions in life. This is also one of the key features among the young Muslim women in ethnologist Pia Karlsson Minganti's doctoral thesis. These religiously active young women of Middle East and West African backgrounds strive to be acknowledged as "independent subjects."[43]

In accordance with the social identity theory, an individual's self-understanding derives from her experience of belonging to social groups.[44] Such a self-evaluation of one's membership in a social group (or groups) would not be possible without any reference to an Other.[45] Consequently, other people will work as a reference point in the process of self-identification. With this said, the feeling of shame, as an experience that involves the self as a whole and as evoked in reference to the Other, needs to be taken into consideration when dealing with social identity formation.

SOCIAL BELONGING – RELIGIOSITY AS A DECIDING FACTOR?

Initially, the topic of religion was not one of my main themes of interest within the frame of my project. However, as I conducted the interviews and analyzed the material, I realized that this issue is important for the participants, and perhaps for many other youths of immigrant background in Sweden today. Religion in Sweden has become an increasingly

infected subject in official debates over the past decade or so. Considering the recent debates on honor-related violence and discussions about
the role of religion in this matter, my interviewees seemed to feel an urge
to ventilate their thoughts on religiosity.

Similar processes can be found elsewhere in Europe, for instance,
in France. Trica Danielle Keaton has examined the everyday life experiences of Muslim girls living in French outer cities.[46] In this study, the
young Muslim women of primarily North African origin are part of
the French immigrant youth, which has become a category of people
whom the French public has been "taught to fear." In the ongoing process
of reshaping French society into a multicultural country, these youths,
among them Muslim girls, have been treated as "suitable enemies" – at
least on political and media levels.[47] What characterizes the experiences
of the Muslim girls in Keaton's study is the ambivalence toward identifying as "simultaneously socially excluded and culturally assimilated
while being defined as a threat to the 'national identity.'"[48] Particularly,
Muslim girls who wear the veil are excluded from an imagined French
national identity. One of the participants in Keaton's study, called Aïcha,
expresses her self-understanding in this way: "Listen, let me put it to you
in this way. When I am in Morocco, people call me French, and when
I live in France, they call me a dirty Arab. So I prefer to identify myself
as 'Aïcha.'"[49] Keaton argues that the young women in this study face an
identity dilemma: "On the one hand, being French can imply 'oppressor'
to the girls and their families, since they place it in opposition to African,
Arab, or Muslim, the 'oppressed.'"[50]

Like the young women in the French context, my interviewees experience a dilemma in their sense of national and cultural belongingness.[51] In contrast, religious identification was more rigid. Religious
identity was discussed as both a uniting and a segregating factor. For
Yasmin and Linda, their religious differences had a subordinate significance when discussing family values, female respectability, relations to
parents, and related issues. Their fairly equal sense of religiosity appeared to transcend their religious differences.[52] The following quota-
tions – in response to a question about similarities between Muslim and
Christian families – can illuminate such identifications across religious
differences:

Linda: Yeah, we still live in the same country, Christians and Muslims.

Yasmin: I think like this, that Christians, Muslims and Jews all have the same basis. . . . We all have the same foundation, what is right and wrong. . . . Some things are wrong for everyone. I don't think that you [Linda] are allowed to do more things than me, for example. 'Cause both of us still are, like, religious.

Instead of claiming differences between immigrant groups of different religious backgrounds, the participants experience that Swedes and immigrants approach religion in divergent ways. The participants experience that Swedes in general celebrate religious holidays solely on the basis of tradition; these young immigrant women feel that Swedes show insufficient religiosity and are contradictory to the purpose of the holidays. They experience a difference in how Christians of immigrant background embrace their religion in comparison to, for instance, the Swedish celebration of Christmas and Easter:

Yasmin: But like, a Christian, a Christian Swede, I wouldn't take him as seriously as, like, an Arab who says he's a Christian. 'Cause, if a Swede comes and says, "I'm a Christian" . . . I do understand. I respect that he's a Christian, but I don't think that they are as strict as, like, an immigrant-Christian would be.

Linda: Exactly. It's like that.

Yasmin: 'Cause, they [immigrants] have more limits.

Linda: There is a difference . . . between Protestants and Catholics and . . .

Yasmin: Yeah, that's what I mean. But, like, Protestants, I haven't seen it as real. . . . I don't see it as real Christians. [pause] Or, I don't know . . . like, some are Protestants and are real Christians, but most of them I have known who say that they are Christians, I think, go against the religion.

What is striking in these discussions is the notion of "realness," which Yasmin and Linda think characterizes "immigrant-Christians" but not Swedish Protestants. However, it is not only some groups of Christians who can be viewed as "not really religious." Some Muslim girls, even some who wear the veil and cover their body shape, do not automatically qualify as "real" religious people because they can take advantage of the visible symbol of their religious devotion. Since the veil is such a powerful symbol for purity and religiosity, girls can use that symbolism to cover up religiously improper behavior. Fatima explains this by referring to a fictive Muslim girl: "She wears the veil, she wears long clothes. She does all these rules that she is supposed to do, that is a must, in front of people. . . . But they [people in general] have no idea about what she's really doing." These girls are rarely questioned about their religious sincerity. But Swedish people who claim to be religious are not easily regarded as serious about their religious intentions, even if they would claim to be deeply religious.

COMPLEXITIES OF SOCIAL IDENTITY FORMATION

According to social identity theory, the individual will strive for a positive self-image that derives from her identification with an in-group (or groups). Therefore, the individual will seek to engage in groups recognized as positive and ascribed a higher status. This approach further implies that identification with a relatively low-status group causes lower self-esteem for the group member. Since the self-conception is formed within the intergroup context, the status of one's in-group has significant impact on the person's self-image and self-esteem.[53]

Living in Sweden and growing up with parents originating from the Middle East, the young women in this study express mixed feelings of attachment to several collective groups. However, the participants show a trend toward positive identification with a low-status group, combined with an individual high self-esteem. They generally evaluate their Middle Eastern background as positive. To some extent, they reject the norms and values of the majority, high-status category of ethnic Swedes. This tendency contradicts Tajfel's theory regarding the correlation between low-status group and low self-esteem. Since the participants predominantly socialize with other members of Middle Eastern immigrant groups in their daily lives, they feel greater distance toward Swedish people (the high-status group) as a whole. This adds to the already strong identification with their family background and, in some cases, also religion and memories of the "home country." Conclusively, the immigrant identity is salient more frequently than the Swedish part of their self-concept. Somehow the low-status group identity – as a person of immigrant background – is reformulated and turned into something positive for the individual.

Departing from the social identity approach, I would suggest that social identity as an analytical tool should be regarded as a multidimensional process that is negotiable in everyday life. Building on the interview material, young people of an ethnic background other than the majority society define themselves along a range of identity categories. My interviewees conveyed shifting feelings of ethnic identification that can be interpreted as various degrees of social attraction to a group depending on the situation. The boundaries between each salient group become blurred in practice, whereas, in theory – when the participants speak in general terms – clear distinctions are made between Swedes, Arabs, Kurds, Iranians, Christians, Muslims, and so forth. They recognize similarities between themselves and other members of their constantly changing in-group. However, as they strongly feel the need to claim independence – to be the opposite of the victimizing stereotype – they simultaneously detach themselves from the assumed prototype of their non-Swedish, ethnic in-group. Based on these findings, I agree with Marilynn B. Brewer's statement: "Group identities allow us to be the same and different at the same time."[54] Brewer has developed a model for balancing between these contradictory and parallel identity motivations. The model is called the *optimal distinctiveness theory,* and it assumes that the two opposing processes of self-categorization operate simultaneously. On the one hand, people will strive for inclusion or *sameness* (depersonalization), which is achieved by strong group identification. On the other hand, people are also driven to stand out in a crowd, to be *unique* (differentiation).[55]

With Brewer's model in mind, I see a struggle between individualistic and collectivistic value systems embedded in the experiences of these young women. These two ideologies look on the individual and her place in the world in relation to others in opposite ways.[56] From the collectivistic perspective, which dominates the participants' family values, a young woman who aspires to become an independent individual is viewed negatively. From the individualistic perspective, which dominates the Swedish culture, a young woman holding on to traditional, family-oriented values is not considered to live by individualistic values. The participants find themselves at both ends at the same time. Both poles are exposed to reinterpretations on a daily basis. Perhaps, this very fluctuant sense of one's self-image causes uncomfortable emotions such as anxiety and worry about the future. Important to bear in mind is that the two perspectives are not exclusive of one another, as the participants' life stories show. Either one or the other will dominate in a given situation. Psychologist Harry C. Triandis argues,

> There is a constant struggle between the collectivist and individualist elements within each human. It is useful to think of culture as a "tool kit" that contains elements that are individualistic or collectivistic, which define a situation as *interpersonal* or *intergroup*. People sample elements from this tool kit to construct the meaning of situations, which determines their behavior. In cultures where most relationships are seen as *interpersonal,* we have individualism; in cultures where most situations are defined as *intergroup,* we have collectivism.[57]

It is obviously necessary to consider both these social patterns or tool kits as negotiable and highly present in the everyday lives of the participants and perhaps among many other young women and men with similar backgrounds.

CONCLUDING REMARKS

The findings of the present study thus far point to the complex processes of identity formation that have been illustrated to some extent in previous, related studies, both in Sweden and elsewhere. What is especially interesting with my results is how the participants use different strategies to cope with at times conflicting situations in their everyday lives. I have illuminated the intersections between several identity categories as the driving force behind such strategies of formulating social identities. Religion and female sexuality have been paid particular attention here.

The overarching theme throughout the chapter goes under the concept of *doing belonging.* My use of the concept is meant to capture the social aspects and ongoing processes of identity formation in the lived experiences of the participants. The "doing" part of the concept points to an active process of self-identification, which is continuously reshaped on a daily basis. Based on the analysis, my conclusion is that the participants' experiences of ethnic identification, and other factors contributing to their social identity as a whole, rely on personal negotiations in everyday life. In relation to different places, times, and various social groups (for example, the family, peer groups), these young women construct their self-images through various strategies. For instance, they have to deal with cultural conflicts concerning their freedom of movement. Also, they need to balance between integration in society and maintaining the relatively traditional values of their parents. At the same time, they wish continuously to make individual choices in the future, even though this might cause problems within the family. Yet that is a risk they are willing to take.

By intersecting several identity components such as gender, ethnicity, sexuality, nationality, and family ties, we can better understand these negotiable and border-crossing practices in the young women's lives. To understand the constructions of ethnic boundaries, we must analytically treat them as products of both individual and collective processes. My final point is that social identity constructions are never unilateral and must be analyzed theoretically as context-sensitive social processes.

NOTES

1. The empirical material is based on two separate qualitative group interviews with a total of six participants who all have an ethnic background in the Middle East. The first interview had four participants, whereas the second interview only had two participants (originally planned to include a third). Each participant was interviewed once. The interviews were carried out at their school. The language used in the interviews was Swedish. All quotes have, therefore, been translated by me from Swedish to English. Another essay that has been drawn from this same research is "'It's my own stuff': The Negotiations and Multiplicity of Ethnic Identities among Young Women of Middle Eastern Backgrounds in Sweden," in *Exploring Transculturalism: A Biographical Approach,* ed. Wolfgang Berg and Aoileann Ní 'Eigeartaigh (Wiesbaden, Germany: VS Verlag, 2010).

2. Four participants were born in Sweden. The other two immigrated to Sweden at the ages of two and eight, respectively.

Here is a list of the participants:

· *Fatima,* eighteen, born in Iraq, came to Sweden at the age of eight; her mother tongue is Arabic, and she is a Muslim.

· *Nadia,* seventeen, born in Iran of Kurdish descent, came to Sweden at the age of two; her mother tongue is Kurdish (Kurmanji), and she is a Muslim.

· *Sarah,* sixteen, was born in Sweden to parents from Iran; her mother tongue is Persian, and she is a Muslim.

· *Aisha,* seventeen, was born in Sweden to parents from Kurdistan (Iraq); her mother tongue is Kurdish (Sorani), and she is a Muslim.

· *Linda,* seventeen, was born in Sweden to parents from Syria; her mother tongue is Arabic, and she is a Christian.

· *Yasmin,* seventeen, was born in Sweden to parents who were born in Syria but were originally from Palestine; her mother tongue is Arabic, and she is a Muslim.

3. My research project as a whole includes twenty-four young women of Middle Eastern backgrounds, although only the six first interviewees are included in the analysis in this chapter.

4. My approach and use of the concept "doing" belonging is inspired by the theoretical perspective of "doing gender." See Sarah Fenstermaker and Candace West, *Doing Gender, Doing Difference: Inequality, Power, and Institutional Change* (New York: Routledge, 2002).

5. Henri Tajfel, *Human Groups and Social Categories: Studies in Social Psychology* (Cambridge: Cambridge University Press, 1981); Richard Jenkins, *Social Identity* (London & New York: Routledge, 2004).

6. The only way to access the lived experiences of these individuals is by the spoken language that will be the material for analysis here. However, my intention is not to analyze the language per se as discursive practices. To reach an understanding of the Other, verbal communication is required. My method to attain such an understanding of the lived experiences of the participants is by applying (empirical) phenomenology. It can be added that this approach corresponds to the general notions of social constructivism. See Patrik Aspers, *Markets in Fashion: A Phenomenological Approach*, Routledge Studies in Business Organizations and Networks (London: Routledge, 2005). See also Irving Siedman, *Interviewing as Qualitative Research: A Guide for Researchers in Education and the Social Sciences*, 3d ed. (New York: Teachers College Press, 2006); Clark Moustakas, *Phenomenological Research Methods* (Thousand Oaks, CA: Sage, 1994).

7. Alfred Schütz, *The Phenomenology of the Social World,* trans. George Walsh and Fredrik Lehnert, Northwestern University Studies in Phenomenology & Existential Philosophy (Evanston, IL: Northwestern University Press, 1967).

8. Aspers, *Markets in Fashion;* Schütz, *Phenomenology of the Social World.*

9. Aspers, *Markets in Fashion,* 172.

10. Catrin Lundström, *Svenska latinas: Ras, klass och kön i svenskhetens geografi* (Göteborg: Makadam, 2007); Fanny Ambjörnsson, *I en klass för sig: Genus, klass och sexualitet bland gymnasietjejer* (Stockholm: Ordfront, 2004); Åsa Andersson, *Inte samma lika: Identifikationer hos tonårsflickor i en multietnisk stadsdel* (Eslöv: B. Östlings bokförl. Symposion, 2003); Pia Karlsson Minganti, *Muslima: Islamisk väckelse och unga muslimska kvinnors förhandlingar om genus i det samtida Sverige* (Stockholm: Carlsson, 2007).

11. For instance, Sara in Umeå in 1996, Pela from Stockholm who was killed in Iraq in 1999, and Fadime in Uppsala in 2002. See, e.g., Pia Strand Runsten, "'Hedersmord,' eurocentrism och etnicitet: Mordet på Fadime – en fallstudie," in *Mediernas Vi Och Dom,* ed. Leonor Camauër and Stig Arne Nohrstedt, Rapport av Utredningen om makt, integration och strukturell diskriminering, SOU 2006:21 (Stockholm: Statens Offentliga Utredningar, 2006).

12. Ann Towns, "Paradoxes of (in) Equality: Something Is Rotten in the Gender Equal State of Sweden," *Cooperation and Conflict* 37 (2002): 157–79.

13. Ylva Brune, "Nyheter på gränsen: Tre studier i journalistik om 'invandrare', flyktingar och rasistiskt våld," diss. Göteborg University, 2004.

14. Ibid.

15. Eva Karlsson, *Att se sig själv: Nio flickors tankar kring massmedias bilder av 'invandrarflickor', samt deras syn på sig själva* (Norsborg: Södertörns högskola, Etnologi, 1999).

16. The story of Fadime has also gained much political attention in Sweden and forced the government to take measures to prevent young women (and men) from being subjected to honor-related violence.

For a thorough examination of Fadime's case, see, e.g., Unni Wikan, *En fråga om heder* (Stockholm: Ordfront, 2004).

17. Eva Reimers, "'En av vår tids martyrer': Fadime Sahindal som mediehändelse," in *Olikhetens paradigm: Intersektionella perspektiv på o(jäm)likhetsskapande,* ed. Paulina de los Reyes and Lena Martinsson (Lund: Studentlitteratur, 2005), 141–59.

18. Towns, "Paradoxes of (in)Equality," 158.

19. See, e.g., Brune, "Nyheter på gränsen"; Gunilla Hultén, "50 år med främlingen," in *Journalisternas bok: 1901–2001,* ed. Agneta Lindblom Hulthén (Stockholm: Svenska Journalistförbundet, 2001); Anna Bredström, "Gendered Racism and the Production of Cultural Difference: Media Representations and Identity Work among 'Immigrant Youth' in Contemporary Sweden," *Nordic Journal of Women's Studies* 11:2 (2003): 78–88.

20. See, e.g., Aleksandra Ålund, *Multikultiungdom: Kön, etnicitet, identitet* (Lund: Studentlitteratur, 1997).

21. It would have been interesting to explore how young Swedish women view this issue. But the aim of my research project does not allow me to expand the selection of participants further than just young women of Middle Eastern backgrounds.

22. The purpose of my research does not allow me to further explore the situation for young men of similar backgrounds as my interviewees.

23. Schütz, *Phenomenology of the Social World,* xxvᴠii.

24. Especially important in phenomenological research is bringing into light the researcher's part in the interactive knowledge production – here based on face-to-face interviews – and reflecting on what constitutes the "We-relationship" between interviewer and interviewee. My personal experience of the interviews is that the participants felt comfortable

revealing information about themselves in my presence largely due to my own immigrant background. Also, the fact that I am a woman and not much older than the participants (about ten years to be specific) probably contributed to their tendency to perceive me as one of them. I am not sure if it would have been as easy for the participants to tell their stories in such an open and honest way had I been ethnically Swedish. The sense of a "We-relationship," developed during the interviews, must, however, be dealt with carefully from the researcher's point of view. There is a fine line between maintaining the role as a professional and losing it when the role as a friend to the interviewees takes over completely. Although the atmosphere of the interviews was friendly and open thanks to the shared identity categories between me and the participants (immigrant background, gender, age), I believe that my insider perspective gave me a great advantage professionally. I probably have these shared identity categories to thank for my instant access to the empirical field and the quick gain of trust among the participants.

25. Schütz, *Phenomenology of the Social World,* xxvii.

26. See further Tajfel, *Human Groups and Social Categories.*

27. Paulina de los Reyes and Diana Mulinari, *Intersektionalitet: Kritiska reflektioner över (o)jämlikhetens landskap* (Malmö: Liber, 2005).

28. Mehrdad Darvishpour, "'Invandrarflickor' som fyrdubbelt förtryckta? En intersektionell analys av generationskonflikter bland 'invandrarfamiljer' i Sverige," in *Bortom stereotyperna? Invandrare och integration i Danmark och Sverige,* ed. Ulf Hedetoft, Bo Petterson, and Lina Sturfelt (Göteborg: Makadam, 2006), 198.

29. An interesting feature of the above quotation is Yasmin's and Linda's laughter at the end. Their laughter can be interpreted as a form of insecurity or hesitation

regarding their statements. But in the interview situation, they seemed to be keen on creating a consensus between them. As a result, they stuck to the same perspective on the subject. Perhaps the subject of sexuality is so sensitive to discuss among friends that it becomes difficult to express conflicting individual opinions that can jeopardize a sense of shared identity within the in-group.

30. Annick Sjögren, *Här går gränsen: Om integritet och kulturella mönster i Sverige och Medelhavsområdet*, 2d ed. (Stockholm: Dialogos, 2006).

31. M. W. Buitelaar, "Negotiating the Rules of Chaste Behaviour: Re-interpretations of the Symbolic Complex of Virginity by Young Women of Moroccan Descent in the Netherlands," *Ethnic and Racial Studies* 25 (May 2002): 464.

32. Bo Lewin, "Sexualities of the World," in *Sexology in Context: A Scientific Anthology*, ed. Bente Træen and Bo Lewin (Oslo: Universitetsforlaget, 2008), 336.

33. Andersson, *Inte samma lika*.

34. The concept of "dis-identify" is borrowed from Beverley Skeggs, *Formations of Class and Gender: Becoming Respectable* (London: Sage, 1997).

35. Margareta Forsberg, *Brunetter och blondiner: Sex, relationer och tjejer i det mångkulturella Sverige* (Lund: Studentlitteratur, 2007).

36. Ibid.

37. Buitelaar, "Negotiating the Rules of Chaste Behaviour," 466.

38. A further analysis of Fatima's choice to wear the veil has not yet been made up to this point, mainly because the format of the group interview did not allow me to ask detailed questions about Fatima's choice to wear the veil in the first place. However, as I have proceeded with an individual interview with Fatima more than a year after the group interview, the circumstances surrounding Fatima's choice to wear the veil will become clearer when the individual interview has been analyzed.

39. Vessela Ivanova Misheva, "Shame and Guilt: Sociology as a Poietic System," diss., Uppsala University, Dept. of Sociology, 2000.

40. Ibid., 53.

41. Ibid., 46.

42. Ibid., 76.

43. Karlsson Minganti, *Muslima*, 56.

44. Tajfel, *Human Groups and Social Categories*.

45. Cf. Misheva, "Shame and Guilt."

46. Trica Danielle Keaton, *Muslim Girls and the Other France: Race, Identity Politics, and Social Exclusion* (Bloomington: Indiana University Press, 2006).

47. Ibid., 2.

48. Ibid., 4.

49. Ibid., 35.

50. Ibid., 46.

51. However, it should be remembered that Sweden does not share a history of colonialism with France. For the young people of immigrant background in France, the colonial heritage contributes to shaping their self-images. See Keaton, *Muslim Girls*. This is not the case for my interviewees.

52. Cf. Karlsson Minganti, *Muslima*, 138ff.

53. Tajfel, *Human Groups and Social Categories*.

54. Marilynn B. Brewer, "The Social Self: On Being the Same and Different at the Same Time," *Personality and Social Psychology Bulletin* 17 (1991): 477.

55. Ibid. See Figure 2.

56. See, e.g., Sjögren, *Här går gränsen*; Harry C. Triandis, *Individualism and Collectivism* (Boulder, CO: Westview Press, 1995).

57. Triandis, *Individualism and Collectivism*, xiv.

FIVE

To Be or Not to Be a Minority Group? Identity Dilemmas of Kashubians and Polish Tatars

KATARZYNA WARMIŃSKA

THE TRANSFORMATIONS FOLLOWING THE DRAMATIC POLITICAL
changes of 1989 have had a substantial impact on the situation of national
and ethnic communities in Poland. In respect to minorities, the last
twenty years have resulted in stabilization of a formal and legal frame of
their activities. Minority groups have delineated the way they expressed
their ethnicity on both collective and individual levels, as well as in private and public spheres. In the early stages after 1989, we could observe
a renaissance of ethnicity in Poland, then setting up the rudiments of
ethnic relations in democratic Poland. Nowadays, the collective interests
of the minority groups are gradually stabilizing and crystallizing, and
they are geared toward attaining certain aims and interests (material,
sociocultural, media-related, and educational) which are to a large extent
based on institutionalized actions.

At present, a small percentage of the inhabitants of Poland constitutes the persons who belong to ethnic or national minorities. According
to the statistics, in the interwar period over one-third of the population
(out of 32.1 million) was of other than Polish national identity. Data from
the 1930s list Ukrainians as the most numerous national minority group
(5 million), followed by Jews (3.1 million), Byelorussians (2 million), and
Germans (0.8 million). In the 1920s, the authorities would solve nationalistic issues based on working out the relations on the idea of uniform
national citizen loyalty. The 1930s brought a change in this scope. The
relations on the dominant group/minorities line took on a more confron-
tational character, on the part both of the emancipating communities of
the minorities as well as of the state, which intensified Polonization ac-

tions. A nationalistic spirit started gaining strength. World War II and its effects brought fundamental changes to the ethnic composition of Polish society. First of all, one has to mention the losses among civilians (the Holocaust of the Jewish population). In addition, the war's end brought a change in the state borders. A significant part of the eastern territories inhabited by Ukrainians and Byelorussians now was outside Poland. The shift of the western borders toward the West brought about a compulsory out-migration of the population of German descent. Consequently, Poland became, in fact, a more monocultural society after World War II, when compared with the preceding period.

The policy toward ethnic and national groups after 1945 was a derivative, as Sławomir Łoziński writes, of a new national shape to the population, yet an ideological vision of the Polish state as a culturally homogeneous one. Its derivative was that the rights to preserve and communicate cultural separateness of individual groups were limited, the minorities issue was excluded from the public sphere, and assimilation became a way of social integration. At that time, officially recognized expressions of minority-group ethnicity amounted, most of all, to folklore. Even such expressions functioned through cultural, educational, or social organizations that were under the auspices of the state, and their operations were limited.[1]

At present in Poland, according to the Central Statistical Office based on the results of the 2002 census, out of the total population of 38.2 million, 96.7 percent (36.99 million) declared Polish nationality; 1.2 percent gave a nationality other than Polish (0.47 million), while another 0.775 million (2 percent) did not respond to the national affiliation question.[2] In the report of 2002 to the secretary general of the Council of Europe, the number of these minority communities was estimated at about one million (2–3 percent of Poland's population).[3] The following are the official and estimated number of selected groups in thousands:[4] Germans (152.89/300–500), Ukrainians (30/200–300), Byelorussians (48.7/200–300), Roms (12.86/20–30), Silesians (173.2), Jews (1.13/8–10), Kashubians (5.062/300–500), Tatars (0.495/5).[5]

To return to the most important issue of this article, the two key moments for the shape of ethnic discourse in Poland were the National and Housing Census of 2002 and the Regional Language, National and

Ethnic Minorities Act of 2005, that is, when the official, state's vision met the one represented by the minorities.[6]

The census of 2002 in Poland was crucial because, for the first time since World War II, a question about a national identity of citizens was posed. The question was to reveal the actual head count of individual ethnic and national groups. The results of the census showed quite a different picture of diversity than the one that was assumed in the context of estimated data (provided by the minorities themselves and by different state institutions). The chasm between the estimates and the census data was substantial (that is, in many cases, there was a tenfold revaluation of the head count) as the above-cited numerical data show.

It should be noted that the logic of the census question – "What is your nationality? 1) Polish; 2) non-Polish (specify)" – specifically indicated the choice; it did not give the respondent any possibility to represent his or her ethnocultural characteristics in a more complex way. Rather, it made the respondent define him- or herself in a clear-cut way: "Are you a Pole or not?"[7] Also, the census questionnaire included a separate question about citizenship and the language used at home.[8]

The act of 2005, on the other hand, aimed at amending constitutional provisions of 1997 and at final regulation of the legal situation of representatives of ethnic or national minorities and communities that used a regional language (those with a Polish citizenship and whom the Polish State considered as so-called traditional national minorities as listed in the act).[9] Such a formal institutionalization of an ethnic status indicated a plane within which ethnocultural differences could be accepted and protected.

The events mentioned above were a strong stimulus for the minorities to become active in the politics of identity. At a very fundamental level, the policy touches, first of all, the issue of gaining acknowledgment of a given identity status quo on the part of the majority: that is, the vision of itself the community articulates. As a consequence of their complex histories and their earlier identity choices, the Kashubians and Polish Tatars faced the necessity of clearly defining the frames of their ethnocultural characteristics. Their choice located them either on the side of the Polish national majority or on the side of a minority identity, be it national, ethnic, linguistic, or regional. In the case of the Kashubians, it meant occupying the status of a community using a regional language; for the Tatars, it meant occupying the status of an ethnic minority.

It is important to mention that, in the case of the Kashubians and Polish Tatars, we are dealing with complex constructions of ethnocultural identities. The majority of members of the two communities define themselves as Kashubian-Poles, as Tatar-Poles, or simply as Poles. This state of affairs is the effect of, in both cases, many factors, especially historical and political ones. The two kinds of identity – minority and Polish – are not mutually exclusive. Such declarations leave room for manipulation or negotiation of the meanings they contain. The impulse for such activities can be initiated by the group that wants actively to shape its identity resources. The minorities conduct their cultural politics in pursuit of creating such self-descriptions or symbolic representations, which, in the public sphere, will allow them to achieve group and individual goals. Most often, however, such activities are a response to what is happening in the national discourse about ethnicity that takes place outside the group.

The process of a gradual stabilization of the state policy toward minorities, especially in its formal, legal aspects, was connected to the issue of the dominant ideology regarding the attitude toward minorities. This was especially the case in the matter of national integration of the state, whose roots are in an ideology of a homogeneous national identity. As the sociological research shows, the Polish thinking about the nation and the state is dominated (on both popular and official levels) by a strong ethnic component, and a mixture of Polocentrism enforced by the communist state's vision of a monoethnic nation still functions in the consciousness of many Poles. The citizen element in a liberal version or a communitarian version of understanding Polishness is marginal in comparison to the ethnic, communal element.[10]

This is a challenge for minority groups, which stress their ethnocultural separateness and which, at the same time, postulate Polishness at the level of national identity. They face a situation of a homogeneous Polish ethnic vision of the nation and citizenship, which requires an unambiguous declaration regarding community ties because, in the national discourse, such ties communicate the scope of loyalty toward the national state.[11]

In the Polish national project, whatever is ambiguous is not tolerated and stirs distrust. Therefore, there exists a conviction that one can only be a Pole or not a Pole. One cannot be a Pole and not a Pole at the same time in the ethnic category (the census question reflects this logic very clearly). Meanwhile, the members of the groups under discussion in this chapter, an overwhelming percentage, *do* feel Polish and Polish-Kashubian or Polish-Tatar at the same time.

Therefore, it should be interesting to look into the effects of the meeting of the official identity discourse as seen by the authors of the census and legislative procedure with the subtle nature of ethnicity.

For the purposes of the analysis, I chose two groups that differed from each other in many respects – their size, cultural features, descent (Kashubes are an indigenous group, while the Tatars are migrants). Despite the differences, they experience the same identity situation, namely, their members carry a similar identity situation in the ethnocultural aspect, and one of their significant common elements is coexistence in self-description of Polishness and ethnic identification. Furthermore, in both communities for the last twenty years, discussions have been taking place about the character of cultural resources that they have at their disposal, and different identity options have been postulated as regards the ethnic "us." Also, within their own community and in intergroup relations, they undertake actions that can be defined as politics of identity with the aim to give a positive shape – from the point of view of a given fraction – to the configuration of identity. Thereby, they are a good example of a struggle with the situation of a minority and its complex identity.

KASHUBES AND POLISH TATARS

The Kashubes, who are one of the subjects of this paper, are an ethnic group of a regional/indigenous character. The estimate data created by researchers and the interested party say that nowadays there are about half a million people identified as Kashubes. They live mainly in the area stretching from Gdańsk toward Łeba and the areas of the Tuchola Forest, that is, in the northwest part of Poland. The Kashubians are descendants of the Western-Slavonic Baltic tribes. Over its complex history, this community has found itself between cultural, social, and political influences of two strong groups: Polish and German.[12]

The situation, on the one hand, caused penetration of dominant Polish values into the ethnic Kashubian culture by Polish state and national organs. On the other hand, it situated this community in the position of a minority as the border with Germany fluctuated because its ethnocultural distinction was visible in both the Kashubian-German context (for example, Slavic origin and partly Catholic religion) and Kashubian-Polish (for example, no knowledge of the Polish language and culture, enculturation through the educational system into the German culture). Some researchers write about a specific Polish-German rivalry for Kashubes or the strategically important Pomeranian region that they inhabited, and others write about Germanization and Polonization pressures.[13]

It is important from the point of view of the problem discussed in this paper that, during the rise of many nationalisms in the nineteenth century, the Kashubes failed to join the trend where identities of many small nationalities were crystallizing around them in this part of Europe. Attempts to awaken Kashubian separateness evoked no response, although some ideas emerged that aimed at saving and reinforcing Kashubian culture and consciousness. Still, the Kashubes were not powerful enough to expand their ethnic and cultural community into an autonomous political and national group.[14] They established strong national ties with neither the Polish nor the German group.

The twentieth century brought about significant changes when the majority of the area inhabited by Kashubes was incorporated into the Polish state in 1920. At that time, the group developed its elites. These began building ideological programs, mainly around the question of the national status of the Kashubes (Polish, Polish-Kashubian, or separate Kashubian). During the communist period, the Kashubian people were treated by the state in almost the same way as national minorities or some other socially distinct group. Despite the limitations of that era, the group established the Kashubian-Pomeranian Association, which still exists. Their ethnic culture, especially its folklore, developed in a limited scope under the supervision of the state. After 1989, the group mobilized itself ethnically, focusing first on preservation of its ethnic resources: the language (codification, education, the press, literature, and translation of the Bible) and the preservation and enrichment of its cultural and ethnic identity.

Then, the discussion on the national status of the communities was gaining momentum. Its peak came in the period just before the year 2002 and the National Census. This revealed different concepts toward national self-definition on the part of the group's members. In the census, we can find only fifty-one hundred declarations of Kashubian nationality, yet fifty-three *thousand* people declared they used the Kashubian language at home.

Adopting the act on national and ethnic minorities and regional languages of January 2005 and recognizing the Kashubian language as a regional language, rather than an ethnic one, are the reasons that the Kashubes do not now have the status of a recognized national or ethnic minority. In the act, they are referred to as a community using a regional language. They do enjoy some of the legal regulations for minorities, which pertain for the most part to teaching their regional language at state schools and using it in state institutions.[15] The new status was contested by some activists already during the process of adopting the act (they suggested placing the group on a list of recognized ethnic and national minorities). The discussion is ongoing to this day.

The Polish Tatars are a group created by migration. They appeared in the Grand Duchy of Lithuania and other parts of the Kingdom of Poland in the fourteenth century. They were descendants of the settlers from the Golden Horde and the Tatar Khanates. The Tatars who settled in Lithuania received privileges of personal liberty and freedom of religion (Islam). They were given land on the condition that they would serve in the army. The head count of this group in the fourteenth century did not exceed seven thousand; in the nineteenth century, it had reached almost thirteen thousand members. There were six thousand Tatars in Poland in the interwar period, most in the eastern part of the country. After World War II, the Polish borders were changed, and the region where most Tatars lived was incorporated into the Soviet Union. Some of the Tatars preferred to remain where they were born, while others joined the migration of Poles from the Soviet Union into the Polish Regained Territories. These migrants first moved to the western regions, but later to the eastern part of the country. One can say that, over the history, this community has shared the fate that is typical for immigrants on two occasions. The first time it happened was when they arrived in the Grand Duchy of Lithuania and the other time after the end of World War II. However, in the first case, the group concentrated mostly on the territory of the Grand Duchy of Lithuania (later the Polish-Lithuanian Commonwealth), whereas, in the other case, the group was dispersed and this situation continues still today. Although divided by state borders, nowadays the Polish-Lithuanian Tatars (as under this historical name they function in the scientific literature) inhabit the territory of Lithuania (3,000), Belorussia (5,000–10,000) and Poland (4,000).[16]

At present, there are about four thousand Tatars living in Poland. Today, the Tatars can be found in such cities as Białystok and its surroundings (2,500), Warsaw (100), and Gdańsk (200).

The Tatars who came to Poland six hundred years ago were the followers of the Sunni Rite of Islam. As a result of marriages with Catholic and Orthodox partners, some of them became Christians and assimilated. Now there are nine Muslim communities in Poland, dominated by Muslim Tatars. They have three mosques and several cemeteries. The publication of religious books and systematic religious teaching for children are at present a common practice. The Tatars lost their language in the sixteenth century and have used neighboring languages ever since. They are associated in two organizations: a religious one – the Muslim Religious Association, which has operated for over eighty years – and the Association of Polish Tatars in the Republic of Poland, established in 1992. Polish Muslim Tatars have always been recognized as a distinctive group in Poland because of their religion and origin, and the group leans toward endogamy. During the census of 2002, 495 of them declared their Tatar national identity. Under the act of 2005, the Polish Tatars obtained the status of a recognized ethnic minority.

ETHNIC STATUS OF KASHUBIANS AND POLISH TATARS

First of all, from the etic point of view, both groups maintain features of cultural minorities as they hold a marginal position in the society and they are aware of their separateness from the majority. Moreover, they undertake public actions toward realization of their own group interests, and demand from the majority certain rights in relation to their ethno-cultural separateness.

As I have mentioned, the Tatars are a recognized ethnic minority, which seems to be accepted by most of the group's members, as one interlocutor said: "There . . . now I can be this minority. . . ."[17] This does not bridge, however, the dilemmas that are the derivatives of gaining the official status of a minority. One of my interlocutors noted that this pro-vision unnecessarily divides people, excluding some by granting them rights. To quote his words,

> The act secludes certain communities from the Polish society – there is a legal regulation that gives somebody something, and when all citizens have a specific legislative position and all of a sudden a group is separated from this act, and rights are given. . . . This is such dividing people.

The drawbacks of the act of 2005 come from, first of all, unnecessarily underscoring ethnicity (Otherness) at the expense of Polishness – such was the sense of this statement. However, the opinions occurred in my interviews with the Tatars that the act is necessary because they as a group may grow: "we can feel the same in the place we are now; nobody will uproot us from here."

Yet, the answer to the question whether the Tatars are a minority causes certain difficulty in my interlocutors. First, it makes them reflect on the Polishness of their group. If it means that they are on a par with such communities as Germans or Byelorussians, then they negate the sense of their being a minority because, in their opinion, in contrast with other groups of this type, they have always been loyal to Poland. A state-ment could be heard that they are more an ethnic group than a minority because they are also Poles (from one generation to the next): "We are *our own*, that is, the Poles."

Second, the sort of minority they may be is problematic: ethnic, national, or religious? One can notice a peculiar duality in this case. On the one hand, the group's separateness and its striving for preserva-tion or strengthening and its being a small population make the group a minority in a nominal (sociological) sense. On the other hand, it was difficult for my subjects to accept their status as a minority if it means their exclusion from the national community. An attempt to reconcile the sameness and separateness is referring to the civil understating of hegemonic Polishness; that understanding allows them to be different ethnically and yet similar nationally without a conflict.

In the process of adopting the act, the Kashubian leaders filed a petition to enter their group on the list of the recognized ethnic minorities, but the petition was rejected by the legislature, as described above. Granting the group the status of a separate language community was supposed to be a compromise.

The Kashubes, however, have an ambivalent attitude toward their minority status, which they have not gained on the legal level despite the fact that they intensely discussed the possibility. In my opinion, this is a result of, first of all, different visions of the "Kashubian Us" constructed in terms of ethnic variables. On the basis of the statements of this community published in the ethnic press and expressed during my research, a few kinds of arguments can be distinguished.

On the one hand, they can clearly see the cultural differences in relation to the Polish majority (for example, their language is considered to be a fundament of their being Kashubian, and the group has taken many actions to maintain it, which markedly emphasizes the ethnic borders), and they want to protect their separateness. In this context, such strategic considerations speak in favor of the status of a recognized ethnic minority as gaining access to statutory financial means purposed for this type of a community.

The pursuit of preserving cultural identity is accompanied by another need: that is, to ensure the Kashubes, in their opinion, a peaceful, uncontested, and beneficial functioning within Polish society. And this induces searching for a specific compromise with the majority. This has shown itself, for instance, through the invalidation by some activists in a public forum of national aspirations on the part of some Kashubes and emphasizing those postulates that fit into the vision of the Kashubian community as a group that is distinct yet deeply rooted within Polishness. Another idea that is strongly written into the Kashubian ethnic discourse is one dating back to the nineteenth century and that states, "There is no Cassubia without Polonia and Polonia without Cassubia." For instance, the Kashubes often mention an argument that their endeavors to maintain their Kashubian separateness are an expression of a right of each community to self-determination, but not separatism nor any move against Polishness, of which they are often accused. As one of the Kashubian publicists said, "Is the will to speak our fathers' language an antinational [that is, anti-Polish] symptom?"[18]

Some leaders choose the path of building a strong regional identity. According to some members of the group, as broader in meaning than ethnic in the direct sense, this path excludes their community from the debate about its possible location as a minority. As they say, they are at home in their "small mother country" (in Kashubia), but it is part of a "larger mother country" (Poland). Furthermore, as they say, they are a numerical majority in many places within the Kashubia region.

There is yet another reason for which the minority status is not approved. It is the historical memory that speaks about marginalization of the group that is strengthened by the so-called Kashubian complex. By this, they mean a feeling of inferiority, being a derivative of the treatment that the Kashubians and their culture received at the hands of the majority (Polish and German). They complain of being regarded by both majority populations in turn as a people who are poor, rural, and primitive. Therefore, the status of a minority has deepened and indirectly confirmed the inferior position of the group and has discouraged some of its members from claiming Kashubianness.

The answer to the question of why Kashubes do not want to be a minority can be found in the self-description of the members of the community. During interviews, they communicate their dual Polish-Kashubian identification, considering them complementary. In this context, the minority position is a denial of the identification set up. Thus, the concept of being an ethnic group seems to the members of the Kashubian group (as to the Tatars) a desirable categorization. It stresses a distinct ethnocultural character of Kashubians, and it allows them to claim ethnic recognition. In both Kashubians' and the Tatars' opinions, this category is neutral, in the sense that it does not specify directly or impose the status of a minority. However, such a self-description does not fit into the frames of the official discourse.

Second, the members of both communities are bearers of multiple identities in the ethnocultural context. Not only do the interested parties talk about this situation, but also the results of research on the ethnic identity of the Polish Tatars and Kashubes clearly show it. In the case

of the Kashubes, we can talk about a dual Polish-Kashubian identity as
inseparable elements. Whereas being Polish is decided by history, indigeneity, and usually by Catholicism and other formal criteria such as
citizenship, in contrast, being Kashubian is determined by language, origin, historical memory, indigeneity within that region, ethnic traditions,
and material culture.[19] As far as the Polish Tatars are concerned, their
being Polish comes from the fact of their acquisitive prescription (over
six hundred years), cultural community (the language), historical traditions (especially the military ones), historical memory, and citizenship.
Their being Tatars, however, is determined by their origins, historical
memory, and traditions, but most of all by their religion (Islam), which
delineates the ethnicity of the group very strongly.[20]

Third, in the area of their Polishness, the Kashubians and Tatars share
in the majority of the cases their postulating of each as belonging to a
common ethnos. The argument for this postulate is different in the two
cases because the borders that delineate ethnicity of the groups are different (for example, language among the Kashubes versus Islam among
the Tatars).[21]

One can, however, notice similar identity mechanisms connecting
those dimensions of the identity that, based on the Polish discourse, fail
to contain themselves in the image of a "true Pole." For the most part, in
each case, it amounts to a redefinition of the criteria of Polishness, their
hierarchy of importance, its core, its history, in order to justify a vision
of a complex Polish-Kashubian or Polish-Tatar identity.

The existing identifying status quo is a result of both identity choices
(for instance, after World War II, some Kashubes chose the German
option) and also a certain historical logic, which meant that, in respect
to their identity, they are not anchored in their own, other than Polish,
national community. Polishness locates itself, metaphorically speaking,
between an obligation and fate. The fact of having lived in Polish society
for long decades brought about a far-reaching enculturation into Polishness within the aspect of popular culture and also within the national
canon of values, attitudes, visions of the history, everyday life patterns,
and festive codes. This finds its expression in the manner of argumentation for being Polish, which is deeply rooted in the traditional and dominating discourse, although the citizen element is becoming stronger over

the recent years, and it is stressed in many declarations that citizenship
and nationality are two separate issues.[22]

As I mentioned before, for such groups as Kashubes and Tatars, the census and the process of adopting the act of 2005 constituted important
stimuli that mounted unique challenges to their models of multiple identity. The issue of national self-identity became a topic of politics on the
part of the state, which, through the use of such tools as the census, not
only counts the population but also shapes the manner in which individuals perceive themselves and how they act by imposing on them available identification categories. The logic of the census question regarding
nationality did not allow a person who is constructing an ethnocultural
vision of him- or herself to fit in a complex identity between the imposed
frames. Besides, if we assume that the criteria of national identity can be
either more political or more cultural, then the person, when answer-
ing the census question about nationality, could deem that he or she
was expected to define him- or herself at the level of a large imagined
community, such as the Polish nation (understood as an exclusive eth-
nogenealogical community of one language, one religion, one history,
and the like).[23] In this vision, such minorities as Polish Tatars-Muslims
and Kashubes place themselves outside the Polish group. To take such a
stance, a respondent could have been under the impression that he or she
had already been asked about his or her citizenship in the questionnaire,
which, as a consequence, could suggest that nationality and citizenship
are two different identifications.

Therefore, we can say that this forced the group leaders to undertake
identity politics to initiate and then to organize identity discourse within
the groups so that they could realize the groups' interests and also that
their identity interests were in agreement with their constituents' everyday experienced vision of themselves.

As a result, in the case of both groups, we dealt with the critique of
a census procedure and the way the question was formed, which did not
allow one freely to declare one's national identity, especially a complex
identity.

The leaders encouraged people to choose an option that was in agreement with the consciousness of each individual, on the one hand. But, on the other, they also called for taking the stance that bore responsibility toward the group. So, discussions took place whether to choose the Polish nationality or the Kashubian one or the Tatar one, respectively. The arguments for each of the options had a historical-, scientific-, world-outlook character. Yet, they also had an instrumental character, in accordance with the rule "Will it pay off?" for "us," the Kashubes or the Tatars. We can articulate this dilemma differently: the choice of Polishness threatened to hasten the fading of minority ethnicity, while the choice of asserting a Kashubian or Tatar ethnicity threatened people with being labeled alien non-Poles, which would also contradict a part of their self-awareness and the group's public identity declarations. In the case of members of some ethnic minorities like Kashubians and Tatars, the choice was between Polishness, which safely places an individual on the side of the majority, and a minority ethnicity, which communicates autonomy but also foreignness.

We must keep in mind, however, other contextual variables, such as the nature of Polish nationalism at various times, the experiences of the minorities under communism (distrust toward the state and its agendas, the fear of making one's separateness public), and the history and character of each minority's relationship with the Polish majority.

When analyzing the results of the census, we could assume that Polishness for the majority of members of the groups discussed in this paper is such an enduring, permanent, and deeply internalized element of identity that its declaring either has never been subject to reflection or that it has been a conscious choice because of the hierarchy of the shared images of the self. The same can be said about revealing one's other-than-Polish nationality. But declarations pertaining to the Kashubian or Tatar nationality have also appeared.

In the case of the Polish Tatars, the census could be treated as an opportunity to answer the question whether the Tatars are or are not a separate group, which holds to the traditions and which is not an exotic relic. Strategic reasons, such as a potential access to financial resources for organizational and educational activities (which are reserved only for minorities) were also crucial.

Those among the Kashubes who chose to mark themselves as Kashu-bians, just as the Tatars strove on the one hand to stress their separate-ness, also aimed at finding a new formula for their ethnic status. Prior to the census, an idea emerged among a small group of activists that the Kashubes constitute a separate nation. This idea was actively imple-mented by their propaganda and widely accompanied by argumentation pertaining to the history of the group as well as scientific theories of ethnicity and nationhood.

After the results of the census were published, another important point in the minority-versus-majority relations was creating and adopting the act of 2005. As far as the Tatars go, it was known from the very begin-ning that they would be included in the list of the minorities referred to as "old," thus deeply rooted in the history of the state. They also fulfilled the criteria that the legislature accepted as defining them as an ethnic minor-ity. In reference to this fact, the group's leaders pointed to the marginal status of their group, to their small impact on decisions pertaining to the shape of the legislation, and also to the potential disadvantages result-ing from their being a minority. The division into national and ethnic minorities and, consequently, different rights, bigger ones for the former, also caused some doubts. It seems, however, that the existing status quo has been accepted.

The situation is much different as far as the Kashubes are con-cerned. As I have already mentioned, they have undertaken some ac-tions to enter their group on the list of recognized ethnic minorities. We can say that the census revealed a variety of identity options (national Kashubian, national Polish, a model of dual identity), which function within the group. The census also propelled a discussion within the group, while the legislation reopened the question about the possible ethnic status of the community, both in relation to the dominating self-description characteristic for the interested group itself and to the categorizing frames used in relation to them by the state and group interests.

The results of the actions in the form of recognizing the Kashubes as a community using a regional language do not satisfy part of the Kashu-bian elite, although they have entered a phase of intensive actions within the politics of identity directed both outward and toward the Kashubian group. It is a community that, as one of a few like it in Poland, has been dealing with its ethnicity on the symbolic level very intensively. The aims of Kashubian politics are more and more clearly defined by Kashubian leaders, although, due to the variety of their views, it is hard to determine which choice within the accessible options the group will decide to make. For sure, in their case, the borders within which the state is willing to recognize the group's postulated model of separateness are clear. Kashubian Polish identity discourse is negotiating the existence to which Kashubian leaders aspire, within the limits that majority Poles are willing and ready to grant.[24]

In his book *Citizenship and National Identity*, David Miller points to an interesting aspect of minority-majority ethnic relations, which partly explains the actions of the members of the Tatar and Kashubian groups. In his opinion, ethnic minority groups that have complex and multiple identities, in their pursuit to obtain recognition and respect, are not always interested in a model of a collective ethnic identity that clearly stresses their separateness in relation to other fellow citizens. Recognition of separateness may not be entirely consistent with the group interest and the group's vision of its relations with the majority, but instead may destroy the existing identity configurations as realized by the members of the community. Political recognition potentially joins and integrates the community into the state and, by granting it the status of a minority, legitimizes and strengthens its existence as a separate whole. This dynamic is especially significant in a situation where the group's ethnic borders are not certain or clear.[25]

Yet, there is another side to this coin: If a community becomes enclosed within a given definition of its status, within specific borders, then it closes its members off to some degree from the freedom to shape their own feeling of their selves. In other words, it too imposes certain frames. At present, ethnicity is in many cases – and such is the case of Polish Tatars and Kashubians – one of the identity options. At times, individuals and ethnic elites employ minority identity openly for strategic ends. At others, depending on individual needs, biographical factors, the discourse inside or outside the group, they may hide their minority identity. Ethnic groups and their membership are not destiny, but sometimes they constitute one of the strategic alternatives.

In light of the approaching National Census of 2011, in which, quite certainly, the question about the nationality of the citizens of the Polish state will return, we can expect intensified discussions among the groups on the topic of the status of the Kashubes. As one of the activists stated, "The reflection on the Kashubes' identity is not a discussion which effectively deflects the attention from principal Kashubian interests.... It is an issue which in a direct way pertains to each Kashube.... We can't plan our actions if we don't know who we are – and so far there is no agreement between us on that. By not knowing who we are, we will let the road lead us, and the road can lead as astray."[26]

To sum up, I would like to stress that the meeting of the official identity discourse delineated by the creators of the census and legislation procedures with the subtle nature of ethnicity has brought about identity dilemmas in the case of Polish Tatars and Kashubes and has raised questions such as "Who are we?" "Who should we be?" and "Who do we want to be?" The situation has also induced reflection on identity assets, which, in turn, released actions aimed at implementing options in agreement with the needs and interests of each community.

We should also stress that the census and legislative rhetoric are based on an approach that categorizes and tends to reduce the issue of identity, even when accepting subjective criteria when understanding ethnicity. It always simplifies the reality and does not reflect its entire complexity, despite the fact that it might as well reflect and adhere to an individual's self-description. It can fail to reflect the complexity of social identities taking place in many specific interactions and within different networks of interdependence, as it disregards the complex reality of identity choices by assuming that different categories of people share the same identities in their shape and content.[27]

NOTES

1. See Sławomir Łodziński, *Równość i różnica: Mniejszości narodowe w porządku demokratycznym w Polsce po 1989 roku* (Warszawa: Wydawnictwo Naukowe SCHOLAR, 2005).

2. http://www.stat.gov.pl/gus/8185_PLK_HTML.htm, accessed August 2, 2012.

3. Łodziński, *Równoś Równość i różnica.*

4. The first number is the census data published in 2003, and the other one is the estimated data for secretary general of the Council of Europe in 2002. Łodziński, *Równość i różnica.*

5. Ibid.

6. In the case of some minorities, the visions meet, for instance, in relation to the German or Roms minority, when a simple census question (what is your nationality?) well writes into the members' national identifications; then, the answer is, respectively, German or Roms. They are not compatible in the case of those groups whose members share a multiple identity and where, in the self-description except for the ethnic identification, there is also a strong Polish component (e.g., Kashubes, Polish Tatars). The issue of complex self-descriptions, which appear in the 2002 census, was in a way solved in the 2011 census where two questions were introduced, as discussed later.

7. It should be kept in mind that statistical studies, inclusive of the census, in particular, in the issues that have a great social significance are not neutral but rather reveal certain political visions or preferences concerning the characteristics of citizens and the manner they are studied. In the case in question, a vision of a nation as postulated by the authorities appeared. It clearly showed that, in Poland, one can be either a Pole or **"Other."** For some members of Polish society, such a model of identity turned out not only "too narrow" to be able to express their identity but also threatening, as, potentially, it located them among Others/strangers. And in an almost uniform national state, such a status is potentially discriminating.

8. The Central Statistical Office decided to examine the national identity adopting the following understanding of this notion: "Nationality is a declarative (based on a subjective feeling) feature of every person, expressing his/her emotional, cultural or genealogical (due to the origin of the parents) ties with a certain nation." See http://www.stat.gov.pl/gus/8185_PLK_HTML.htm, accessed August 2, 2012.

9. The act states that the Polish state regulates in a special legal act matters related to the preservation and development of national and ethnic minorities and the development of a regional language, regarding as a national minority the citizens of Poland who are smaller in number than the remaining part of the population of the Republic of Poland and who, in a marked way, differ from other citizens in their language, culture, or tradition; who strive to preserve their language, culture and tradition; who have an awareness of their historical community and are directed toward its expression and protection; who have lived on the territory of the Republic of Poland for at least one hundred years; and who identify themselves with the nation organized in its own state. On the other hand, an ethnic minority is the one that fulfills the above criteria, except for the last one, being a lack of identification with a nation. See http://www.stat.gov.pl/gus/8185_PLK_HTML.htm, accessed August 2, 2012.

10. See Joanna Kurczewska, "Nationalism in New Poland: Between Culture and Politics," in *Transitional Societies in Comparison: East Central Europe vs. Taiwan – Conference Prague 1999* (Frankfurt am Main: Peter Lang, 1999), 193–208.

11. See Grzegorz Babiński, "Mniejszości narodowe i etniczne w Polsce w świetle spisu ludności z roku 2002," *Studia Socjologiczne* 1 (January 2004): 139–52.

12. See Cezary Obracht-Prondzyński, *Kaszubi: Między dyskryminacją a regionalną podmiotowością* (Gdańsk: Instytut Kaszubski w Gdańsku, 2002).

13. One can say that the Kashubes persisted on their indigenous territory while the state borders kept moving. The terms *Germanization* and *Polonization* pertain to the assimilation pressure exerted by individual state organisms, in this case on the Kashubes in the course of history.

The term *Germanization,* similar to *Russification,* has a negative connotation in the Polish national discourse as it is associated with the period of partitions when the Polish state was divided between three dominating monarchies – Russian, German, and Austro-Hungarian, each of them conducting intensive actions to impose their own culture. In the case of *Polonization,* the sense of the term is equally pejorative; however, here the context changes into the minority, and, from the perspective of these groups, it shows analogical actions toward them on the part of the Polish state.

14. At that time, in the majority, the Kashubes were forming a country community, with a small elite able to formulate national postulates. They were rather inclined to live in relative isolation from the center in their "small mother country," as they used to call the Kassubia. It was a typical, marginalized, borderland community.

15. The issue of locating the group formally in the circles of individual categories translates into the scope of entitlements they have been granted. Being a language community, the Kashubes receive funds only for those initiatives that are connected with activities aimed at preserving their language; for other ethnic initiatives, there are none.

16. I give only estimates based on my own research.

17. The quotes come from the interviews collected during field research among Polish Tatars I have been conducting continuously since 1991, including ones collected between 2002 and 2004, as well as research among the Kashubes which I have been conducting since 2004 until today.

18. See Anna Szpony, "Separatyzm czy regionalizm," *Pomerania* 12 (2006).

19. See Brunon Synak, "The Kashubes' Ethnic Identity: Continuity and Change," in *The Ethnic Identities of European Minori-*

ties: *Theory and Case Studies,* ed. Brunon Synak (Gdańsk: Wydawnictwo Uniwersytetu Gdańskiego, 1995), 155–66.

20. See Katarzyna Warmińska, *Tatarzy polscy: Tożsamość religijna i etniczna* (Kraków: Universitas, 1999).

21. We do not have room here to show how, at the level of identity and ideology, narrations of given visions of separateness and commonality are communicated and justified (for instance, being a Polish Muslim or being a Pole who wishes to speak Kashubian).

22. It is interesting that, in both communities, the scientific discourse that postulates an existence of multiple identities goes hand in hand with the declarations of the members of the communities and, to a certain degree, is used reversibly for self-description. So one can say that it has become an element of a reference knowledge.

23. Babiński, "Mniejszości narodowe i etniczne."

24. For instance, one of the arguments used by politicians toward Kashubian proposals is that, in Poland, we do not need new nations because it does not serve integration of the state.

25. David Miller, *Citizenship and National Identity* (Cambridge: Polity Press, 2000).

26. Tomasz Piechowski, *Dylematy kaszubskich koniunkturalistów,* http://naszekaszuby.pl/modules/artykuly/article.php?articleid=96, accessed September 24, 2012.

27. When writing this text, it was known that the next census would include ethnic questions. Indeed, in the census of 2011, two questions appeared in the questionnaire whose wording "reached out" to the expectations of some minorities and which was a result of numerous consultations between their representatives and the government and GUS [Central Statistical Office]. The first question was "What is your nationality?"; the second was "If

regardless of nationality declared you also identify with another national or ethnic community than that indicated in the previous question, please define it." Each question was accompanied by a list of options to choose from. The results had not been published at the time this book went to press. When available, they will show whether the change of the self-description formula has changed the Polish ethnic landscape. It must be stressed that the minority organizations, in contrast to the year 2002, were intensively engaged in activities within the identity politics and they were consciously encouraging their members to declare to be on a given side, suggested by their leaders, of their group's vision of ethnicity.

SIX

"When You Look Chinese, You Have to Speak Chinese": Highly Skilled Chinese Migrants in Switzerland and the Promotion of a Shared Language

MARYLÈNE LIEBER AND FLORENCE LÉVY

WHILE COMMONSENSE UNDERSTANDINGS USUALLY CONSIDER ethnic and racial identities as natural, researchers have long shown that identity is the unstable, nondefinitive result of social processes involving a very broad range of dimensions. Instead of focusing on the meaning or the acceptance of a type of *cultural* or *ethnic identity,* which necessarily varies among people, place, and social contexts, current research analyzes the processes of identity formation.[1] As ethnic identity is by nature fluid and multilayered, people's identity choices depend on the situation, the community, and the individuals involved. According to Pei-te Lien, "Thus, ethnic self-identity labels preferred by individuals of Chinese and other Asian descents may be varied and the negotiated outcome of several competing forces, such as between assimilation and ethnic attachment, or between identification with a specific place or ethnic origin and a pan-ethnic, racialized entity."[2]

In this paper, we will analyze these processes of cultural representation of identity as they play out among Chinese migrants settled in Switzerland. Chinese culture and Chinese language appear to be two crucial notions that, for our interviewees, play a determining role in the definition of Chineseness. Thus, despite the fact that practices of people who consider themselves as Chinese are far from homogeneous, almost all the persons we interviewed subscribe to the idea that, as "Chinese," they share the same culture and the same language. They participate in presenting a very unified and ahistorical vision of what it means to be "Chinese." We will focus on the issue of language to probe the processes of reinterpretation our interviewees engage in in the migratory context.

More specifically, we will show that, while the various associations that teach "Chinese" for children of "Chinese descent" in Switzerland may look like the product of a natural demand by "Chinese" people living abroad, various stakes are at issue behind the apparently simple question of Chinese language transmission.

By way of introduction, we will present a quick overview of Chinese migration in Switzerland, as it is very different from the situation observed in neighboring countries. Then, on the basis of observations carried out in Chinese schools, in teacher training sessions, and in children's summer camps in Switzerland, and of more than sixty interviews with Chinese individuals, teachers, and officials in Switzerland and in Taiwan,[3] we will present a picture of the different schools designed to teach Chinese to children of Chinese descent. We will analyze the different arguments used by parents and teachers to explain their pressing need to transmit the Chinese language to their children born in Switzerland. By concentrating on language practices, we try to look beyond those arguments that present a natural link between Chinese language and Chineseness. We highlight the slippage and blurring of notions in their discourse and finally show that other issues, of a completely different nature, are at stake in these discursive constructions.

CHINESE MIGRATION TO SWITZERLAND

Highly Skilled Migration

China and Switzerland have never maintained significant ties. Historically, there have been no remarkable exchanges at a governmental level, while links at a business or informal level were not, until recently, substantial. This has consequences for the ways in which populations have circulated between the two countries that are both quantitative and qualitative in nature. In addition, Switzerland has also elaborated quite restrictive residency policies that partially explain why Chinese people have represented a very small presence in Switzerland for a long time.

Despite enormous increases in Chinese migration worldwide, this situation has barely changed in recent years. In 2010, according to the data of the Swiss Migration Office, there were only 8,606 Chinese officially settled in Switzerland, holding either a short- or long-term resident permit. Thus, Chinese represented only 0.5 percent of Switzerland's foreign population. Nevertheless, when compared to the situation as little as ten years ago, there has been a dramatic percentage increase in these figures, as the number of Chinese living in Switzerland has risen by 50 percent over this period. This trend is mainly due to an important influx of students[4] and reflects the general tendency of Chinese migration to Europe where a wave of student migration is also very significant.[5]

If these statistics provide us with an overview of the evolution of Chinese migration to Switzerland, there is still much open to debate. Official figures are based on the single criterion of nationality and only take into account citizens of the People's Republic of China (PRC). Our fieldwork shows that the reality is more complex and that this category adopted by Swiss institutions hides a denser reality that is of central importance to the question of Chinese identity. For instance, Taiwanese people are not counted in these figures, though our estimates show that they represent around six hundred persons, mostly educated women married to Swiss citizens, and that their number remains stable. Neither do these figures capture the reality of persons who have changed their nationality and acquired Swiss or any other European nationality through marriage or a long period of stay. More interestingly, these categories are unable to measure the fact that many people holding other Asian nationalities – Vietnamese, Thai, Cambodian, Malay, or Singaporean – might consider themselves to be Chinese because of a Chinese ancestry that they regard as more meaningful than their actual nationality.[6] Conversely, Tibetans[7] may well not feel concerned with Chineseness but are nonetheless included in these statistics (since 2000).

In addition, the Chinese population in Switzerland appears to have certain specificities when compared with that of neighboring countries in Europe or the United States. Despite Switzerland's small size and the relative porosity of its borders, the patterns of migration and settlement are startlingly different from those found in France, Italy, or Germany, for example. First of all, the organization of the Chinese population in Switzerland is different from that observed in other countries; the types of ethnic organization that are famous in other countries, such as ethnic economic niches or social enclaves like Chinatowns,[8] have not sprung up in Switzerland. This is probably due to the small number of persons involved; with a population of only seven thousand, this migration is far from reaching the critical mass allowing for the creation of an ethnic community that could rely on its own social and economic resources.

Second, the composition and socioeconomic profile of the Swiss Chinese population is also quite different from that found in neighboring countries. Over our three years of fieldwork (2006–2009) with a great variety of individuals, we have met very few undocumented migrants, contrary to our own and other researchers' experiences in countries such as France, Italy, and the United Kingdom.[9] Furthermore, while other European countries with a Chinese migration demonstrate structured patterns of networking based on regional or family ties,[10] with many unskilled migrants concentrated in the so-called ethnic economy (especially the catering and garment industries), in Switzerland most migrants are well educated and, thus, have more resources with which to integrate into the host country. A majority of them have entered Switzerland as students or highly skilled professionals. As white-collar workers, they have often been graduated from Swiss, European, or Chinese universities and now hold highly skilled jobs with Swiss or international firms. In Geneva more particularly, many of them work as international civil servants for international organizations, such as the United Nations. Their income places them squarely at the middle- or upper-middle-class level, and many of them have even bought their own houses in Switzerland. In this respect, the socioeconomical level of the Chinese living in Switzerland differs dramatically from the main Chinese groups found elsewhere in Europe.

As opposed to those populations who need to rely on ethnic solidarity to survive and to achieve a more comfortable situation in the host country, Chinese migrants in Switzerland do not need to rely on other migrants from China. Nor are they much involved in Chinese networks, neither at an occupational nor at a social level. The language barrier that can play such an important role in the lack of integration of Chinese migrants in nearby countries[11] seems to be absent in Switzerland. Indeed, our study shows that almost all our interviewees are fluent speakers of one of the local languages: French, German, or even Swiss German.

Many of them report also using English as a language of communication, in either social or professional settings, or both.

Thus, social confinement due to communication barriers is rarely a problem in our case, and we have observed that the social networks of Chinese in Switzerland are not particularly concentrated on other Chinese. Many interviewees told us that they seldom meet other Chinese; to the contrary, they emphasize the fact that they do not regard nationality as a relevant criterion for making social ties. Most of the time, their friends are made at the university, in the workplace, or in their neighborhoods and include people of Swiss or European nationality. Many of the persons we have interviewed live in very international and cosmopolitan social circles. We can observe no geographic concentration and, though they express a marked preference for urban dwelling, Chinese people are scattered all over the country. Thus, no kind of spatial, economic, or social confinement can be observed in Switzerland; on the contrary, Chinese persons seem to be integrated fully both from a point of view of the labor market and from the standpoint of social interactions.[12]

A Fragmented Community

Beyond this initial picture, it is interesting to observe that, while our interviewees' social networks are not predominantly composed of Chinese people, they cannot be considered completely multicultural. Closer attention must be paid to the type of relation at stake. Thus, for example, very often the circle of close friends and strong social ties, those who can be called on in an emergency, is for most of our respondents composed of other Chinese. In other words, most of our interviewees' "best friends" are also Chinese. They explain this situation by the fact that they share with these friends a common set of interests, habits, and the facilities of communication: "it's more convenient to talk in our own language." Indeed, while there are generally no extensive networks linked by interdependency and shared norms as in other countries, we do observe within this population a division into many informal and small social groups all over Switzerland. These networks coexist and often are not aware of each other's existence. Furthermore, beyond the communality of sharing the same origin or language, it seems that our interviewees make important distinctions between different sorts of Chinese. Analysis of our interview material has enabled us to disentangle the different factors used in the process of this "intraethnic" boundary making that explains the formation of small social groups.

First, place of origin is an important criterion for group formation, especially in regard to the distinction between people coming from Taiwan and from mainland China. Generally speaking, Taiwanese get in touch with Taiwanese, while people from mainland China remain mostly in mainland Chinese social circles. Even if our interviewees report making acquaintances across this boundary, these are exceptions in their social networks. However, there is a unanimous refusal to explain this situation by reference to political conflict between Taiwan and communist China. Rather, our interviewees say that they do not share historical, political, and economic backgrounds. "We don't have common topics of conversation," explains Mrs. Yi[13] from mainland China. The process of boundary making is also obvious as between overseas Chinese from Southeast Asia and persons from mainland China or Taiwan who have very few connections despite their long periods of stay in Switzerland. Surprisingly, we did not notice within these three distinctive communities – mainlander, Taiwanese, or overseas Chinese – other internal distinctions based on provincial origins, often observed in the settlement pattern of the Chinese diaspora in the form of regional associations such as *tongxianghui*. Again, while in France, we used for instance to observe a tendency for people from Zhejiang province to regroup on the basis of shared geographic origin; in Switzerland, this distinction does not seem to be relevant, and it is common to observe sustained relations between persons coming from different provinces.[14]

Time of arrival in Switzerland is a second point of reference that emerges out of our interviews. Thus, persons who arrived twenty or thirty years ago tend to have few connections with newly arrived Chinese. Mr. Wang, who lives in Lausanne, explains that they do not share any "common values." The later comers are considered as "selfish" and "arrogant." Without being able to talk about "waves of migration," as so few people are involved, the earliest settled interviewees distinguish four different periods of influx of Chinese into Switzerland. Many persons who arrived before 1949 and during the 1960s belong to wealthy families and stayed in Switzerland to protect their fortunes after the Communist Party victory in the mainland. During the 1960–70s, as PRC borders were closed, a second but very small wave of people, mainly Chinese from Hong Kong or Taiwan, arrived in Switzerland. They were followed at the end of the 1970s by ethnic Chinese refugees from Laos, Vietnam, Cambodia, and Indonesia fleeing their countries because of the anti-Chinese resentment in their homelands (a reported five thousand were accepted in Switzerland); many of them have specialized in the catering industry. Finally, since the mid-1990s, there has been a continuous rise in the number of university students, both from Taiwan and from mainland China.

This rough typology demonstrates that periods of arrival are interwoven with distinctions based on a third factor: educational and class level. The line between people coming from mainland China and *huaqiao,* overseas Chinese from Southeast Asia, is often explained by differences in educational background. The latter have invested in the catering industry in Switzerland and are often described as being very poorly educated – in comparison to Chinese from Taiwan or mainland China in Switzerland. This is clearly indicated by their level of Mandarin, a language they often speak with a heavy accent. For example, even if Mr. Di feels the need to specify that they "are also Chinese," he told us that he does not usually make friends with *huaqiao:* "It is related to educational and cultural level, and maybe we do not have common interests." This kind of argument seems to have been internalized by some overseas Chinese themselves. Restaurant owners in Geneva, Mr. and Mrs. Shao, who came from Malaysia, only socialize within the circle of restaurant owners and report having many friends from Vietnam; yet they seldom become acquainted with people from mainland China: "Their educational level is higher than ours. It's not annoying, but you have to step back [*tuibu*]. We don't feel comfortable."

Our observations indicate even finer distinctions among the recently arrived students on the basis of different educational levels. PhD or postdoctoral students are supposed to be very hardworking and form a kind of elite among Chinese students abroad. They do not have difficulty finding scholarships and are often courted by the best European universities. Mr. Ding, who is an outstanding PhD student, recognizes that, since he has arrived in Zurich, he has seldom met Chinese bachelor-degree students, even if he often hangs around with Chinese PhD students. The Chinese educational system is based on a very selective process; he believes that people who came to Switzerland for university or professional schools are not good students in China and probably failed the university entrance exam there. This impression seems to be confirmed by some research that demonstrates that these students belong to wealthy families who can afford the huge cost of sending their child abroad to study.[15] Mr. Ding explains: "For them, going abroad represents a second chance to study." This explains, in his view, why the two groups seldom interact.

Educational and economic levels can also intersect with legal status, our fourth factor. For instance, we have observed that housewives who came to Switzerland through marriage with a local citizen seldom meet Chinese professionals who work in local or international companies or organizations. In the same vein, people who have a stable residence permit tend to interact with persons who enjoy the same conditions and almost never come into contact with undocumented migrants from mainland China. Most of our interviewees in Zurich have never met illegal migrants and believe that there are none in Switzerland. In Geneva, we have observed that undocumented migrants form a very tight social network mainly composed of people in the same juridical situation. Most of them are from the province of Fujian and communicate in that local dialect.[16] This selective use of dialect might play a role in the closure of their social circle. Information about available jobs and accommodation and support circulates within their network all around the country. This network intersects with the one composed of undergraduates or students of professional schools – that is, students who have the most precarious residency permits. Work sites play the role of meeting places, as many of them work illegally in the same restaurants: students work as waiters in the dining room, while undocumented migrants work in the kitchens.

This first picture shows that Chinese migrants in Switzerland are socially dispersed. People from various backgrounds, nationalities, mother tongues, generations of migration, and so on do not get along on the single base of shared Chinese origins. Informal social groups are often quite small in size and reproduce processes of boundary making based on geographic and political allegiance, professional and educational level, and even legal status. These observations allow us to confirm that there is no ontological ethnic group called *Chinese* in Switzerland.

The Rise of Chinese Schools

Despite the diversity and the centripetal trends observed among Chinese migrants in Switzerland, there is an attempt to unify this population around a common interest: the issue of culture and language transmission.[17] Indeed, virtually all parents who live abroad for a long or short period and who have to register their children in local schools appear to share a common concern about education of their children. The question of language transmission is intimately related in their minds to the question of Chinese identity. "What am I going to do if they become foreigners [*waiguoren,* or non-Chinese]?" The question that Mrs. Tan frankly asks is a concern for many parents as they observe that their children are more fluent in local languages (either German, Swiss German, or French) than in Chinese. Even the director of a Chinese school in Geneva explained that "French is the mother tongue of my two daughters. When they talk with me, I force them to speak Chinese, pretending that I can't understand French, but as soon as they talk together, they use French." Mr. Wu shares the same feeling: "My son doesn't master the Chinese language. He doesn't like to speak Chinese. With his friends, he speaks French. Even at the Chinese school during the breaks between classes, they speak French. It means that he thinks in French." Surveying the Chinese language level of children born in Switzerland, which he regards as quite low, he told us that he is preparing himself for the fact that his son will never speak perfect Chinese. This corroborates our observation that the children we met in the schools we visited use French or Swiss German to communicate rather than Chinese.

Clearly, not speaking Chinese is regarded by Chinese parents as a loss of identity, and they consider learning Chinese to be the best way to transmit Chinese culture. Indeed, in their discourse, language is presented as *constitutive of* Chinese identity. The desire to transmit their mother tongue to their children is a concern that is presented as completely legitimate and natural for migrants, whatever their origins. Parents of diverse backgrounds, who had never met before, have started to meet and mobilize around this concrete problem, a problem that appears both noncontroversial and nonpolitical.

Thus, over the last ten years, we have seen the creation of many Chinese schools all over the country. There are now more than fifteen Chinese language schools[18] dedicated to teaching Chinese to Chinese children. They have all opened relatively recently and are run by Chinese associations which offer extracurricular Chinese classes for low prices on weekends or evenings. While this number may appear small – and is related to the small number of Chinese living in Switzerland – if we take it in proportional terms, it is seven times higher than that in the United States, where there are about seven hundred Chinese schools for an estimated population of 2.7 million Chinese.[19] In each of the large Swiss cities (Geneva, Zurich, Lucerne, and Berne), there are two or more Chinese schools competing for new students.

The creation of Chinese schools in Switzerland is the result of various and distinct initiatives by parents.[20] Mothers are particularly implicated in the creation of Chinese schools. In interviews, they emphasized the fact that, when their children enter local schools and, therefore, are about to spend more time speaking the local language – either French, German, or Swiss German – than the language spoken at home, many parents start to be afraid that their children will lose their proficiency in Chinese. They feel the need to teach the Chinese language to their offspring. This concern is even more crucial for short-term resident families, such as UN civil servants, for the whole family is supposed to return in China within a few years, and the children are expected to reenter the Chinese educational system. In these families, to maintain children's fluency in Chinese is not perceived as a matter of choice. Mothers, who usually are the ones who take care of children, begin by teaching Chinese at home. All our interviewees mentioned the difficulties they encountered teaching Chinese to their children on their own. That is why some women tried to help each other and started to teach their children together, but still many gave up. The creation of Chinese schools in their cities was regarded by our interviewees as a real relief. It meant that they could transfer this question out of the private parent-child relationship.

Over the years, Chinese schools have grown larger, and their public has diversified; almost all the Chinese schools in Switzerland have around a hundred students registered and manage around ten classes. Most of the schools are managed by parents as nonprofit associations,[21] which rent rooms in local public schools. Teachers are all volunteers, often mothers of the children who follow classes. Indeed, these volunteer pedagogical activities seem to provide extra benefits for these women, who are often housewives and say they are happy to have an occupation and a status.[22]

These schools were first dedicated to children of Chinese migrants either from Taiwan or mainland China. Over the years, the clientele became more diverse. Children of binational couples or ethnic Chinese families of other nationalities were admitted. Subsequently, some schools opened to local children (of Swiss or Western descent) and, very recently, even to adults. With this diversification of their audience, teachers face a complex situation, since the language backgrounds and levels of students are very different from each other.[23] Some are native speakers, as are most of the children of Chinese couples who use Chinese at home. Others are nonnative speakers – for instance, most of the children of mixed families, who do not speak Chinese with their parents. Finally, there are the children of families from parts of China or the diaspora who use another dialect or another language (Cantonese, Vietnamese, etc.) for their daily exchanges rather than Mandarin. As for local children and adults, they have had almost no familiarity with the Chinese language before enrolling in Chinese school and seldom use it outside the schools. These different situations,[24] of course, have an impact on the interest in Chinese and on the pace of language acquisition on the part of students.

THE PROMOTION OF A UNIFIED
CULTURE AND LANGUAGE

Language for Social Inclusion

People define themselves in different ways depending on context and can, therefore, be sometimes quite paradoxical. They can present themselves in a single interview as sharing characteristics with other people from the same country or origin and then deny any kind of common characteristics in the following sentence.[25] Aihwa Ong[26] has underlined the existence of a flexible and strategic cultural and political identity among overseas Chinese, who entertain varying relationships with their host populations. Throughout this research project, we have been confronted with a similar paradox: despite the geographic, social, and political divisions that we observed during fieldwork, the people we interviewed also displayed a widely shared, unifying discourse about language and culture. Chinese parents present their motivations as natural: what is more natural than migrants' attempts to transmit their language and culture to their own children?

The question for us thus became the following: Why do people who in different contexts often emphasize the differences between groups of Chinese suddenly express belief in a unified vision of Chineseness?[27] The question of language transmission, for example, appears to be unquestioned, and, on this, our interviewees seem to share the same point of view. No differences on the language issue can be observed between people from different social backgrounds or from different regions, neither between Chinese parents and mixed couples nor between short- and long-term migrants. Behind this unanimity, however, it appears that things are more complex. Consequently, in what follows we will explore the different meaning of the notions of "language" in circulation and what is at stake behind this fictitious unity.

Four simple themes are recurrent in parents' explanations of their motivations for transmitting Chinese language and culture to their children. "It's a question of roots," explain many of them: they want their children to know about their origins because "they have Chinese ancestors," says Mr. Wu in Geneva. The need to transmit the language is also explained by the necessity for their children to be able to communicate directly with their Chinese relatives, especially grandparents and cousins. Another argument is linked to a question of race: "As Chinese, you have to speak the Chinese language" announced Mrs. Zhang in Biel. Identity is often related by parents as biology: "They have Chinese blood in their bodies. . . . Inside, they are Chinese," reports Mr. Wu. "When you look Chinese, you have to speak Chinese," repeats Mrs. Zhang, and several other interviewees agreed. Another explanation seems to be radically different in nature: parents consider professional opportunities and want their children "to take advantage of being Chinese and of speaking

Chinese in the future." This concern is linked to a common belief that, with China's economic growth, being able to speak Chinese will be an advantage in the job market. Mr. Wu, father of an eight-year-old child, sums up these reasons: "Why do you have to learn Chinese? First, because you are Chinese; secondly, because China is becoming a very important country. Third, nobody can avoid being in contact with China. Fourth, as Chinese you have facilities to learn the language. Considering all these conditions, if you don't learn Chinese, of course, I will be upset."

In these parents' discursive constructions, language is presented as constitutive of Chinese identity. Moreover, there is a complete overlapping between different notions: the isomorphism of the categories of language, culture, family belonging, nation, and race appears to be pervasive. Their meaning is not clear, and it changes, often over the course of a single interview. Indeed, our interviewees often use these different notions as synonyms. We will now analyze all these arguments in turn.

FAMILY COHESION. Many parents hope that migration will not have any impact on their children's affiliations. Even if they have grown up abroad, they feel they belong to their families in Asia. In this perspective, language plays a crucial role linking children born and raised abroad and family members back home. Parents would like their children to be able to communicate directly with other family members. Mrs. Lu in Zurich, for example, is very happy that her sons are able to speak Chinese fluently: "Otherwise, they wouldn't be able to communicate with my parents and my brother. They wouldn't be able to communicate with their family [in China]!" Mrs. Tang, originally from Taiwan, explains why every weekend for the past nine years she has driven two hours every Saturday to bring her sons to the Geneva (Taiwanese) Chinese school: "Our objective is that, when we are back in Taiwan, our children shouldn't need us, shouldn't need our translation support. We want our children to be independent [during their stay in Taiwan]." Apparently, this argument seems unproblematic. Still, during our interviews, we found gaps in this line of explanation, as the link between family belonging and language is often more complex that this image suggests.

Except for people from Mandarin-speaking areas,[28] that is, people from the northern and western regions of China, Mandarin is often not the language used at home, and dialects are more probably the "family

language." Mr. Wu acknowledges that, even if he speaks Mandarin fluently, his "parents can barely speak Mandarin. . . . At home, they never
speak Mandarin. Between them, they speak [the] Shanxi dialect; they
also use dialect when addressing us [his generation], but we answer them
in Mandarin. I barely master the dialect." The same situation is also common for families from Taiwan, as most families use Taiwanese (a dialect
part of the Min group) or one of the Hakka dialects[29] to hold private or
daily conversations. In this regard, the argument that children must
learn Mandarin to be able to communicate with family members is no
longer convincing, since both grandparents and grandchildren would
need to use a foreign language – Mandarin Chinese – to communicate
with each other. If family communication is the goal, it would be more
effective to teach the local dialect directly to grandchildren, which is
seldom the case with the people we have met.

The expectation that children should learn Mandarin also leads to
reinterpretations of family linguistic history. Like many other interviewees, Mrs. and Mr. Shao explain, "Because our ancestors are Chinese,
we want our daughter to study Chinese." As overseas Chinese raised in
Malaysia, they had to learn English and Malaysian, which were compulsory languages at school. They now speak these two languages fluently.
But in private interaction, they generally speak Cantonese with their
parents and friends, and they still use it to communicate with each other
in Geneva. Actually, they are the first generation in their families to
learn Mandarin, and they were sent for this purpose to private Chinese
schools; their grandparents did not even speak Cantonese but rather expressed themselves principally in the Hakka dialect. Thus, we can hardly
call Mandarin their "mother tongue." Still, Mr. Shao purposely uses
Mandarin to talk to his daughter, while he addresses his wife in Cantonese. Clearly, through their family's language history, we can observe
a process of language selection rather than of the transmission of the
"original" family language. They have rather chosen to transmit to their
children the language spoken by the dominant group, that is, Cantonese
(for the generation of the parents), then Mandarin (for Mr. Shao's daughter). This example shows that language transmission and the category
"mother tongue" are far from natural and self-evident, contrary to what
many of our interviewees seem to believe. Indeed, over the course of this

research, we discovered that the tension between the dominant language (Mandarin, now the national language of mainland China, Singapore, and Taiwan) and the "mother tongue" might lead to the erasure of the second in favor of the first, despite the fact that this very process is often simply denied. This situation has been often observed among Chinese migrants in Switzerland, in families with overseas Chinese, Taiwanese, and mainland China origins.[30]

BELONGING TO THE CHINESE NATION. The Chinese language embodies another kind of link: symbolic *inclusion within a nation*. Like many other migrants, Chinese parents are reluctant to acknowledge that their children's affiliations might be more connected to their local experience, that is, to Switzerland, than to their parents' country of origin. Even if children have grown up abroad and have few direct experiences of China, parents want to preserve the link of the "second generation"[31] with "their" nation. It is as if it were necessary to downplay the impact that living abroad might have on their children's sense of belonging and identity formation. In this respect, language embodies the link between individuals and the nation. Mrs. Bai, who came to Switzerland as a visiting teacher for one year, expresses her doubt about the Chineseness of children born abroad. She wonders how her friend's Geneva-born son could be Chinese if "he can't speak a word of Chinese and doesn't even like Chinese food." This kind of concern is very common among the persons we met. Mr. Wu explains: "In theory, a Chinese must speak Chinese.... This is Chinese culture. It is the difference between Chinese culture and Western culture. A Chinese that does not speak Chinese, it is inconceivable. You have to speak Chinese to be Chinese. It is a question of culture, of history." There is an unformulated expectation – we might even say injunction – in this quotation that is widely shared by our interviewees, producing a common racialized vision of language.

The link between language and an almost racialized version of origins was observable in the discourse of parents and teachers alike. Mrs. Zhang of Biel attempts to drive this message home to her students as follows: "Do you know who you are? You are Chinese? You are born here, but you will always be Chinese." In Geneva, Mr. Wu explains: "Why should my son learn Chinese? Because you are Chinese. Maybe later you will have a Swiss passport, but your ancestors are all Chinese. In your body, you have Chinese blood. You can't avoid being thankful to [the] Chinese people. Inside, you are Chinese." This overlapping of language, culture, and origins might be considered as a simple sign of nationalism, were it not for the fact that the host society also plays a role in this process of racializing Chineseness. With its traditionally small population of Chinese, the tendency in Switzerland to assign a foreign identity to any persons who belong to a visible minority – and in our case, the labeling as Chinese of any person with an "Asian" face – is particularly strong. The concern about labeling[32] seems to play an important role in parents' preoccupation. Mrs. Zhang from Canton forces her son to study Chinese because "it's impossible to have a Chinese face and to be unable to speak Chinese; it's ridiculous." Mrs. Chu who comes from Taiwan, explains: "The society, people consider you as Chinese. For them, you have a Chinese face; you are still a Chinese even if you have the Swiss citizenship." As an overseas Chinese from Malaysia, Mr. Shao is fully aware of the contradictions[33] that can result from such processes of labeling: "You have yellow skin; of course, people will say that you are Chinese. They won't even think that you are Malaysian. Why? Because of your yellow skin, of your black hair."

It seems that our interviewees make a clear distinction between nationality and national belonging. The former is seen as relatively flexible,[34] as many of them change their nationality and adopt Swiss or European citizenship. In the family of Mr. Di, his wife remains a PRC citizen, while their two children, born in Italy, and Mr. Di himself have become Italian "because it's more convenient when traveling." But most of our interviewees have a clear idea that they belong to the "Chinese nation" that they define by racial criteria, based on the belief in a specific culture and a common language (Mandarin). In this respect, they forget that both mainland China and Taiwan are multiethnic countries, with fifty-five official minorities recognized by the PRC. They also downplay the existence and role of dialects, even if, as we saw before, they have direct and personal experience of the phenomenon. Mandarin is considered to be the common language of all Chinese, despite the fact that the imposition of Mandarin as the only official language of China is a recent social construction and the result of a political decision.[35] Indeed, this standardization is still in process in mainland China and Taiwan, and

the use of Mandarin varies widely according to one's place, level of education, and generation.

In overseas communities in particular, Cantonese has long been
the lingua franca of all Chinese migrants. It is only very recently that
people have started to promote and adopt Mandarin in daily interactions. This change of common language among Chinese communities
abroad is clearly the result of a power struggle: it points to a change in
dominance as the number of recently highly qualified immigrants from
mainland China (who speak fluent Mandarin), tightly connected and
supported by the Chinese embassy, is progressively exceeding that of
traditional overseas Chinese abroad, most of whom speak Cantonese.
It also reflects the growing influence of mainland China's government
within overseas communities.

Other Motivations Present in the Decision to Teach
Chinese Language to Chinese Children

POLITICAL STAKES. As we have noted, many different kinds of motivation are hidden behind the simple choice to teach Chinese to Chinese children, and language is definitely not an apolitical field. While
both mainland China and Taiwan have adopted Mandarin as the official language, still today two competing written systems exist. In the
1950s, the PRC reformed the written language and introduced "simplified characters" (*jiantizi*) and a system of alphabetized transcription[36]
called *hanyu pinyin*. In Taiwan, the official language continues to use the
traditional characters (*fantizi*), which may be accompanied by a specific
transcription system, the *zhuyin fuhao* or *bopomofo*, which does not use
the alphabet. Schools teaching Chinese abroad must choose between
these two systems, and this option will generally indicate their political
allegiance.[37]

Among Chinese people living in Switzerland, this dichotomy is obvious. In the four big cities, there are at least two competing Chinese
schools: the one run by mainlanders uses simplified characters; the other,
run by Taiwanese or overseas Chinese, is based on "traditional characters." We observed that most parents from mainland China enrolled their
children in the school using simplified characters, while people from

Taiwan supported their own schools. The position of overseas Chinese is more complex: for some of them, the choice of school is linked to an ideological choice; others, along with a minority of parents from the ROC or PRC, explain that they are not concerned by these political struggles between communist China and noncommunist Taiwan and have chosen a school for practical reasons – schedules are more convenient, the school is closer, or they prefer one school's educational methods.

Supporters of both systems have elaborate arguments to legitimate their choice as the more rational one. Debates are passionate. Mainlanders explain that "simplified characters" are easier to write and that children can remember them with less effort than "complex characters." Furthermore, they point out that it is more convenient and rapid to use their alphabetized *hanyu pinyin* transcription system with a computer. Supporters of the traditional characters reject these arguments and explain that the very meaning of the language can only be preserved with traditional characters, which they called "true characters" (*zhengtizi*).

Most of these arguments have also been put forth by governments. For instance, Mrs. Tan, whom we met in Geneva, used exactly the same sentence to promote traditional characters as we heard in the official discourse of a representative of the Overseas Compatriot Affairs Commission (OCAC), whom we interviewed in Taiwan in 2008. Both governments actively promote their respective notions among Chinese communities abroad in order to claim their allegiance. This policy is also pursued by active support of Chinese schools through the PRC's and ROC's embassies and their respective departments in charge of overseas Chinese affairs or education. Basically, the policies of the two governments are similar: embassies are closely connected to schools and offer material and pedagogical support by providing teaching manuals, which, of course, correspond to their respective linguistic systems. Taiwan further offers and sends the books for free.[38]

To ensure a steady and uniform teaching level among schools, both embassies organize teacher training classes, either abroad or in China or Taiwan, directed at the predominantly nonprofessional staff who will become teachers in these schools. Teachers can attend three weeks of courses in mainland China for free. The Taiwanese government organizes nearly identical support each year. It also sends two professional teachers to Switzerland for a training session of two days, which was attended by forty voluntary teachers in 2008.

Since 2007, both governments have been trying to federate these many schools into two parallel Chinese school networks. If both embassies deny that this represents an attempt to influence their activities, we also can observe that the mainland association held its annual meeting inside the office of the PRC embassy and that the entire team of its Education Department attended the meeting; as for Taiwan, the representative of the Taipei Cultural and Economic Delegation in Bern (that is, the ambassador) gave the opening and concluding speeches at the meetings organized by his association. Political affiliation is, thus, clear in both these associations.

Both governments also support target families, as both ministries finance summer camp for children abroad. The PRC organizes two weeks of activities in mainland China dedicated to Chinese children living abroad. All expenses are paid, with the exception of travel fees that are the responsibility of the parents. The director of the Geneva school reported that, in 2008, around five hundred Chinese children from all over the world attended a summer camp in Shenzhen. In 2008, the Taiwanese government sent two teams of three voluntary teachers to Switzerland who offered sports, dance, and arts and craft activities to more than one hundred children in two different summer camps, one organized in a Buddhist temple in Geneva and the second in the countryside near Bern. The involvement of both governments in the Swiss school projects reveals the political issues that are hidden behind the language and culture transmission concern, where the struggle between communist and nationalist governments gives form to the apparently natural need of migrants to have their children learn Chinese.

CHINESE, THE LANGUAGE OF AN ECONOMICALLY POWERFUL COUNTRY. Beyond one's home country nostalgia and political affiliation, parents regularly mention another practical reason for their desire that their children learn Chinese. With the Chinese economy playing an increasing role globally, they consider Chinese to be a critical language for the coming century. Many parents bet that being Chinese and speaking Chinese will be a career advantage for their offspring. Chinese is principally considered to be the business language of the future: "Now

China is a big power. Many people do business with China. My daughter will have a professional advantage. If she couldn't speak Chinese, she would have missed some opportunities," explains Mr. Shao from Malaysia. Even if he does not consider himself Chinese, but Malaysian, Mr. Shao, along with many parents, believes that his child will have a natural advantage that she has to capitalize on in the professional field. We found this argument advanced by all the groups we interviewed.

Furthermore, this interest goes beyond the business field: Chinese is also the language of a powerful country. This is a consequence of the changing status of China in the world arena. Mr. Wu explains this position: "China is more and more important in the world. If you are Vietnamese and only speak French, it's not a problem. But Chinese is a big language; hundreds of thousands of people all over the world learn this language. As a Chinese, if others [foreigners] speak better Chinese than you, it's a shame." It seems that there is a new pride in being and speaking Chinese. Indeed, we observed that many overseas Chinese families, who have historically emphasized learning the local language, have recently changed their attitude toward language and registered their children with Chinese schools. Even adults of Chinese origin who explain that, when they were young, they were not interested in Chinese and could not speak a word of Mandarin, have started to learn this language, which they understand as their own natural language.

Finally, as noted above, this interest goes beyond the clientele of Chinese descent, as almost all the Chinese schools in Switzerland have opened specific classes for local non-Chinese students.[39] In this perspective, language is more than the language of one's ancestors; it is regarded very practically as a useful language and as a strategic and powerful identity.

Children's Views, a Generation Gap?

During our interviews, we noticed a tension between parents' and children's viewpoint: In sum, the former are very concerned about their children's ability to speak Chinese, while the latter do not seem as enthusiastic. We did not have the opportunity to conduct interviews with children. However, through parents' explanations, we understood that the second generation does not (yet?) feel concerned about the link between language and a symbolic inclusion within the Chinese nation. Parents' narratives demonstrate that many children have few concrete experiences of being Chinese. Most of them almost never speak Chinese, even at home.[40] Many of them seldom go back to China – perhaps one month every two or three years – as some parents cannot afford to go back to China on an annual basis. For overseas Chinese, the link with China is even more remote. Mrs. Zhang explains that most of them do not have family in mainland China anymore. Mr. Shao himself, whose family emigrated to Southeast Asia four generations ago, has never been to China, and his daughter has no direct or personal experience with this symbolic homeland. Furthermore, most of the children are simply too young to question their identities. They are connected to their local reality, have no direct experience of racism, and feel Swiss.

Finally, it must not be forgotten that learning Chinese and especially written Chinese is a long and difficult process that can take years. There is little connection between the oral and written languages, such that someone who speaks fluent Chinese at home cannot take advantage of this when he studies the characters. If some of them, often the younger ones, enjoy going to school, for others, it seems to be a burden. Parents recognize that their children would often rather stay at home than go to the Saturday school. "Actually, many children are forced by parents to go to the school," acknowledges the director of the Taiwan school of Geneva. "Why should I go to Chinese school? I hate Chinese!" one child told his mother. Mrs. Yang sums up the situation as follows: "When they are young, you can force them to go to the school, but as soon as they become teenagers, you can't do it anymore." As soon as children enter high school, many give up their Chinese, as they say the workload is too heavy. The director of the Biel Chinese School explains the children's point of view: "Many of them are not interested. They have their reasons. For them, Chinese is a foreign language. Their mother tongue is the local language, French or German. That kind of language [Chinese] is too complicated, too different. Some of them say that it's too difficult, that they don't want to study anymore. For instance, even my son wants to give up." Many teachers complain about the lack of interest on the part of students. According to them, some don't do their homework and are passive during lessons. Teachers are unanimous in highlighting the link between parents' involvement and their children's level. A teacher in Geneva confided to us that all children born in Switzerland have huge difficulties mastering Chinese; they lack the vocabulary and do not use correct sentence structures. It appears clearly that children are not sensitive to the symbolic impact of language; learning Chinese is not the choice of their generation but rather an imposition by their parents.

CONCLUSION

Behind the quite obvious desire to transmit one's mother tongue to one's children when living abroad, wider issues are at stake in the rise of Chinese schools in Switzerland. We have underlined differences in the arguments of parents, teachers, students, and administration representatives and demonstrated how the shifts in meaning lie beneath the use of such notions as language, culture, or identity. Language, culture, race, kinship, and national belonging – even the economy – are often blurred together and used as synonyms, reinforcing the belief in the uniqueness and specificity of Chineseness. The question of language transmission thus represents an exemplary point of entry into the ways in which Chinese people living in Switzerland attempt to find unity despite their diversity: the inescapability of Chineseness "in the blood," the link between "looking Chinese" and speaking it, and the presumption of a common culture barely intelligible to others. In this process, Chinese language and culture are simplified and even reified. To sum up, the Mandarin language embodies different types of capital: a racial and national capital, as well as a cultural capital (roots for "Chineseness"), a social capital (a way to communicate with relatives), and a human and economic capital (such as professional advantage in the future).

As anthropologists and other social scientists have demonstrated, race, community, ethnicity, and culture are not substantial identities but are rather representations widely shared. They are ways of seeing, thinking, understanding, and interpreting the social world. They are results of interactive and cognitive processes that classify, organize, and make hierarchical this social world. Therefore, race, community, ethnicity, and even culture are to be considered as "perspectives on the world," unconscious tools to make the social world intelligible, communicable, or transformable.[41] If we acknowledge this perspective, we then have to shift the analysis from groups as basic units to group making and grouping activities such as classification and identification. We have to focus on those processes that make people deeply believe that they share common interests and, in our case, that they are all Chinese, despite their various backgrounds and living styles. Our point here is not to deny these common interests or shared ways of being, doing, or thinking but to understand the social (and political) processes that allow and enable these communalities to emerge.

We can also question the performative dimension of learning language. Wouldn't children feel more Chinese as soon as they are able to speak the Chinese language? Mrs. Lu in Zurich is fully aware of this symbolic dimension of language: "The most important question is the identity question. If children are not able to speak Chinese, then they couldn't identify with that culture. . . . Of course, language and culture are different. But if children know this language, at least they won't reject this culture. On the contrary, if they don't know this language, they might completely reject this culture. The worst would be that they could despise this culture."

NOTES

1. See Gerd Baumann, *Contesting Culture: Discourses of Identity in Multi-Ethnic London* (Cambridge: Cambridge University Press, 1996); Rogers Brubaker, *Ethnicity without Groups* (Cambridge, MA: Harvard University Press, 2006).

2. Pei-te Lien, "Homeland Origins and Political Identities among Chinese in Southern California," *Ethnic and Racial Studies* 31.8 (2008): 1385.

3. These interviews concentrated on their motivations for running schools or teaching "Chinese language" and "Chinese culture" to children of Chinese descent.

4. Pascal Rocha da Silva, "La population chinoise en Suisse dans l'ère de la globalisation," MA thesis, Université de Genève, 2007, http://www.unige.ch /ses/demog/Publicationsetrapports /Memoiresmaster/Chine.pdf, accessed August 2, 2012.

5. Guochu Zhang, "Migration of Highly Skilled Chinese to Europe: Trends and Perspective," *International Migration* 41.3 (2003).

6. See, for example, Ien Ang, *On Not Speaking Chinese: Living between Asia and the West* (London: Routledge, 2001).

7. Tibetans represent a minority. They counted 515 persons in 2008.

8. See, for example, Jean-Philippe Béja and Chunguang Wang, "Un village du Zhejiang à Paris ?" *Hommes et migrations* 1220 (1999); Gregor Benton and Frank N. Pieke,

eds., *The Chinese in Europe* (London: Macmillan, 1998); Antonella Ceccagno, "New Chinese Migrants in Italy," *International Migration* 41.3 (2003).

9. Chloé Cattelain et al., "Les déclassés du Nord: une nouvelle migration chinoise en France," Revue européenne des migrations internationales 21.3 (2005); Yun Gao, Florence Lévy, and Véronique Poisson, "De la migration au travail. L'exploitation extrême des Chinois-es à Paris," Travail, genre et sociétés 16 (2006); Florence Lévy and Marylène Lieber, "La Sexualité comme ressource migratoire: les Chinoises du Nord à Paris," Revue française de sociologie 50.4 (2009); Ronald Skeldon, Myths and Realities of Chinese Irregular Migration, Migration Research Series 1 (Geneva: International Organization for Migration, 2000).

10. Carine Pina-Guerassimoff, "La Chine et les nouveaux migrants chinois en Europe," *Migrations Société* 15.89 (2003); Frank Pieke, *Recent Trends in Chinese Migration to Europe: Fujianese Migration in Perspective,* Migration Research Series 6 (Geneva: International Organization for Migration, 2002).

11. Estelle Auguin and Florence Lévy, "Langue et vulnérabilité des migrations Chinoises actuelles," *Revue européenne des migrations internationales* 23.3 (2007).

12. The intermarriage rate is around 10 percent. It concerns mainly Chinese women marrying Occidental men.

13. Names have been changed to preserve anonymity to our interviewees.

14. Marylène Lieber, "Chinese Migrants in Switzerland: From Mutual Assistance to Promoting Economic Interests," *Journal of Chinese Overseas* 6.1 (2010).

15. Michael Sztanke, "Pékin–Paris: L'étudiant chinois est-il une marchandise?" *Hommes et migrations* 1254 (2005).

16. The Chinese language is usually described as composed of seven main groups of languages or dialects (*Guan, Wu, Yue,* *Min, Xiang, Kejia, Gan*), but this amount varies between seven and seventeen depending on the classification scheme followed. As a matter of fact, the judgment whether one of the various forms of spoken Chinese is a language or a dialect is more a sociopolitical than a linguistic issue. In this article, to simplify, we will use the notion of dialect to speak of all spoken Chinese languages and dialects that differ from Mandarin or national standard Chinese.

17. Marylène Lieber, "'When You Look Chinese, You Have to Speak Chinese': The Valorization of a Shared Unified Culture and Language," paper presented to the International Forum for Contemporary Chinese Studies, Inaugural Conference, "Post-Olympic China: Globalisation and Sustainable Development," Nottingham, 2008.

18. This research is focused on extracurricular Chinese language schools organized by Chinese associations; it does not take into account classes for local students who teach Chinese as a foreign language in schools or universities.

19. See the web site of the National Council of Associations of Chinese Language Schools, http://www.ncacls.org/index.html, accessed August 2, 2012.

20. Eric Yang observes the same process in the United States. See Wenzhong Eric Yang, "Chinese Language Maintenance: A Study of Chinese-American Parental Perceptions and Activities," *Journal of Chinese Overseas* 3.2 (2007).

21. The main exception to this volunteer form is *Tangren* School, a private company, which has opened classes in ten cities located in the German-speaking part of Switzerland.

22. Being a housewife is often not a choice but the result of different factors: sexual division of work; difficulties having their foreign diplomas recognized in Switzerland; a legal ban on work linked to their legal status as dependent on their husbands.

23. Schools have to choose the best way to organize classes: they can take into account age, but then children will not have the same Chinese level in the same class; on the contrary, they can organize classes in regard to proficiency in Chinese, but then classes will mix children of different ages and interests.

24. The proportion of students of different profiles varies from school to school regarding the composition of the Chinese population of the various cities. For instance, the director of Geneva's "mainland" school estimates that two-thirds of the students have either two Chinese or two overseas parents, while the director of a private Chinese school in Basel estimates that two-thirds of the children come from overseas families (who mainly settled down in the German-speaking part of Switzerland).

25. See Gerd Baumann, "Dominant and Demotic Discourses of Culture: Their Relevance to Multi-Ethnic-Alliances," in *Debating Cultural Hybridity: Multi-Cultural Identities and the Politics of Anti-Racism,* ed. Werbner Pnina and Modood Tariq (London: Zed Books, 1997), 209–25.

26. Aihwa Ong, *Flexible Citizenship: The Cultural Logics of Transnationality* (Durham, NC: Duke University Press, 1999).

27. We use the term *group* in a nonessentialist perspective, adopting the position of Rogers Brubaker and others that groups are the result of a complex and never-ending construction. Rogers Brubaker, Mara Loveman, and Peter Stamatov, "Ethnicity as Cognition," *Theory and Society* 33.1 (2004).

28. Mandarin is a language based on the Beijing dialect, which is part of a larger group of northeastern and southwestern dialects. It differs, often quite radically, from the dialects used in the south of China. Southern Chinese have to learn Mandarin at school, and one can consider it a foreign language. See Viviane Alleton, *L'écriture chinoise* (Paris: Presses universitaires de France, 1984).

29. See note 16.

30. The same process of erasure of dialects can probably be observed in China.

31. This term is contested because these children cannot be counted as migrant: they do not have any experience of migration.

32. For further discussion of this process, see Ien Ang, "Can One Say No to Chineseness? Pushing the Limits of the Diasporic Paradigm," *boundary 2* 25.3 (1998).

33. Note that he also takes advantage of this kind of simplification of identity, as he wants to sell his Chinese restaurant in order to open a Japanese restaurant.

34. See Ong, *Flexible Citizenship.*

35. The use of Mandarin, *guanhua,* literally the "language of officials," has long remained the attribute of small dominant groups. It was only after the end of World War II that governments of the PRC and the Republic of China (ROC, Taiwan) both actively introduced it as the national language and imposed it as the sole language for education, media, and formal interactions. Furthermore, the terms used to refer to this language reflect this political aim. In mainland China, people talk about *putonghua,* which means "common speech" or "standardized language"; in Taiwan, people refer to Mandarin as the "national language" (*guoyu*), while overseas Chinese tend to use the term "Chinese language" (*huayu*).

36. The system of transcription is used to indicate the pronunciation of words and is also one of the means to write Chinese with a computer.

37. This may change, though, as there is a debate since 2009 as to whether Taiwanese schools abroad should use traditional or simplified characters.

38. The choice of manuals used to be quite limited, as both education depart-

ments published and promoted their own teaching materials for overseas Chinese. It seems that today the offerings are more diverse and display fewer political affiliations.

39. Most Swiss who want to learn the Chinese language attend classes at a university; this group is not taken into account in this article.

40. Dialects are often used in overseas Chinese families, while standard Chinese is often not the communication language within double-nationality families – as often one of the parents does not understand it. When both parents come from mainland China, Mandarin would probably be the family language. In this category, though, there is a distinction regarding the length of stay of parents in Switzerland. Short-term sojourners, such as diplomats, will not use the local language at home, while children of long-term resident parents would probably use the local language, learned at school.

41. Brubaker, Loveman, and Stamatov, "Ethnicity as Cognition."

PART THREE

Family Matters

SEVEN

Intercountry Adoption:
Color-b(l)inding the Issues

SAIJA WESTERLUND-COOK

INTERCOUNTRY ADOPTION HAS BEEN REFERRED TO AS THE "quiet migration," highlighting different and sometimes conflicting perspectives not only on children but also on diversity and race. This chapter explores how Finland and England (in policy and practice but also in the social and cultural context) have dealt differently with the same issue: adoption into Finnish and English families of children who come from abroad (Finland) or domestic, transracial adoptions (England) and the population of children in care.

How can reasons for such vast differences be accounted for? Why does Finland seem to favor a color-blind, postracial view, while England favors "same race matching" with domestic adoptions (resulting in an overrepresentation of Black and mixed-race children in care) but does not apply the same rule to intercountry adoption? What does this say about the way questions of race, ethnicity, and identity are dealt with generally and within these two contexts of culture and history?

More importantly, what does this mean for adoptees on a personal level? Are they supported in negotiating and carving out a meaningful identity for themselves, even if it is not necessarily one that fits within the popular discourse? How can mixed race as an area of research and experience contribute to the understanding of the transracial adoption experience? What are the strengths and shortcomings of the current Finnish and English systems, respectively? This chapter aims to bring important insights into the understanding of the ways in which policy processes, discourse on racism, and welfare of children operate within different national contexts.

OVERVIEW

In a united Europe, borders are disappearing, economies and military defenses are merging, and legislation is being streamlined as efforts are made to present a united front to the world. It follows that there are expectations for these homogenizing efforts to filter down to common social policies as well. Whether this can, or should, ever happen is an interesting question on a philosophical and theoretical level, as well as in practical application.

Availability of children for intercountry adoption has been shaped by political upheaval, civil wars, natural disasters, and domestic family policies in the third world, historically, for example, in Korea, Cuba, Vietnam, and Cambodia. More recent examples include Romania, the former Soviet Union, the People's Republic of China, and Thailand. Kirsten Lovelock characterizes these "two waves" of intercountry adoption as the first being a largely humanitarian response to the predicament of children in war-torn countries (in the aftermath of the world wars) and the second one as also being driven by falling fertility rates in the West, coupled with a decrease in the number of healthy Caucasian infants available for adoption domestically. Further, she sums up the waves from the recipient society's point of view as (1) finding families for children and (2) finding children for families.[1] Lovelock explains,

> The concerns and practices of individual[s who adopt from abroad] have contributed significantly to national image internationally, have complemented domestic race relations policy, have helped promote domestic adoption objectives, and have dampened dissatisfaction with domestic adoption policies and realities.[2]

Interestingly, while general concerns about racial harmony shaped the response to criticisms of interracial placements domestically, this did not extend to intercountry interracial adoptions.

POLICY CONTEXT

"The character of policy and practice in both Britain and Finland is determined by the role which it is felt that the state should fulfil."[3] Are children's rights first and foremost to care and protection, or should their rights be compared to those of adults? These questions are the basis for any family and childcare policy. Finland and England seem to have answered these questions differently, as will become evident when comparing the two countries' adoption policies.

"[In the UK] the emphasis is placed on every child needing at least one permanent, secure relationship with an adult. [In Finland] the emphasis is on doing everything to support the biological family."[4] There are obvious differences in policy and practice between the countries. The adoption systems of the two countries have opposing views on whether it is ethically and legally possible (or even desirable) to place children for adoption if the birth parents do not consent. The question is problematic. However, the aim of legislation in both countries – and the one principal view that is universally shared – is that it is in the children's best interest to grow up in a stable, loving environment – regardless of genetic links or lack of them.

Overview of Adoption Legislation and Policy in Finland

The planning and governance of domestic and international adoptions in Finland is the responsibility of the Ministry of Social Affairs and Health, which operates through the Finnish Board of Inter-Country Adoption Affairs. The first Adoption of Children Act came into effect in 1925, a year before England passed similar legislation. The present adoption act dates from 1985 (with a decree in 1997 for Adoption Counseling and Intercountry Adoptions). Finland signed the Hague Convention for the Rights of the Child in 1997.

Under these laws, children are only taken into care and placed in fostering if the environment at home or the child's own behavior is threatening the well-being or development of the child and it is deemed to be in the best interest of the child to be placed in care. The child and his or her parents have a right to be heard before the child is taken into care. Permanent transfer of parental rights is not only "not so much a focal concern" but if anything the opposite: adoption against the will of the biological parents remains exceptional in Finland. In addition, children's wishes are always taken into account, according to the maturity of the child, but if the child is over twelve years of age, he or she *must* be listened to when making decisions.

The new law for child protection, which came into effect in 2008, requires the social workers to map out the kinship network of a child taken into care. As such, any possibility for the child to stay with kin should be exhausted before the child is placed in care outside the family. Also, the law now requires that a care plan be put in place within three months of the child's coming into care. The care plan should be reviewed as needed, but no less than yearly. There are no reliable statistics on domestic adoptions from care, as the official statistics include step-parent adoptions, but the annual number is very low compared to the number of international adoptions.

According to Finnish law, an adopted child (intercountry or domestic) has the same legal position, rights, and responsibilities in a family as any biological children. As soon as the adoption is confirmed, any child under eighteen years of age is granted Finnish citizenship automatically if at least one of the adoptive parents is a citizen and the adoption is deemed valid under Finnish law. Only married couples or single people can adopt; couples who cohabit cannot legally adopt jointly. The welfare benefits for biological and adoptive families are theoretically comparable.

The first intercountry adoptees arrived in Finland in the 1970s. However, those children were privately adopted, and, as such, the numbers were not significant. In 1985 when the Law for Adopting Children came into effect (with a provision for intercountry adoptions), a total of only eleven children were adopted from abroad. Intercountry adoption stipulations are that

1. The adoption be carried out through a recognized adoption agency.
2. The adopters be given adoption counseling and deemed suitable as adoptive parents.
3. The Board of International Adoptions Committee has given consent to the adoption.

The numbers have steadily increased since the introduction of the 1985 law. Between 1985 and 2005, the total number of children adopted from abroad was 2,906. The most popular countries of origin were Russia, Colombia, Thailand, and China.[5]

Overview of Adoption Legislation and Policy in England

Adoption became formally legal in England in 1926 when the first adoption act came into effect. The current adoption act dates from 1976, although it was amended by the Children Act in 1989. The Adoption (Intercountry Aspects) Act of 1999 provided a statutory basis for the regulation of intercountry adoptions for the first time, which, in practice, means that the same process and standards now apply for domestic and intercountry adoptions. The Adoption and Children Act of 2002 brought adoption legislation in line with the Children Act of 1989. The U.K. signed the Hague Convention for the Rights of the Child in 1994.

Social services departments have powers to obtain emergency orders so that they can act to protect a child, but, under the Children Act (1989), local authorities cannot remove children from the care of their parents without a court decision. A placement order authorizes a local authority to place a child for adoption where there is no parental consent or where consent should be dispensed with. The welfare of the child outweighs parental rights. When a child is taken into care, adoption plans are made simultaneously to alternative care plans. After four months in care, a plan for permanence is made. However, if a child has not been adopted within twelve months, parents can apply for the placement order to be revoked on the grounds of wishing to resume parental responsibilities. Once a child is adopted, all legal ties with the birth parents are severed. Approximately three thousand children are adopted annually in England (3,700 in 2006) with only around three hundred intercountry adoptions.[6]

England and Wales have led the way in making adoption a central part of childcare policy, with the government actively seeking to reduce the number of "looked after children" (children in care). Currently, the main form of adoption in England is of older children or children with special needs. There has also been a move toward open adoptions. "The Prime Minister's Review of Adoption," followed by the white paper "Adoption, New Approach," both of which appeared in 2000, set in motion what is promising to be the biggest overhaul of the system for decades.[7] Unlike Finland, unmarried couples in the United Kingdom can legally adopt, provided that their relationship is deemed to be stable. Paid adoption leave is currently under consideration.

About half of all adoptions in England are from looked-after children; the other half is made up of step-parent and intercountry adoptions. Intercountry adoption was relatively rare in England until the 1990s. As such, it is more useful for the purpose of this paper to focus on the changing policies and practices on transracial adoptions. (This was not discussed in the section on Finland, as there are virtually no domestic transracial adoptions.)

A Brief History of Transracial Adoption in England

The British Adoption Project was created in the mid-1960s, with its main aim to secure adoption placements for Black children. At the time, it was thought that the best way to achieve racial assimilation was to place Black children in White families. During the 1970s, criticisms of the practice gradually started surfacing, but it was only in the 1980s that the Association of Black Social Workers and Allied Professionals launched an organized campaign opposing transracial adoptions, effectively reducing the numbers of such placements.

Currently, the government has left the policy on "same race matching" open for interpretation by individual local authorities and social workers. While the Children Act of 1989 states that "due consideration" (a vague term at best) is to be given to the racial, cultural, religious, and linguistic needs of children when making decisions regarding their placements, the white paper on adoption, mentioned above, can be seen as an attempt to reverse (without actually doing so) the previous guidelines by stating that "the best family for a child will be one that reflects their birth heritage – no child should be denied loving adoptive parents solely on the grounds that the child and parents do not share the same racial or cultural background."[8] It is worth mentioning that, in an attempt to reduce the number of non-White children who are in care, the fostering and adoption teams across the U.K. have made considerable efforts to appoint more Black social workers and target recruitment drives to ensure more Black and Asian potential adopters.

THE RIGHTS OF THE CHILD

Adoption laws and practices in Finland and England are governed by the UN Convention on the Rights of the Child. Article 3:1 of the convention states that the best interests of the child shall be a primary consideration in all actions concerning children, whether undertaken by public or private social welfare institutions, courts of law, administrative authorities, or legislative bodies.[9] Both countries are also governed by the Hague Convention on Intercountry Adoption, which, in attempting to safeguard the long-term "best interests" of the child, sets out options in a hierarchical order:

- **Family Solutions** (return to the birth family, foster care, adoption) should generally be preferred to institutional placement.
- **Permanent Solutions** (return to the birth family, adoption) should be preferred to **Provisional Solutions** (institutional placement, foster care).
- **National Solutions** (return to birth family, national adoption) should be preferred to **International Solutions.**[10]

Wendy Stainton Rogers is calling for a willingness to recognize that child protection is both a moral and a political endeavor. She explains that the social construction of child concern is dual: there are a discourse of welfare and a discourse of control. Within the discourse of welfare, there are two main assumptions: that the child is entitled to a good childhood and that the child needs protection. According to Stainton Rogers, this is the discourse currently influencing social policy toward children as well as the law about children's care and upbringing in England. Arguably, the same is true for Finland. The discourse of control rests on the assumption that children lack self-control and need to be regulated. According to Stainton Rogers, this discourse mainly informs educational policy.[11] However, perhaps it could also be argued that it is implicit when it comes to adoption policy – or specifically transracial adoption policy in England and taking the child's wishes into account in Finland (a point to which I will return in the section titled "Inconvenient Truths" below).

Over the last decade or so, there have been an ideological and theoretical reconstruction of childhood and a shift in how children are acknowledged, in both research and practice. In line with the United Nations Convention on the Rights of the Child (1989), children all over the world are increasingly viewed as active participants in society and accorded rights. There is a growing emphasis on children's right to take part in decision making and research: children have gone from being objects of concern to being active participants.

Priscilla Alderson identifies different ways to view the child in the wider context of society. Not so long ago, the dominant view saw the "child as object," a perspective that neglected understanding the child as a social actor in his or her own right, rather assuming children were dependent. In the past, the majority of research involving children was mainly concerned with the impact they had on the lives of adults, as children were not considered to be interesting social actors in their own right. A more child-centered starting point for research is the "child-subject" perspective. This perspective sees the child as a person with subjectivity, but it comes with a different set of problems as it relies on the researcher's assessment of the child's cognitive and social abilities. Finally, there is the perspective of the "child as a social actor," where the child is seen to act, take part in, change, and become changed by the world in which she or he lives. This perspective does not take for granted a distinction between adults and children. The final perspective of the child as a social actor is the one that underpins the discussions and analysis of existing research as well as of the social and cultural context of policies in this paper.[12]

SOCIAL CONSTRUCTIONISM AS A TOOL

When comparing and analyzing adoption policies and research, David Howe's four principles for applying social constructionism practically are helpful:

· **Pluralism:** entails acceptance that there will always be a conflict between interests, perspectives, and standpoints and that no professional agency or group can ever claim to know the universal truth. As a result, different positions need to be encouraged to be expressed: conflicting views must be managed constructively and respecting diversity.

· **Participation:** if the assumption is that nobody has a monopoly of "truths," decisions and actions need to be taken in such a way that all those involved or affected participate in the process.

· **Power:** constructionism highlights the issue of power and demands that there is an acknowledgment of how power is deployed and by whom. Conversely, constructionism also reminds us that everybody has some avenues to power.

· **Performance:** How is the power managed, institutionally and bureaucratically? What is done (rather than just said) and what are the consequences of that?[13]

Following these principles, it is evident that a comparative study on adoption policies should not, and cannot, definitively conclude which approach is correct or establish what exactly is in the best interest of the child. The comparison is valuable in its own right. Howe's principles could certainly be applied in advocating a more child-centered approach when it comes to researching adoption and implementing policies. According to the principle on pluralism, it seems futile simply to argue who is right and who is wrong or to point fingers at failures elsewhere. General acceptance that there is probably not a universal truth might free up resources, and it would tend to make people see and do things differently. According to the principles on participation and power, more could certainly be done to include the children in any and all decisions made with regards to their welfare. Finally, and crucially, the principle on performance might enable a more critical look at where the road paved with good intentions actually leads the children – they, after all, are the ones who should matter most in the equation.

WHERE ARE THE CHILDREN?

One of the questions posed at the start of this research was why intercountry adoptions are favored in Finland. The question might be answered simply: It is the only available option. But other questions then follow: Why are there no domestic children available for adoption? Where are the children? The aim was also to find out how the same population of children is treated in the two countries. Statistics on children in care should provide some answers. As suggested by Peter Selman, it is also interesting to look at fertility rates and their impact on adoptions.[14] This approach does indeed highlight differences between the two countries.

It is worth pointing out that the statistics can only be seen as indicative, as domestic adoptions include step-parent adoptions (and, in England, also intercountry adoptions) in the total annual numbers. To complicate matters further, Finland keeps a national register of citizens, which means that population numbers are reliable and accurate. However, racial or ethnic data are not collected by the Finnish government or the local authorities, while England relies on data from the census for population numbers, and those include data on the ethnic makeup of the population.

Statistically Speaking: Finland

As of December 2008, a total of 16,608 children were classed as being "in care" in Finland. Out of these, 33 percent were in fostering (with relatives or other kin or a foster family), 19 percent were in "professional family homes" (licensed family homes or child welfare institutions), 34 percent were in "residential care" (child welfare institutions, family rehabilitation units, residential schools, institutions for substance abusers, or institutions for people with intellectual disabilities), and 14 percent were in other care settings. The National Institute for Health and Welfare in Finland points out that the number of children in care is exceptionally small compared to the rest of the Nordic countries and the European Union, only 1 percent of all children under eighteen.

Abortion statistics can also be used to gauge the impact on children available for adoption. In 2006, the total number of abortions per one thousand fertile women was 8.9. For women in the age group 15–19, the number of abortions per one thousand was 14, with a decrease from the previous year.[15]

Statistically Speaking: England

As of March 2009, approximately 60,900 British children were in the care of local authorities. Seventy-three percent of these were in foster care, 10 percent were in children's homes, 7 percent were with their parents, 4 percent had been placed for adoption, and 3 percent were cared for in residential settings. Foster care is clearly the favored approach in England.

According to the abortion statistics for England and Wales in 2006, the total number of abortions per one thousand fertile women was 18.3. For women under eighteen, the figure was similar at 18.2 per one thousand, with an increase from the previous year.[16]

It is worth pointing out that, under the Finnish classification, "young" women are classed as 15–19, whereas in England and Wales, the classification is under 18. This is likely to skew the numbers somewhat, as women in the age bracket 20–24 have the most abortions.

Lessons Learned

As the high number of abortions is seen as a problem in England, it is interesting to speculate why there is such a vast difference in the number of abortions between the two countries. When looking at all women of fertile age, the number of abortions in England and Wales is more than double that of Finland.

The laws governing abortions in the two countries are quite similar. The low rate of abortions in Finland might be attributed to a number of things (such as sex education in schools being part of the Finnish national curriculum). But it is also interesting to note that birth control in England and Wales is completely free, whereas in Finland, there is a substantial charge for birth control pills and condoms (the favored methods of contraception for young people). When comparing the rates of abortion to the rates of domestic adoptions, one might conclude that the number of unwanted pregnancies in Finland is altogether lower than in England.

However, when rates of abortion are compared to children in care a different picture emerges. England may have an abortion rate that is double that of Finland, but England also has proportionally half of the number of children in care, with a far larger proportion of children actually adopted from care. In reference to the total population of children under eighteen, the percentage for England is approximately 0.55 percent, which makes the Finnish claim of "exceptionally small numbers" seem questionable, especially in light of the fact that 4 percent of English children in care were placed for adoption. No reliable statistics are available for the proportion of children adopted from care in Finland, but, with the total number of domestic adoptions of children under nineteen years of age in 2008 at 189, even if every single one of them was adopted from care (which is extremely unlikely), the percentage would be only 1.2 percent of the population of children in care.

INCONVENIENT TRUTHS

Finland

"It might be argued that many of those children in long-term placements could and should be adopted, but this is against the dominant tendency, in Finnish society, in support of family preservation."[17] Considering that, in England, 75.8 percent of children are placed for adoption within twelve months of the decision that this is in the best interest of the child, the Finnish policy of reviewing the care plan "as needed, but no less than yearly" seems not to quite cut it, especially in light of the admission that a child in care is likely to have several different placements during the course of a year and that the official statistics only reflect the last known placement of a given child in a given year. It seems that a "plan for permanence" (which is put in place in England after four months) is missing in Finland.

Further, Finnish law clearly states that children's wishes are always taken into account, according to the maturity of the child, and, if the child is over twelve years of age, he or she *must* be listened to when making decisions. The importance of the child being involved in each step of the process of making a care plan was further highlighted in the updated law of 2008. Yet the sad truth is that, while this may well be the case in theory, in practice the picture is far from child-centered.

Let's take another look at those statistics: of all the children taken into care in 2008, only one-fifth was taken into care against the will of the parents or the child over twelve years of age. The overwhelming majority are, therefore, in care without objections. It seems sad, with this in mind, that so few children are actually adopted each year. It does make you wonder to what extent the children really do have a say in what happens to them. It seems unlikely that any child would choose multiple placements during the course of a year rather than a permanent family home. The more plausible explanation is that the "family preservation" mentioned earlier trumps the wishes of the children concerned.

Why else would the number of children cared for in other than family settings steadily increase (ten years ago, nearly half of the children in care were in a family setting, compared to the current third)? Consider, then, the case of one particular child in care. He was under twelve, but he had spent most of his life living with the same foster family. Not only did he have a loving home, he was also very much part of the community and had established friendships at school. Every few weeks, he was required to spend a weekend with his biological mother – something he often was anxious about doing. After each visit, he acted out both at home and at school, obviously distressed by the experience. Eventually, the foster family tried to adopt him, only to have the mother demand that the child be moved to a children's home closer to her. The child eventually ended up moving out of a home, away from the friends and school he knew and loved. He was placed in an institution with teenagers, in a Finnish-speaking environment, despite previously having lived in a Swedish-speaking one.[18]

Why rob a child of a family, culture, and language that are virtually the only ones he has ever known and dump him in an environment that can only be described as second-best in every respect?

Finally, as it is estimated that, in England, around 20 percent of all placements of children from local authority care breaks up within five years or before the child reaches adulthood, it seems strange that no such data could be found for Finland. I called one of the most prominent adoption agencies in Finland to ask informally about this lack of data. I was met with astonishment and told that adopting a child is no different from having a biological child and that, as such, the relationship cannot break down. This is perhaps an admirable viewpoint, but, as the adopted child by default is proof of the fact that (even) biological relationships do break down, it seems debatable. Further, as I discussed this with the manager of a children's home, I was met with equal astonishment, for

that particular home alone has had several adoptees in care over a relatively short space of time. It seems that these relationships do indeed
break down – the extent is obviously not known, but it seems fair to re-
evaluate the need for statistics on such an important matter.

England

While England has done comparatively well in the data analyzed above,
it is important to remember that there is also a significant number of
children in care who are not yet part of the success story.

In 2001, the Department of Health published statistics on the ethnicity of looked-after children. In England, 18 percent are from ethnic
minority groups; of these, 36 percent are of mixed heritage.[19] According
to the first report in the National Adoption Register, there were roughly
equal numbers of children and adoptive families with Black or Asian
heritage on the register. However, there was a mismatch between the 510
children of mixed heritage (making up 17 percent of the total number of
children on the register) and the 190 mixed-heritage families seeking to
adopt.[20] As the population of looked-after children is steadily increasing, with children spending longer in the system, it is expected that the
discrepancy between the number of children waiting to be adopted and
the available, racially matched adoptive parents will also increase. The
result will be even longer waiting times spent in temporary arrangements
for an ever-growing population of racially unmatched children.

This is a serious concern. There is a stronger association of placement
breakdown with age at placement than with placement of children of
minority ethnic origin in White families.[21] There have, in recent years,
been recruitment drives specifically targeting ethnic minorities. Despite
these groups representing only 8 percent of the total population, they
make up approximately 40 percent of the children under five years of
age waiting to be adopted.

The reasons for the dearth of matching families are numerous; for
example, while it is common for Black families to arrange informal adoptions, they tend to view formal adoption arrangements with suspicion,
partly because the fostering families do not wish to cut off the ties to the
child's biological families but also because the checks performed by the

adoption boards are seen to be intrusive and unwarranted, often tainted with negative presumptions:

> Some see the collateral issues of whether there are sufficient families of color to adopt available children of color as tied up in a battle between racial groups over whose standards should be applied, with critics of transracial adoption saying that White standards and values close the door to many potentially excellent adopters in communities of color.[22]

In England, the current consensus is that there is no clear evidence to demonstrate a difference in rates of disruption for transracial and matched placements, although there is limited evidence that placements are more successful when the environment is mixed. However, the Performance and Innovation Unit review concluded that there was "No reason to change perception that same race placement is first choice, although it should not be so at the expense of the child getting a permanent family."[23]

Mixed Race and Mixing Race?

While "mixed race" as an experience or area of research does not currently feature in the public awareness or discourse in the Nordic countries, it deserves attention as it contributes to the understanding of the transracial adoption experience, which in itself can be seen as mixing race. In the English context, it is particularly pertinent as a way of explaining the current policy of race matching and the consequent overrepresentation of Black and mixed-race children in care.

Andrew Bebbington and John Miles have found that a child of mixed race is two-and-a-half times more likely to enter care than a White child, all other factors being equal.[24] This can be seen as evidence of a lack of mixed-race adoptive parents. Perhaps more controversially, it suggests unease when it comes to "mixing" races in families.

With all due respect to "due consideration" given in England to the child's ethnic background, this policy is not without pitfalls. Even with the best intentions it can backfire.[25] One anecdote serves as a useful example (and is far from an isolated incident). An Indian Muslim boy was placed with an Indian Sikh family for reasons of racial matching. However, the religious dietary restrictions (Muslims do not eat pork, and

Sikhs do not eat beef) and the language barrier (they only had English as a common language, which the boy's parents did not speak fluently) contributed to the placement being disrupted. When this was brought to the attention of the local authorities, they were surprised, as they had specifically matched the boy with an Asian family.[26]

Jill Olumide warns against "operationalisation of race thinking. . . . any thought or action proceeding from the view that race is a meaningful division of humankind is to be counted racist."[27] Her viewpoint, though perhaps controversial, presents a powerful argument against race matching in adoption. Olumide identifies five features of the mixed-race ideology:

- **An ambiguous social location:** there is no legitimate space for identification with more than a single racially defined group. The ambiguity is constructed through this social situation and not by those who are considered to be mixed or mixing race.
- **A contested site:** struggles to define "mixed race" in the example of transracial adoption discourse have led to children and families perceived as "mixed race" being part of a contest over professional practice.
- **Induced dependency:** welfare agencies have been instrumental in defining and organizing groups of people trapped by changing political strategies in relation to "race mixing." The discourses arising from such institutions construct "mixed race" in terms of inadequacy, ineffectiveness, and menace.
- **A conditional state:** the very presence of "mixed race" has been dependent on changing social circumstances. Where the condition of acceptance is silence, "mixed race" may have to endure lavish racism with the occasional assurance "not you, you are one of us."
- **A point of articulation:** in the ordering of race, gender, and other divisions. For the most part groups perceived as mixed or mixing race have been dependent on more powerful social groups for allocation (or denial) of social space.[28]

It is interesting to return to Wendy Stainton Rogers's discourse of control, the assumption that children lack self-control and need to be regulated. It could be argued that the discourse of control is implicit in the policy on transracial adoptions. It certainly seems to sit well with Olumide's induced dependency and point of articulation. The conditional state is also reminiscent of the gaze Anna Rastas speaks of when discussing transracial adoptees' experiences of racism and the "oh, you are ok because you are not really Black" reactions.[29]

"Although the exploration of context [and its influence on adolescents' ethnic identity formation] is critical, the specific elements of context that are relevant may vary across cultures."[30] The increase in immigration over the last decade has made the multiculturalism debate topical and necessary in Finland. However, as Anna Rastas points out, it is made difficult as the definitions are imported and, therefore, carry with them the social context and history of the places from which they came. Issues discussed under the label "racism" in the English-speaking world have been labeled "tolerance" in Finland.[31]

Research into racism has indeed found a new dimension in transracial adoptees: the discrimination faced by adoptees cannot be attributed to cultural differences or lack of language skills, since adoptees have grown up in the dominant culture and are different only on the outside. Rastas's research on the racism experienced by young Finnish people who either had a foreign parent or were transracially adopted equally highlights the need for antiracist strategies and, arguably, better post-adoption support services.

According to Rastas, Finnish multiculturalism can be classed as "authority-led," whereas multiculturalism in Britain rests on the ethnic communities themselves. Although there has not been much academic debate on "tolerance" in Finland, in popular discourse it is usually seen as the aim or mission statement for politics, policy, and societal state of being. Rastas further points out that it is difficult to research racism comparatively, as racism is tied to a particular time, place, and context.[32] However, it is nonetheless important to make such a comparison, as it gives us a better understanding of the phenomenon known as racism. While this chapter is not about racism as such, racism is clearly pertinent to the debate about transracial and intercountry adoption and essential to understanding the policies and the discourse within the social and cultural context. Interestingly, in Finnish (as other Scandinavian) academia and research, the general consensus is that *race* as a term should not be used. It is thought that, if the word is not used, then the ideology behind the word will not be perpetuated. However, as Olumide points out, "The salience of race ideology in lived experience cannot be denied. It must, therefore, be addressed."[33]

Perhaps the following examples from popular culture might be helpful in providing a snapshot of context. The Finnish population is becoming increasingly multicultural (dare one say "multiracial"?), but only in recent years have voices of protest been heard on matters of everyday racist practices. There has been a recent debate about whether it is still acceptable for popular chocolate sweets to be called "nigger kisses." After a heated debate, the consensus is to rename them "chocolate kisses." Nonetheless, the nation's favorite licorice still has a logo that can only be described as a "golliwog." From the outside, in a global context, the notion of such "acceptable" racism seems absurd. Even multinational corporations seem to be playing by different rules in Finland. A recent Kahlua advertisement that was displayed all over the Helsinki Metro reads, "If your sweetheart tells you they have fallen in love with a black Russian, ask if they have tried a white one!" These examples are small, but they serve to illustrate how far removed even the Finnish popular culture is from the English one, where a *Big Brother* contestant was disqualified for using the N-word.

Negotiating Identities

Transracial adoptees face additional and unique challenges when it comes to identity development:

> The person may ask, "How do I deal with issues of cultural difference and with the disparity between how I look and how my adoptive family looks or perhaps between how I look [Black] and how I feel inside [White]." Transracially adopted children will have to consider questions such as "Who am I? Can I fit in? Where do I want to fit in? To which group do I have responsibility or allegiance? Must I choose, or can I live in both worlds? Will society let this be my free choice?"[34]

An anthology by Sarah Armstrong and Petrina Slaytor illustrates these points beautifully. Their informant Amara said, "I have never really thought about being adopted from a different culture because I have always felt so accepted – I am Black, they are White, and we are family." On the other hand, their informant Bev said, "I have never really felt a part of my adoptive family, due to my skin colour and because I lacked the blood connection."[35]

Conclusions based on these very different experiences and feelings on the same subject are determined by whether the reader is likely to place the blame or credit with the adoptive parents or the adoptee. Projection of negative events and feelings to the most obvious cause is tempting and easily done but not always right.

In a study done by Howard Altstein and Rita J. Simon, a sixteen-year-old Black girl commented at the end of the interview, "I don't really see my family as a White family. Each of us is colour blind." In another family, a child described his adoptive brother: "I don't look on him as a person of a different race. I look at him as a brother." Yet another commented, "Race doesn't matter. Love is what is important."[36] Or, as Diran Adebayo observed on living in England as an ethnic minority, "Until someone tells you different, what you feel you're living *in*, is a culture. And race and culture are not the same thing. Race is on the outside, culture is on the inside."[37]

Pamela Anne Quiroz states that the adoption arena's version of color-blind discourse argues that race should not matter in adoption and that racism can be eradicated through transracial adoption. White parents adopting children of color (or not adopting them) is seen as a matter of individual taste and lifestyle, as color-blind individualists look to transracial, intercountry, and minority adoption as partial solutions to poverty and family disruption.[38]

An opposing viewpoint was expressed by one of the people Jill Olumide interviewed. She likened such assertions of color blindness to saying, "I don't see wheelchairs; I see people" and pointed out how this is convenient, since not seeing wheelchairs would mean you do not have to see the need for ramps. She concluded, "To treat everyone equal, you can't treat them all the same."[39] While she raises a valid point, especially the latter one, the analogy is one that sits uncomfortably. It equals color or race with a disability. In doing so, it essentializes race. Disabled people do need special equipment to get around. Regardless of race, in a color-blind world (utopian as the notion may be), you would certainly get by without any special equipment. It would only require bridge building with very different kinds of requirements!

Perhaps even more problematic is the "need" of society to define transracial adoptees because common standards will not allow a person to define him- or herself as belonging to more than one of the categories of race within which society by and large operates. As in Olumide's fifth dimension of mixed-race ideology, it is a question of being dependent on more powerful social groups for allocation (or denial) of social space. Olumide also asks why it is that a mixed-race child's perception of "Whiteness" is pathologized and taken as an indication of "identity problems."[40] This is something that transracial adoptees are often accused of, if they identify more strongly with the culture of their adoptive (White) parents. Most often, transracial adoptees identify with the culture in which they were brought up – that is, *their* culture – rather than with the culture society associates with the color of their skin. If it is deemed unhealthy for a black-skinned transracial adoptee who was raised in a White family to perceive herself as White (because, in society's eyes, the child is Black), then why would it not be equally unhealthy for the child to perceive herself as Black? Going back to Adebayo, "Race is on the outside, culture is on the inside." If what is on the outside becomes the only criterion and that criterion solely determines how one should feel on the inside, then it takes all agency away from the individual, relying completely on society to define the identity of a person, irrespective of her or his own self-perception or life experience.

Tobias Hubinette raises the point of racialization and racism coming from the outside. It is not connected to the origin of the adoptee but to society being racist. When adoptive parents start to acknowledge the differences in forms of roots and origin instead of denying them, as with the color-blind approach, they also give up the antiracist and democratic idea of sameness and instead make use of the concept of difference grounded within racist and nationalist ideologies. It is a precarious balance to keep. In Hubinette's words, "The ideological standpoint is suppressed in favour of pragmatic reasons."[41]

While several models of satisfactory identity development have been posed, others have argued that mixed-race or double ethnicity (as in the case of intercountry or transracial adoptees) is not sustainable as an identity, for the number of people belonging to this group is too small to be considered a community. This is ludicrous. If size of the group is the criterion of identity, does that mean one cannot be Jewish in Germany today or Korean in France? It is often precisely the small numbers that enable members of a given community to feel a sense of belonging and togetherness, creating an even stronger identity.

Toyin Okitikpi reminds us that all identities are problematic, with their own challenges and promises. Identity is not fixed; rather, it is an ongoing process.[42] Maria Root sees such adaptability as strength, rather than a sign of confusion. Why should multiethnic children have to choose between two polar identities, especially if the choice of one necessitates rejecting the other?[43] What is wrong with "situational ethnicity"? Is this not something, after all, that we all perform day in and day out, with our different roles in society, anyway? Many children and adults alike struggle to make sense of who they are, what they want to do with their lives, where they belong, and which people are important to them. This is not a condition that comes with being adopted or being mixed race.

While mindful of the fact that Internet discussion boards and support groups need to be used with caution and should not be taken as representative of a given group of people, I would, nonetheless, like to quote an adoptee who wrote on the subject of negotiating identities in an Internet support group for transracial adoptees (or "abductees," as the subscribers called themselves). While the name of the support group highlights a clear bias against transracial adoption, it still gives a platform for voices that deserve to be heard:

> Transracial Abduction is an "authentic" person of color experience. Other people of color need to listen to how abductees analyze our experiences of radical displacement, and learn from our strategies for survival and resistance; we've had to develop a wide variety of them, and we often have unique perspectives on white culture, the construction of families and how to cope with racism and isolation.[44]

It is often argued that White adoptive parents cannot experience minority status and that, therefore, they will inevitably bring up a child who is ill-equipped to understand or deal with the realities of a racist society. While it may be true that White adoptive parents have probably not had to face racism personally, the claim cannot be extended automatically to include minority status. Being White does not exclude also being part of a minority. Discrimination is often, but far from always, on racial grounds. It is also important to keep in mind that such claims are disempowering to the child, as is evident from the quote by the adoptee above.

Could it not also be argued that, regardless of race or ethnic background, the children of today will have to face the world on their own? In a world that is changing as rapidly as ours is, can any parent or family, regardless of background, really be considered competent to equip its children to deal with life out in the real world? Isn't it true that all children, much like the adoptee above, will need to learn their own strategies for survival, while inhabiting a culture that will in many ways be unfamiliar to their parents?

CONCLUSION

Within the adoption triangle of biological parents, adoptive parents, and the child, it seems difficult, if not impossible, to offer sufficient support to all parties in a respectful way. Children can be viewed as commodities, and adoption can be seen as beneficial only to the adoptive family and not to the birth family. Adoptive parents are assumed to be altruistic, giving a home to a child who is not biological, but the birth parents are at the very least equally altruistic, giving up a child in the hope that he or she can have a better life. Signe Howell speaks of the "naked child," a child who is socially denuded of all kinship and meaningful relatedness, regardless of whether its identity is known or not.[45]

When I initially started researching intercountry and transracial adoptions, I was puzzled by why countries such as the United States and England, each of which has a diverse ethnic makeup and a multicultural society (and where, consequently, transracial adoptees would most certainly have access to "racially matched" role models, if not within the immediate family, then definitely within society), are also the ones where transracial adoption is opposed most strongly. If, as it seems, transracial adoption works in the Nordic countries, where arguably the issues around positive racial or ethnic identities should be more pronounced (Finland has the lowest number of foreign citizens in the EU), why would it not work in a potentially more hospitable environment?

All children have the right to be provided for, and, at the moment, there are too many left behind. Both Finland and England have a population of children in care that could be significantly reduced by examining again the balance between parental versus children's rights and the due consideration given to the children's ethnic background, respectively.

The intention of this chapter has not been to discover which country is right in its approach to adoption and children in care or the issues surrounding adoption, race, and ethnicity. It should be clear that such an approach is unnecessary and unhelpful.

It is evident that, to ensure that the best interests of children are met, the debate needs to move away from the issues around race and ethnicity and toward ensuring that no child is denied the right to a permanent home on grounds of policy or practice that is (or may be) counterproductive. That is not to say that race and ethnicity are nonissues or should be treated as such.

Race is an invention, a social construct. Nonetheless, with that invention came racism, and it is, therefore, an invention that desperately needs to be addressed: both in terms of addressing the denial and disregard of racism in Finland and also bringing the mixed-heritage issues into the public debate and in terms of acknowledging that, while the intentions are good, the outcomes of the race-matching policy in England are arguably not in the best interest of *all* children, as so many are left waiting. The current numbers of children in care (domestic in Finland, minority children in England) should be a national source of shame for both countries.

Acknowledging the need and right for a child to have a positive social identification is crucial, and making provisions for such identification is paramount.

Undoubtedly, we cannot give what we do not have. White parents cannot *give* a non-White child an identity other than White – but then identity is not really something that is given anyway. Just as surely, regardless of the skin color of any family member, parents can provide a safe, loving environment in which a child can be supported, even in establishing a positive racial or ethnic identity on his or her own, with the family's support. Therefore, the emphasis should be on figuring out how both adoptees and their families (birth as well as adoptive) can be helped in achieving that.

"If we are to work towards achieving a better quality of life for children – we need the vision to imagine what better childhoods might be and the determination to achieve the conditions that will make these better childhoods possible."[46]

NOTES

1. Kirsten Lovelock, "Intercountry Adoption as a Migratory Practice," *International Migration Review* 34.3 (2000): 907–49.

2. Ibid., 910–11.

3. Paul Michael Garrett and Jari Sinkkonen, "Putting Children First? A Comparison of Child Adoption Policy and Practice in Britain and Finland," *European Journal of Social Work* 6.1 (2003): 28.

4. Ibid.

5. Finnish Ministry for Social Affairs and Health, http://www.stm.fi/etusivu, accessed August 4, 2012. See also http://www.valvira.fi/luvat/adoptio/tilastot.

6. Department for Education, http://www.education.gov.uk/researchand statistics/statistics/a00196857/children-looked-after-by-local-authorities-in-engl, accessed September 24, 2012.

7. [UK] Department of Health, "LAC (2000) 16: The Prime Minister's Review of Adoption: Report from Performance and Innovation Unit," http://www.dh.gov.uk/en/Publicationsandstatistics/Lettersand circulars/LocalAuthorityCirculars/All LocalAuthority/DH_4005024, accessed August 4, 2012.

8. [UK] Department of Health, "Adoption, A New Approach – A White Paper" (December 21, 2000), http://webarchive.nationalarchives.gov.uk/+/www.dh.gov.uk/en/Publicationsand statistics/Publications/Publications PolicyAndGuidance/DH_4006581, accessed August 4, 2012.

9. http://www.unicef.org/crc/, accessed August 4, 2012.

10. Pam Foley, Jeremy Roche, and Stan Tucker, eds., *Children in Society: Contemporary Theory, Policy and Practice* (New York: Palgrave, 2001). See also http://www.hcch.net/index_en.php?act=conventions.text&cid=69, accessed September 24, 2012, for a text on the "Convention of 29 May 1993 on the Protection of Children and Co-operation in Respect of Intercountry Adoption."

11. Wendy Stainton Rogers, "Constructing Childhood, Constructing Child Concern," in *Children in Society*, ed. Foley et al., 26–33.

12. Priscilla Alderson, "Children as Researchers: The Effects of Participation Rights on Research Methodology," in *Research with Children*, ed. Pia Christensen and Allison James (London: Palmer Press, 2000), 276–90.

13. David Howe, "Modernity, Postmodernity and Social Work," *British Journal of Social Work* 24.5 (1994): 513–32.

14. Peter Selman, "Intercountry Adoption in the New Millenium: The 'Quiet Migration' Revisited," *Population Research & Policy Review* 21 (2002): 205–25.

15. http://www.stakes.fi/NR/rdonlyres/DCF23E53-4FC3-49D1-B210-6CD F3AAC3322/0/Tt06_07.pdf, accessed September 24, 2012.

16. http://www.statistics.gov.uk/hub/population/births-and-fertility/conception-and-fertility-rates/index.html, accessed September 24, 2012.

17. Garrett and Sinkkonen, "Putting Children First," 21.

18. Field notes.

19. [UK] Department of Health (2001), http://www.dh.gov.uk/en/Publication sandstatistics/Statistics/StatisticalWork Areas/Statisticalsocialcare/DH_4086825, accessed September 24, 2012.

20. *National Adoption Register* (2003), http://www.adoptionregister.org.uk/ UserFiles/File/Adoption%20Register% 20Annual%20Report%202005.pdf, accessed September 24, 2012.

21. June Thoburn, Liz Norford, and Stephen Parvez Rashid, *Permanent Family Placement for Children of Minority Ethnic Origin* (London: Jessica Kingsley Publishers, 2000).

22. Michael E. Lamb, *Parenting and Childcare in Non-Traditional Families* (Mahwah, NJ: Lawrence Erlbaum Associates, 1999), 267.

23. www.cabinetoffice.gov.uk/media/ cabinetoffice/strategy/assets/adoption .pdf, accessed August 4, 2012.

24. Anthony Bebbington and John Miles, "Background of Children Who Enter Local Authority Care," *British Journal of Social Work* 19.1 (1989): 349–68.

25. Anthony Douglas and Terry Philpot, *Adoption: Changing Families, Changing Times* (London: Routledge, 2003).

26. Field notes.

27. Jill Olumide, *Raiding the Gene Pool: The Social Construction of Mixed Race* (London: Pluto Press, 2002), 27.

28. Ibid., last chapter.

29. Anna Rastas, "Rasismi," in *The Finnish Guestbook: How to Deal with Multiculturalism*, ed. Anna Rastas, Laura Huttunen, and Olli Löytty (Tampere: Vastapaino, 2005), 69–116.

30. Adriana Umana-Taylor, Ruchi Bhanot, and Nana Shin, "Ethnic Identity Formation during Adolescence: The Critical Role of Families," *Journal of Family Issues* 27 (March 2006): 408.

31. Rastas, "Rasismi."

32. Ibid.

33. Olumide, *Raiding the Gene Pool,* 179.

34. Lamb, *Parenting and Childcare,* 179–80.

35. Sarah Armstrong and Petrina Slaytor, *The Colour of Difference* (Sydney: The Federation Press: 2001), 27, 45.

36. Howard Altstein and Rita J. Simon, *Transracial Adoptees and Their Families: A Study of Identity and Commitment* (New York: Praeger, 1987), 65.

37. Diran Adebayo, "Race in Britain," *The Observer*, November 25, 2001.

38. Pamela Anne Quiroz, "Color-blind Individualism, Intercountry Adoption and Public Policy," *Journal of Sociology and Social Welfare* 34.2 (2007): 57–68.

39. Olumide, *Raiding the Gene Pool,* 176.

40. Ibid., 171.

41. Tobias Hubinette and Carina Tigerwall, "Contested Adoption Narratives in a Swedish Setting," paper presented at the International Conference on Adoption Research (2006), http:// www.uea.ac.uk/swp/icar2/pdf's/Tobias %20Hubinette.pdf, accessed August 4, 2012.

42. Toyin Okitikpi, *Working with Children of Mixed Parentage* (Lyme Regis, UK: Russell House, 2005).

43. Maria P. P. Root, "Within, Between, and Beyond Race," in *Racial Mixed People in America*, ed. Maria P. P. Root (Newbury Park, CA: Sage, 1992), 3–11.

44. http://www.transracialabductees. org/politics/backtalk.html, accessed August 4, 2012.

45. Signe Howell, *The Kinning of Foreigners* (Oxford: Berghahn Books, 2007).

46. Stainton Rogers, "Constructing Childhood," 33.

EIGHT

The Children of Immigrants in Italy: A New Generation of Italians?

ENZO COLOMBO AND PAOLA REBUGHINI

SPECIFICITIES OF THE ITALIAN CASE

This chapter is based on five years of national research (2004–2009) around the teenage children of immigrants in Italy.[1] The principal aim of this research was to look into the processes by which these young people construct identities and claim citizenship. Our aim was also to assess whether and to what extent the prevailing research perspectives currently used to predict the future of second generations can be applied to a context where the migration phenomenon is relatively recent, compared to other European countries.

Italy, in fact, switched from being a country of emigration to being one of immigration only as recently as the 1970s. At least until the 1980s, immigration was considered a national domestic matter, and immigration from abroad was completely absent from public debates; at that time, Italy still perceived itself as a country of emigrants, recently enriched and industrialized. As a matter of fact, since the start of the industrial development of the country, Italy has mainly been characterized by internal fluxes of immigration, from rural areas in the south to the industrialized regions of the north. Immigration from abroad started slowly at the end of the 1970s when other European countries such as France and the United Kingdom were closing their borders because of industrial crises. During these years in the industrial areas of the north of Italy, immigrant manpower, coming from very different countries, became less expensive that Italian, even if internal immigration has never completely stopped.

Such configuration has been defined as a "Mediterranean" or "post-modern" model[2] of migration, characterized by a later development of immigrant fluxes, by a pluralistic and fragmented differentiation of immigrant's characteristics (culturally, economically, and professionally), and by a strong difference in gender (immigrant men and women present different patterns of inclusion and family formation, different provenances, and different goals).

To understand the specificity of the Italian situation in the wider European landscape of immigration fluxes, it is necessary to consider that the historical delay in the arrival of consistent numbers of immigrants on Italian soil overlaps with the weakness of an Italian sense of the nation and feelings of "Italianness."

In the introduction to this volume, Paul Spickard says that "every modern European nation is founded on an idea of ethnic homogeneity that is thought to reach deep into its past"; in Italy, things happened in a slightly different way because the idea of a common ethnic homogeneity is far from being accomplished and because immigration was becoming an important topic – especially for some right-wing or localist political parties – for strengthening an otherwise weak nationalism. In fact, Italy is one of the youngest European nation-states, even if its linguistic unit is much more ancient. Italy has been culturally decentralized for centuries, and, since the country unification in 1861, it has been difficult to construct an Italian identity out of the diverse regional cultures and city-states that preceded national union. Hence, Italy's varied and regionalized cultural heritage has brought forward a more complex construction of the sense of nationhood that has never been reified or transformed in a powerful identity rhetoric. Pluralism is part of the Italian history, and this now influences the process by which Italy is becoming a multicultural nation, in a different way compared to other older European nation-states.

In some way, the historical delay of Italian modernization can today have some positive effects on the demand of institutional and cultural transformations imposed by globalization processes and immigration flows. Particularly, a weak identification with the idea of nation and national pride, the multicultural and fragmented history of the different geographical regions, and the absence of a technocratic tradition have resulted in a certain elasticity of the contexts, favoring pluralism and encouraging a situated interpretation of the rules.

However – as the introduction of this book points out – discrimination and racism remain the hearts of darkness of every meeting process among different populations, habits, religious values, and identities. Despite its multicultural foundation and the positive influence of Catholic culture (or simply its rhetoric), Italy is not a European exception in the matter of discrimination and prejudice.

Being a country in which colonialism has been considered as an incidental – and largely forgotten – component of national history, Italy has not developed a "politically correct" culture, and racist proposals can be explicit among political parties that prey on the fear of immigrants in order to gather consensus.

FIRST AND SECOND GENERATIONS OF IMMIGRANTS

We said that, in Italy, the immigration flux from abroad increased in visibility only at the end of the 1980s; moreover, since its beginning, immigration has been characterized by tremendous diversity: today the five million immigrant community (which accounts for nearly 8.5 percent of the population) is made up of people from over 180 different countries, and no single group accounts for more than 20 percent of the total foreign population (the biggest communities are those from Romania, Albania, and Morocco).

Although the majority of the immigrant population lives in the north of the country (63 percent), no national community is large or well organized enough to form a highly distinctive "ethnic" group. Frequently, on the contrary, associations and groups are formed of a pan-national character, sharing a common language (especially those from Central and South America) or religion (as is especially the case with believers in Islam). Also, although characterized by rising hostility and large use of stereotypes based on ethnic and national categorization, the perceptions held by the indigenous population do not appear to focus on fixed ethnic hierarchies, with their representation of different groups being quite changeable and tending to vary according to crime reports and political discourses. So, migrants enter a fluid representation system of ethnic relationship that assumes different meanings for different social groups and different temporary situations.

Concerning the role of the media in the representation of immigrants, Italy presents another sort of delay: despite a history of almost three decades of migration fluxes, the debate around immigration continues to be dominated by rhetorical "emergency" issues and has, therefore, focused on reducing and quashing illegal immigration. As a result, in the last ten years, political elections have been heavily influenced by immigration and security matters and migrants have been mostly considered as manpower, wanted but not welcome.

We can say that Italians have only recently begun to realize that the migration process is going to become established. The rise of family reunions and of children of immigrants born in Italy and receiving an Italian education is self-evident proof that migrants and their families have become an important and permanent part of the nation. Moreover – as Paul Spickard affirms in the introduction – immigrants are the main protagonists of the recent growth of the Italian population. Particularly, minors now represent more than one million people, and they grow by around one hundred thousand every year. In 2009 in the main towns of the northern regions, where migrants are more concentrated, almost one newborn in every three had one or both immigrant parents. Around 50 percent of the one million minors without Italian nationality are born in Italy, but they are only "foreign" from a juridical point of view because it takes a long time to obtain Italian citizenship and the fact of being born on the territory does not convey automatic citizenship (see below).

As a consequence, the presence of these youngsters is also growing in Italian schools. Today, foreign students represent 7 percent of the national scholastic population, but this presence is more marked in the larger cities such as Rome, Milan, or Turin and in the north and eastern areas of the country. The current seven hundred thousand foreign pupils in Italian schools are geographically concentrated in areas where their parents can easily find work – such as big cities and industrialized areas – but, even where their presence peaks, there is no corresponding ethnic concentration.

On the local level – for example, in Milan – we find areas of the town in which students with immigrant origins are more concentrated (up to

80 percent in some primary schools), but, in any case, within this concentration, different ethnic characteristics and nationalities are always present.

Today, the educational integration of young foreigners is constantly increasing, and although the number of children of immigrants born in Italy has become considerable, their increasing presence and visibility are sometimes perceived as a "social problem," especially in schools and in some urban areas of industrial towns where their concentration is more evident.

However, the growing importance of the second generation in Italian society concerns not only educational matters but more widely public life and public debates on difference and equal opportunities. Particularly, young people with immigrant origins have started to discuss racism and discrimination, citizenship and social rights, especially within their associations. These associations are mainly based on web sites and online forums that expand their member group's social visibility. Associations such as "Young Muslims of Italy" show that this new generation has started to stake a claim for social and political participation in Italian public life. Moreover, adolescents involved in these local and national associations as well as in cultural activities are mostly second generation, as they were born in Italy. On the contrary, youths who entered Italy during adolescence seem less interested in such social activities and debates (a phenomenon also seen in other European countries).

THE IDENTIFICATION MODELS OF YOUNG
ITALIANS WITH IMMIGRANT ORIGINS

The researches we present here explore the experience of a specific segment of children of immigrants: those attending high schools beyond compulsory education. They usually come from families with high cultural capital, are fluent in the Italian language, are interested in planning their future in Italy, and normally do not feel themselves different from their Italian peers, with whom they share the same patterns of consumption and most of school and free time. We looked into the ways these youths narrate their everyday experience, the models of self-identification and belonging they use to talk about themselves, their plans for the future, and the way they perceive and integrate into the Italian context. Considering the characteristics of the Italian situation, our researches adopted a *generational* rather than an ethnic perspective. They considered the teenage children of immigrants as sharing a similar "generational location,"[3] which goes to support the perception that they share a specific historical and biographical experience; starting from this point, they tried to assess the relevance of ethnic and national belonging.

More specifically, we investigated to what extent, if at all, the interpretive patterns developed to analyze a "Fordist" context of immigration – typical in countries with a long immigration history – can be useful for understanding second-generation youths' pathways of inclusion in the Italian immigration context.

We have seen that Italy, like other southern European countries, is going through a new form of immigration fluxes – the "Mediterranean model" – that in many ways is not comparable to the Fordist model. It, therefore, seems important to analyze how, if at all, the analytical tools developed for studying and understanding the old immigration flux into countries experiencing a phase of huge industrial growth are still useful in trying to analyze a new form of immigration in more fluid and global contexts. New research questions arise. What will the pathway of inclusion be for second-generation youths in countries like Italy that experience immigration in the contest of widespread globalization? Are they going to achieve complete assimilation and become Italians without being "different"? Or will they maintain their differences and contribute to the creation of a society where differences, indifferences, lack of unity, and potential conflicts will constitute a normal feature of social coexistence?

Contemporary research on the second generation is dominated by two approaches: the segmented assimilation theory on one side and the emphasis on transnational dimensions or the development of new forms of cosmopolitism on the other.

The first approach at least partially tries to recover the concept of assimilation.[4] These scholars, although they recognize the association of the word *assimilation* with a normative program, imposed by the nation-state and oriented to eradicate minority cultures, nevertheless think the concept of assimilation can be valued and used as an analytical tool in an effective way to indicate a spontaneous and often unintentional social process characterizing every prolonged contact between majority and minority groups. They are mainly interested in social and economic factors (the abandonment of formal and informal ethnic associations in favor of equivalent nonethnic social institutions concerning familiar and conjugal patterns, jobs and professions, religious attitudes and values, political associations and behavior). They support the concept of assimilation because it counteracts an excessive positive appraisal of difference and because it can give an account of processes that do not take place on an individual level (transformation of identity, values, and personal behavior), but on a collective one, involving several generations or the whole society.

The idea of "segmented assimilation"[5] is used both to indicate that the assimilation process is all but taken for granted, without problems, unavoidably oriented toward upward economic and social mobility, and to stress that economic and social inclusion can be disjointed from the acculturation process.[6] On the contrary, a strong tie with the ethnic network and a fluent bilingualism constitute solid premises for upward assimilation.[7] Second-generation youths who can rely on a consistent and pluralistic ethnic network have more opportunity for scholastic and professional achievement,[8] while second-generation youths living without the support of a strong ethnic network are more likely to experience the processes of downward assimilation, pushing them to associate with the urban underclass. Starting from these premises, the segmented assimilation theory designs three different outputs:

(1) a first pathway of complete and successful inclusion into the mainstream of the autochthon host society in which the premise for upward social mobility is the complete abandonment of any claim of difference
(2) a second path marked by downward mobility due to an anachronistic self-recognition with the traditions and the networks of their parents, showing a difference that is hostile toward the dominant culture
(3) a third path in which the retention of strong ties with their parents' ethnic network and culture works as a resource for upward social mobility.

The perspective of segmented assimilation, although useful for understanding inclusion processes in countries with a long immigration history, seems less effective in capturing the fate of the second generation in Italy. Here, in fact, both the rise of a new underclass characterized by isolation and institutional discrimination and the economic and social success due to ethnic closure seem to be marginal possibilities. Diversity in the place of origins and a largely inclusive welfare system seem to support the creation of a marginal middle class, characterized by *subaltern integration*[9] at the economic level (marginal jobs with low wages and low status), an everyday interaction with the indigenous population, and the necessity of a never-ending engagement in order to avoid or reduce exclusion and discrimination. In this marginal position, keeping identities open and mobile while being able to call for closeness with the Italian community as well as underlining difference becomes a resource that cannot be given up.

The second perspective, transnationalism, sees the inclusion pathway of second-generation immigrants within the wider context of globalization. For the majority of scholars of transnationalism, migration processes create new social fields connecting spatially separated places and groups and a new category of social actors – the transmigrants[10] – who maintain strong instrumental and affective ties over national boundaries.

The experience of transnationalism does not require living in two different countries; it is based on the feeling of permanent, deep, and lasting ties – based on exchange, reciprocity, and solidarity – between different places. This feeling allows the creation of social cohesion and collective symbolic representations.[11] Transnationalism has to do with a space of imagination,[12] communicative and affective fluxes, movement of goods, news, and pictures, rather than with a specific and lasting spatial collocation.[13] The relational and imaginative dimensions, rather than the spatial one, make the space people experience as personal meaningful, a necessary base for the feeling of being "at home." This meaningful space is constructed by a dynamic synthesis that links territorial dimensions with the routines of everyday life (made of habits, friendships, love, consumption, and trivialities), the memory (made of relationships, obligations, reciprocities, biographic experiences, respect, and self-esteem), and the future (made of expectations, ambitions, dreams, and projects). Within this context, far from being the simple extension of their "native land" or their "traditional roots," second-generation youths negotiate and create collective identities that can be somewhat dissociated by ethnic and cultural membership. They take their symbols for identification from everywhere possible, from the global cultural flux as well as from local specificity, both from the country of their parents and the country where they live.[14]

Emphasis on transnational dimensions can carry different weights. In its more radical version, it risks overestimating the space for individual freedom and creativity. In so doing, it transforms difference into a never-ending process in which it becomes irrelevant, a mere exercise of aesthetic construction, the manifestation of a sterile creative omnipotence by subjects oriented only toward immediate, selfish gratification. The emphasis on the mixing processes risks sliding into a normative dimension that hides the power relationship and always presents the hybrids in a positive form, a type of emancipation from former powers and ties, a desirable condition for a wider consciousness, and a stronger warranty for freedom and justice.[15] It also risks representing group identification as pure contingency, without any stability or consistency. All this sounds in sharp contrast with social situations in which the recognition of collective belonging seems to be a basic point for struggle and a factor capable of moving passions, animating conflicts, and creating exclusions.

In its weaker version – a version we share – it underlines how new second generations – no differently from any other youngster growing up in a globalized context and having a sufficient set of cultural and social resources – learn to put themselves into relational and cognitive horizons that transcend the national dimension and, in an innovative and creative way, bind the local and the global. Transnationalism has less to do with the ability to cross borders or subjective creativity and more to do with being accustomed to finding a synthesis in every different context – which can never be changed with just individual will or creativity – to be able to use different codes in different situations to achieve different goals. The capacity to manage ambivalence, to fit different contexts, to recognize that rules and expectations hold in specific circumstances, and to show or conceal difference in order to expand personal opportunities become generational skills. Showing complex identifications and multiple belonging, which shift and change over the course of time and changing circumstance – as Paul Spickard observes in the first chapter of this book – do not eliminate discrimination and racism but become a necessary competence to oppose fixing negative labels externally imposed. Young people show the capacity to manage and use difference and belonging in a tactical way[16] – that is, taking advantage of the moment when the opportunity presents itself, finding new ways to obtain something, according to circumstances, possibilities, and personal goals.

Consumption behavior and the representation of citizenship appear to be two interesting starting points for analyzing how people can make a tactical use of difference and self-identification. In both these domains, the skill of modulating practices, values, and belongings on the basis of contexts and goals seems to be a constant for children of immigrants in Italy. We choose to present here these two important parts of our research analysis – consumption behavior and citizenship's representations – because, inside our interviews, these are the two features of daily life and personal biography that the children of immigrants have more valorized as "trials" in which difference and belongings are at stake.

CONSUMPTION STYLES AND IDENTIFICATIONS

The analysis of consumption styles is indeed particularly useful to understand the link between identification practices, tastes, moral values, emotional belongings, and everyday lifestyles among the children of immigrants.

Consumption styles in Western countries have usually been considered as a typical reference point of White, bourgeois, mainstream culture.[17] Hence, the construction of cultural difference has also been developed through the claim of different consumption styles and the rise of so-called ethnic youth subcultures. On the one hand, we have a literature speaking about *consumer acculturation* into Western references; on the other hand, there is another kind of literature – sometimes linked to cultural studies and postcolonial studies – that specializes in the relationship between ethnic identity and consumption styles. In the first case, the "dominated" social position of migrants and their children is reflected in the passive assimilation of a Western and national consumption culture; in the second case, consumption style and aesthetics are at the base of identity claims.

Our research shows that, although the Western culture hegemonic position indeed enforces migrants and their descendants to position themselves socially *within* it,[18] this never happens in a simply passive and neutral way. The analysis of their dealings with Italian material culture shows us that there is much more than either being enchanted and tamed by brands and commercial visions as the unique means of integration or closed within their ethnic group, sharing common deprivations. This is why it is important to pay close attention to the *ambivalent* role played by material culture in structuring the relationship between consumption and identification.

If it is true that – in Italy as in other European countries – young people with immigrant origins are usually overrepresented within the lower social classes (because their parents have been integrated mainly in the Italian labor market of low-skilled professions) and the lower educational pathways (usually "professional" schools or vocational training as opposed to the more prestigious high schools such as lyceums, highways toward university), this does not mean that they could be considered as systematic victims of subaltern integration or downward assimilation. The majority of them do not live isolated inside their communities; on the contrary, they are engaged in daily interactions with Italian friends (and other young people with foreign nationalities) in order to manage different forms of identity and belonging.

Our investigation on their consumption patterns shows that Italian culture as "the predominant group," especially in the area of consumption styles, is not an established and shared dominant model for these young people. There are not only two options, however: on the one hand, successful assimilation of the Italian way of life and consumption style; on the other hand, downward assimilation, where cultural difference becomes a tool to oppose the host society and its rules in the presence of economic difficulties. On the contrary, consumption styles represent an open space of "transnational" strategies, cutting across cultural borders and interconnections within cultures.

Of course, consumption is also a way to stress frontiers and build ethnic enclaves and national networks of reference (to listen only to Latin music, to watch only Chinese films, and so on); however, our research shows that, even among those recently arrived in Italy, consumption styles are a way to build a transnational perspective and that they are the products of a dynamic synthesis (for example, references to U.S. hip-hop clothes can be mixed up with Latino music or a passion for Japanese manga).

Even though we must be careful not to make an excessive claim for individual freedom and creativity, consumption choices are not a mere aesthetic exercise. Statements of double and hyphenated belonging can be expressed through clothes, accessories (a typical example is the color of the headscarf according to the color of clothes), and the choice of specific brands. These connections allow young people to at the same time be members of one group without giving up other possibilities of belonging. These forms of identification highlight a desire for participation and openly demand access to community life without discrimination or exclusion.

> When I came at first, I would only listen to the music I had brought with me, salsa . . . everything came from there, I wouldn't listen to anything from here . . . that is, there were music programmes on the radio or on TV and I said, "No! That's horrible, forget about it!" Then, all of a sudden, I started watching them more and more; now, I still have my tapes but I don't usually listen to them, I don't take them with me to play on my Walkman, while you bet I take my Walkman and my Italian music tapes with me when I go out . . . Because now I like it. (*Milagros, eighteen years old, Peruvian parents*).

Young people who recognize themselves as having a double belonging appear to share the lifestyles that are assumed to be typical of contemporary Italy; nevertheless, they do not want to give up their multiple identification, which is considered to be a factor of prestige: some symbolic reference to their difference is usually present in their accessories or clothes. They do not want to hide difference or be recognized for it only in private; on the contrary, they claim to exhibit and acknowledge it openly in the public sphere through consumption styles. In other words, through an inclusive rather than a substitutive process, they "retrieve" a sense of belonging of which they have often never had firsthand experience (especially if they were born in Italy) but which takes on a powerful symbolic meaning.

Looked at from the point of view of consumption, differences are considered as positive resources: consumption offers a field in which it is possible to play with different references and claim multiple belongings. In organizing their consumption styles, these young people are able to hold worlds together that are apparently so different and so far apart. Consumption choices can also be *ironical*,[19] especially in front of Italian-born friends who sometimes do not understand the relativistic approach and the rejection of the fundamental and lasting value of differences expressed through specific symbols (the headscarf as a fashion accessory, for example). Through consumption specificities, rules, traditions, and allegiances do not have an absolute value, but they hinge on specific times and places: the "ironical" consumption choice is closed to the cosmopolitan model. The cosmopolitan is the person who can apply the right codes at the appropriate times and places and with the right people. Through the grid of consumption, identifications and differences appear to be perceived as "local rules."

In our research we also noticed a different relationship with money and sometimes a critical view of the consumption style of Italian schoolmates. Saving practices particularly involve rather more complex changes in intergenerational relationships, as care-giving responsibilities between parents and their children tend to be reversed in respect to their Italian peers:

> because, you know, in order to have fun ... over there [in Santo Domingo] *you just don't need money*.... I mean ... I know a lot of friends of mine, in Italy ... and they always tell me stuff like...."Do you know what I like about your folks? ... It's that people like you, at your place, even if you happen to wake up in the morning without a penny, you can be happy anyway.... It's not like here in Italy," they used to tell me, "because we Italians ... even when we wake up with 100 euros, then we want more and more, always thinking where to find some more," and so on ... and I think it's true ... I mean ... to me ... simply staying with my boyfriend and some of his friends, that's enough to be happy ... for me ... (*Lisa, seventeen years old, in Italy for four years, born in Santo Domingo*).

> I mean ... I don't think you can just get to buy the most expensive stuff, as the first thing ... you know ... I'd just think to what I might need ... yes ... just that in the beginning ... (*Alex, sixteen years old, in Italy for twelve years, born in Russia*).

Our research shows a particular socializing process into Italian commercial culture that seems to be far from a linear process of "acculturation" into Western consumption culture, following rather more the path of a situated encounter between the commodities they find in the consumer society and the embodied experience they bring with them from their families and personal experience of migration.

However, if consumption styles seem to confirm the presence of transnational, hyphenated, and cosmopolitan attitudes, there is another domain, that of citizenship, in which the problem of boundaries becomes a more evident matter of inclusion and exclusion. If consumption can create symbolic spaces of freedom and the self-construction of identifications, the legal issue of citizenship is still relevant for the effective recognition of civil, political, and social rights.

THE CLAIM FOR CITIZENSHIP AMONG THE CHILDREN OF IMMIGRANTS

The part of the research dedicated to citizenship tried to understand how the children of immigrants – either born in Italy or who arrived during their childhood – represent and claim citizenship, how much they are interested in claiming it, what kind of motivation they advance for its achievement, how they value it. The research dwells on the idea of citizenship presented by the children themselves.[20]

Due to a long emigration history, the idea of citizenship in Italy is deeply rooted in a *jus sanguinis* perspective, valuing blood community ties more than the free will to participate in its construction. So, for the children – second, third, or even fourth generation – of Italian emigrants living abroad and with only sporadic ties with the Italian life, it is easier to obtain Italian citizenship than for youths born in Italy with foreign parents who have never left Italy in their lives. The children of immigrants born in Italy can ask for Italian citizenship when they come of age, but it is only granted if they can demonstrate that they have lived in Italy without interruptions throughout their childhood. The arbitrariness of the recognition of citizenship is always high, and, even for children who fulfill all the request criteria, there is no guarantee of success.

It is also important to highlight that all immigrants who wish to stay in Italy legally (including those under age) have to ask regularly for a permit that requires a long bureaucratic process. This permit needs to be renewed periodically; this often means extenuating queues and a long list of necessary documents. The time required for renewal is long, and it is not unusual to receive the official renewal a few months before its date of expiry. People whose permit is near to its expiry date may have huge problems returning to Italy after a trip abroad.

Due to the bureaucratic complexity and arbitrariness of obtaining an official permit to stay in Italy for anybody not considered part of the blood Italian community, it is not surprising that all the children of immigrants interviewed show a strong interest in obtaining Italian citizenship.

Our interviewees often just see citizenship as a way of obtaining (useful if not necessary) formal documents, particularly represented by the passport, for the practical advantages they can assure.

The practical dimension of citizenship is overwhelming: it allows one to live legitimately and without an excessive grade of discrimination. Citizenship is first of all a *document*, attesting the recognition of equality, the possibility to be considered a human being, attesting the rights to *exist*, to *stay*, and to *live* legally in a specific place.

The emphasis on the *legal* dimension of citizenship, on its ties with a legal permission to stay in Italy, is easy to understand if the context of long and uncertain bureaucratic procedures is taken into consideration. The children of immigrants, especially those born in Italy, consider their obligation to have a permit to stay regularly in the country an unequal and oppressive request, making a not understandable or justifiable distinction between them and their peers with Italian parents, who are perceived as similar, and with whom they share the same everyday life, the same style of life, and the same dreams for the future.

In its formal dimension, citizenship is considered above all an instrumental resource. It allows the children of immigrants to *stay* legally in Italy and bypass the bureaucratic procedures outlined above and to be considered equal to their Italian peers, especially concerning the opportunity to *travel*, a right that is regarded as a fundamental and sacred freedom of all human beings.

As a right to stay and to travel, citizenship has to do with mundane, daily questions. Nonetheless, this everyday dimension can have central relevance and affect many other aspects of personal experiences:

> With citizenship comes the possibility to vote ... identity papers, so I can go everywhere in Europe without showing my passport. ... Then there is also the passport that allows you to travel easier ... so, they are ... we can say they are small things, but they can also turn over a new leaf (*Loum, born in Italy, with parents from Senegal, waiting for Italian citizenship*).

Citizenship also represents an important document for recognition and participation. The right to be recognized as members of a specific community, to be entitled to all the rights connected with that belonging, to be legitimate to stay and to have a say, to participate in taking common decisions, all represent concrete factors for inclusion or exclusion. Even more so, citizenship – that is, recognition as member of a specific group, the right to stay in a specific place and the right to travel without excessive restrictions – is considered as a central element of *personal capacity:*[21] a set of resources a subject can use in order to think of herself and to act as a subject, to be recognized as a subject by others, and to invest energy into her personal realization as a human being. Citizenship, from this point of view, represents not only a strategic instrumental document but also a prerequisite for full and concrete *agency.*

As well as these things citizenship represents a relevant and needed element for adequate personal recognition. Without citizenship, in many situations, an individual is not considered as a person. So citizenship constitutes a central element for self-definition and a required resource for a complete and nondiscriminating recognition; it not only conserves a strong relevance for its instrumental and formal dimensions, but it also represents a vital issue for the symbolic dimension.

> To have citizenship also means to be treated in a different way; I would like to have Italian citizenship. It would be great; if I had Italian citizenship, maybe at customs they see I have an Italian passport and they would let me go by without stopping me; usually they stop me and check me; with Italian citizenship I would seem one of them ... and then they see at you from another point of view, they look at you as a person (*Albena, born in Bulgaria, in Italy since she was ten years old*).

Citizenship is still important because it entitles one to a series of political and social rights that cannot be otherwise fully guaranteed at a supranational or local level; it is also important in order to be recognized as "equal" in the right to be present in a particular place and to participate in community life.

This second aspect is particularly relevant for the youths born in Italy. For them, citizenship as a recognition "to be Italian" is something "natural," due. Non-recognition of this belonging is seen as groundless discrimination.

Citizenship allows actual participation in community life, it allows personal agency, to have a say in common decisions. Citizenship ensures the capability to shape the form of the future, to affect the definition of situations; it allows one to make oneself heard, to express preferences, to fully exercise the *voice* option.[22] Without citizenship, it is impossible to be the master of one's own future, impossible to participate equally, impossible to be a protagonist, an auto-directed subject. Of course, in many cases, citizenship alone does not prevent discrimination. Phenotypic traits matter and dark skin or almond-shaped eyes are often reasons for racist comments, vilification practices, and inordinate police controls. Having Italian citizenship does not eliminate experiencing racism, but not having it is perceived as a form of unjustifiable discrimination.

In this case, the denial of citizenship is perceived as a significant reduction of personal resources, the set of tools allowing people concretely to exercise their capacity of agency, to give form to the contexts in which they operate in order to adapt to their necessities and goals. A person who is not allowed to have a voice and to participate is not only stigmatized by a discriminating difference but is also deprived of her essential capability of agency and autonomy. She is dispossessed of the possibility to participate – on equal terms – in building her life and her future.

THE AMBIVALENT TIES BETWEEN CITIZENSHIP AND IDENTIFICATION

While the importance given to the formal recognition of citizenship and participation in community life evidences how the "classical" dimension of citizenship could still be relevant,[23] the ties between citizenship and identification seem more articulated and more complex. Identification is felt as something deeper, more personal, and more complex than the formal recognition of political and social rights or respect for the possibility to participate. Even if citizenship represents a central, often perceived as fundamental, part of the identity construction processes, it is not able to express the complex articulation and the dynamic, contextual dimension of personal loyalties and belongings by itself.

> I'm happy to have Italian citizenship. . . . When I think that my father came here a long time ago, he worked hard, he made a lot of things, and only at the end got citizenship, I mean, I did nothing to have citizenship. . . . It's a great thing to have Italian citizenship, but at the same time my origin is always Egyptian, I mean, also if someone said to me, "No, you are no more Egyptian," I always feel Egyptian. . . . It is not a paper that can change my feelings. . . . It's the same for the Italian side; I would also feel Italian if I didn't have citizenship, because I have been living here for a long time now, I stay here, I know how people live here, I know how to speak to the people . . . so I feel Italian and also Egyptian (*Silvana, born in Egypt, in Italy since she was three years old and with dual citizenship: Italian and Egyptian*).

Mostly, citizenship first and foremost makes sense as an *additional* recognition. For this reason, it recognizes the Italian side without forcing anyone to give up other identifications and other ties. Citizenship cannot be considered as an abandonment of previous identification in order to embrace a new one. On the contrary, it is seen as the necessary deploying of the irreducibility of one's own identity into a unique dimension. Double citizenship constitutes the recognition of the deeper character of identity, inevitably hybrid and plural:

> Look, I really feel like this: Italian and Moroccan . . . because after all . . . I'm what I'm . . . I mean, also if I say "I'm of this or that extraction" . . . at the end, everyone can see that I'm in this way: Italian and Moroccan. . . . Yes, and after all I like it . . . I love my culture, I love the fact that I'm Arabic, I'm proud of this, I don't want to keep it secret. So, yes, I'm Italian and Moroccan. . . . I strongly feel Italian too; otherwise, I wouldn't have all this hope of obtaining Italian citizenship (*Kenza, born in Morocco, in Italy since she was two years old*).

Citizenship is never fully equivalent to identity; the youths interviewed make a sharp distinction between, on one side, the recognition of formal rights and the bureaucratic dimensions that legitimate their presence in a specific community and, on the other side, their feeling of belonging and national identification. While the first factors can have direct influences on the personal capabilities and life conditions, the second ones have to do with the symbolic and affective dimensions. These two aspects of citizenship are not necessarily in conflict with each other, but the indispensable recognition of equality and human rights cannot be reduced to the constraint to have one single passport or to the request for total loyalty and total recognition of a unique national belonging:

> Citizenship has to do with the future you are going to construct, both for yourself and your children. If you want to have your future in Italy, you have to be a citizen; you cannot say, "I live here," without thinking about having citizenship. Citizenship means that you are part of that community, that you are engaged with and committed to that community. Citizenship means that you have all the rights and all the duties of being a member of that community. After that, if you want to conserve your ties with the place where you were born, that is another question. In this case there is always a tie.... In my opinion, citizenship and identity are not strongly tied to each other, because, if I take Italian citizenship, I still remain what I am, I still hold all the ties with the country where I was born. I don't change as a person. To be a person is not connected to a document upon which it is written who I am. Citizenship is just bureaucratic stuff, which can help you both at the economic level and for better integration with other people, but what you are is bound to your family, the place where you were born, where you come from (*Amed, born in Egypt, in Italy since she was eight years old*).

So, in our interviewees' narrations, we often find a clear distinction between these two dimensions of identity (recognition and belonging) that are perceived as acting on two different planes and are differently connected with citizenship.

While citizenship is perceived as an indispensable and central element for complete recognition – and its absence represents one of the mainly contemporary forms of discrimination for most of the children of immigrants born in Italy – on the other hand, it represents only one of the multiple constitutive elements that make up identification and belonging. These are always plural, differentiated, open to change, and adaptable to the situation, fully coherent with the everyday experience of living in contexts that are changeable and dynamic; that multiply social positions, networks, and reference groups; and that require a plurality of involvements and the continuing ability to adapt one's own position and identification.

On the basis of the interviews, it is possible to affirm that citizenship is still considered very important by the children of immigrants born or raised in Italy. Citizenship is still fundamental for the right to *stay*, to be *present* legitimately – that is, to be allowed to participate, on grounds of equal consideration and recognition, in common daily life. To be able to participate in the definition of the everyday contexts of life, to have *voice* and to have the opportunity of expressing real agency are all central elements for a full development of personal capacity and to construct a complete and autonomous identity. But the ties between citizenship and identification seem more complex. On the one hand, citizenship seems to be a relevant element for personal identity, something "evident" and "natural," something people have to recognize without asking proof of loyalty or complete identification. The simple fact of being born or living in a specific community, with the will to stay and to participate, should be enough to obtain citizenship, which is detached from any strong tie with blood or ancestral loyalty. On the other hand, citizenship cannot fulfill the complexity of contemporary identification; identity is perceived as always in progress, dynamic, changing with contexts, goals, and public. A satisfying identification is always plural, made of different elements that come from different experiences and different networks.

People must have the opportunity to have full citizenship – that is, the right to be included, to be a part of a process, to be a protagonist – without having to give up their most personal specificity. To be able to manage inclusion, mostly based on an equal recognition, and differentiation, mostly based on the possibility to be different, constitutes a necessary skill for becoming a person, a master of one's own future. The possibility of claiming both the similarity given by citizenship and the difference tied to a presumed original specificity constitutes a necessary resource for developing real agency.[24]

People learn to use citizenship's claim to support inclusion requests, asking for equal recognition, and to combat discrimination and racism, using difference to support personal recognition and respect, or to support their own goals:[25]

> I usually introduce myself as Egyptian, because I'm not a really Italian . . . I mean, yes, I am because I was born here, I spent all my life here, but actually my origins are Egyptian. . . . I always introduce myself as Egyptian, but if I find a guy

who offends foreigners, then I say, "Listen to me, I'm Italian too; you shouldn't behave in that way." . . . With people with prejudices it is important to show your passport and say, "Look, I'm an Italian citizen" (*Moussa, born in Italy with Egyptian parents*).

These youngsters learn to consider culture and traditions as important but not rigid. The capacity to stay tuned in with the context is more important than showing an irreducible coherence. To be able to understand the right code to be used in each specific situation to avoid exclusion or discrimination is a diffused skill:

> Parents' traditions should never be forgotten, because knowing where we come from is to know the history of mankind. Why do we study history? To know what humans did before, the same as with the history of our parents. For me, it's important to know tradition, but it is also important to be able to fit into every situation. It's a fusion of these two aspects: to be able to come to terms with life, never forgetting where we come from. It's what I'm trying to do (*Titus, born in the Philippines, in Italy since he was eight years old*).

> I don't think people should be too attached to their traditions, I mean, people have to learn to fit in, as I do . . . to fit into Italian culture and not to impose his own. I'm not saying that people have to give up their culture, but they have to know how to adapt it in order to fit the context (*David, born in Peru, in Italy since he was three years old*).

CONCLUDING REMARKS

From our research it emerges that the majority of the children of immigrants present in Italy are usually able to use their difference as a resource: the boundaries of their identifications are permeable, their consumption choices and their descriptions of themselves are demotic and context-related. The characteristics of Italian context – with its later, pluralist, and scattered immigration fluxes – and the postindustrial and globalized historical phase in which the second generation has grown up can, at least partially, explain such attitudes.

Despite this, we have seen that citizenship and equal opportunities are still a fundamental matter and a potential source of disappointments and conflicts. The recognition of Italian citizenship represents an important aspect for identification: it is part of their feeling "Italian," being very much like their "native" peers for capability, lifestyle, and projects for the future. But it is rarely enough: this aspect of their identification needs to be completed with new meanings, new loyalties, and new belongings that do not dismiss Italian identification but make it more complex and more articulated.[26] The specifics of their social position are expressed by thinking of themselves through composite categories – Egyptian *and* Italian; Chinese *and* Italian, etc. – to show multiple identification and a plurality of belongings, identifications and belongings that cannot be easily summarized in a unique category. They show a strong tension toward inclusion and, for this reason, active participation, without having to homologize completely to the majority patterns and rules. A certain degree of difference is as important as equality because it constitutes a specific "mark" that can improve personal resources and capabilities. To be both Italians *and* foreigners does not constitute a claim for the recognition of an incommensurable and insuperable diversity; rather, it means to be part of the mainstream without giving up one's own specificity. It is relevant when it works as a relational tool rather than as a stigma.

To be able to conserve a certain grade of continuity with the parents' traditions does not assume the form of a *symbolic ethnicity,*[27] a pure individualistic expression of identity and belonging that can be felt without having to be incorporated in everyday behavior and without involving undue interference in other aspects of life. Neither does it assume the form of an *instrumental ethnicity* – as supporters of segmented assimilation theory are inclined to think – a shelter, a protected space in which people can find both protection from outside hostility and resources for their personal social success.

Rather, it highlights the space for a possible *tactic ethnicity,* that is, an ethnicity that takes contexts into account, which can use different languages in different situations. Tactic ethnicity is instrumental as well as reactive. Tactic is characterized by the capacity to fit contexts, to find tricks to achieve a goal, to take advantage of the circumstances, to thread its way when it finds a small opening. So tactic ethnicity is neither a completely auto-directed project nor a totally hetero-directed imposition. Rather, it signals a continuing tension toward the construction of multiple identities that are ongoing processes and always subject to redefinition, identities that can be sectionalized and differentiated on the basis of situations, actors, and goals. Its essential aim is "to be everywhere at the center" or "to be everywhere at home."

All this is quite evident in the case of consumption styles. Managing ambivalence is more important than coherence: to fit the context in order not to reduce personal chances is more relevant than showing an integrity that is not affected by the situation. Tactic ethnicity can be built with changing raw materials, and it is always ready to change, to select, to distill from plural references.

Being able to use difference, identification, and belonging in a tactic way does not mean that children of immigrants are totally free to construct their experience and their reality as they will. They can only use meanings, symbols, languages, and practices that are already there in the contexts in which they act and that are embedded into structural asymmetries, racist assumptions, and power differences. Nevertheless, these children of immigrants seem to learn to translate them into the specific exigencies of the different contexts, managing ambivalences and taking advantages from the complexity and plurality characterizing their particular generational position in a global and interconnected world.

NOTES

1. The study made from 2004 to 2005 involved 105 adolescents, aged between fourteen and twenty-one years old, attending Italian higher secondary school in Milan, northern Italy. A second study (2007–2008) about the consumption patterns of these young people involved one hundred students aged between sixteen and twenty-one years old. The study about the claim of citizenship (2007–2009) involved 150 young people attending high schools in Milan (during the same research, fifteen hundred questionnaires have been collected among the students – both indigenous and children of immigrants – attending the last two years of technical and professional school). Given the peculiarities of the current Italian migration situation among adolescents, only a relatively small percentage of respondents (around 25 percent) actually belong to the "second generation" of immigrants, while most of them came to Italy during childhood. When selecting prospective respondents, we tried to mirror the various ethnic and national origins characterizing the current picture of Italian schools. For a presentation of methodology and main results, see Enzo Colombo and Paola Rebughini, *Children of Immigrants in a Globalized World: A Generational Experience* (Basingstoke: Palgrave, 2013); Enzo Colombo, Luisa Leonini, and Paola Rebughini, "Different but Not Stranger: Everyday Collective Identifications among Adolescent Children of Immigrants in Italy," *Journal of Ethnic and Migration Studies* 35.1 (2009): 37–59.

2. Martin Baldwin-Edwards and Joaquin Arango, eds., *Immigrants and the Informal Economy in Southern Europe* (London: Frank Cass, 1999); Enrico Pugliese, *L'Italia tra migrazioni internazionali e migrazioni interne* (Bologna: Il Mulino, 2002); Nikos Papastergiadis, *The Tur-*

bulence of Migration (Cambridge: Polity Press, 2000).

3. Karl Mannheim, "The Problem of Generations," in *Collected Works of Karl Mannheim,* vol. 5 (London: Routledge, 1997), 276–320.

4. Richard Alba and Victor Nee, "Rethinking Assimilation Theory for a New Era of Immigration," *International Migration Review* 31.4 (1997); Herbert J. Gans, "Toward a Reconciliation of 'Assimilation' and 'Pluralism': The Interplay of Acculturation and Ethnic Retention," *International Migration Review* 31.4 (1997); Rogers Brubaker, "The Return of Assimilation? Changing Perspectives on Immigration and Its Sequels in France, Germany, and the United States," *Ethnic and Racial Studies* 24.4 (2001).

5. Alejandro Portes, ed., *The New Second Generation* (New York: Russell Sage Foundation, 1996); Alejandro Portes, Patricia Fernández-Kelly, and William Haller, "The Adaption of the Immigrant Second Generation in America: A Theoretical Overview and Recent Evidence," *Journal of Ethnic and Migration Studies* 35.7 (2009).

6. Nancy Foner, "The Immigrant Family: Cultural Legacies and Cultural Changes," *International Migration Review* 31.4 (1997); Alejandro Portes, "Immigration Theory for a New Century: Some Problems and Opportunities," *International Migration Review* 31.4 (1997); Min Zhou, "Growing Up American: The Challenge Confronting Immigrant Children and Children of Immigrants," *Annual Review of Sociology* 23 (1997).

7. Alejandro Portes and Julia Sensenbrenner, "Embeddedness and Immigration: Notes on the Social Determinants of Economic Action," *American Journal of Sociology* 98.6 (1993).

8. Alejandro Portes and Rubén G. Rumbaut, "Introduction: The Second Generation and the Children of Immigrants Longitudinal Study," *Ethnic and Racial Studies* 28.6 (2005).

9. Maurizio Ambrosini, *La fatica di integrarsi* (Bologna: Il Mulino, 2001).

10. Peggy Levitt and Nina Glick Schiller, "Conceptualizing Simultaneity: A Transnational Social Field Perspective on Society," *International Migration Review* 38.3 (2004).

11. Peter Kivisto, "Theorizing Transnational Immigration: A Critical Review of Current Efforts," *Ethnic and Racial Studies* 24.4 (2001).

12. Arjun Appadurai, *Modernity at Large: Cultural Dimensions of Globalization* (Minneapolis: University of Minnesota Press, 1996).

13. Thomas Faist, *The Volume and Dynamics of International Migration and Transnational Social Spaces* (Oxford: Oxford University Press, 2000); Steven Vertovec, "Conceiving and Researching Transnationalism," *Ethnic and Racial Studies* 22.2 (1999).

14. Stuart Hall, "New Ethnicities," in *Stuart Hall: Critical Dialogues in Cultural Studies,* ed. David Morley and Kuan-Hsing Chen (London: Routledge, 1996).

15. Cornel West, "The New Cultural Politics of Difference," in *Out There: Marginalization and Contemporary Cultures,* ed. Russell Fergusson, Martha Gever, Trinh Minh-ha, and Cornel West (Cambridge, MA: MIT Press, 1992); Floya Anthias, "New Hybridities, Old Concepts: The Limits of 'Culture,'" *Ethnic and Racial Studies* 24.4 (2001).

16. Michel de Certeau, *The Practice of Everyday Life* (Berkeley: University of California Press, 1984).

17. John Brewer and Frank Trentmann, eds., *Consuming Cultures, Global Perspectives: Historical Trajectories, Transnational Exchanges* (Oxford: Berg, 2006).

18. Pamela Perry, "White Means Never Having to Say You're Ethnic: White Youth and the Construction of 'Cultureless' Iden-

tities," *Journal of Contemporary Ethnography* 30.1 (2001); Paola Rebughini, "Consommation et cultures de la différence chez les jeunes descendants d'immigrés: le cas Italien," *Revue Européenne des Migrations Internationales* 27.2 (2011).

19. Richard Rorty, *Contingency, Irony and Solidarity* (Cambridge: Cambridge University Press, 1989).

20. Enzo Colombo, "Changing Citizenship: Everyday Representations of Membership, Belonging and Identification among Italian Senior Secondary School Students," *Italian Journal of Sociology of Education* 4.1 (2010); Enzo Colombo, Lorenzo Domaneschi, and Chiara Marchetti, "Citizenship and Multiple Belonging: Representations of Inclusion, Identification and Participation among Children of Immigrants in Italy," *Journal of Modern Italian Studies* 16.3 (2011).

21. Alberto Melucci, *The Playing Self* (Cambridge: Cambridge University Press, 1996), 52.

22. Albert O. Hirschman, *Exit, Voice, and Loyalty* (Cambridge, MA: Harvard University Press, 1970).

23. Rogers Brubaker, "Immigration, Citizenship, and the Nation-State in France and Germany: A Comparative Historical Analysis," *International Sociology* 5 (1990); Irene Bloemraad, "Who Claims Dual Citizenship? The Limits of Postnationalism and the Persistence of Traditional Citizenship," *International Migration Review* 38.2 (2004).

24. Melissa Butcher, "Universal Processes of Cultural Change: Reflections on the Identity Strategies of Indian and Australian Youth," *Journal of Intercultural Studies* 25.3 (2004); Anita Harris, "Shifting the Boundaries of Cultural Spaces: Young People and Everyday Multiculturalism," *Social Identities* 15.2 (2009).

25. Giovanni Semi, Enzo Colombo, Ilenya Camozzi, and Annalisa Frisina, "Practices of Difference: Analysing Multiculturalism in Everyday Life," in *Everyday Multiculturalism*, ed. Amanda Wise and Selvaraj Velayutham (London: Palgrave, 2009).

26. Colombo et al., "Different but Not Stranger."

27. Herbert Gans, "Symbolic Ethnicity: The Future of Ethnic Groups and Cultures in America," *Ethnic and Racial Studies* 2.1 (1979).

NINE

Possible Love: New Cross-cultural Couples in Italy

GAIA PERUZZI

CROSS-CULTURAL[1] COUPLES ARE ONE OF THE MOST EMBLEMATIC examples of the transformation resulting from the union between natives and immigrants living together in the same territory. In fact, a man and a woman of different nationalities and cultural backgrounds who decide to live together are a living laboratory of the building of multiple identities, a challenge to the mentalities and the conservative traditions of the local societies, a political project for the cohabitation of diversities grounded on the backbone of all human societies: the family. It is not by chance that the historian Fernand Braudel affirmed that there is no integration without intermarriage.[2]

At the end of the first decade of the new millennium, binational couples are also an emerging phenomenon in Italy, thus announcing crucial changes in the social and cultural life of the country. What are the specific characteristics of these unions in comparison to those formed by two Italian partners?

This article attempts to answer these questions by using data from two sources. First, profiles of the new mixed couples as they emerge from the most recent statistics (made available by ISTAT, the Italian National Institute of Statistics[3]) of marriages celebrated in the country will be sketched out. Second, this paper will explore the problems, the choices, and the negotiations of the protagonists of these experiences through the stories of eleven couples that have been collected by the author between 2005 and 2008. All the couples, whether married or "only" living together, were formed by an Italian man or woman and a foreign partner. Keeping the newness of the topic in mind, the research was conceived

Table 9.1. Typology of marriages celebrated in Italy, 2008

Types of couples					
Marriages with wife and husband both Italian	Marriages with at least one foreign partner	*Italian husband and foreign wife*	*Foreign husband and Italian wife*	*Wife and husband both foreign*	Total marriages
Absolute values					
209,695	36,918	*18,240*	6,308	*12,370*	246,613
Percentage values					
85	15	7.4	2.6	5	100

Source: ISTAT 2010

as an exploration, and the sample included many different nationalities.[4] All the couples lived in Tuscany, a region in central Italy characterized by relevant rates of immigrants and binational marriages. More, all the families lived in mid-sized to small towns: this choice was made to privilege the dimension of provinces, which is a typical Italian context. For each couple, the researcher interviewed separately (but using the same questions) both partners, when possible at their home. The analysis of these life stories will be organized along the *fil rouge* of age difference and gender that will emerge as unavoidable variables as explained in the following paragraph.

NEW ENTRIES IN THE ITALIAN MARRIAGE MARKET

How many binational couples are there in Italy today? The administrative and census sources available in Italy do not offer a precise answer to this question. We are only provided with the flux data about new marriages celebrated annually in the country.

According to the national statistics published by ISTAT this year, in 2008, out of 246,000 new registered marriages, there were 36,918 unions made involving a foreign partner, that is, 15 percent.[5] A glance at the tendencies of the last two decades makes these data more significant.

In 1996, new marriages involving a foreign partner were little more than 4 percent of all new marriages; after four years, they reached 7 percent; in 2003, they exceeded 10 percent; and in 2006, they made up 14 percent of all marriages. Clearly, the presence of foreigners in the Italian marriage market is increasing rapidly.

For some years, new mixed marriages involving an Italian and a foreign partner have been regularly divided into the following proportions: three out of four binational couples are formed by an Italian husband and a foreign wife, while only one out of four is formed by an Italian wife and an immigrant partner. As shown in Table 9.1, the data from 2008 do not present an exception to this rule. It is evident that marriage is a way to integration in the Italian society more accessible to foreign women than to foreign men: immigrant women are better able to penetrate private spheres of Italian people, and, on the other side, Italian families seem to accept more easily a foreign woman than a foreign man entering their houses (in questions of love as in domestic work). Moreover, it must be borne in mind that the presence of men and women is not balanced in the foreign national groups: seeing the first twenty immigrant nationalities in Italy, the groups characterized by a great woman's prevalence are Ukraine, Poland, Moldova, Peru, and Ecuador, while Morocco, Tunisia, and Egypt are the most important fluxes with a stronger male presence. It is clear that cultures from East Europe and South America are closer to Italian society than those from North Africa and Asia, probably another reason that the number of foreign women married to Italian men is three times the number of Italian women with immigrant men.

The distribution of binational marriages within the country is quite heterogeneous.

The majority of mixed marriages between an Italian man or woman and a foreign partner are in northern Italy (27.6 percent), with the region of Liguria being at the top of the list (15.4 percent). While all regions of central Italy (Tuscany, Umbria, Marche, and Lazio) are already "mixed," in southern Italy and in the islands (Sardinia and Sicily), the numbers of binational marriages collapse. Puglia, the heel of the boot, is the back marker with just 4.1 percent of binational marriages celebrated there in 2008. Moreover, big cities like Rome and Milan have higher concentrations of binational marriages than do rural or provincial contexts.

When we consider the profiles of these couples, we can immediately see that the mixing processes on this sphere proceed along specific

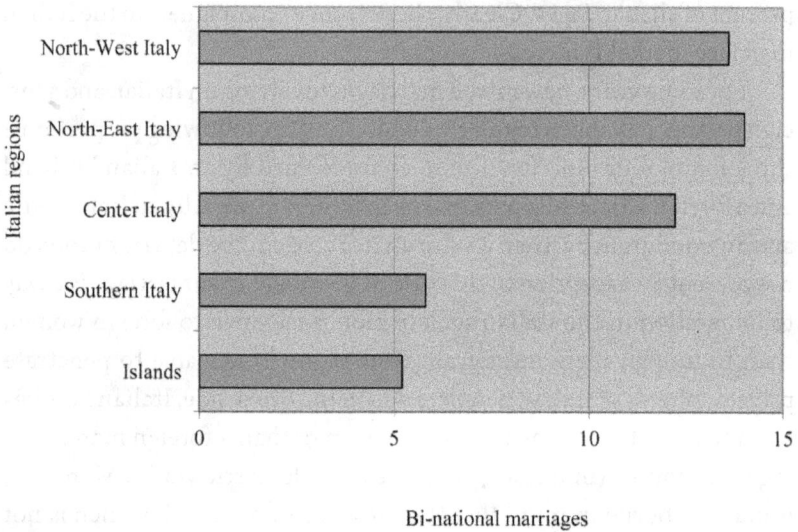

Figure 9.1. Distribution of binational marriages in Italy, 2008. *Data from Istat (2010).*

routes. In fact, only some foreign nationalities participate in the local marriage market.

The large majority of immigrant brides come from Eastern Europe: the Romanians, Ukrainians, Poles, Russians, and Albanians dominate the Italian marriage market. Latino women of Central and South America, particularly Brazilians, Ecuadoreans, and Cubans, belong to the second-largest category of foreign wives. By contrast, many immigrant husbands of Italian women come from North Africa (Moroccans, Tunisians, and Egyptians together make up 37 percent of all immigrant men partners). The second large area of origin of foreign male partners is Eastern Europe, lead by Albania or Romania. Table 9.2 clearly shows that the great majority of foreign partners come from the countries characterized by strong pressure to migrate. It is important to remember that, according to the Islam religion, a Muslim woman cannot marry a non-Muslim man: this is the reason that we find only an African nationality (Morocco) in the first column of Table 9.2.

The last statistics from ISTAT that we are analyzing do not make available the data about the age of the newlyweds. However, let us consider all the other data presented in this article that seems to confirm

Table 9.2. First ten nationalities of foreign partners in binational marriages with an Italian husband or wife, Italy, 2008

Italian husband with foreign wife Wife's nationality / Percentage values		Italian wife with foreign husband Husband's nationality / Percentage values	
Romania	13.7	Morocco	22.2
Ukraine	10.6	Albania	9.0
Brazil	9.6	Tunisia	7.6
Poland	6.7	Egypt	6.1
Former Soviet Union	5.3	Brazil	4.6
Moldova	4.7	Senegal	4.5
Morocco	4.5	United Kingdom	4.3
Albania	4.0	Germany	2.9
Peru	2.7	France	2.8
Ecuador	2.4	United States	2.8

Source: ISTAT 2010

many constant tendencies in the profile of these couples. Various surveys are in agreement that marriages between an Italian partner and a foreign man or woman are typically characterized by larger age gaps than the unions formed by only Italians.[6] That being the case, we will also report some information regarding this aspect.

Native Italian couples are generally made up of husband and wife of a similar age: that is, a maximum difference of three years. Sometimes the husband is five or six years older; only in rare cases, he is more than ten years older. The binational relationships are generally characterized by much wider age gaps between the partners.

More specifically, the widest gap is registered in the marriages of the type Italian husband–immigrant wife. Indeed, in many couples, he is ten or more years older than she, and there are relevant percentages of cases in which the husband is even twenty or more years older. On the other hand, even though the gaps are less accentuated in the case of marriages between Italian wives and foreign husbands, there are still two-digit percentages of wives who are older than their foreign partners; this is a very infrequent case in the unions among local people. It is important to point out that these anomalous age asymmetries only concern marriages between foreign people and Italians, but not the couples in which both partners are immigrants. So, the gaps seem to be a characteristic of this mixing.

Table 9.3. Education level of partners in different types of marriages, Italy, 2008

Husband's education level	Level of instruction of the wife				
	University	High school	Junior high	Primary	Total
Percentage values					
BOTH ITALIAN PARTNERS					
University degree	51.1	9.7	2.7	3.4	15.6
High school diploma	37.9	67.5	17.8	7.7	46.9
Junior high school diploma	10.4	22.2	75.8	26.3	34.7
Primary school diploma	0.6	0.6	3.7	62.6	2.8
Total	100	100	100	100	100
ITALIAN HUSBAND and FOREIGN WIFE					
University degree	28.9	9.7	2.5	3.5	10.8
High school diploma	34.2	55.2	18.4	13.8	35.8
Junior high school diploma	29.8	30.2	71.5	41.1	43.6
Primary school diploma	7.1	4.9	7.6	41.6	9.8
Total	100	100	100	100	100
FOREIGN HUSBAND and ITALIAN WIFE					
University degree	59.3	12.7	10.3	12.7	19
High school diploma	29.0	60.1	19.5	12.3	35.7
Junior high school diploma	8.7	22.4	56.0	24.4	33.6
Primary school diploma	3.0	4.8	14.3	50.6	11.7
Total	100	100	100	100	100

Source: ISTAT 2010

Statistics show that the level of education is also a very interesting variable: in fact, while in the couples formed only by indigenous people, the woman is inclined to marry a man with an equal level of education or immediately higher, there are very different percentages in the binational marriages.

In 2008, 90 percent of Italian wives with a primary school diploma married a man with no more than a junior high school diploma; almost 94 percent of Italian women with a junior high school qualification married a man with the same diploma or a high school diploma; more than 77 percent of wives with a high school diploma married a man with a high school diploma or a university degree. Finally, half of the Italian wives with university degrees chose a husband with an equal level of education, and 38 percent chose a partner who had an immediately lower level of education.

It appears evident from the third table that the mixed couples are more heterogeneous.

When the woman is an immigrant, the percentages we have just seen decisively go down: foreign brides who married Italian men with an equal or a directly higher certificate are 82.7, 89.9, and 64.5 percent of the women with a diploma, respectively, from primary school, junior high school, and high school. Moreover, among the university graduates, only 29 percent of women married a fellow graduate, as 30 percent have an Italian partner with a junior high school diploma and more than 7 percent a husband who only attended primary school. The percentage of Italian women with degrees marrying Italian men with a primary school certificate is only 0.6 percent!

On the other hand, in the couples in which the man is the immigrant partner, the differences between the partners are still more accentuated and the gaps have opposite signs: 12.7 percent of Italian wives with the lowest degree and 10.3 percent of those having a junior high school diploma married foreign men with university degrees.

To complete our overview, the following graphs regarding wedding rites outline yet another interesting aspect of mixed marriages. While a vast majority (72 percent) of Italian couples chose to have a religious ceremony in 2008, binational couples chose the opposite: 85 percent of the new unions were celebrated by civil rites and only 15 percent by a prelate. The proportion is relatively the same for both types of mixed marriages involving foreign partners. Why do binational couples so often get married through a civil ceremony? Having two different religions cannot be a problem in the everyday life of the couple (as many interviewees of the qualitative research told us), but surely it is an obstacle to a religious rite. Second, for many Italian husbands, the union with a foreign partner is the second marriage.

We find differences between Italian and mixed marriages also when we consider first and second marriages. While almost 90 percent of the new Italian couples married in 2008 were having a first experience, 81.3 percent were first unions between a foreign husband and an Italian wife, and only 63.4 percent were first unions for the Italian husband and the foreign wife. The binational marriage is the second chance for many Italian men and foreign women.

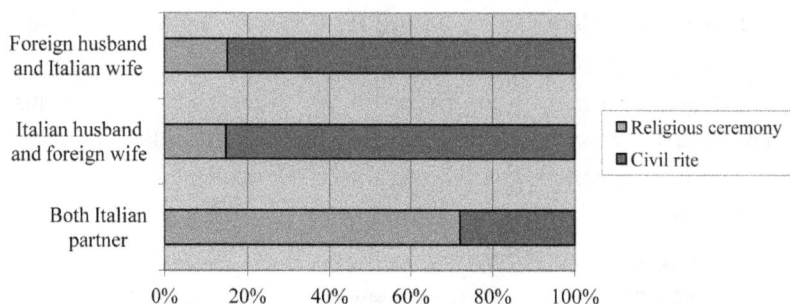

Figure 9.2. Wedding rites, Italy, 2008. *Data from Istat (2010).*

Just a note to conclude this section. Another distinctive feature of these couples seems to be their instability. The latest available statistics affirmed that the number of separations and divorces is increasing among binational couples, too. It was also calculated that the life span of a binational marriage in case of divorce is nine years, while it reaches fourteen in Italian couples.[7]

We will now attempt to explore beyond the data to discover the way in which these differences are reached by understanding the daily life of these *mixité*[8] and cross-cultural couples.

AT THE ORIGINS OF CROSS-CULTURAL LOVE

Where do Italian and immigrant men and women meet?

The stories of the partners collected by the author, together with ones of other researchers recently conducted in Italy,[9] are characterized by the recurrence of specific elements allowing us to sketch a map of fertile zones for *mixité,* considering the age of the partners and of the two genders of coupling (Italian husband and immigrant woman, Italian wife and foreign man).

Emerging from the accounts of the interviewees, we know that the majority of meeting places is common among the immigrants. First, streets, benches, bars and cafés, squares, ballrooms, and all the public places of the city dedicated to passersby and meetings. The sample protagonists of two senior couples (both of the type he Italian / she foreign) reported that they met in the street by chance.

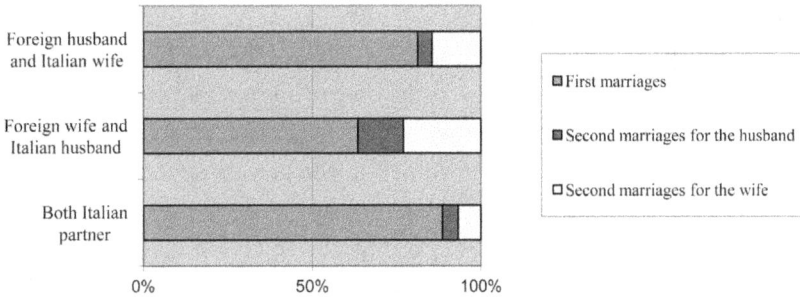

Figure 9.3. First and second marriages, Italy, 2008. *Data from Istat (2010).*

> I was waiting for a friend; we were meeting in a bar. By chance I met Mario. He
> came in and sat down at a table, and on the table, I saw a piece of paper, like a
> napkin with writing on it, saying "Bon appetite." I like learning the Italian lan-
> guage and I was reading "Bon appetite," and my [future] husband was very kind;
> smiling, he said "Yes. Yes, that's right." So I went near him and asked him some
> words and he taught me some, very kind . . . (*Zyang, Chinese, forty-five years old,
> wife of Mario, fifty-five*)

The recurring accounts of the casualness of the meetings and the
nature of these urban spaces open to mingling and mixing could be mis-
leading. Instead, by thoroughly analyzing the interviews, it has been
well understood that Italian men, particularly lonely and aged ones, and
foreign women meeting in these places probably met less by chance than
they recounted. That is, at least some of them, more or less consciously,
took into account the possibility of meeting an Italian man or an immigrant woman by spending time in these places. In Zyang's long interview,
there is a passage that perfectly exemplifies what has been stated above:

> When I arrived here [in Italy], everything was difficult for me, very difficult. I
> even went to church to ask Maria for help. . . . I am a Buddhist, I know . . . people
> say that, if you are a Buddhist, you cannot go into a church, but I think that, even
> if you are a Buddhist, God is the same; he helps poor people. . . . So I asked for
> help, that they find me an Italian job, an Italian man . . . and after fifteen days, I
> met my husband: yes, I had asked Maria for an Italian husband, and from then I
> always keep her in my heart and I still thank Maria. (*Zyang*)

For a lonely, immigrant woman, an Italian partner can represent
a chance to find an accommodation, a way to integrate into local society, even to become a citizen. In another part of the interview, Zyang

explained that an Italian husband is also a great boost in stature in the community of Chinese immigrants.

Not only is the city a crossroads where different cultures every now and then manage to intertwine, but Italians are also exposed almost daily to foreigners, especially women in the private sphere. This takes place above all in the houses where immigrant women work as house-keepers or family assistants. For example, when Guido, a university stu-dent, was thirty-one years old, he met Rosa, a Romanian woman who was three years younger than he and was working in his uncle's home:

> We met because she was working as an assistant to the elderly at my uncle's house, in the apartment above mine . . . so she didn't really pop out of nowhere; she was there working as an assistant at my uncle's house. We met for the first time while getting the bread that gets delivered to all the people in the building every day. But she was cold, all arrogant; she got on my nerves. . . . The first time that we spoke a bit was at a lunch at a relative's house . . . but she was a bit . . . I didn't really like her much. . . . She seemed nicer when I had the chance to talk to her a bit more, she was a bit less haughty than usual, always kept a little to herself; but, anyway, at my mother's birthday, when she had a party for her fiftieth birthday, we ended up, well, maybe they put us together, it seems like they put us together, beside each other. . . . My cousin made it that we ended up beside each other, because it seems that she, Rosa, wanted to get to know me. (*Guido*)

Guido's story is a meaningful example of how daily contact and a direct acquaintance can promote the meeting, communication, and mixing among native inhabitants and new residents. In fact, as clearly emerges from the report above, not only is the birth of the relationship made possible by repeated encounters, but, most importantly, the fact that Rosa already lived with a family member makes for the best antidote to the prejudices and the fears that Guido's parents and relatives might have had when the couple announced their engagement:

> The funny thing is that Rosa practically met my mum before me. Like I said, she was looking after an old lady in my uncle's house, on the floor above us. . . . Rosa almost never left the house, and it was my mum who talked to me about her, even before meeting her: "Oh, this girl is so good! She's careful, she really capable." Initially, she made a good impression on my mum and on my dad too, but less on my sister . . . but, anyway, my whole family, apart from some prejudice from some of my uncles and aunts . . . there are four families, four brothers that live in the building . . . her first impact on the family was positive, very positive. Then, when we told the others that we got together . . . apart from some of my uncles and

aunts that lived upstairs and that were quite racist, so some "little comments"...
and my dad a little cold about it, you know, a foreign girl, very noticeable...you
know? A beautiful girl...maybe one of those who was trying to set herself up by
finding a man.... my dad, it was understandable that the thing disturbed him a
bit, but...well, he didn't ever say anything...because, you know, my uncle, the
family she was working for, they were all happy, they had a great opinion of her,
they respected her a lot...because she was a hard worker.... My uncle's house,
which was a chaotic place, because there was my uncle, his mother-in-law, my
cousins, the wife had died.... the house was tremendously filthy...and she,
Rosa, when she arrived put everything in place, like new.... The old lady then,
nobody wanted her, was in a state that you could get near her because of the
stink, [Rosa] even polished her nails, she took her out, she looked like the old
lady from the ACE bleach [TV spot]....so even my family, apart from the bit of
fear at the beginning that she might be using me, well, apart from that, with her,
with her as a person, it was okay! (*Guido*)

The doubts of Guido's family about the new cross-cultural relationship are emblematic of a widespread prejudice against women coming
from Eastern Europe. As they arrive in Italy alone and quickly install
themselves in Italian houses (as domestic workers or partners of Italian
men), immigrant women from the former Soviet Union, Poland, and
Ukraine have often been labeled as exploiters and prostitutes.

The third setting for mixed meetings revealed by our research is organized by nonprofit organizations promoting intercultural exchanges
and solidarity. Four sample couples, all made up of Italian women and
foreign men, reported that they had met in this type of setting: an Arabic
language course for Italian people, a political association fighting for immigrants, a social club organizing intercultural football tournaments, a
street market frequented by many Black people. The recurrences in the
profiles and in the accounts of the partners, especially of the women,
are very strong, even curious. All these women more or less explicitly
declared that, before having met their present partners, they had an "old"
interest in the African or Eastern cultures. Then, three of them worked as
social or cultural mediators in projects aimed at immigrants. Moreover,
by considering all the stories we have the impression that the women
played the role of protagonists in the beginning of these relationships:
at least in three cases, they first approached the men or provoked the
encounters, and in all the couples, they wanted to initiate a cohabitation
sooner and with stronger conviction than their fiancés.

Well, we met because I signed up for an Arabic language course for Italians. . . .
I had wanted to study Arabic for a long time; I was fascinated with the sound,
the writing, the music . . . so, seeing that I like Battiato [an Italian singer] and
he knows Arabic things, no? Well, I had always had this passion for Arabic, I
don't know why. . . . So it happened that, one evening while speaking with some
friends, [one of them] said that she was attending this Arabic course . . . even free!
And I said, "Oh, my God! I'm coming too!" And so I went, but with a friend, not
alone . . . also, in X [she mentions a town about 20 km from where the interview
was taking place] . . . I went and, nothing, I started this Arabic course with this
teacher that, I don't know, was interesting right away . . . he was really interesting. . . . Sometimes after the lesson, we'd go to a bar to talk with all the others
from the course, and we'd talk about lots of different things, and I had a load of
fun telling him what I thought. . . . I don't know. . . . One time, for example, he was
telling us about fixed marriages or about what is taught to children [in] Qu'ranic
schools . . . because he knew the whole Qu'ran by heart, and so sometimes he'd
recite some verses. . . . I was spellbound, a little because I loved listening to him
recite, and then I'd say to myself, "God, how can he know it?" . . . So he told us
that, when he was four, he was sent to this Qu'ranic school where every week,
they were taught a verse and until they learned to recite it and to write it down
on a slab; they wouldn't go on and sometimes they were punished, understand?
Like teachers from the past that would strap you. . . . I naturally had fun telling
him that they were stupid for doing these things to children. . . . Then the
discussions would start. . . . wow, what discussions! He kept to his opinions on
religion, on culture, and on music, very Muslim position, and so this interested
me even more, and then from there . . . (*Sandra, forty-five years old, divorced with
a daughter, about her first meeting with Hibrahim, Moroccan, forty-nine*)

The passion for the exotic that frequently emerges in the interviews
materialized in an explicit reference to a physical attraction toward a
foreign man only one time, in Nicoletta's account, below. Nicoletta is
attracted by Black men and surely sought them out. She describes the relationship with a Black man as a way to know and to appropriate faraway
cultures and styles of life. But she "cannot" openly speak about her preferences because she fears to be considered a girl of loose morals: in the
Italian popular imagination, the main frame in which a Black man and a
White woman will be "explained" is surely the discourse about race and
sexuality. So, it is clear that, because of embarrassment, she only touches
on this subject. The impression of the author is that physical attraction
can play a role in these unions. Similar to the way a Black man may have
a fascination with White women, so European women seem to evoke
images of freedom and sexual coolness in African men. But from this

second front, the men's stories were still more reticent, and the analysis had to be limited to the unsaid and pending phrases.

> With Himed . . . no, it wasn't the first time I was with a foreign guy. . . . I actually had more than one . . . but they never lasted as much as with Himed. . . . First I was with a guy from Senegal, with one from Morocco, and . . . well . . . this way it sounds like . . . well, I wish this will remain anonymous, otherwise, you know, "This girl knows all these foreigners." Well, you can imagine that now it is not difficult for me to do this type of job [because] I am a cultural mediator . . . but also previously I had some problems with the thing of foreign men. . . . My mom as well was in a mixed couple . . . and, well, . . . I think Black men are really handsome . . . I think . . . what represents for me, Africa. . . . I also live through them [through the partners], and going to Senegal I understood this even better. . . . This is my feeling, when I feel the drums playing, I feel my most carnal and earthly self is being nurtured. (*Nicoletta, thirty-two years old, Italian, ex-partner of Himed, Senegalese, thirty-six years old*)

Another frontier in this geography of *mixité* is identified by the marriages of young people. It all started with the Internet for two sample couples; even in this case, they are curiously similar to each other. They are Paula and Stefano, respectively, Brazilian and Italian, thirty-one and thirty-six years old; she is a language teacher, and he is an employee. The second couple, Cintia and Gianni, twenty-four and thirty-three, have the same nationalities as the previous couple; she is a university student, and he is a future lawyer.

As in the stories we examined above, in these interviews, the womanly initiative and, above all, the greater breeziness with which the wives told of their experiences surprised the readers. While the husbands were very embarrassed to speak about the beginning of their relationships, Paula and Cintia felt more free and easily said, "We met during a chat session!" It is evident that they were both assiduous participants in chat rooms and that they conceived of the Internet simply as a medium for meeting friends at a distance, especially men.

> *How did you meet Paula?*
> Through the Internet. . . . [silence] . . . My second job is working as a computer technician; you see, I am very into computers, and . . . once I was looking for some info, for my job. . . . I opened the browser, and this other web site popped out that had nothing to do with that . . . where there was a certain Paula that, like that . . . [silence]
> *Would you often chat on the Internet?*

Never! I've always been against it! Completely against it! I even scolded some friends for joining chats online!

Excuse me, I had imagined you were passionate about it . . .

I was completely AGAINST IT! Or better: I always thought that people whom you'd meet on the Internet would be lonely people, people that . . . that basically can't find anything else. . . . that's why I don't even know why she and I are married! Anyway, she on the contrary, she spent her entire life online . . . while I was searching for things for my job, and this web site came out, and so I said to myself, "Why not try to write something?" Just to try . . . so I wrote her, she replied, we began writing, I was like being a bit stupid, you know? Here is a girl writing me, why not see who this is? Also because I like getting at the juice of things . . . so I tried videoconferencing, with a webcam. . . . Every single night we were standing in front of the computer chatting, with the webcam . . . and then there was Christmas, and it just happened that I went to Brazil! (*Stefano, Italian, thirty-six years old, software programmer, future husband of Paula*)

How did you meet Stefano?

Through the Internet. I had lots of relationships, if not exactly friendships, let's say. . . . I, since I was studying Italian in an Italian company, so I was interested in getting to know people of the Italian race. . . . I was curious to get to know him personally, an Italian man . . . but, I didn't think I would meet him this way. (*Paula, Brazilian, thirty-one years old, language teacher, future wife of Stefano*)

So, where did you meet?

Well, so . . . [silence]

Where, how, I mean, if you remember . . .

Well, to tell the truth . . . we always say in London because that's where we actually met, concretely we met there the first time . . . in London in February 2001. . . . I went to London to visit a friend, and I took advantage of the occasion . . . because, you see, actually I knew who I was going to meet . . . because we knew each other before . . . from the Internet. . . . I mean . . . I had met her in 1999 on the Internet, like, well . . . which I didn't use at all . . .

Therefore you knew her . . .

Since 1999, yes, June '99. Actually, yes, but not physically, though . . . well, she was at her home, in Brazil. . . . It was weird, weird because I always knew. . . . I don't like the Internet very much, I don't like computers in general, I never got into it, but I use them at work. . . . I fight with them daily because I don't have a lot of . . . I am not an expert. . . . But, well, I must tell the truth, in that moment, I had just come out of a tough period, and I knew that when I joined the chat . . . maybe something really good could come out of it . . . I could feel it, I can't explain why, well, . . . and, well, nothing, we just emailed each other, we exchanged pictures, "Come see me in Brazil," but I absolutely couldn't go. . . . Then in 2001, it had been already a year since we wanted to meet . . . [and] she was going to London to study abroad, so . . .

So you met...
It was ... look, it was a ... trauma. A TRAUMA. I'm telling you, it's a trauma. Because you are supposed to act like a boyfriend with the person, right? We had been in touch for two years now, for a year we spoke over the phone ... well ... but when we were there, when we met, there is the technical-practical problem that, we wouldn't even hold hands. (*Gianni, Italian, thirty-six years old, clerk, husband of Cintia*)

Where did you meet Gianni?
He must not know ... so, we met on the Internet. Then, once, two days before I arrived here, in England, he said, "Look, about this, I am going there to see a friend of mine." So I said, "Well, maybe we'll meet then. ..." Because for him chatting is for idiots, he said I should swear that I never said, so officially we met in a pub ... because actually in England we met for the first time in a pub ... and this will be the official version ... because, you see, he wasn't used to chatting, he really doesn't want to say ... while I had friends all over Brazil ... we always chatted. And he, the first time he tried, I found him immediately! (*Cintia, Brazilian, twenty-four years old, university student, wife of Gianni*)

In addition to the opportunity offered by the world of digital media, there is yet another platform for binational love that has emerged from our sample couples: the existence of transnational organizations that promote the meeting of men and women from different countries and generally organize the arrival and the settling in of the future wives in the cities of the husbands. It can be noted in pioneer studies that this is a widespread phenomenon on an international scale in which relatively formal and specialized agencies and intermediaries of different natures create complex international networks and act as channels for negotiating and organizing journeys and marriages. Legal or illegal, sometimes profit-oriented, sometimes only directed toward the maintenance and reinforcement of a group beyond national borders, these activities of mediation seem to play a more and more important role in the fluxes of contemporary migration.[10]

In these networks, the questions of love and money are mixed so easily and ambiguously that sometimes it is difficult to distinguish them from the traffic of prostitution. Moreover, these shadows contribute to creating fears about binational couples, combined unions that can deceive poor foreign women and old people.

In our story, the protagonists are Beppe, a retired man who is seventy-five years old and Kathia, a pediatrician, twenty years younger than he. The brokers are a middle-aged woman and a priest engaged in the organization of holidays in Italy for children who were victims of the Chernobyl catastrophe:

> My present wife is a result of a joke played on a woman who comes from a little town near here. This woman, who is Russian, together with the priest, who I think is not really Catholic, anyway ... were organizing trips for Russian kids holidaying with Italian families. My first wife and I hosted a Russian girl for years, seeing that we couldn't have children but loved them so much ... just think that once we even went there, in Russia, to visit her.... anyway, I've known her [the woman who organized the trips] since '91, and I've felt attached to this woman, even after my wife died, because she doesn't have a car and sometimes when she needed some favors done, she'd call me and say, "Oh, Beppe, could you bring me some things?" And I would go and take things to her. And three years ago I went to do one of these favors. She was going to Russia for Easter, and when she was about to leave, she said, "Now tell me, Beppe, are you still alone?" And I responded, "Yes, I'm alone." And then I say, "Oh, you know what you should do? Bring me one of you back, because if not I...." And so, just like that I was joking ... and I didn't think about it anymore. And instead, when she came back, she called me, "Come for a visit!" She brought me a passport, a photo, and gave me a telephone number. I say, "Excuse me, but this girl is young! Did you tell her how old I am?" She says, "I told her, listen, I told her ... she knows everything: what you're like, what you're not like ... and she wants to come to Italy. Do as you like, if you call...." And I started to dial the number. (*Beppe*)

The network filtering through Beppe would seem informal. While it would be wrong to speak about trafficking, because there are no traces of money transfers or pressures on the two partners, many elements in the entire story (the promptness with which the request of an encounter is accepted, the accuracy with which the two women had already organized many details prior to the meeting) make us perceive the lack of spontaneity in the nature of the actions that prepared the grounds for the first contact between the partners, Kathia's journey, the stay in Italy, and the marriage.

At a final glance at our map, what appears immediately to be evident from this simple classification is that the territories where the mixing processes began taking place are spaces that already were permeable, opened, and available to the contact and the meeting between natives and immigrants or, as in the last case, between distant partners.

Table 9.4. Differences within new cross-cultural couples

<<communication language	< less problematic		more problematic >		conflicts >>
	meals food and habits in meals	religion	domestic duties and women's role	money bounds and relationships with ex-partner	future perspectives

PUTTING THE *MIXITÉ* TO THE TEST IN EVERYDAY LIFE:
OLD DIFFERENCES AND NEW PROBLEMS

Which are the differences that create problems or opportunities for communication and cohabitation inside the new cross-cultural couples living in Italy today? Do they follow the same criteria transmitted to us by traditional literature on binational marriages?

This study is the report of a journey to the land of cross-cultural relationships, inside the private lives of the partners, to verify whether or not the problematic factors suggested by traditional studies (for example, differences of language, diet, religion, gender) are still topical difficulties in today's couples and, if so, to update them.

As explained before regarding the method of research used, we have tried to find answers to these questions by analyzing and comparing the stories of wives and husbands, and some ex-partners, of recent cross-cultural couples, who were all interviewed separately on the same issues. The vastness and the complexity of the project obliged us to make some choices. Because we were mainly interested in the relations between genders and generations, we focused our research on the relationships between the partners, leaving issues concerning children in the background.

Obviously, in this article, it is not possible to report all the detailed results of the inquiry, so, we will dwell on the aspects that are most influenced by the age and the dynamics between the women and the men.

The different occurrences of the same problems in the life stories of the sample led us to the building of a continuum that orders emerging elements to range from a less problematic pole, in which differences seem to stimulate curiosity and communication between the partners, to the opposite extremity, in which diversities provoke serious tensions and conflicts threatening the stability of the relationship.

More, in this continuum, we can see a crescendo of tensions from *symbolic differences* to *material issues,* that is, from some areas of the life deputed to the exchange and the socialization to the questions directly concerning the processes of individualization.

Look closer. At the left pole, we find less problematic differences, which are language and meals. Even though these are considered to be milder issues, we did find a few tracks of misunderstandings between the partners provoked by these dimensions. But, on the whole, it seems that bilingualism and the exchange of culinary cultures are, especially in the first period of the relationship, an opportunity to experience and compare two different worlds and lifestyles.

No partner explicitly spoke about conflicts caused by using two languages. Instead, all women, both Italian and foreign, said that they were interested or engaged in learning their husbands' languages. Learning Italian is an obsession for Kathia, who is Russian. It is as if only a perfect mastery of the new language could assure her a good job and full integration into this new context. Every night before going to sleep, she compels her elderly husband to repeat together the lessons she has been studying during the day. Maria often reproaches her boyfriend Patrick, who is Senegalese and does not speak Italian fluently, although he has been in Italy for many years. By contrast, Rosa, who is Romanian, speaks Italian very well. She confessed that she is often afraid of making a bad impression in public because of her Romanian accent. Other researchers reported analogous examples among new immigrants in Italy of what we define as an out-and-out determination for assimilation demonstrated by some women and foreign groups.[11] It is interesting to note that the answers of men were completely different: no Italian man declared himself to be interested in knowing the original language of his foreign wife, and no immigrant male partner was overly involved in learning the Italian language as eagerly as were the foreign women.

The food and meal habits seem to be another possible field of experimentation for new cross-cultural practices. Similar to the point mentioned above, women are more enthusiastic promoters of the mixing processes. In fact, all the partners of foreign men wanted to learn to cook African or Asian food; sometimes, they had tried doing it even before having met the foreign husband.

When analyzing the behaviors of the partners in the kitchen, we found some differences related to the age of the interviewees. The younger ones appeared to be more willing to experiment with new dishes and diets, whereas older partners, especially Italian men, declared themselves to be rather unwilling to change their customs after marrying a foreign wife. If necessary, they preferred to find separate solutions. However, even in these cases, all the problems in our families were rapidly solved:

> I was already cooking, even before meeting Patrick, food that was a bit Oriental, I mean different . . . vegetables, for example, a little strange. He doesn't like it. . . . He absolutely loves pasta, even more than me. Look, he's awfully Italian, a real *Italian*! Now, when he goes to Senegal, he takes . . . it's crazy! He would take spaghetti in his suitcase . . . like Italians in the old days, you know. They used to have spaghetti in their suitcases. . . . He takes pasta because he dies for spaghetti, garlic, oil and hot pepper . . . he'd eat it every day! (*Maria, thirty-one years old, partner of Patrick, Senegalese*)

> Each of us eats what we like: if Zyang wants to make Chinese food for herself, she does. If she wants to go to a restaurant, she does. When we eat together, at home, usually, seeing that she's not really able to cook – this is not my personal opinion, I even have confirmation from the Chinese community! – So I usually cook. Or she makes soup for herself, that I see even the son eats in a disgusted way . . . if not, we go out, and obviously each of us decides for ourselves. (*Mario, fifty-five years old, husband of Zyang, Chinese*)

Despite the fact that for the couples mentioned above, the problems about food are not serious, this is not always the case. Some tensions have been reported by a few young foreign wives about the obligations concerning Sunday dinners that the Italian in-laws tried to impose on the new couple. However, it is clear that, in these cases, the real object of discussion is not the food but the autonomy of the newlyweds (particularly of the son) from the Italian family. Furthermore, the division of duties between husband and wife is yet another point of contention and is more difficult to resolve:

> I've heard about the cultural stupidities that caused terrible fights at the beginning . . . for example, this way of sharing our time with the family. . . . I'll give you an example: at the beginning on Sundays, we'd spend the day together, going around Siena together, and I, being a tourist, twenty-two years old, would say, "Let's take backpacks, and maybe we could go to Pisa." No! Because at eight we have to be home to eat! These are things I couldn't digest. Sometimes

we go to his parents' to eat for convenience, because I don't feel like cooking. But these are things that I still don't deal with very well, the fact that we have to be there at one, have to be there at eight.... if I get there at 8:20, I might as well not go at all because the mom has a long face, because we're late. These are things that I have always told him: "Listen, if you marry me, I don't cook in the evening; each of us can open the fridge and eat what we like, because, at my house, it was like that!" At the beginning, we'd fight about these things, too, ... but now I've changed, by staying with him. It's not something that I find so traumatic anymore; it's even nice to all sit together ... because, at my house, my mom worked, we all had different schedules; for me that worked well, but now I see that there is another way that works just the same. If it's not making me suffer, if it comes naturally ... about other things, though, no. Like for example, the fact of cooking: One time it's my turn, but what about him? For me it's normal, but he says, "Well ... sometimes it's okay, but not that it gets to be a habit, because [she imitates his voice] it's not a natural thing! (*Cintia, Brazilian, twenty-four years old, wife of Gianni, thirty-two*)

According to my research, the most difficult variable to be positioned in the continuum is the difference of religion, which is one of the most frequently mentioned points of contention in the study of this phenomenon. I have positioned this variable near the center because it seems to have different effects in different situations.

First of all, many Italian partners declared themselves to be "non-believers, non-churchgoers, or indifferent" about the issue of religion. Contrarily, foreign women and men, even if they seemed more attached to their credo in some cases, all clarified that their faith and religious practices are private matters and must not interfere with the couple's life. So, many signs would seem to indicate that the processes of secularization are softening the conflicts generated by religious factors.

However, we noticed that, in the few cases in which the partners recognized that religion is an important dimension in their lives, the negotiations and the creation of a mixed couple can follow very difficult paths and that the tensions become so strong as to threaten the possibility of living together. The choices about the wedding ceremony and the thought of children's education most often provoke explosions of this kind of conflict.

The following story illustrates very well the complications that can arise when religions are different. Gianni and Cintia are both Christian churchgoers, but he is Catholic and she is Evangelical. When they decided to get married, they had to face a serious crisis of identity . . . and when it seemed that all the problems had been solved, the decisions about the ceremony brought out new family tensions:

> The rites . . . we'll do hers. Even if I am Catholic, we can solve this because we have the bishop's notes for mixed marriages and for the noncanon law . . . that is already, difficult to have: we have to find, even within the church, people who are willing, we absolutely have to find them! We found one by chance, we found a Salesian priest who has been working with us a lot. . . . he really, really helped us saying that, from the point of view of the faith, we are . . . he always calls us, he says that we are "a living prophecy." . . . See, the point is this . . . well, there was a first phase where "Yes, well, this problem of different religions is big, but we care for each other, love each other, we can face it." There was a second phase where "We still love each other; let's see if we can really face this problem," and we started to face it. There was a third phase where we said, "We've faced it; there's no way we can stay together, let's break up." . . . We said it more than once. "There's no way to solve this; we'll break up!" Then there was the breaking point of the situation . . . where we ended up, both she and I, . . . listen, I can tell you that many, many times during that period we said, "Okay, let's just break up." We did break up, so go figure . . . but then, I must say, we both got to the point. . . . I like to say this: "They turned us inside out like a sock!" . . . because we got to the root of the person, both me with myself and her with herself. I can tell you in words like this, but it's difficult. . . . Okay: we took away all the ruffles and when we got to the root of the person, we understood, with pain and suffering, we understood that this design, the fact that we are together was not only about will but, there, this is what calmed us down, from this point of view we were calm, even with the problems that remained . . . because they remain. . . . I don't know what will happen when the kids are born. . . . I always say, "What are we going to do? Where are we going?" (*Gianni*)

> The wedding will be in Brazil, an Evangelist ceremony . . . not without trauma, not without tears . . . in Brazil, in my country. . . . Gianni came to Brazil twice, but he was alone. . . . I insisted on having the wedding in Brazil because I have a family of about forty billion people, all close relatives . . . not distant ones, or distant cousins. . . . we see each other all the time, I have all four grandparents that are still alive. They [Gianni's family] are a handful. . . . I told him . . . for economic reasons, my relatives can't come here. . . . they would have all come willingly, but you know . . . how can we do that? Gianni's parents took it badly, very badly . . . first, for the religious thing, because they believe that marriage is a sacrament, so they saw it as a second-class marriage, mine that is, the one in Brazil. . . . also because, at the beginning, we went to some priests who advised him not to marry me. . . . now it seems that they, his parents, well . . . are starting to understand . . . but the problem now is this long journey, that they have never taken an airplane. . . . the trip itself . . . and then there's the dog: "Who are we

going to leave the dog with?" says his mother. . . . she cries every day for the dog
. . . she's a little depressed. . . . I told her to leave it in a hotel for dogs, but she says
no . . . just think that they don't go further than fifty kilometres from home on
holiday . . . and even then, there are problems. So, you see, Brazil. (*Cintia*)

After religion, we move toward the end of the continuum where we
find the most serious differences. The second-strongest and most widespread source of tension between the partners is the division of domestic
duties. In fact, many couples saw this question as the reason for struggle
within their private life. The arguments over domestic duties often cover
up divergences about the woman's role and freedom.

We have registered accusations coming from all the sides.

Some Italian men declared to have been surprised by the spirit of
independence and the feminist claims of the partner coming from Eastern Europe or South America. These foreign wives demand more than
Italian women! But similarly, on the other hand, the immigrant women
are often disappointed by the Italian man's traditional and obsolete vision of women . . . these Italian husbands continue for many years to be
"mommy's boys"!

These tensions can easily become heightened in couples in which
the male partner is African. Two Italian women from our sample rose
against the restriction of women's freedom expected from their African
partners and, above all, by their families and friends.

Sandra is fascinated by the exotic world of her partner Hibrahim and
mixes with great pleasure with Moroccan people during public events
required by his profession; but she cannot tolerate the male chauvinist
behaviors of Hibrahim's friends at their house. First of all, she had never
taken into consideration the idea to introduce her friend to her older
parents, because she fears their reaction in front of a foreign, Muslim
partner.

The same difficulties that Sandra has with the African friends of the
partner have been denounced by Nicoletta.

Finally, there are immigrant men divided by the requests of the Italian partners and the "recall" to the original culture and families:

He never wanted to come to dinners organized by my friends. . . . It was me who,
he closed me in his world . . . but I couldn't do it, I couldn't bring him into mine.
. . . Instead I went with them, and how! To tell the truth, he took me around like

a sort of . . . I don't know how to say it . . . not like a trophy . . . but something to
show off about, no? One thing that distinguished him from the others . . . he took
me to places where the others didn't take their women . . . [and] I wasn't only
taken, but taken in full regalia. . . . He introduced me as his wife . . . then in front
of his friends, it so happened that I obliged him, I obliged him to put up with
things that weren't expected of them . . . like when he, if there were friends at our
house, he ordered me . . . at times he expected to give me orders, like, "Bring me
some tea! Bring us some tea. . . . Better yet, if he was with his friends: "Make us
some tea!" And I didn't do it, because if you ask saying please, if I have time, and
if I feel like it, I'll make it. Then, sometimes I'd find myself at these dinners with
only men, where the women were confined to the kitchen. . . . These men would
come to the house, alone, without women, and, according to him and his friends,
I was supposed to stay in the kitchen. . . . I would just get out of there! I mean:
I won't put up with this! So, he'd get mad. . . . Once for a similar reason, I even
left him at a restaurant! But then, not really his fault, I must say, as much for his
friends' fault, the men would gang up and the things that happen among men,
they'd drink, they'd start talking, and I'd get pissed off, and at times I'd leave
him there . . . disputing about guerrillas! (*Sandra, forty-five years old, ex-partner
of Hibrahim, forty-nine, Morocco*)

We'd get together with some of his friends; yes, . . . he had a few really sweet,
nice friends. They were really laid back, they'd come to visit me with him, and
when he was there, or when we went out sometimes, we'd see them . . . like that,
two or three friends, laid back. But there was one, one of his friends, though, if I
could have thrown something at him . . . because you know what he used to do?
He'd come to visit, he'd sit down . . . in the meantime he'd speak in their dialect,
African, not Italian . . . in front of me, obviously excluding me . . . and he'd start,
"Nicoletta, do this, do that, Nicoletta, make me a coffee!" . . . Without even, I
mean, speaking in dialect! I saw this as something prearranged about this thing
about men, but I took it in a way, well . . . about males and females! And, he,
Himed, he, when we were alone, agreed with me, he understood . . . but he didn't
say anything in front of him. This was the point: he understood and even agreed,
but he didn't ever want to contrast. (*Nicoletta, thirty-three years old, ex-partner of
Himed, Senegalese, forty*)

The struggle to manage these types of conflicts can lead to very different outcomes: from the irreparable break of the couple to the negotiation
obtained by the slow and exhausting reversal of the positions.

The most interesting processes that emerged from the analysis of
the gender conflicts were the transformations concerning aged Italian
men. Beppe and Piero, seventy-four and sixty-six years old, husbands, respectively, of Kathia (Russian, fifty-five) and Lynn (Filipino, forty-five),
both said that, after having refused to do any housework for years during

their first marriages to Italian women of their same age, they now have accepted to collaborate with their new young immigrant wives, to save relationships based on completely new rules and roles. In these stories, the age gap between the partners, that at the beginning of cohabitation is surely a problem, seems to be reversed and transformed into a resource: the aged husbands, just for the fact that they are aware of the great age difference with their wives and by the maturity that comes with full adulthood, radically change their behaviors and truly renew their own identities.

A further step to the right of our continuum and we arrive at the divergences about the management of money, which appears to be yet more threatening than the previous ones.

In the foreign woman / Italian man couple, almost all immigrant partners declared their career and their economic independence to be their first priorities, and, as these are conditions that enable them to stay in Italy, they cannot be sacrificed. While many Italian partners declared that they were open to accepting this clause, and often would even help their wives find a job, they were less favorable about allowing the women to manage an independent budget when the economic situation of the family was not good. Here, quarrels easily erupted. For example, Kathia, who has a degree in medicine, is willing to accept any work in Italy, on the condition that she can have money, making her a free woman:

> Some discussion we had for money . . . not for big spending, just small problems, for different lifestyles. . . . For work, Italians have different opinions about woman . . . for example, I'll give you an example. He, my husband, at first he couldn't understand why I wanted to work; he said, "We don't need, we have enough money to eat." But just to eat for me is not okay; I am an animal if I just eat! One needs to work for independence, to feel one's freedom, to go. . . . We used to fight at the beginning because I would go to the market, and I always buy something, small things, a shirt for him, for example, even if there is no need. . . . He says to me, "But why do you buy? You always need to buy. . . ." We fought; for me it was difficult: I had no job, not my own money, you understand? But I want [to] feel free, I don't want to ask [for] money to buy something, it's not okay. . . . I said, explained . . . now he understands, he says, "That's fine," he understands. Before, no. . . . He helps me in all ways to find a job. . . . He says, "I want to do for you all that I can!" He's good, but I said to him, "If I knew that I couldn't find a job, I didn't come!" Because I think women need to work and be equal to [the] husband. Sometimes when I fought I said, "That's it, I leave, I don't want anything, I want to leave!" Maybe he has some thought that I could do . . .

because I am a free person. I [am] free. I feel this way, that I can do what I like. For this reason, I want to work. (*Kathia, fifty-five years old, doctor in Byelorussia, unemployed in Italy, wife of Beppe, seventy-four, retired*)

There are many similar tensions in the couple type of Italian wife / foreign husband when faced with the question of the remittances to the native country of the immigrant partner. Indeed, the African and Arab men keep sending remittances to their country regularly even after starting a family in Italy. The Italian wives from our sample appear to be well disposed toward this rule, considering it proof of the husband's sense of responsibility. However, these dynamics work nicely as long as the couple does not face economic problems; the matter becomes even more complicated when the husbands send remittances to ex-wives and children rather than to their families of origin.

Finally, there is the uncertainty of the future. In many passages of the interviews, the partners openly said, or implied, that the Italian partner fears that the other partner might go back to her or his native country, if things went wrong. On the other hand, the words and the tone of the immigrants sometimes let the feeling of homesickness become apparent. So, even if fragility has been pointed out as the new characteristic of sentimental relationships of the contemporary liquid societies, the fact that one partner is an immigrant, always belonging to two lands, to two worlds, causes many cross-cultural couples to live with an additional daily feeling of uncertainty.

FALSE MARRIAGES OR POSSIBLE LOVE?

Returning to our exploration of the new mixed sentimental relationships that are spreading in the Italian marriage market, we can reach some conclusive impressions about the significance of the phenomenon.

First of all, the numbers speak out loud: binational couples are an emerging topic in Italian society. In fact, the trend is constantly increasing. A glance at other Western European countries with a longer tradition of immigration suggests that a social and cultural revolution is just beginning. Traditionally elitist events, characteristic of privileged social classes and professions (diplomats, professors, artists, politicians), cross-cultural sentimental relationships are becoming a popular fact.

Moreover, if we consider that immigrant people today make up about six percent of the Italian population and that the percentage of binational couples celebrating new weddings every year is already a two-digit number, it is clear that the marriage market is a very important place of mixing and integration between natives and new residents, where the distinctions that formulate the equation "immigrant = foreign person" begin to be made publicly.

The second interesting aspect is that binational marriages are an important, but very selective, way of integration. The combination of gender and nationality of the immigrants turns out to be decisive for their access to the dating market. For example, it is easy to note that the Chinese and other African or Asian groups that began to arrive in Italy noticeably sooner than other nationalities are not at the top of the list of the mixing processes. We also see that women and men coming from the same foreign countries can have very different accesses to meeting Italian people. With the only exception of Muslim women, on the whole, immigrant women are clearly favored in participating in the Italian marriage market. They play a protagonist role in the changes of the family landscape.

So, this sentimental route seems to be able to draw paths toward integration that are not so greatly influenced by the variable "duration of stay."

The last considerations will concern strange asymmetries between the partners. We found anomalous differences of age and education between the partners of a notable proportion of these unions, both in the statistical analysis and in the couples interviewed during the qualitative research.

This recurring characteristic in mixed couples is announced by the literature, which explains that it depends on a compensatory mechanism allowing the foreign partner to gain access to the marriage market of the new country. In other words, by accepting to marry a much older or a less educated partner, a foreign person can barter his condition of immigrant status, which is considered low if not a negative stigma in the new society, and compensate the native partner for having accepted it in mate selection. From the opposite point of view, these anomalous unions could be seen as new chances for some Italian men or women, who normally would be relegated to the margin of the marriage market due to their age or to specific personal attributes, in taking part in mate selection.

This issue involves very delicate social implications.

First, the presence of these strong differences in a considerable number of the binational marriages suggests that, nowadays, Italian society is not indifferent to the origins of people living in its territory: if many foreign women and men have to use a younger age or a higher education to access the game of partner selection, it means that some zones of the marriage market are regulated, silently but effectively, by racist prejudices and rules.

Second, these asymmetries raise the question of the ambiguity of (binational) couples. These anomalous asymmetries in the profiles of the partners often function as a spy hole: they uncover the dynamics of convenience and calculation that, more or less consciously, exist in all sentimental relationships. The problem is that it is very difficult to acknowledge the presence of these negotiations for the inhabitants of contemporary societies, when consumed with a romantic idea of love, made up only of passion and sentiment, where there is no place for rationality and for usefulness. As marriage today can be a matter of love alone, a union that openly shows the components of convenience, or an arranged union, automatically becomes a false marriage in the eyes of the public. In fact, this is what often occurs today in Italy to mixed couples.

The impression of the writing is that the issue is much more complex than common sense proposes.

The couples made up of natives and immigrants are concentrations of many differences and tensions. The excesses of asymmetries and problems and uncertainties make them the "black box" of the marriage, a place revealing augmented and exploded underground dynamics among genders and cultures.[12]

This *function of mirror* can explain the ambiguity we spoke about above.

These couples consist of a mix of different cultures reintroducing in our societies forms of interaction and lifestyles that have been already seen in the past but that are worked out and exist in completely different contexts today. Like the age gaps, which we noticed could consequently create unexpected new identities, we are reminded that marriages are

not pure relationships, exclusively founded on sentiment, and that arranged unions are not necessarily false marriages, rather, sometimes,
possible loves.

NOTES

1. *Cross-cultural* and *binational* are
not synonymous terms in the strict sense
of the words. However, in this paper, seeing that there is no room to delve into
the question and, above all, as we will
take into account couples whose partners
come from different nationalities and
cultures, we will use the two adjectives
interchangeably.

2. Fernand Braudel, "L'immigration
étrangère: Un problème récent," in
L'identité de la France, vol. 2, *Les hommes
et les choses* (Paris: Arthaud-Flammarion,
1986), 185–201.

3. To profile cross-cultural couples
living in Italy, we used the official data on
resident population, immigrants, and families regularly published by ISTAT on the
site *Geo.demo Istat.it – Demografia in cifre*
(http://demo.istat.it/index.html), also
available in English (http://demo.istat.
it/index_e.html), both accessed August
5, 2012. We referred both to the statistics
presented in the periodic reports and to
the rawer data of the tables.

4. A synthetic profile of the couples:

- *Zyang* (Chinese, forty-five, Buddhist, employee) and *Mario* (Italian, fifty-five, secondary school
graduate, nonbeliever, public
employee);
- *Kathia* (Russian, fifty-four, university graduate in the former Soviet
Union, Orthodox Christian but
rarely a churchgoer, ex-pediatrician,
now unemployed family assistant)
and *Beppe* (Italian, seventy-four,
elementary school, Catholic but not
a churchgoer, retired shop owner);

- *Paula* (Brazilian, thirty-one, university graduate, nonbeliever,
teacher of English) and *Stefano*
(Italian, thirty-six, not a churchgoer, employee);
- *Cinzia* (Brazilian, twenty-four,
practicing Evangelical Christian,
university student, baby-sitter) and
Gianni (Italian, thirty-three, practicing Catholic, university student
and appretice clerk);
- *Maria* (Italian, thirty-one, university student, Catholic but not a
churchgoer, university student and
cultural mediator) and *Patrick* (Senegalese, thirty-six, secondary school
graduate, does not regularly practice
Islam, factory worker);
- *Sabrina* (Italian, thirty-three, dance
school graduate, Catholic education, social operator) and *Salem*
(Bangladeshi, forty-one, secondary
school graduate, "only formally"
Muslim, manager and owner of
restaurant);
- *Lynn* (Filipino, forty-five, unemployed family assistant) and *Piero*
(Italian, sixty-six, nonbeliever, retired trader);
- *Nicoletta* (Italian, thirty-three,
nonbeliever, university student
and cultural mediator) and *Himed*
(Senegalese, forty, secondary school
graduate, hawker);
- *Sandra* (Italian, forty-five, nonbeliever, trader) and *Hibrahim*
(Moroccan, forty-nine, graduate,
"leader" of a religious Islam community, teacher of languages);

· *Daniela* (Italian, thirty-seven, secondary school graduate, unemployed) and *Karim* (Tunisian, twenty-six, secondary school graduate, ex-pusher now in rehabilitation);
· *Guido* (Italian, thirty-one, university graduate, Catholic, social operator) and *Rosa* (Romanian, twenty-eight, university graduate, family assistant).

It was not possible to interview *Lynn, Daniela,*and *Hibrahim.*

Some other details: eight out of the eleven couples were living together at the time of the interviews; instead, the witnesses of three couples told about the failures of their mixed relationships. The selection of the sample has been made by multiple channels. The couples did not know each other.

5. ISTAT, *I matrimoni. Dati relativi agli anni 2004–2008,* April 8, 2010, http://demo.istat.it/index.html, accessed August 5, 2012. See also http://www.istat.it/it/archivio/1786, accessed September 29, 2012.

6. Caritas/Migrantes, *Immigrazione. Dossier statistico 2009. XIX Rapporto* (Roma: Idos, 2010); Gaia Peruzzi, *Amori possibili: Le coppie miste nella provincia italiana* (Milano: FrancoAngeli, 2008); ISTAT, *Il matrimonio in Italia. Un'istituzione in mutamento. Anni 2004–2005,* February 12 2007, http://www.istat.it/salastampa/comunicati/non_calendario/20070212_00/testointegrale.pdf, accessed August 5, 2012.

7. Caritas/Migrantes.

8. We use the French word *mixité* to indicate the character of heterogeneity of binational couples deriving from the overlapping and the mixing of two sexual genders and of different cultures, habits, and languages. The choice of this word has emerged from a deep examination of the international vocabulary of the mixing of cultures: the noun of the root *mix* appeared the most suitable term to "fix" simultaneously the idea of a heterogeneous nature and the one of a process. *Mixité* does not have a perfect equivalent in English; the author proposed its use in the Italian language of family and migration, too (Peruzzi, *Amori possibili*).

9. Rossana De Luca and Maria Rosaria Panareo, *Storie in transito: Coppie miste nel Salento* (Milano: Guerini Scientifica, 2006); Valentina Furri Tedeschi, *E se Romeo si chiamasse Alì? Le coppie miste italo-mussulmane* (Civitavecchia: Prospettiva editrice, 2006).

10. Hong-zen Wang and Shu-ming Chang,"The Commodification of International Marriages: Cross-border Marriage Business in Taiwan and Viet Nam," *International Migration* 40.6 (2002): 93–116; Barbara Ehrenreich and Arlie Russell Hochschild, eds., *Global Woman: Nannies, Maids, and Sex Workers in the New Economy* (New York: Metropolitan Books, 2002).

11. De Luca and Panareo, *Storie in transito;* Vincenzo Romania, *Farsi passare per italiani. Strategie di mimetismo sociale* (Roma: Carocci, 2004).

12. Augustin Barbara, *Les couplet mixtes* (Paris: Bayard, 1993).

PART FOUR

Modes of Multicultural Success?

TEN

Divided Identities: Listening to and Interpreting the Stories of Polish Immigrants in West Germany

MIRA FOSTER

GERMANY HAS BEEN A COUNTRY OF IMMIGRATION AND emigration since long before its foundation as a nation-state in 1871. People came from the east and south, whether they were the Polish mine workers at the end of the nineteenth century who came to the Ruhr region or the guest workers from Turkey and Italy who arrived in West Germany during the second half of the twentieth century. Germany has also been a place where people left for different parts of the world, as far away as Central Asia or the Americas. Strangely enough, the historical narrative of Germany as a country of migrants plays only a marginal role in history schoolbooks and in the country's collective memory.

On the contrary, the romanticized notion of the German people, *Volksgemeinschaft*, as an ethnically, linguistically, and racially homogeneous nation has been the prevailing ideology for most of the last century. This ideology found its official expression in Germany's citizenship laws as early as 1913.[1] Based on the *jus sanguinis* principle, or the descent principle, German citizenship sharply distinguished between those who were granted and those who were not granted political membership. For decades, individuals who were not of ethnic German origin could not become legal Germans even if they were born, raised, and permanently lived in the country.

In the West Germany of 1989, this policy governed the lives of nearly five million immigrants. The majority of them immigrated from countries in southern Europe, such as Greece or Italy, or from Turkey.[2] Starting in the 1950s, these immigrants came as guest workers, *Gastarbeiter*, a euphemism explicitly referring to their status as temporary foreigners.

Despite the fact that, over decades, the guest workers and their families permanently settled in West Germany, they remained foreigners, *Ausländer*. On the other hand, people born and raised thousands of miles outside Germany's borders, as far away as Central Asia, who could document German ancestry, were granted citizenship and invited to join the German community. The German government welcomed them as ethnic Germans, or resettlers, *Aussiedler*, while the terminology implied their right to return to and settle back in their ancestral homeland. This ideology, which privileged ethnic descent over place of birth as the key to the right of citizenship, perpetuated the rhetoric of Germany being a nonimmigration country.[3] Furthermore, the *jus sanguinis* principle continued shaping the illusion of Germany as a nation of ethnically and racially homogeneous people.

The German immigration policies excluded millions of *Ausländer*, foreigners, and at the same time included millions of *Aussiedler*, resettlers.[4] Between 1945 and 1990, during the era of the communist regimes, over two million migrants came to West Germany from Eastern Bloc countries, such as the former Soviet Union, Poland, Hungary, the former Yugoslavia, and Romania. Over 50 percent of those immigrants originated in Poland.[5] Upon documenting their German ethnic background, the overwhelming majority of the Eastern European immigrants received German citizenship and were absorbed into the German society as "ethnic Germans," *Aussiedler*. Although officially considered Germans, these people still had to establish their lives anew while coping with a genuine immigration situation.

Shifting focus from the German citizenship policies, which allowed for the legal inclusion of the resettlers into German society, this chapter examines the impact of immigration laws on the personal experiences and changing identities of the newcomers.[6] It takes a close look at the Polish resettlers who came to West Germany during the 1970s and 1980s, the last two decades before the breakdown of the Eastern Bloc. Despite being the largest part of the ethnic German migration, the Poles remained fairly invisible in the immigrant arena. Scholars attributed this invisibility partly to the immediate grant of German citizenship, which made the Poles disappear from immigration statistics, and partly to their cultural, religious, and racial similarities to the Germans.[7] This meant that the Poles identified with Western European values, they were Christians (mostly Catholic), and their skin color did not differ from the Germans around them. Simply said, they did not stand out as immigrants or as an ethnic community.

Nonetheless, on an individual level, the immigration experience left visible traces; I argue that, in personal memories and individual life stories, the Poles deconstruct their invisibility by articulating their experiences and giving Polish migration a voice. In oral history interviews, they talk about their immigration motives, their struggles, worries, and disappointments. They also share their achievements and successes. This chapter draws attention to the voices captured in oral histories and points to the nuances in the experiences of the Polish resettlers, while elucidating their immigration history. The interviews provide rich sources that highlight the variety of ways in which people acted and reacted to their life circumstances. Using personal narratives, this article examines the human agency from the perspective of the actors. Instead of analyzing immigration from above by focusing on immigration polices, political agendas, and ideological debates, this study reaches out to the stories from below and shows how those macrofactors influenced the newcomers, their membership in the society, and their concept of who they are as resettlers from Poland living in Germany.

LISTENING TO THEIR STORIES: ANNA

My children, they feel.... Truly, I don't know who they feel like. My daughter argues she is Polish. Me, my entire life here, I was never ashamed. Many people in our community are ashamed to say they are from Poland, or they are ashamed to say they are Polish. I have been stressing it from the beginning. Some thought I was crazy, but at least I was me, and true to myself. Even now, even if it is [to] an officer, whoever, [I say] I am Polish. Despite having the German passport, which is only a paper, I always stress the fact that it is only a paper, which allowed me to live here, but it is not me, this is not what I feel. Me, being German, ... never in my life will I identify with Germany, never.[8]

Anna left Poland for a trip to West Germany in the fall of 1981.[9] She and her husband came to visit friends for just a few weeks. They had their five-year-old son with them. The youngest child had to stay back in Poland with his grandparents, as human collateral. It was common practice of the Polish government to issue passports and travel permissions for only a part of the family as a way of ensuring the return to Poland of those who traveled abroad. During the few weeks of Anna's absence, the situation in Poland changed dramatically. On December 13, 1981, the Polish government silenced the anticommunist movement *Solidarność* by declaring martial law, "state of war." In an attempt to suppress the political opposition against the regime, the communist government arrested thousands of people and radically restricted normal life. For many Poles, the defeat of the *Solidarność* movement confirmed the unshaken power of the communist regime while weakening their hope for democracy and a better life in Poland.

After learning about the circumstances in their home country, Anna and her husband decided to remain in Germany and postpone their return until things quieted down. Their parents urged them to stay abroad as the situation in Poland was politically unstable and economically hopeless. They would take care of Anna's son left in Poland. At that time, Anna contacted her cousin who had immigrated to West Germany a few years earlier. Anna recalled, "I told her about the problem we had [in Poland], and she said, 'Well, I received my German citizenship after my father. My father and your father were brothers, which means you could receive the citizenship as well. Why don't you apply, get some help and support, and wait.'" Anna applied and received German citizenship. During the interview, with tears in her eyes yet a smile on her lips as a disguise of her sadness, she said, "When we got these papers, I thought ... Jesus, for the first time in my life I drank till oblivion because of the hopelessness. It was horrible, I could not accept it. But that's what it was like."

Growing up in Poland, Anna did not know much about her family history. She was aware of the fact that her grandmother married a German man. Anna was also curious about her last name, which did not sound Polish but rather German. However, no one spoke about those issues in the family, and they seemed a bit of a "family mystery," as Anna recalled. It was shortly before her grandmother's death that Anna learned more about her own past. During World War II, some of her grandmother's children, who at that time were young adults, supported Poland, but others backed Nazi Germany. Having a Polish mother and a German father, the children had divided identities. Some felt strongly about Poland, as they identified with their Polish mother. Some joined the German army and fought against Poland because they took the German nationality from their German father. The family broke apart over the national and political loyalties of the siblings. One of the sons was Anna's father. He felt strong patriotism for Poland during the war and after. The loss of his brothers in war combat, paired with his patriotism for Poland, made him a silent man with regard to his personal history. Awakening the consciousness that her German citizenship was directly connected to this painful family history, Anna realized that, once again, her family was divided between borders and nationalities. Her parents and child were left in Poland; her husband, son, and she herself were now in Germany. The German papers, as Anna refers to her citizenship documents, linked her to the German nationality and the German part of her family, both distant and foreign to her.

Anna's newly received German citizenship ensured her legal membership in the German community. Her family was eligible for an apartment, welfare support, and a German language course. Like many other Poles who immigrated to Germany during the 1970s and '80s, they did not speak German. Socialized and educated in Poland, they had Polish biographies and were familiar with neither German custom nor culture. Many of them had never visited a country on the other side of the Iron Curtain. Their German roots were merely a distant family history put aside or even forgotten due to the prevailing memories of the Nazi invasion and destruction of Poland during World War II, as well as the nationalist pressure in communist Poland.

Anna's family was, thus, part of a larger migration movement from Poland to Germany that took place between 1950 and 1990. Over a million Polish people migrated to West Germany during this time, more than half of them during the 1980s. Over 80 percent came as resettlers with the claim to German citizenship. At the turn of the millennium, scholars described the Poles as the second-largest ethnic minority in Germany, after the Turks.[10] Despite being a fairly large ethnic group, the Poles have never attracted nearly as much attention as the Turks. Generally, in immigration debates, the Poles remained relatively invisible – until just a few years ago when sociologists and historians began to examine the Poles and their invisibility. Furthermore, the press and scholarly literature have often interpreted the invisibility of the Poles as an indicator of their successful integration into the German society.[11] From an ideological standpoint, this argument made sense, as being invisible or not standing out meant blending in with the German society, hence, becoming German. Exploring individual stories sheds light on what it meant for the Poles to blend in. Examining Anna's biography negates the notion of being invisible as a Pole while complicating the assumption of successful integration.

After a year of separation, with the help of the International Red Cross, Anna's younger son was able to join his parents in Germany. One of the conditions for allowing the child to leave was that the Polish government would confiscate the family apartment in Breslau, Poland. With resentment toward the communist regime for the difficulties in reuniting the family and the loss of their home in Poland, Anna and her family decided to stay in Germany. Life went on. Anna's husband pursued his career as a goldsmith. Anna did not work in her profession as an interior designer but helped her husband on and off while raising their two, later three children. Anna hoped to return to Poland eventually. However, as her husband became professionally successful and her children identified more with their German environment than with their mother's Polish memories, the thought of leaving became increasingly unrealistic. After living for nearly thirty years in Germany – more than half of her life – Anna still referred to herself as Polish. Although her documents stated her German ethnicity and German citizenship, she distanced herself from the imposed and expected Germanness. Because Germany defined itself as a monoethnic nation, there was no place for people with multiple national identies. The "either-German-or-not-a-part-of-the-society" ideology excluded people like Anna, who proudly chose to remain Polish and to stress her Polish identity while she chose to live in Germany.

CROSSING BORDERS – BACK AND
FORTH AND BACK AGAIN

Anna's story is complex and multidimensional. It is unique and, at the same time, similar to many other resettlers' stories. Without a doubt, certain episodes resemble subjective perceptions, individual choices, and personal opinions. Other elements of the story resurface and repeat themselves in most of the resettlers' narratives. One of these elements is the German ethnic background that each of the resettlers had to declare upon their immigration to Germany. Hence, to understand the recent Polish immigration to Germany, it is worth going back to review its historical origins and highlight the role ethnicity had played.

Historically, pre-1990 Polish immigration fits into a context of larger migratory movements, such as the German eastward expansion and the west–east migration.[12] Recent Polish immigration to Germany connected with both the long-standing tradition of Poles migrating westward and the influence of German migrant communities spreading throughout Eastern Europe. Both migratory movements had influenced Polish migration to the West during the last decades of the last century. Although it may seem strange to begin with the eastward expansion of the Germans, a rough outline of this movement will suffice to communicate its importance in later history.

Beginning in the Middle Ages, Germans migrated eastward, to the Baltic region and Hungary, creating numerous German colonies. A unique characteristic of these German settlements was that these people did not assimilate into the local community. On the contrary, they preserved their German language and German culture as well as their German ethnic and (later) national identity.

In addition to German people crossing borders, German borders also crossed people. Sandwiched between Russia, Austria, and Prussia (later Germany), Poland's territories have often been consumed by its neighbors, while the Polish state disappeared from European maps, as was the case between 1795 and 1918. Prussia and later the German Reich incorporated nearly one-third of Poland's western territories and residents. Germans inhabited these regions for decades or even centuries.[13] It was only in the summer of 1945 at the Potsdam Conference of the United States, the United Kingdom, and the Soviet Union that Germany's national borders were newly established to define the country's territory as we know it today. As the borders shifted, so did the citizenships of the people living in these regions. Those who experienced these events remember:

> I was born in '32. Before Hitler. [I lived in Beuten and Beuten was] German. Only
> German families lived there. The Poles weren't there. They came only in '45, when
> the Red Army came. They marched in, the Poles, and they surrounded us.... The
> Russians gave it [Beuten] to the Poles. And from that time, we were under the
> Polish rule.[14]

The eastward movement of Germans and the shifts of borders continued until the end of World War II. The year 1945 marked the turning
point; the Allied Forces in control of the events after the war defined
Poland's territories anew and expelled the German population from the
regions that now became Polish. Between 1945 and 1946, some twelve
to fifteen million German expellees and refugees fled westward, as they
were forced to leave the occupied territories and the eastern parts of the
former Reich. At this point in history, their previously German homeland became a part of Poland.[15] These events ended the centuries-long
eastward expansion of the Germans.[16]

What role did the eastward expansion of the Germans and the border shifts play in the context of Polish immigration to Germany? These
events provided what later would be the legal grounds for the migration of ethnic Germans back to their ancestral home country. As some
intermixing and interaction took place especially in the borderlands,
culturally and ethnically diverse families formed. In the oral history interviews, the Polish resettlers often recall vague images of their families'
dual national past:

> I come from a mixed family where, after the war, we didn't talk about it as it wasn't
> well regarded.... In my family, it was the women who had the German names,
> Brandt, Fischer ... and men Polish [names].... My grandma, for example, was
> Brandt. There was a bunch of Brandts in Tczew [my hometown], also lots of
> Fischers, and so on. In short, although we stayed [in Poland] after the war, there
> was always this division, father wanted to stay in Poland, mother was drawn to
> Germany.... So, they stayed [in Poland] and got Polish identification documents,
> of course.[17]

From 1945 on, in addition to the Polish-German families, there were
also those Germans who did not leave at the time of the massive postwar expulsion. Estimates of the number of Germans who remained in
the newly established Poland vary from one hundred thousand to one
million.[18] It would be their children and grandchildren who, during the
1970s and 1980s, would leave Poland and immigrate to West Germany.

Decades after 1945, the ability to trace an ethnic German background provided the legal foundation for immigration for thousands of Poles who came to West Germany.[19]

When listening to their stories, the distant and often unknown past reemerges in resettler biographies at their point of immigration to Germany. The family history that was dormant, or even unknown, becomes meaningful in understanding and dealing with the new German identity. This identity has not been chosen or slowly incorporated into one's perception of self, but rather is presumed by the immigration policy and expected by German society to be performed by the newcomers. Since German society, culture, and language were foreign for most of the Polish resettlers and German ethnicity was an expected criterion for the privilege of citizenship, the identification with the individual family history was often the only way to fulfill external expectations. Although distant and foreign, the ethnic German element in the family history became the center against which identities were reshaped. Whereas the resettlers' policies represented the governmental pressure to identify as German and could be rejected as an external force, the family histories were personal, internal motives, and had to be incorporated into one's biography. Individual stories speak about the different ways in which people negotiated their identities between these external and internal influences. Anna stands as an example of a person who reformed her identity by rejecting the expected Germanness despite both the knowledge of her German family history and the official verification of her German nationality through citizenship. For other resettlers, the family past allowed them to bridge the gap between their personal Polish biographies and their new lives in Germany. Jan, a man who left Poland in late 1970s, explained:

> [Germany] was my faraway, my second homeland, in a sense. [It is because] when I was still a child, a lot came from my grandparents. They never talked about it aloud, because you had to be cautious after the war. But looking at it today, my grandmother prayed in German, she counted in German – because you count differently [in German – from the back]; she counted "one and twenty" and not "twenty one" [as you do in Polish]. . . . Some poems, pictures, religious pictures with German signatures, kitchen utensils [had German names], "Messer, Gabel, Salz" (knife, fork, salt). Or the neighbors, Neuman, Guenter, well, you didn't talk about it, but the atmosphere was German in a sense, an

atmosphere that remained with me, that somehow shaped me. . . . And, in 1975,
I remembered all that I experienced as a child. And I realized that my history is
also a part of German history, despite the fact that, until 1974, I have not thought
for a second about emigrating and I absolutely identified with Poland.[20]

LISTENING TO THEIR STORIES: JAN

Unlike Anna and her family, Jan and his wife made a conscious decision
to emigrate. Jan was a scholar who had recently finished his doctorate in
chemistry. While pursuing professional advancement at the university,
Jan was finally told not to bother and to start looking for a job elsewhere. The reason for being denied a promotion was his involvement
in students' religious life. He was told that "the socialist youth must be
protected from such elements [as religiously active people]." The Polish Catholic Church grew to be a strong opposition to the communist
regime in Poland. Official participation in religious life was a political
statement for which Jan had to pay with his professional career as a
scholar. Jan left the university and found another job. He did not last
long; he remembered, "The corruption that was going on was shocking."
For Jan, it was the denial of professional opportunities and the lack of
religious freedom that influenced his wish to emigrate. Realizing he
might qualify to immigrate to Germany as a resettler, Jan applied for
emigration permission. After being denied three times between 1975
and 1977, he and his family were finally granted exile in 1978. One of the
conditions for leaving was that they renounce their Polish citizenship.
The permission to emigrate was permanent – a one-way ticket to Germany. As the borders between the Eastern and Western Bloc countries
were still virtually impermeable, chances of a future family reunion were
rather slim. Within three months, Jan, his wife, and their two children
had to pack up, dissolve their existence in Poland, and leave for West
Germany.

Jan was not the first in his family to emigrate from Poland. One
of his sisters immigrated to West Germany in 1971. She left with her
husband who was of German ethnic origin. Now, almost a decade later,
Jan could connect with her, which made his arrival easier. The immigration stories of Jan and his sister, Anna, and her cousin reflect a continuity of Polish migration to Germany and should be placed in the larger

historical context of east–west migration. Economically advanced and industrially developed, Germany has been one of the major destinations for immigrants, not just recently but since its industrial revolution in the last quarter of the nineteenth century. Industrial centers such as the coal-mining and steel-producing Ruhr Valley, as well as agricultural and urban hubs such as Berlin, Dresden, and Hamburg, drew permanent immigrants and seasonal migrant workers from Poland as early as the nineteenth century. Between 1871 and 1910, the number of foreign migrant workers within the territories of the newly founded German Reich increased from 207,000 to 1,259,880.[21] Poles, who made up 10 percent of the population, established Polish communities and well-functioning social networks. Whether they were well integrated or merely tolerated remains a topic of historical debates; nonetheless, Poles were visible as an ethnic community and a part of the social and cultural fabric of the German Reich.[22]

During the interwar period, the number of Poles in Germany decreased greatly. The majority of the Polish migrants returned to the newly established Polish state or emigrated to France. Furthermore, in September 1939, Polish organizations were banned, as Hitler's race politics legitimized all forms of discrimination against racially inferior peoples, including the Poles. The next wave of Polish migration into Germany took place during World War II. This time the migration was forced. Apart from the Polish Jews forcibly deported to work and to concentration camps, the Nazis also deported nearly two million Poles to the Reich and employed them as forced labor for the German war effort. After the war, more than 90 percent of these forced workers returned to Poland. Less than 10 percent (about one hundred thousand) remained in Germany as displaced persons.[23]

During the late 1940s and the 1950s, the Polish communist government strictly controlled emigration from Poland so that the numbers of emigrants remained minimal. A small window of opportunity opened between 1956 and 1959 for ethnic Germans – those who had not left immediately after the war – to leave the Polish territory and settle in Germany. However, the liberal emigration policies were discontinued within a few years, making the numbers drop again.[24] Under the official label of "family reunification" – an effort to unify the families who separated during the period of post–World War II expulsion and remained divided by the Iron Curtain – the migration from Poland to Germany resumed during the 1970s.[25] Although the migration originated from Poland, the people who left Poland relatively soon after World War II were de facto Germans. Some scholars argue that neither the 1950s nor the 1970s migration wave should be considered Polish. The people who left during this time were born in what was German territory prior to the 1945 border shift and spoke German, grew up as, and were socialized as Germans. They saw themselves and were identified by German law as Germans rather than Poles.[26] This group differs from the resettlers described in this study, in that, although they were living in Poland, they did not identify as Poles but rather as Germans. Most of them experienced strong German influence in terms of cultural norms, tradition, and language within their immediate families.

Beginning in the second half of the 1970s and through the 1980s, emigration from Poland to Germany increased, as the Polish government relaxed travel polices. During these two decades, nearly one million Poles migrated to West Germany, not just as resettlers but also as migrant workers and as asylum seekers. Among the over one million Polish immigrants, the resettlers constituted by far the largest proportion, over 80 percent.[27] In the fall of 1989, the communist regimes of Eastern Europe collapsed, while the borders between the East and the West dissolved. With open borders to the east, Germany could no longer deny its reality of being an immigration country. In 1991, new immigration laws concerning the resettler status stipulated that ethnic Germans must apply for German documents in their country of residence. The prospect for democracy and a better life in Poland, paired with this new legal hurdle, greatly diminished the number of Polish resettlers immigrating to Germany after 1991.[28]

When connecting these various migratory movements from Poland, a tradition of continuous Polish presence in Germany becomes apparent. Poles lived in and were a part of the social and cultural fabric in Germany for over 130 years. For more than a century, multiple waves of migrants moved to Germany motivated by different social, economic, and political circumstances. During each wave, the political makeup and ideology of both the Polish and the German governments determined the char-

acter of the migration experiences. These changing migration circumstances created a heterogeneous group of Poles in Germany. Lacking an
ethnic Polish community that would preserve their Polish heritage and
cultural identity and being erased from Germany's collective memory
and historical narratives, for many Poles, immigration became an individual experience shared mostly among family and close friends.

ORAL HISTORY: THE VOICES OF THE PEOPLE
AND THE ECHOES OF SOCIETY

In this study of Polish resettlers in Germany, oral histories provide access to the personal experiences and individual memories of immigration. The use of the oral history method also offers further advantages;
due to the recency of this research topic, most of the relevant archival
material will not be accessible for at least another decade. Furthermore,
since Poles constitute a minority group, traditional archival sources may
have little information about these people. More importantly, oral history offers insight into motivations and feelings, personal judgments,
and subjective experiences. Even if archival sources exist and are open
to the public, they simply may not hold this information. Here oral history provides a unique tool to gain access to this specific kind of knowledge – knowledge about mentalities, motivations, rationalities, and ir-
rationalities and how these translate into actions. In other words, oral
histories allow for a deeper understanding of human agency – the ways in
which people made sense of their circumstances and the variety of ways
in which they acted on and reacted to them. The immigration experience of the Polish resettlers was determined by German immigration
law, which ultimately required Poles to be German before being granted
legal membership in German society.[29] However, the impact of this legal
policy on individuals differed among the resettlers, as their oral histories
testify, from a total rejection of the externally expected Germanness, as
expressed in Anna's narrative, to a strong identification with it, as the
next story reveals.

Piotr escaped Poland in 1981, at the age of eighteen. He went on a bus
trip to Czechoslovakia and never returned. From Czechoslovakia, he
made it to Vienna where he reached the German consulate. Piotr knew

his father was German, had served in the German army, was a prisoner of war, and returned to Poland in 1947. Piotr had his father's army documents with him to prove his German descent. It took a few weeks before Piotr was granted German citizenship, and then he was sent to northern Germany. Hannover was his city of choice because of an extended family member, his brother-in-law's father. Piotr does not like to talk about this time in his life. During the interview, his answers to my questions were short. After few minutes of single-word answers, Piotr finally concluded,

> This time, I want to say, I don't want to have to process it again ... because it was difficult, for the psyche. . . . Gone from the family at eighteen. That hurt. That hurt. Somewhere there was a breaking point. I say, sometimes you [lay] down and asked yourself, "why?" And then you would get up and say, "I have to. I want to." That's how it was. But to process it all again ... it is difficult. Difficult.[30]

Eventually, life became easier for Piotr. He started with a one-year-long language course provided for all resettlers by the German government but discontinued it after three or four months when he found a job. He met local people and had a German girlfriend. Inclusion and participation in the world around him meant integration as opposed to isolation in immigrant communities. He had to adapt to his environment, had to "learn to accept certain things," as he stated, for example, the fact that he felt ashamed when he spoke his native Polish language in public. People would look and point with their fingers. "Don't speak too loud, and so . . . [and if you do, do that] in hiding." Piotr noted that this was around 1980, the images of cold-war enemies were still a reality, and Poland was on the other side of the Iron Curtain. Speaking Polish in public immediately marked him as a foreigner from the communist East. Not wanting to be identified as such was an attempt to fit into the ethnically, racially, and linguistically homogeneous German society where being different meant being foreign and, hence, an outsider.

Beyond access to the individual, oral histories also offer insights into social and cultural realms. Piotr's personal memories project a picture of the environment of which he was a part. His life and, hence, his personal narrative are embedded in a social and historical context and reflect the intersections of individual life and larger social and historical dynamics.[31] Piotr's hesitation to speak Polish and his effort not to stand out as a Pole represented the social pressure to blend in. Unable to perform the legally and socially expected Germanness, the resettlers often conceal their Polish background in public and sometimes even at home. These social and cultural expectations were yet another force against which the resettlers had to reform their identities. Piotr feels proud to be a part of German society. After nearly three decades in Germany, he identifies as German:

> [I feel clearly that I am German.] And I never had a problem, let's say, even less as self-employed, when someone says – some still say it – "Are you from over there?" or "Where are you from?" Because of the pronunciation, or accent, and such. But you are accepted by the Germans. No one has said yet, "You Pole." ... Earlier, yes, but not in the last TEN years. No one has said it to me, you Pole, or so, no. I personally could not adapt to life in Poland anymore. Because, for me, everything there is more or less foreign. ... At this time point, I feel good here. I work, and business is here, money is here. I am accepted in the neighborhood. ... I built my life here; this is important. I achieved something here.[32]

CONCLUSION: DIVIDED IDENTITIES

Although Poles are the second-largest group of immigrants in Germany, they have remained invisible as an ethnic community. Being invisible translated into trying to blend in with the social environment and not standing out as an outsider, a concept that corresponded with the ideology of Germany being an ethnically and nationally homogeneous country. Successful integration was measured by the ability to adhere to this ideology. How did Poles blend in, and what did it mean for them to be invisible?

As this essay has demonstrated, the answers to these questions can be found in personal narratives constructed by the resettlers. Their stories display a spectrum of immigration experiences and strategies that helped these people cope with their situations. The narratives allow us to observe how the same policies and laws influenced people differently – for example, how the process of fitting in was less a personal choice and more a reaction to the external social pressure of the environment. A multitude of historical, political, and social forces that shaped the resettler identities become apparent in their stories. Furthermore, focusing on the individual memories provides insight into the process of identity transformation. The study of Anna's, Jan's, and Piotr's narratives reveals the essence of their identities, which are fluid, not solid, divided between the private and the public, the individually decided and the socially expected. Through the lens of personal stories, we can follow the process in which the self-image is being redefined. The narratives also reflect on the social, cultural, and political context in which these processes took place. Historical developments such as the monoethnic ideology or the lack of immigration history within Germany's collective memory resurface in each of these individual oral histories.

Studying the resettlers not as a uniform group but rather as individual actors allows us to deconstruct the stereotypes, such as invisibility or successful integration, which are used to define this group. By listening to oral histories, we can generate knowledge about a multitude of emigration motives, immigration experiences, and integration strategies, while replacing the statistically driven generalizations of policy reports. The personal interviews present the Polish resettlers as a heterogeneous group of individuals who differ in degree of integration and personal identification with their German nationality. As a group and as individuals, they can be characterized as divided – divided from the experiences of the earlier Polish migratory movements due to their resettler status but also divided between their Polish biographies and their part-German family histories. There is a division between those resettlers who chose to identify with their German nationality and those who identify as Poles with a German passport. These divisions, which become apparent through the study of the personal stories, were shaped by and thus represent the complexity of Polish and German histories and the ways in which they are interconnected.

Finally, by adding the voices of Polish resettlers to the immigration historiography, this study not only makes these migrants visible but also helps create the understanding of Germany as an ethnically, nationally, and culturally diverse society.

NOTES

1. For more in-depth treatment of German citizenship, see William A. Barbieri Jr., *Ethics of Citizenship: Immigration and Group Rights in Germany* (Durham, NC: Duke University Press, 1998); Rogers Brubaker, *Citizenship and Nationhood in France and Germany* (Cambridge, MA: Harvard University Press, 1992).

2. *Statistik kurz gefasst. Bevölkerung und soziale Bedingungen 8/2006* (Statistics Made Short. Population and Social Conditions) (Europäische Gemeinschaft, 2006), http://www.eds-destatis.de/de/downloads /sif/nk_06_08.pdf, accessed June 6, 2012. For example, prior to the unification in 1990, the more than 1.6 million Turks formed the largest foreign immigrant community in West Germany, representing one-third of all foreigners.

3. On the paradox of Germany being a nonimmigration country, see Klaus Bade, *Migration in European History* (Oxford: Blackwell Publishing, 2003), 243–44; Barbara Marshall, *Europe in Change: The New Germany and Migration in Europe* (Manchester: Manchester University Press, 2000), 5.

4. In my research, I use the term *resettlers* rather then *ethnic Germans*, which is used in most of the English-language literature. I reject this term for its connotations. Since my work explores the very concept of *German ethnicity*, its historical context, the political, social, and personal meaning, I will break with the traditional terminology and use a more neutral name. *Resettler* simply emphasizes a physical movement of a person indicating neither nationality nor ethnicity.

5. Heinz Fassmann and Rainer Munz, "European East-West Migration, 1945–1992," *International Migration Review* 28.3 (Fall 1994): 520; Bundesverwaltungsamt, Anlage 4 zum Integrationsbericht LK-GF 2008-06-09 *Aussiedlerstatistik seit 1950* – Bundesverwaltungsamt, III Stabsstelle, Statistik–Dokumentation, Köln.

6. The term *experiences* describes here the entire spectrum of events from the decision to emigrate until the present. Likewise, the expression *identities* refers not to a rigid self-concept, but rather the processes of ongoing transformation of the self according to the personal and social circumstances that the individual encounters.

7. The following works address aspects of Polish invisibility and social perception: Cornelia Krampen, *Zuwanderung aus Polen und die katholische Kirche in Bremen. Migration und Religion in der modernen Gesellschaft* [Immigration from Poland and the Catholic Church in Bremen: Migration and Religion in the Modern Society] (Hamburg: Verlag Dr. Kovac, 2005), 11; Christoph Pallaske, ed., *Die Migration von Polen nach Deutschland: zu Geschichte und Gegenwart eines europaischen Migrationssystems* [Migration from Poland to Germany: A European Migration System in Past and Present] (Baden-Baden: Nomos Verlagsgesellschaft, 2001), 9, 13; Furthermore see Agata Cybulska, "Das Bild der anderen" [The Picture of Others], in *Standpunkte: Zum Verständnis deutschpolnischer Probleme* [Standpoints: Understanding the Polish-German Problems], ed. Wolfgang Drost and Marek Jaroszewski (Siegen: Akademisches Auslandsamt der Universität Siegen, 1999), 55–70; Frauke Miera, "Transnationalisierung sozialer Räume?" [Transnationalism in Social Spaces?], in *Die Migration von Polen nach Deutschland*, ed. Pallaske, 141; Katarzyna Polikowska, "Die deutsche Minderheit in Polen, die Polen in Deutschland" [German Minority in Poland, Poles in Germany], in *Standpunkte*, ed. Drost and Jaroszewski, 81; Rosemarie Sackmann, "Migranten und Aufnahmegesellschaft" [Migrant and the Receiving Society], in *Zuwanderung und Städteentwicklung* [Immigration and Urban Development], ed. Hartmut Häussermann and Ingrid Oswald (Opladen, Wiesbaden: VS Verlag für Sozialwissenschaften, 1997), 42–59; Anna Wolff-Poweska, "Paradigmen der gegenseitigen Wahrnehmung von Deutschen, Russen und Polen" [Paradigms of Mutual Perception, Germans, Russians, and Poles], in *Die deutsch-polnischen Beziehungen: Bilanz nach fünf Jahren Nachbarschaft* [German-Polish Relations: Accounts of

Five Years of Neighborship], ed. Claus Montag and Andrzej Sakson (Potsdam: Brandenburgische Landeszentrale für Politische Bildung, 1996), 23–32.

8. Anna M., of Bockhorst, Germany, interview by author, August 7, 2008, Bockhorst, Germany, digital recording, University of California, Santa Barbara. The interview is a part of a larger collection of oral history interviews conducted during my research trips to Germany in 2008 and 2009. The collection encompasses over thirty hours of interview material. The collection documents life stories of twelve resettlers, focusing on the experiences of immigration to Germany. All of the twelve interview partners left Poland for Germany between 1970 and 1989.

9. The names of all interview partners have been changed to protect their identity. All information about the interview partners is based on multiple oral history interviews conducted during research trips to Germany in summer 2008 and spring 2009.

10. Christoph Pallaske, *Migrationen aus Polen in die Bundesrepublik Deutschland in den 1980er und 1990er Jahren: Migrationsverläufe und Eingliederungsprozesse in sozialgeschichtlicher Perspektive* [Migration from Poland to Germany: A European migration system in past and present] (Münster and New York: Waxmann, 2002), 12f.; Andrzej Kaluza, "Zuwanderer aus Polen in Deutschland" [Migration from Poland to Germany], *Utopie kreativ* 141/142 (2002): 699; Katharina Stankiewicz, "Migranten aus Polen – unsichtbar gemacht? Die Folgen der Aussiedlerkategorisierung im Schatten der deutschen Einwanderungs- und Integrationspolitik" [Immigrants from Poland – made invisible?] (Frankfurt: Diplomarbeit, Europa Universität Viadrina, 2003), 13.

11. See Adam Soboczynski, "Wir Unsichtbaren, Wie funktioniert Integration? Eine ganze Generation polnischer Zuwanderer bemüht sich dabei zu sein, ohne aufzufallen" [We, the invisible: How does integration work? An entire generation of Polish migrants tries to participate without standing out], *Die Zeit*, August 17, 2006.

12. Heinz Fassmann and Rainer Münz, "European East-West Migration, 1945–1990," in *The Cambridge Survey of World Migration*, ed. Robin Cohen (Cambridge: Cambridge University Press, 1995), 472. See also Pallaske, *Migration aus Polen*. 31–32.

13. See Brubaker, *Citizenship and Nationhood*, 128–37.

14. Stephanie G., of Bremen, Germany, interview by author, March 16, 2009, Bremen, Germany, digital recording, University of California, Santa Barbara.

15. Fassmann and Münz, "European East-West Migration, 1945–1990," 470.

16. Marshall, *Europe in Change*, 5. See also Wolfgang Benz, "Fremde in der Heimat: Flucht – Vertreibung – Integration" [Foreigner in the homeland: Escape – expulsion – integration], in *Deutsche im Ausland, Fremde in Deutschland* [Germans abroad, foreigners in Germany], ed. Klaus Bade (München: C.H. Beck, 1992), 374–86.

17. Jan J., of Bremen, Germany, interview by author, July 20, 2008, Bremen, Germany, digital recording, University of California, Santa Barbara.

18. The numbers represent a highly politicized issue, here that of German minorities in Poland; the Polish authorities recorded lower numbers, while the German government preferred higher estimates.

19. This is a very rough outline of the migration streams between the east and the west. However, it illustrates how interconnected these migratory movements were and how it is difficult to understand one without looking at the other.

20. Jan J. interview.

21. Klaus Bade, *Vom Auswanderungsland zum Einwanderungsland? Deutschland 1880–1980* [From a country of emigration to a county of immigration? Germany, 1880–1980] (Berlin: Colloquium Verlag, 1983), 29; F. Burgdörfer, "Die Wanderungen über die deutschen Reichsgrenzen in letzten Jahrhundert," in *Allg. Stat. Archiv 20* (1930), 539, cited in Bade, *Vom Auswanderungsland zum Einwanderungsland?* 130; Klaus Bade, "Labour, Migration, and the State: Germany from the Late 19th Century to the Onset of the Great Depression," in *Population, Labour, and Migration in 19th and 20th Century Germany,* ed. Klaus Bade (New York: St. Martin's Press, 1987), 63.

22. On Polish communities in Germany during the first half of the twentieth century, see Richard Murphy, *Gastarbeiter im Deutschen Reich. Polen in Bottrop 1891–1933* [Guest workers in the German Reich: Poles in Bottrop, 1891–1933) (Wuppertal: P. Hammer, 1982); and Christoph Kleßman, *Polnische Bergarbeiter im Ruhrgebiet 1870–1945. Soziale Integration und nationale Subkultur einer ethnischen Minderheit in der deutschen Industriegesellschaft* [Polish miners in the Ruhr region, 1870–1945] (Göttingen: Vandenhoeck und Ruprecht, 1978).

23. See Ulrich Herbert, "'Ausländer-Einsatz' in der deutschen Kriegswirtschaft, 1939–1945" [Foreign Labor in the German War Economy, 1939–1945], in *Deutsche im Ausland,* ed. Bade, 354–67; Bade, *Migration in European History,* 206–13; Barbara Malchow, Keyumars Tayebi, and Ulrike Brand, *Die fremden Deutschen: Aussiedler in der Bundesrepublik* [The foreign Germans: Resettlers in the FRG] (Reinbek: Rowohlt, 1990), 32–35; Czeslaw Luczak, *Polscy robotnicy przymusowi w Trzeciej Rzeszy podczas II. Wojny Swiatwej,* (Forced Polish Workers in the Third Reich during the Second World War) (Poznan: Wydawn. Poznańskie, 1974); Ulrich Herbert, *Fremdarbeiter. Politik und Praxis des*

Ausländer-Einsatze' in der Kriegswirtschaft des Dritten Reiches [Foreign workers: Politics and practice of the foreigner service in the German war economy during the Third Reich] (Bonn, Berlin: Neuauflage, 1980).

24. Whereas nearly 140,000 people per year were able to leave Poland during 1957 and 1958, the number of emigration dropped to less than 40,000 in 1959 and continued to decrease yearly until the 1970s. Piotr Korcelli, "Emigration from Poland after 1945," in *European Migration in the Late Twentieth Century: Historical Patterns, Actual Trends, and Social Implications,* ed. Heinz Fassmann and Rainer Münz (Brookfield, VT: E. Elgar, 1994), 173.

25. Ibid., 171–85.

26. Pallaske, *Migrationen aus Polen in die Bundesrepublik Deutschland,* 11; Pallaske, ed., *Die Migration von Polen nach Deutschland,* 37.

27. Over eight hundred thousand came as resettlers, while the remaining two hundred thousand came applying for political asylum and were granted an exceptional leave to remain, based on the 1966 East Bloc refugee agreement, *Ostblockflüchtlings-Regelung,* which stipulated that East Bloc refugees cannot be rejected or deported. See Pallaske, *Migrationen aus Polen in die Bundesrepublik Deutschland,* 10–11, 50, 70–79.

28. In 1989, the number of Polish resettlers arriving in West Germany reached a quarter million. In 1990, the number dropped to 133,872, and, in 1991, only 40,129 individuals came to Germany from Poland. See Bundesverwaltungsamt, *Aussiedlerstatistik seit 1950.*

29. Legal foundation was provided by German Basic Law: *Deutsches Grundgesetz, Artikel 116 (1), Deutscher im Sinne dieses Grundgesetzes ist vorbehaltlich anderweitiger gesetzlicher Regelung, wer die deutsche Staatsangehörigkeit besitzt oder als Flüchtling oder Vertriebener deutscher*

*Volkszugehörigkeit oder als dessen Ehe-
gatte oder Abkömmling in dem Gebiete des
Deutschen Reiches nach dem Stande vom 31.
Dezember 1937 Aufnahme gefunden hat.* (2)
*Frühere deutsche Staatsangehörige, denen
zwischen dem 30. Januar 1933 und dem 8.
Mai 1945 die Staatsangehörigkeit aus politischen, rassischen oder religiösen Gründen
entzogen worden ist, und ihre Abkömmlinge
sind auf Antrag wieder einzubürgern. Sie
gelten als nicht ausgebürgert, sofern sie nach
dem 8. Mai 1945 ihren Wohnsitz in Deutschland genommen haben und nicht einen entge-
gengesetzten Willen zum Ausdruck gebracht
haben.*

Further laws concerning the resettlers
are the *Bundesvertriebenen- und Flücht-
lingsgesetz (BVFG)*, Expellees and Refugee
Settlement Law, from August 10, 1949; *So-
zialhilfegesetz* (SHG), Law for Immediate
Assistance, from August 8, 1949, replaced
in 1952 by *Lastenausgleichgesetz* (LAG),
Law for the Equalization of Burdens, ter-
minated by *Kriegsfolgenbereinigungsgesetz*
(KfbG) Law to Settle Consequences of
War. See Marshall, *Europe in Change*, 6–7.

30. Piotr. P., of Achim, Germany, inter-
view by author, August 10, 2008, Achim,
Germany, digital recording, University of
California, Santa Barbara.

31. Mary Jo Maynes, Jennifer L. Pierce,
and Barbara Laslett, *Telling Stories: Use of
Personal Narratives in Social Sciences and
History* (Ithaca, NY: Cornell University
Press, 2007), 45.

32. Piotr. P. interview.

ELEVEN

The Politics of Multiple Identities in Kazakhstan: Current Issues and New Challenges

KARINA MUKAZHANOVA

SINCE KAZAKHSTAN DECLARED INDEPENDENCE ON DECEMBER 16, 1991, along with adjusting to the new political environment, the country faced the challenge of transforming the entire economic system, adjusting its legislative and social policy.

The main objective of the politics of multiple identities remained the same – to promote mutual understanding and respect among representatives of different nations and ethnic groups living on the vast territory of the second-largest post-Soviet country. In spite of the number of different interpretations and controversial issues about the politics of multiple identities, it is undeniable that, today, Kazakhstan is emerging as one of the economically and politically stable countries in the Central Asian region. It has done well to build tolerance and mutual understanding among its diversity of nationalities and ethnic groups. However, many issues still need to be considered when analyzing the politics of multiple identities in Kazakhstan.

The economy of the country is the fastest evolving in the Central Asian region. The oil and gas industry is considered to be its leading economic sector. Kazakhstan holds about four billion tons of proven recoverable oil reserves and three trillion cubic meters of gas.

According to industrial analysis, the expansion of oil production will enable the country to produce as much as three million barrels per day by the year 2015. Today, the country is one of the main world exporters of oil and gas in the international trade arena. The developing industrial sector played a significant role in revitalizing the country's economy after the collapse of the Soviet Union. The transition period of the country that was the last to declare its independence from the former Soviet Union was accompanied by declining average incomes, increasing unemployment rates, and deteriorating social services. Since this low point, the country has gradually recovered due to reforms that were implemented to ensure macroeconomic stability and improvement in social services, including privatizing state enterprises, developing the banking sector, defining a labor market policy, and reforming the pension system and social insurance. In 2004, the government of Kazakhstan increased its revenue of oil deals by increasing taxation of new oil projects. Later, the Law on Subsoil and Subsoil Use was adjusted by the government to protect the economic security of the country. The amendments give the government the right to annul or amend subsoil contracts if the contracts pose a danger to the country's national economic security interests. Political stability within this multinational country also plays a significant role in creating a steady platform for its sustainable development. As a member of the fifty-six-state Organization for Security and Co-operation in Europe (OSCE), Kazakhstan was the first post-Soviet Central Asian republic with a Muslim majority given the OSCE chairmanship in 2010. According to many critics, to be able to promote democracy and the rule of law in the region, Kazakhstan must continue upholding democratic principles and human rights within the country. Nevertheless, there were some positive changes made in the country during Kazakhstani chairmanship of the OSCE.

The government of Kazakhstan has instituted reforms to promote dynamic growth of its society, based on equal progress of nationalities and unity of its people. However, there is a question as to how these reforms have been implemented in practice and what the results of the implementation are. It is undeniable that precise realization of the politics of multiple identities within the state is a crucial factor for its further stable economic and social development as well as its external political success.

NOSTALGIA ABOUT THE SOVIET PAST
AND NATIONAL IDENTIFICATION

Nostalgia about the Soviet past still persists among a large portion of the older generation in the post-Soviet area. Most of the people of different nationalities older than thirty-five feel homesick about the shared Soviet past. This is one of the crucial factors that unite people of the post-Soviet countries.

Self-identification with the Soviet legacy has its reasonable ground. In most post-Soviet countries, there is no solid alternative ideology that can substitute for the one that persisted in the Soviet Union for decades. The social memory of a shared historical past that united people of different nationalities during the Soviet era still persists among older people: "It was good times when we were Soviet people – all members of one big family. I do not feel such unity among people today. This wild market made us suspicious towards each other. The main concerns of young people are to be more competitive, not to be united," says Natalya, a fifty-one-year-old Russian woman. "I miss the old good days. At the same time, I see that there are a lot of opportunities our children have today, to study abroad, get international experience, for instance. Maybe for us, the older generation, it is hard to adapt to new things. But I believe, our children feel much more comfortable," says Damira, a forty-eight-year-old Tatar woman.

It is true that, after the collapse of the Soviet Union, revitalization of the national identification processes was achieved not only among Kazakhs but also among Russians, Ukrainians, and representatives of other nationalities living in the post-Soviet countries. Perhaps primarily, it was an unconscious reaction to the post-Soviet chaos, followed by the collapse of the centralized command economy. The situation was rapidly changing, and people did not feel safe and comfortable anymore. And then, this homesick feeling transformed into a deeper and complicated process: national identification.

Identities are not something steady and permanent, but changeable and unpredictable. The word *identity* finds its roots in the Latin *idem* – sameness. Thus, to find the sameness and identify themselves as a group, people need to draw a line between "Ourselves" and "Others." The process of otherness "is the way 'we' construct ourselves, through discourse, as different from the other."[1] It is an essential category, which belongs to a specific time and place where "the self" is always related to "the Other." On the contrary, postmodern perception excludes the Other as an indispensable component of the identification process. Postmodernists emphasize that "it should be possible to avoid negative forms of identity creation and that creation of the identity should be possible without using an 'Other' as a comparison."[2] However, usually a nation is defined "through an emphasis of attributes that set it apart from other national groups."[3] Therefore, it is hard to avoid divisions, and even alienation, within a multiethnic state among people who belong to different nationalities and ethnic groups.

The unity of the nation is also strengthened by sharing common symbols and myths. Through myths, people are provided understanding of who is the Other; at the same time, it could be the reason of subdivision within the multicultural state. Hobsbawm emphasizes that myth and invention are essential for the politics of identity by which groups of people today, defining themselves by ethnicity or religion, try to find some certainty in an uncertain and shaking world by saying, "We are different from and better than Others."[4] Therefore, on the one hand, common myths and symbols consolidate people within the state and strengthen their shared patriotism, while, on the other hand, these same myths could reveal internal subdivisions.

Furthermore, to be identified as a nation, people need to be attached to one territory. In other words, they need to identify themselves in geopolitical meanings. The notion of a "shared homeland" stands as a fundamental brick in the process of national identity formation. Giddens claims that nations only exist when there is a state administration that reaches over the territory over which the state has claim of sovereignty.[5]

Considering multicultural and multiethnic backgrounds, as well as historical and cultural features of the multiethnic state, the picture of multiple identity formation in Kazakhstan is not uniform. The official main objective of the politics of multiple identities is to provide each citizen a sense of belonging to one state – the ideology where being Kazakhstanian goes beyond ethnic identification. At the same time, the government supports by all means preserving and developing the diverse cultural heritages and different languages of people of different nationalities living in the country. The Kazakhstanian version of unity-in-diversity can be expressed in the formula "We are different but we all are Kazakhstanians."

Under a decree of President Nursultan Nazarbayev, the Assembly of the Peoples of Kazakhstan was founded on March 1, 1995. The Assembly Member Court was formed among the representatives of national cultural regional centers and veterans' councils. The assembly's activity is directed to solving the following tasks:

· to encourage the maintenance of interethnic concord and social stability;
· to support cultural and spiritual development of every national and ethnic group on the basis of the principle of equality;
· to provide for consideration of multilateral ethnic interests within the national policy;
· to search for compromises to settle the social conflicts arising in the society.

The assembly contributed to equal development of cultures of all Kazakhstanian people. Moreover, the initiatives of the national-cultural centers find great support in state structures. According to the modification in Paragraph 51 of the Constitution of the Republic of Kazakhstan, "nine deputies of Mazhilis [the lower chamber of the Parliament] are selected among representatives of the Assembly of the Peoples of Kazakhstan."[6] The organization was created as a unique institution that confirmed its significance as an important actor for political stability in the multiethnic society. May 1, the former Day of Solidarity of Workers, or Labor Day, was transformed and renamed to a Day of the Unity of the Kazakhstanian People (not "Peoples" or "Nations" but "People"), which is supposed to symbolize the idea of integration and unity of the people of Kazakhstan. On this day, national-cultural associations perform their cultural shows in traditional festivals that recall solemn Soviet marches with images of people of different nationalities in national garments holding hands. The assembly was created primarily for coordinating social and cultural events: promoting unity in diversity through protecting the uniqueness of the cultural heritages and languages of the people of different nationalities. However, some critics assume that the Assembly of the People of Kazakhstan remains only a formal political institution that does not play a significant role in consolidating the nation.

CREATING INTERCULTURAL SYNERGY

Although Kazakhstan occupies a vast territory while being the eighth-largest country in the world, its population is only about 15.5 million people. The two major religions in Kazakhstan are Islam and Christianity (with 57 and 40 percent of all believers, respectively). Most Muslims in Kazakhstan belong to the Sunni denomination of Islam, while most Christians belong to the Russian Orthodox Church. In addition, there are more than 4,551 religious organizations in Kazakhstan, which together represent the principles of another forty confessions. Kazakhstan is recognized as a multinational and polyconfessional state. The majority of the population is either Kazakh (58.6 percent) or Russian (26.1 percent); in addition, more than 130 ethnic groups together make up 15.3 percent of the population. There are 2,195 Muslim mosques, 257 Orthodox churches, 89 Catholic cathedrals, 10 synagogues, 546 Protestant prayer houses, and one Buddhist temple.[7] However, such diversity of religious confessions is not necessarily the sign of the religious revitalization of the entire population of the country. After the collapse of the Soviet Union and the loss of an ideological base, many people became more attached to their church and mosque communities. In most cases, it was the instance of self-identification through association with the group of people who shared the same ethnical and traditional values, the same national and linguistic patterns. Since Kazakhstan declared itself a secular state, none of the religion confessions can be described as dominating or influencing the politics of the country, and religious self-identification remains the personal choice of every citizen. The people of Kazakhstan have never been fanatical in their faith, but rather tolerant toward other faiths. However, because of the lack of knowledge of religion, many young people are highly receptive to imported religious teaching and practices. According to researchers, the threat of spreading extremism in Kazakhstan is increasing. There are some organizations, especially in the western part of Kazakhstan, that teach radical ideas and foster fanatics of the fringe religion under the guise of spreading Islam. In fact, these organizations are just pursuing their own political and economic goals. That is why it is important to take various preventive measures, which first of all should include improving the educational level of the population about religion and different religious organizations. The chairman of the Agency for Religious Affairs of the Republic of Kazakhstan, Kairat Lama Sharif, believes that the spread of extremism in Kazakhstan has to be countered intellectually through cooperative efforts of humanitarian and religious scholars, the community, and the state. Even though the current religious situation in the country is stable, it is important to continue tracking the activities of religious associations and missionaries.

The first Congress of Leaders of World and Traditional Religions, which drew widespread support from political leaders of both Western and Asian nations, was held in Astana in September 2003. Kofi Annan, in his message to the participants of the conference, emphasized the importance of interreligious dialogue in the United Nations in order to maintain peace and international cooperation.[8] However, in spite of what many saw as a positive impact, some critics called the congress a self-promotion campaign organized to draw the attention of the world community to Astana, the capital city.

The Assembly of Peoples of Kazakhstan has significantly contributed to the process of turning multinationality into a strategic advantage. The Institute of National-Cultural Associations established after the collapse of the Soviet Union also plays an important role in creating a positive environment in this multinational state. They were established by representatives of different diasporas and supported by the Assembly of Peoples of Kazakhstan.

Among the main priorities in the activities of the Institute of National-Cultural Associations are

- protecting the rights and interests of the representatives of different diasporas
- strengthening intercultural cooperation
- supporting diaspora activities
- assisting native languages revitalization
- developing original art, music, and literature.

Today more than 470 national-cultural associations are officially registered in the Republic of Kazakhstan. One of the missions of the Assembly of the Peoples of Kazakhstan is to promote mutual understanding and religious acceptance among all these groups, as well as to encourage the maintenance of a diverse cultural heritage. Centers play an important role in strengthening cross-cultural understanding, while also providing an opportunity to representatives of different nationalities to preserve and develop their cultural heritage. National-cultural centers provide the platform for cooperation and communication for people of different nationalities through offering various linguistic and dance courses, time-exchange practices, poetry and drama clubs, educational programs abroad for young people, etc. It is undeniable that Institute of National-Cultural Associations is a strategically oriented project of the successful realization of the politics of multiple identities in Kazakhstan. While Kazakhstan remains our shared homeland, it is important to provide an opportunity for each Kazakh, irrespective of his or her nationality, ethnicity, race, or gender, to preserve his or her national-cultural heritage, to practice his or her religion, and learn his or her language.

Nationhood building and national identity formation are complicated and controversial processes in such a multiethnic society. Cultivating a common sense of belonging among its diverse communities is a long-term challenge. One must consider the historical background of post-Soviet countries and the political priorities and cultural features of various ethnic groups that cannot be simply excluded or underestimated.[9]

Some critics emphasize that the politics of multiple identities in Kazakhstan is just a distorted version of Soviet internationalism. Under the Soviets, Russians enjoyed the status of being privileged among other nationalities. Being a titular nation means enjoying "informal social privileges" such as getting better job opportunities based on national and linguistic principles. Representatives of the titular nation enjoy being native speakers of the official language of the state (for example, the Russian language during the Soviet period) when there is no need to learn the indigenous language or any other languages to succeed in a career. In the Kazakh version of internationalism, according to these critics, privileges are given to Kazakhs as the titular ethnic group of the country, while other groups are being unintentionally oppressed. Thus, Edward Schatz argues that, if in the Soviet period "internationalism had a Russian face then the weak post-Soviet state [Kazakhstan] turned Soviet-style internationalism on its head by offering a normatively appealing discourse to its non-titular population and a diffuse and ill-defined set of privileges to titular Kazakhs."[10] Schatz describes the "internationalism with a Kazakh face," ruled by strong clans and kinship networks that remain powerfully embedded both in state societal and economic structures in all five post-Soviet republics. Furthermore, he emphasizes that the newly independent state perpetuates these types of social organizations, both intentionally and unintentionally. In spite of the fact that the growing market economy is undermining kinship networks rather than causing them to persist, he argues that kinship networks persevere as a means of allocating scarce resources. Therefore, he says, "better performance of the Kazakh economy in comparison with its neighbors leads to the question of how much longer this will continue."[11] Moreover, Schatz underlines the observation that concerted attempts to consolidate a united ethnic front had reinforced salient subdivisions among ethnic Kazakhs. Therefore, instead of consolidating nations, there is an opposite effect as a result of a multitiered ethnic redress practiced by the state elite: "Managing these reconstituted identities is one of the central challenges for independent Kazakhstan."[12]

Jakob Rigi, in his controversial book *Post-Soviet Chaos: Violence and Dispossession in Kazakhstan* (which he published under the name of Joma Nazpary in July 2001) presented his anthropological vision of how the transition to a market economy and wild capitalism affected ordinary people. In spite of quite controversial content and examples provided in his book, Nazpary/Rigi has some remarkable points. He emphasizes that the notion "Kazakhstani people" he uses in his book designates "people who oppose the elite."[13] In other words, he divides Kazakhstanians into two categories: oppressed ordinary people and rich powerful elites. He believes that dramatic polarization between wealth and poverty caused nationalistic prejudices, ethnic conflicts among different nationalities, and internal subdivisions among Kazakhs themselves. It is true that the post-Soviet crisis and reforms that attended the building of the new state have made the conditions of life extremely unpredictable. As a result, many people have been disoriented not only because of economic instability but also because of uncertainty caused by losing their identity of belonging to "homo-Sovieticus."

A brief retrospective review will clarify the origins of subdivisions among Kazakhs. There are subdivisions among Kazakhs based on their belonging to different *zhuz* and *ru,* which are rooted in their nomadic past. The nomadic way of life of the ancient Kazakhs was predetermined by the harsh climate of Central Asia. The culture of nomadic people featured hierarchy and social relations based on territorial belonging and occupation rather than class or gender. The etymology of the word *zhuz* is from the Arabic *Juz,* which means "section." In the Kazakh language, *zhuz* also means "hundred" and "face," which adds a fascinating dimension to understanding its origins. According to anthropologists, nomads adopted a *zhuz* division to develop migration routes within natural borders of the geographical zones formed on the territory of ancient Kazakhstan.

The Kazakh people have been divided into three *zhuz* (tribes): *Uly Zhuz* (Great Zhuz), *Orta Zhuz* (Middle Zhuz), and *Kishi Zhuz* (Little Zhuz). Historically, Great Zhuz nomads inhabited the southeastern part of Kazakhstan. Representatives of the Great Zhuz were skillful in governing and uniting the Kazakh people. Middle Zhuz nomads, who were known as famous poets and intellectuals, lived mostly in the central, eastern, and northern parts of modern Kazakhstan. Warriors from Little Zhuz mostly occupied western Kazakhstan.

Each *zhuz* has its subdivisions – *ru* – the number of which varies. *Rus* were also divided into small groups down to the size of average families. The question that Kazakhs ask each other when meeting for the first time is "What *ru* do you belong to?" or "What is your *ru*?" These divisions played an important role in ancient Kazakh society since it was important for people to know their lineage and to be able to find members of the big extended family (clan) in different *auls* – nomadic tribes' settlements – and control migration routes. As Kazakhs practice exogamy, each person is expected to know his or her ancestors up to the seventh forefather – *Byr Ata*. Marriage within *Byr Ata* in nomadic culture was considered to be incest, a taboo.

The process of collectivization under the Soviets fundamentally transformed the nomadic traditions of Kazakhs. The Soviet government aimed to eliminate these divisions, not only from the political sphere but also from the social life of the indigenous people. Nonetheless, according to some scholars, these divisions among Kazakhs still persist and play an important role in modern Kazakhstani society.[14] Moreover, in the light of the revitalization of the national identification process, many Kazakh people tend to identify themselves according to their belonging to *zhuz* and *ru*, especially in the southern part of Kazakhstan. However, the antagonism among Kazakhs based on *ru* membership is more intensified among so-called elites than among common people.

In spite of the consequential realization of the politics of multiple identities, there are many cases of subdivisions among Kazakhs according to *ru*. These divisions exist alongside tensions between Kazakhs as the titular nation of the state and the other 130 nationalities within the Kazakhstan population, in particular Russians who used to get privileges as the titular nation during the Soviet period. Therefore, there are two factors that constitute the main obstacles to the successful realization of the politics of multiple identities in Kazakhstan. The first one concerns the possible oppression of representatives of different nationalities. The second deals with internal opposition among representatives of different Kazakh *ru*.

The mainstream of Kazakhstanian politics of multiple identities should focus on the establishment and strengthening of the institutions of unity consolidation, which implies unity and reinforcement among a diverse population.

Currently, the politics of multiple identities in Kazakhstan focuses on the promotion of tolerance among citizens of the country. However, the word *tolerate* (which takes its roots from the Latin *tolerantia* – "forbearance," "patience," "mercy") does not comprehend the complexity of the interethnic and international relationships within the multicultural state. It is not enough just to be tolerant toward representatives of other nationalities and ethnic groups. Multicultural diversity requires mutual understanding based on accommodation and assimilation of norms and traditions of different cultures. It is important to provide equal rights for each citizen of the multicultural state, irrespective of his or her nationality, ethnicity, religion, gender, or race. There are some obvious prerequisites for creating such an ideological line in Kazakhstan. Moreover, there are many positive changes in the country regarding this issue. If adaptation of the society to the trade market economy relations is to be successful in Kazakhstan, harmonization of social relationships within the state will require a longer period of adjustment and more effort. To avoid replaying Soviet internationalism in the politics of multiple identities, Kazakhstan should create the new form of "syncretic amalgamation," which implies equal development of all ethnic groups. In this case, I believe that the idea of institutional syncretism – the term used by Dennis Galvan in his book *The State Must Be Our Master of Fire* – must be adopted and implemented as a main objective of the politics of multiple identities. Galvan uses the term "institutional syncretism" to describe the process of culturally sustainable development in Senegal. The author identifies syncretism as a process of "creative bricolage, whereby the elements that make up new and old institutions became raw material in fabrication of new, blended, innovative institutional arrangement at all levels of institutional structure."[15] Institutional syncretism, according to Galvan, is the process of refashioning all levels of institutional structure (administrative hierarchies, formal rules, informal rules, habits, and values) by drawing on elements from both newly imposed institutional structures and "remembered" traditional arrangements.[16] Galvan claims that institutional syncretism is a "recipe for sustainable modernity," which creates recombination of institutional elements with distinctive cross-hatching at every level of the institutional structure. In other words, institutional syncretism implies that different institutional structures should not compete, dominate, or oppress each other but merge in a syncretic way to enhance, elaborate, and enrich each other to form a new type of intercultural cooperation and encourage ethnical coexistence. Further, we will discuss the potential Kazakhstanian version of institutional syncretism – Eurasian unity.

EURASIAN UNITY VS. SOVIET INTERNATIONALISM

President Nazarbayev emphasizes that Eurasian integration is necessary for state security. He points to the "three whales" or political expressions of the Eurasian idea that were created under the initiative of Kazakhstan: the Eurasian Economic Community (EurAsEC), the Shanghai Cooperation Organization (sco), and the Conference on Interaction and Confidence Building Measures in Asia (cicbma). These are three different expressions of how the Eurasian idea works in practice. Nazarbayev's goal is for Astana to become the spiritual capital, the heart of Eurasia.[17] It should be mentioned that Kazakhstan, as the country with the most successful economic development and the most stable social and political situation among the post-Soviet Central Asian countries, aspires to leadership in the Central Asian region.

The idea of Eurasian integration means integration of different ethnic groups in a polyethnic state, "as the state where synthesis of Turk and Slavic ethno-social groups and also many other ethnical groups are presented."[18] Edward Schatz skeptically calls the Eurasian idea "ambiguous cultural categories designed for universalistic appeal and broad resonance, just the vision of *homo sovieticus*."[19] Some scholars also put forth skeptical prognoses regarding multiethnic states. Ernest Gellner claims that the nation is something stable and inflexible and, therefore, that multiethnic states are conceptually incoherent and inherently unstable.[20] On the contrary, Paul Spickard emphasizes that ethnicity or even "race is not a thing or condition but a process."[21] Furthermore, Paul Gillespie and Bridig Laffen believe that identity is "social and relational rather than solitary or atomized; it is not immutable or unchanging, but continually constructed and narrated. It is multiple, not singular. And in its national setting it has to adapt to changing circumstances in which new transnational identities may emerge."[22]

The multiethnic society requires a flexible approach, which implies syncretic amalgamation of the institutions. National identity revitalization provides more challenges for nationhood building in a multiethnic state. People need to share a common history (a remembrance of the past), a common culture (an understanding of the present), and a common destiny (a vision for the future) to be united while preserving cultural diversity. The politics of multiple identities in Kazakhstan encourages diversity while building the Kazakhstanian nation. Irrespective of their nationalities, Kazakhstanians share a common past, present values, and future aspirations: "We are all different but we are one nation" – the formula that reminds one that the Canadian version of multiculturalism ideally should work for Kazakhstan.

Along with sharing common codes and symbols, which are based on recognition and assimilation of different cultures, sharing a common language is one of the crucial criteria for unifying the nation. This is quite a controversial issue in post-Soviet Central Asian countries, since, during the long Soviet period, indigenous languages were not popular among Soviet authorities, for whom the Russian language was the symbol of education and cultural development. Today, the fact that the Kazakh language was almost forgotten by the new generation of Kazakhstanians is another challenge for nation building in Kazakhstan.

THE LOST GENERATION AND THE KAZAKH LANGUAGE REVIVAL

Til zhok zherde ult zhok.
Where there is no language there won't be a nation.

KAZAKH PROVERB

Language is a very important factor in national and ethnic integration and identification processes. There are many russophones among the urban population of Kazakhstan, especially ethnic Russians who are "acculturated in Soviet-values and [are] unable to justify their existence without close links with Russians or with Russia."[23] Some scholars argue that, if during the Soviet period there was russification of the state, the aspiration of the new government is to reinforce the process of Kazakh-ification of the country. They claim that many people of non-Kazakh nationalities living in Kazakhstan claim that the politics of the Kazakh language revival amounts to an oppression of other nationalities,[24] while others recognize that the process of Kazakhification of the state is a re-flex reaction against the politics of russification that was imposed by the Soviet government for many years.[25]

Alevtina, a young Russian woman, claims, "I've received a denial from several prestigious companies in Astana when I tried to find a high-paying job there. I do not know the Kazakh language, and that's become the main obstacle. I do not think it is fair. Why should I learn it if I have no wish to do so? Moreover, many native Kazakhs do not know their language, too."[26]

"Most young Kazakh people speak Russian at home, in the office, at the university, at meetings with their friends and relatives, even though they are all native Kazakhs. I think the new generation of Kazakhs does not even realize that they are disclaiming their culture when refusing to speak Kazakh," says Maral, a university teacher of the Kazakh language.

Here is one more example of how people feel toward the revitalization and promotion of the Kazakh language. One day I was traveling by train from Astana to Karaganda. A small Russian girl of nearly six years old sat with her grandmother just next to me, looking over the postcards she took from the Astana Oceanarium. "Granny," she said, "I cannot read these letters." The old woman took the card and tried to read aloud what was written there. It was a description of the rare fish, given in the Kazakh language. After unsuccessful attempts to explain what was written on the card, she suddenly shouted, "Why they do not provide a translation into the Russian language?" Then she added, "Earlier, my dear, all *normal people* used to speak Russian only." This is an obvious example of how people of the older generation can influence young children's perception about not only language politics but also intolerance toward the Kazakh language.

There are many other examples that show how people try to adapt to the new environment. Natalya and her husband are a young Russian couple living just next door to me. Their three-year-old son Nikita attends a Kazakh group in kindergarten. When I asked Natalya about how hard it was for Nikita to adapt, given that he was the only Russian boy in his group and not skilled in the Kazakh language, she answered, "We want our son to speak fluently both the Kazakh and Russian languages. We lack knowledge of the Kazakh language ourselves, but we want Nikita to be accustomed to speak Kazakh and feel comfortable among Kazakh-speaking people."

There are many TV shows and intellectual programs that promote the image of nonnative Kazakhs who speak Kazakh fluently as people who deserve respect and admiration. "When I see on TV a blond girl with a European appearance who is the same age as me and who perfectly speaks a literary Kazakh language, I feel a bit ashamed because I realize that my native language skills are limited to understanding the common words and phrases. And, of course, it inspires me to learn it in a proper way!" says Madina, a twenty-one-year-old student of Karaganda State University.

The politics of ethnic language revival is one of the main directions of the realization of the politics of multiple identities in Kazakhstan.

Considering new ethnopolitical conditions, the aspiration to raise the status of the Kazakh ethnic language is a natural process.[27] However, in comparison with other post-Soviet Central Asian countries, Kazakh language revitalization is a multiple-value and ambitious process.

Central Asian political cultures, as well as national identities, were shaped by the Soviet experience. "While pre-revolutionary Russian rule did not significantly alter Central Asian traditions, Soviet rule transformed the indigenous cultures," says Charles E. Ziegler.[28] However, there is something, according to many scholars, that puts Kazakhstan and the Kazakh people in a unique position among the other post-Soviet states. During the Soviet era, Slavs predominated in the territory of Kazakhstan due to a longtime politics of settlement of Russians in Kazakhstan. Therefore, the process of cultural and linguistic russification of native Kazakhs was historically determined: "Kazakhs aspired to active integration into the new Soviet order as the best means of survival."[29] All Central Asian republics experienced an influx of ethnic Russians, but, according to many social scientists, Kazakhstan was unique in the extent to which nationality was diluted by Russian immigrants. Schatz claims that Kazakh people "tend to be more assimilated to Soviet-Russian culture than other Central Asians."[30] Therefore, urban Kazakhs of the central and northern parts that, during the Soviet period, were mostly occupied by migrants from Russia tend to be more russified. The population of the southern and western parts of the country is still considered to be more nationalistic. Another feature of this process is russification of the elites during the Soviet period. It was prestigious to be fluent in the Russian language and receive a higher education in Russian universities and academies. Therefore, not only political elite but also intellectuals were fostered mostly by Russian culture.

Bhavna Dave emphasizes that there was no nationhood in nomadic Kazakh society because "nationhood [was] impossible [due to] the lack of industrialization and modernization," and then, in "post-colonial" Kazakhstani society, the russified national elite started to create an "imagined national community."[31] As a result, Soviet nationality politics has had an influence over the Kazakh ethnic elite and developed into a special form of national identity. The Russian language was promoted as the language of international communication. Russians, the carriers of this language, enjoyed the privilege of feeling at home everywhere when crossing the territory of the great motherland, because they did not need to learn local languages: "Soviet-era internationalism reserved a special role for Slavs (especially ethnic Russians) as the missionaries, emissaries, and technical specialists of Soviet rule," Schatz states.[32] Therefore, indigenous peoples' languages were mostly disregarded, often displaced by Russian and sometimes even forgotten. The Russian language gradually became a symbol of enlightenment and progress. This marker of higher social status made the Kazakh language unpopular during the Soviet era.

Here is a story described by a friend of mine:

> At the end of the seventies my mother and her friend [an ethnic Kazakh] came to the public library in Almaty. They took some books from the librarian who was an ethnic Russian and started to prepare for the seminar. As both of them were Kazakh natives, they spoke Kazakh with each other. Afterward, the librarian made a note that it is a public library and that they were supposed to speak Russian there, as all other educated people do. She also added, "If you want to speak the Kazakh language, you'd better go to your *auls*" [village, farm]. My mother said she is still burning with shame because she did not say a word to that woman who actually humiliated her and her friend.

Speaking the Kazakh language symbolized that a person was an uneducated rural dweller. Consequently, urban Kazakhs were ashamed to speak their own language in public places.

Here is another story of Saida, a young Kazakh woman:

> When we were pupils, we used to play in the schoolyard after classes. During the games, boys from the upper classes, who obviously belonged to Slavic nations, usually told our Russian classmates to keep a distance and not play with "these stupid rural Kazakhs." I was not able to rebel like some Kazakh boys did. I remember I was just ashamed to be Kazakh.

Such attitudes toward the Kazakh language make it unpopular among native Kazakhs. As a result, many people, especially in urban areas, felt alien in their own country. Perhaps it was not the consequence of the official version of Soviet politics. However, many people paradoxically felt oppressed in their own homeland.

Today, the Kazakh language revival is one of the main tasks of the governmental policy and an important instrument of nation building in a multiethnic Central Asian country. It is believed that sequential and systematic realization of the state language revival policy strengthens the sovereignty of the newly independent state. Moreover, it is "shaping ethnic, cultural, political, civic and geopolitical identities."[33]

According to the Paragraph 7 of the Constitution of the Republic of Kazakhstan of August 30, 1995,

1. The official language of the Republic of Kazakhstan is the Kazakh language.
2. In state organizations and institutions of local government, both the Kazakh and Russian languages are officially used.
3. The state is concerned for the creation of conditions for study- ing and developing all languages of the people of Kazakhstan.

Paragraph 19 of the constitution says that each Kazakhstanian has the right to use her or his native language and culture; everyone is free in his or her choice of language of communication, education, study, and creativity.

According to the Languages Development State Program for the period 2001–2010, there are several steps in a language-development strategy: to develop social and communicative functions of the official language of Kazakhstan, to preserve cultural functions of the Russian language, and to develop the languages of other ethnic groups.[34]

In spite of such decrees, there is a big gap between the official status of the Kazakh language and its actual position.[35] The percentage of docu- ments written in the Kazakh language in central state institutions is just 20–30 percent; overall, document circulation is 45–50 percent. There are more than 2,300 newspapers and magazines published in Kazakhstan. However, only 458 of them are in the Kazakh language. Only five of 215 central and local television and radio programs are in the Kazakh lan- guage. Moreover, many electronic mass media realize the law about the use of language just on a formal level.[36]

According to other statistics, 80 percent of Kazakh schools are situ- ated in rural areas. In other words, only 20 percent of the schools where pupils can study in the Kazakh language are situated in urban areas. The problem of deficiency of high-quality textbooks, manuals, and methods in Kazakh schools, colleges, and higher educational institutions adds to the urgency. Today, the Kazakh language is spoken by 52 percent of the population. The Russian language is spoken by almost everyone, as a language of interethnic communication in Kazakhstan. The other problem is that the young generation of urban Kazakhs, especially in the northern and central parts of the country, has only a very basic, limited knowledge of the Kazakh language and still prefers to speak Russian with each other.

One of the positive reforms in language policy is the "Unity of Three Languages" project. Trilingual politics implies promotion of the Kazakh, Russian, and English languages among the population. According to the goals of this project, each Kazakhstanian should be at least trilingual; that is, each should speak Kazakh, Russian, and English fluently. The Kazakh language is an official language of the state, Russian is the language of interethnic communication, and English is a language of successful integration into the global economy.[37] At the same time, President Nazarbayev emphasizes the preservation of the Kazakh language as an official language that identifies Kazakhstan as an independent state: "Each country has its official state language that consolidates and unites the nation. In Kazakhstan, it is the Kazakh language. It cannot oppress other nationalities."[38]

There are many Kazakh language centers that have been established in cities and towns. Free Kazakh language courses are offered in governmental organizations, universities, and other institutions. However, people complain that the quality of knowledge that they get when studying these courses is low.

According to official statistics, 56.2 percent of the population of Kazakhstan is ready to send their children to a Kazakh school; 27.6 percent of them are Kazakhs, while 28.6 percent are non-Kazakhs.[39] The motivation for learning the Kazakh language by the younger generation of russified urban Kazakhs and people of other nationalities is stimulated by giving career prerogatives to those who speak Kazakh, Russian, and English fluently. Usually, instead of providing work for several people, the employers prefer to hire one person who knows all three languages. Therefore, many ambitious young people learn the Kazakh language not because of a high level of patriotism but just because they aspire to get a prestigious, well-paid job.

At the same time, President Nazarbayev emphasizes that the Russian language, used as the language of communication among ethnic groups, plays a significant role in stabilizing and strengthening inter-ethnic relations.[40]

To sum up, there are many positive reforms in the language develop-ment sphere. However, there are some obstacles to its realization. First of all, many Kazakh people simply lack the sense that the Kazakh language is their mother language. Some Kazakh language defenders claim that those young people are a lost generation, while others concede that re-alization of the language revival reforms needs time and patience. How-ever, violation and other enforcement activities could not only cause the inverse effect but also could provoke recurrence of the same phenomena of oppression toward the other 130 nationalities living in Kazakhstan. To inspire people to learn the Kazakh language, there is supposed to be a well-established motivating system for teaching the Kazakh language, in school and university programs as well as in short-term and long-term courses for those who wish to learn by themselves. Another factor is the scarcity of appropriate textbooks and practice materials, which does not reflect the significance of the issue.

PEOPLE WITH INTERETHNIC LINEAGE

The phenomenon of people with interethnic lineage is the inevitable con-sequence of the previous historical internationalization, as well as of the modern integration processes. Due to the international and interethnic character of Kazakhstani society, there are many cases of international marriages in Kazakhstan. The fact that there are many people with inter-ethnic lineage in Kazakhstan demonstrates the multiethnic character of the state. Usually, people with interethnic lineage are a mix of Turkic and Slavic ethnic backgrounds and assimilate and accommodate the tradi-tions, languages, cultures, and even mentalities of two and sometimes several ethnic groups. There are many different, sometimes completely unexpected, variations of multiethnic lineage that result from the pat-terns of social mixing in different historical periods.

People with multiethnic lineage usually enjoy being unique and are proud of their exclusive appearance and original heredity. Most of the people whose parents belong to differing ethnic groups and religions are considered to be more tolerant and accepting toward people of other nationalities. Zhanna is a twenty-six-year-old student in the Medical Academy:

> The question of self-identification is rather complicated to me. I cannot say that I belong entirely to Kazakhs or absolutely to Russians. Both cultures are close and relative to me. I speak Kazakh with my father and Russian with my mother. When people ask me about my nationality, I usually say that I am *métis* [*ka*]. However, when I changed my passport last year, I put "Kazakh" to the box "Nationality," even though it was my right to leave it empty or to choose any other nationality.

People with multiple lineage usually know and respect traditions and religions of both parents. At the same time, the picture of the identification processes of people with interethnic lineage is not uniform. People with interethnic lineage in Kazakhstan could be conventionally divided into three groups. The first generation includes those who were born during the Soviet period before 1970. They usually identify themselves as Soviet people, irrespective of their ethnic belonging. The second generation is those who were born during the last decade of the Soviet period. And the last group includes those who have been born since 1991.

Identity formation for the people with multiethnic lineage is related to the modern processes of cultural and ethnic integration, as well as to nationhood and the nation-building process in Kazakhstan. However, the issue goes far beyond the generally accepted considerations of institutionalized integration processes. Interplaying of multiple identity formation considering various social, cultural, and economic factors, as well as national ideology and other interests and conditions that incite people to transform their identity, are to be analyzed. The issue of people with multiethnic lineage assumes multidisciplinary analyses in order to reveal the features of sociocultural as well as psychological adaptation of people with unique lineage considering different features of social reality. This question is important in the light of modern globalization and integration processes, where the limits and boundaries among states and markets, cultures, ethnic groups, and even races may be disappearing. Moreover, multiple identities as a form of alternative identification of individuals with multiethnic lineage reveal debates about the important issue of supranational state existence.

CONCLUSION

Today, Kazakhstan is emerging as the most dynamic economic and political actor in Central Asia. Having gained independence barely more than
two decades ago, Kazakhstan stands a chance of becoming a "spokes-
country" for Central Asia to the West.[41]

The strategically important direction of the politics of multiple identities in Kazakhstan is to preserve and strengthen multinational concord. Since Kazakhstan gained its independence, the process of creating
Kazakhstanian unity has been one of the main and challenging tasks,
along with adapting to a market economy and building stable political
institutions. Kazakhstan, as well as other post-Soviet countries, cannot
simply extrapolate Western patterns of economic liberalization and follow established models. On the contrary, considering its unique past
and multiethnic diversity, Kazakhstan needs to create its own model of
a sustainable, united, multinational state.

As Charles Ziegler states, "Kazakhstan would seem to build a vi-
brant civil society, diversified marked economy, and functioning democracy. It is also significant that Kazakhstan has considerable human
capital, which has been nurtured by the state."[42] Today, thousands of
Kazakhstanian students are sponsored by the presidential program *Bo-
lashak* (Future) and pursue graduate and postgraduate degrees in the
world's best universities. Many students are also nominated to other
types of scholarships and continue their education in business, engineer-
ing, and the social sciences in the best universities of Europe, the United
States, New Zealand, and Australia, mostly at the graduate level. In addition, there are many other programs that provide young Kazakhstanians
the opportunity to study abroad, gaining postgraduate education and
international and cultural experience, and then to apply this knowledge
in the development of different spheres of their homeland.

In spite of criticism regarding the realization of some aspects of the
politics of multiple identities, Kazakhstan has great potential and prerequisites to create multinational unity where each citizen, irrespective
of his or her nationality, ethnicity, gender, or race, will fully recognize
his or her belonging to one nation. Creating institutional syncretism or
Eurasian unity as a new form of multinational unity, where all ethnic

groups have equal development opportunities, can be successfully implemented in Kazakhstan. To avoid replaying Soviet internationalism,
the new form of national unity should be based on respect of cultural
diversity while strengthening common symbols of belonging to one
united nation. President Nazarbayev has stated, "With a number of the
states which are interested in expansion and a deepening of dialogue
of civilizations, we could act in common with the large international
initiatives directed on rapprochement of understanding between the
East and the West."[43]

There are two issues that have increasingly attracted academic attention over the last decade. The first is multiple identity formation, which
is affected mostly by social relations. The second concerns the features
of the Eurasian integration. Both of these issues are logically linked with
each other. Having formal signs of commonality, such as territory, borders, law, and political institutions, sovereign states also propose an informal sociocultural identity that is the basis for their existence. For
many Central Asian countries, the identification process has become a
defining factor not only in preserving stability of government and network systems but also as the cornerstone for their further development.

Political stability, civil peace, and interethnic and international consensus, including spiritual consolidation of the society, are major conditions for progress and crucial for the successful development of Kazakhstan. Sustainable development of a multicultural society is quite a
complicated process where certain challenges and obstacles can modify
the scenario of further development of the multinational state. That is
why, in spite of positive transformations, there are still many controversial issues to face in the realization of the politics of multiple identities
in Kazakhstan.

NOTES

1. Johanna Johansson, *Learning to
Be a Good European: A Critical Analysis of
the Official European Union Discourse on
European Identity and Higher Education*
(Linköpings, Sweden: Linköpings Univer-
sitet, 2007), 47.

2. Ibid., 49.

3. Jan Aart Scholte, *Globalization: A
Critical Introduction*, 2d ed. (London: Palgrave Macmillan, 2005), 227.

4. Eric Hobsbawm, *On History* (London: Weidenfeld and Nicolson, 1997), 7.

5. Anthony Giddens, "The Nation as a
Power Container," in *Nationalism*, ed. John

Hutchinson and Anthony D. Smith (Oxford: Oxford University Press, 1994), 34.

6. The Constitution of The Republic of Kazakhstan, Paragraph 51 (modified on May 21, 2007).

7. *The Decree of the Government of the Republic of Kazakhstan*, 701 (July 17, 2008).

8. Kofi Annan, greeting to the participants of the Congress of Leaders of World and Traditional Religions, http://akorda .kz/www/www_akorda_kz.nsf/sections ?OpenForm&id_doc=C143ED5D655 D2EBC462572340019E5F3&lang=ru.

9. Bhikhu Parekh, *Rethinking Multiculturalism: Cultural Diversity and Political Theory* (London: Palgrave, 2000), 231.

10. Edward Schatz, "The Politics of Multiple Identities: Lineage and Ethnicity in Kazakhstan," *Europe-Asia Studies* 52.3 (2000), 496.

11. Ibid., 499.

12. Ibid., 502.

13. Quoted in Schatz, "Multiple Identities," 152.

14. Edward Schatz, *Modern Clan Politics: The Power of "Blood" in Kazakhstan and Beyond* (Seattle: University of Washington Press, 2004), 21.

15. Dennis Charles Galvan, *The State Must Be Our Master of Fire: How Peasants Craft Culturally Sustainable Development in Senegal* (Berkeley: University of California Press, 2004), 216.

16. Ibid., 220.

17. Address of President Nursultan Nazarbayev at the Eurasian National University: source – Official site of the President of the Republic of Kazakhstan – www .akorda.kz, accessed July 5, 2012.

18. Zhanna Kadyralina, "Evolution of National Idea in Kazakhstan," http:// www.ia-centr.ru/expert/1294/ (2007), 3, accessed August 5, 2012.

19. Schatz, "Multiple Identities," 491.

20. Ernest Gellner, *Nations and Nationalism* (Ithaca, NY: Cornell University Press, 1983).

21. Paul Spickard, "Race and Nation, Identity and Power: Thinking Comparatively about Ethnic Systems," in *Race and Nation: Ethnic Systems in the Modern World*, ed. Paul Spickard, 1–29 (New York: Routledge, 2005), 12.

22. Paul Gillespie and Bridig Laffen, "European Identity: Theory and Empirics," in *Palgrave Advances in European Union Studies*, ed. Michelle Cini and Angela Bourne, 131–50 (London: Palgrave Macmillan, 2006), 135.

23. Bhavna Dave, *Kazakhstan: Ethnicity, Language and Power* (London: Routledge, 2008), 1.

24. See, for example, Schatz, "Multiple Identities"; Nazpary, *Post-Soviet Chaos.*

25. Donaka O'Biken, *Kazahizatciya i yazikovaya politika v Post-Sovetskom Kazakhstane* [Kazahization and language politics in post-Soviet Kazakhstan] (2007), 12.

26. Interview by the author, Karaganda, 2008.

27. K. Nugmanova, "Yazik i grazhdanskoe samosoznanie v grazhdanskom obshestve" (Language and civil consciousness in civil society), *Sayasat-Policy* 5 (2003): 51–52.

28. Charles E. Ziegler, "Civil Society, Political Stability and Economic Development in Kazakhstan," presentation at the ISA Annual Convention, San Francisco (March 26–29, 2008), 4.

29. Ibid., 3.

30. Schatz, "Multiple Identities," 492.

31. Bhavna Dave, *Kazakhstan: Ethnicity, Language and Power* (New York: Routledge, 2008).

32. Schatz, "Multiple Identities," 502.

33. Galiya Dosmukhambetova, "Yazikovaya politika kak instrument gosudarstvennogo stroitelsva: problemy i perspektivy" [Language policy as an instrument of state-building: Problems and prospects], *Kazakhstan in Global Processes*, academic edition, 3.17 (2008): 114, http://

iwep.kz/uploads/files/Magazine/3–2008
.pdf (accessed August 5, 2012; abstract in
English).

34. Ruslan Zhangazy, "Ob osnovnyh
tendenciyah yazikovoi politiki" [About
General Tendencies of the Language
Politics], July 11, 2006, http://www.kisi
.kz/site.html?id=3726, accessed August
5, 2012.

35. Dosmukhambetova, "Yazikovaya
politika," 113.

36. Ibid., 114.

37. Nursultan Nazarbayev, address of
the President of Kazakhstan, New Kazakhstan in the New World, http://akorda.kz
/www/www_akorda_kz.nsf/sections
?OpenForm&id_doc=BC3DF7C6FB
65732E46257291002A9331&lang=en,
March 2007.

38. Interactive lecture of the President
of the Republic of Kazakhstan Nursultan
Nazarbayev, September 3, 2007.

39. Decree of the Governmental of the
Republic of Kazakhstan, 701, July 17, 2008.

40. R. Zhangazy, "Ob osnovnyh tendenciyah yazikovoi politiki" [About general tendencies of language politics], July
11, 2006, http://www.kisi.kz/site.html?id
=3726, accessed July 5, 2012.

41. Anna Wolowska, "The OSCE Chairmanship – Kazakhstan's Self-Promotion
Campaign?" Centre for Eastern Studies,
2010, 2, http://www.osw.waw.pl/en/publik
acje/osw-commentary/2010-01-11/osce
-chairmanship-kazakhstans-self-promo
tion-campaign, accessed July 5, 2012.

42. Ziegler, "Civil Society," 7.

43. Speech by President of the Republic of Kazakhstan Nursultan Nazarbayev
at the XIII session of the Assembly of the
People of Kazakhstan: source – official
site of the President of the Republic of
Kazakhstan – www.akorda.kz, accessed
June 5, 2012.

TWELVE

Chinese Americans, Turkish Germans: Parallels in Two Racial Systems

PAUL SPICKARD

THE HISTORICAL DEVELOPMENT OF THE SOCIAL POSITION OF
Turkish Germans from the 1960s to the 2000s bears a striking resem-
blance to the development of the position of Chinese Americans from
the mid-nineteenth century into the twentieth. This chapter explores
comparative aspects of similarity and highlights certain salient differences. Of course, there is a difference of time scale between the two
groups' experiences. The trajectory I am tracing for Chinese Americans
took place over nearly a century and a half, while, for Turkish Germans,
it has only been about forty years. But the crucial item – the formation
of a second generation – was delayed for nearly a century in the Chinese
American case on account of anti-Chinese immigration and citizenship
laws. By contrast, the formation of a German-born Turkish generation
occurred in quite short order. So, the time scale difference is much less
significant than it would appear at first glance.[1]

Several people have suggested that an apt parallel exists between
Turkish Germans and Mexican Americans.[2] While I recognize certain
elements of similarity between those groups, the social position of Mexican Americans historically has been more complex than that of either
Chinese Americans or Turkish Germans. Some Mexican Americans
are descendants of families that have lived in the American West since
before there was a United States; others immigrated yesterday. Sometimes some Mexican Americans have asserted a claim to Whiteness
(and, therefore, full citizenship); most of the time, they have been relegated to social Brownness (and, therefore, a marginal position vis-à-vis
membership in U.S. society).

By comparison, the generational structures of Chinese Americans and Turkish Germans are very similar, as they both consist mainly of an immigrant generation and a single American- or German-born generation. Finally, the current U.S. climate of public opinion fails to recognize that complexity, both historical and contemporary, and insists on casting Mexican Americans as a semipermanent, alien underclass. I believe that highlighting a Mexican-Turkish parallel may have the effect of legitimizing similar racist attitudes toward Turkish Germans as those directed toward Mexican Americans; that is something I am writing specifically to undercut. There is plenty of racism directed toward Chinese Americans, to be sure, but, over the last generation, they have begun to find a place in the social life of the American middle class that parallels a possibility I see for Turkish Germans in Germany.

Both Chinese Americans and Turkish Germans came to their new countries initially as the shock troops of the industrial order. Both were temporary laborers recruited to do hard, dangerous, faceless, and not-very-well-paid work. Beginning in the 1850s, young men from South China were hired through ethnic Chinese recruiters to do body labor in the United States, digging in the mines for gold and copper, building the railroads that knit the country together, cutting down forests to make lumber and clear farmland, canning fish on the Northwest coast.[3] Beginning in the latter 1960s and especially the 1970s, young men from Anatolia were hired through Turkish recruiters facilitated by both Turkish and German governments to do body labor, going down in the ground to dig for coal and working in steel factories, car assembly plants, and other industrial venues.[4]

Initially, both the Chinese and the Turkish young men who went abroad thought of themselves as sojourners – temporary laborers who intended to go out to work for a time, make some money, and then go back home where the capital they had acquired abroad would enable them to buy land or otherwise raise their family's standard of living. Many in each group did just that, and it came to pass that, in villages across Anatolia and South China, there lived men who had made modest fortunes abroad and returned home to spend the remainder of their lives.[5]

Some among both groups, Chinese and Turks, stayed on after their initial commitments and found other work. In the American West, Chinese formed the majority of the farm labor force in the latter decades of the nineteenth century. Chinese gang laborers filled in the mudflats around San Francisco. Others went into service work, in laundries and restaurants in cities and towns.[6] For Turks, some of those who stayed took apprenticeships and entered trades. Others opened small shops and restaurants, particularly the ubiquitous döner stands one finds in every German city and town.

Neither Chinese nor Turks were initially conceived of as candidates for membership in the host society. From the first citizenship law in 1790, the United States embraced a racial definition of national membership: in order to be naturalized, one had to be a "free White person." If a non-White person was born on U.S. soil, then that person was entitled to U.S. citizenship by the principle of *jus soli*, but non-White people could not apply for naturalization. Any child born to a citizen was entitled to citizenship because the United States also embraced the principle of *jus sanguinis*. There was a long-standing hierarchy among various kinds of White people, but the absolute bar to membership fell between Whites and non-Whites, and Chinese fell on the non-White side of that line – they were racially ineligible for naturalization.[7] Until the second half of the twentieth century, the United States failed to develop a language of immigration that included non-White peoples as potential members of the republic. Only during World War II, when alliance politics made the anti-Chinese bar embarrassing, did the United States change the rules to allow for Chinese people to become naturalized, and it was another generation before Chinese Americans were routinely regarded as normal members of American society.

It is equally true that the vast majority of ethnic Germans have never considered Turkish immigrants and their children as candidates for full membership in German society. Even more than the United States, Germany has been wedded to a notion of citizenship that is centered in the myth of the *Volk*. That myth is expressed in the music of Richard Wagner, in the philosophy of Friedrich Nietzsche and Arthur Schopenhauer, in the founding documents of the German nation, and in the ideology of National Socialism. The sense of Germany as a nation made up only of ethnic Germans is very strong. In the 1990s and 2000s, people whose ancestors moved from Friesland to the Ukraine long before there even was a German national government (and often from places that never became part of the German nation)[8] were admitted into the country on a fast track for citizenship, on the grounds they were *Aussiedler* – evacuees who presumably were returning to their home from abroad in exigent circumstances.[9]

At the same time, Germany has developed no language of immigration. Chancellor Helmut Kohl famously declared that Germany is not a nation of immigration, no matter that that declaration flew in the face of demographic reality. Germany has only very recently, haltingly and with many bureaucratic impediments, come to accept the possibility that nonethnic Germans might become German citizens, and there is still little social acceptance for such people, even if they be German born. In a 1999 by-election campaign in Bavaria, the Green Party, which was sure to lose, placed an unusual billboard on Munich streets. Three babies in diapers appeared with their backs to the camera – one Black, one White, one Asian – over the legend "In Deutschland geboren. In Deutschland zu hause" (In Germany born. In Germany at home). It was a radical sentiment then, and it is not much less radical today.

Both Turkish Germans and Chinese Americans have had to survive anti-immigrant movements that directed discrimination against them and sometimes turned violent. The anti-Chinese movement that reached its height in the 1880s, yet persisted as late as the 1990s, has been the subject of many studies. Highlights of the earlier period include the 1850 Foreign Miners Act that levied a tax on non-U.S. and European miners working in the California goldfields; it was directed against the Chinese. A White race riot broke out in Los Angeles in 1871 that killed twenty-one Chinese immigrants. San Francisco outlawed the queue, a uniquely Chinese hairstyle mandated by the Chinese government, to harass Chinese immigrants and to try to get them to go away. Anti-Chinese race riots rocked many western cities and towns during the 1880s, from Denver to Seattle to Rock Springs, Wyoming, where twenty-five Chinese working men died in a mob assault. In 1882, the U.S. Congress passed (over a presidential veto) a law that effectively excluded all Chinese people except for a tiny upper-class fringe from entry into the United States.[10]

Much less remarked thus far has been the campaign of rhetorical and physical attacks that has been launched against Turkish Germans and other immigrants, especially Muslims, in the last two decades. Some examples: In 1992, in Mölln in Schleswig-Holstein, people whom some called "right-wing extremists" threw Molotov cocktails and killed two girls and their grandmother. The following year, in Solingen, arsonists firebombed a Turkish German house and killed two women and three girls. In 2005, in Ludwigshafen, arsonists set fire to an apartment house and killed nine people. In the summer of 2009, Marwa al-Sherbini, an Egyptian pharmacist, was stabbed to death in a Dresden courtroom, while her family and court officials looked on, in an explicitly racist, anti-Muslim hate crime. No major German media outlet covered the story until some days later when huge anti-German demonstrations in Egypt attracted international attention.[11]

The propaganda of the American anti-Chinese movement had several distinctive themes. Chinese immigrants, it was said, were either incapable of learning or unwilling to learn the English language. They were unable to assimilate culturally to American ways of living. They had ongoing ties to their homeland and did not intend to stay. They did not understand American values like democracy. They were dirty and brought disease. The then current generation of American feminists focused especially on the status of Chinese women. The literature of the time (from the 1870s until the 1930s at least) depicted Chinese women as degraded people, forced into prostitution, the victims of Confucian patriarchy. It told tales of horror visited upon women in Chinatowns by Chinese gangsters. The widespread assumptions that Chinese women all were oppressed and that many were prostitutes provided one of the primary justifications for the Chinese Exclusion Act of 1882. On the other hand, Chinese American women could be rescued if heroic U.S. feminists like San Francisco settlement house worker Donaldina Cameron came to their rescue.[12]

The themes that surround the German anti-Turkish movement are not all that different, and they permeate German society, even among those who are liberally disposed toward immigrants. Turkish Germans, it is said, resist learning German, and they do not learn it well when given the opportunity. In 2009, I took a fourth-level German language course in Münster. The twenty students included a few Japanese on extended holidays, the spouses of a couple of medical researchers from China, a

Somali married to a German woman, seven immigrants from Turkey, and me, the only native speaker of English. Our teacher, a young liberal who said she votes for the Greens, tried to give us a curriculum relevant to our circumstances. That fall there was a lot of talk – in magazines like *Stern*, which we read together, and in our class – about the new test of German cultural knowledge that was to become part of the process for acquiring citizenship. At one point, she told us, "You know, the problem with the Turks is that they just don't want to learn German." At that moment she was looking at a class, one-third of whose members were German, none of whom had been in the country longer than three years, yet all of whom had achieved fourth-year proficiency, and all of whom worked an eight-hour job across town and then took a bus over to her three-hour class. Of course, they were working very hard to learn German, but she could not see otherwise, no matter what the evidence before her face.

Other stereotypes are equally pervasive and persistent. Turkish Germans, they say, are culturally too different ever to fit into German society; they do not understand the essence of the German character and sensibility. In any case, Turkish Germans do not intend to stay; if they did, they would shed their ongoing ties to their homeland, change their food and clothing, and speak perfect German. Turkish Germans, it is said, do not understand core German values. They are unhygienic. In particular, there is a focus on Muslim women's status by the current generation of German (and, for that matter, European and North American) feminists. There is a rich literature of women's degradation as prisoners of Muslim patriarchy, tales of horror at forced marriages and honor killings – images that are very much at odds with the actual lives of most Turkish and other Muslim women in Germany. Every German publisher wants a book by Seyran Ates, Necla Kelek, Ayaan Hirsi Ali, or some clone calling on society to rescue Muslim women from themselves, their men, and their culture.[13]

In both cases, the lives of second-generation, Western-born-and-raised Chinese Americans and Turkish Germans did not look very much like the anti-immigrant imagery. Yet both second generations were affected by that negative imagery, nonetheless. For several decades, because of the tiny percentage of Chinese Americans who were women and the ban on Chinese immigration, the American-born generation also remained tiny. Gradually, the numbers grew, but they did not begin to form a significant second generation until the decades after World War II. Chinese American young people grew up mainly in urban centers of the West (along with New York, Boston, and a few other eastern cities).

There they went to public schools. Frequently, their places of residence in poor urban areas meant that they were limited to elementary education at inferior schools. Those schools generally made no provision for English language learning. When I attended such schools in the 1950s and 1960s, I was well aware that my teachers were not prepared to see academic competence in Chinese American children, even as they were quite prepared to see it in me, a White child, to lavish attention on me, and to set challenges before me so I would learn and grow. I ended up at Harvard while smarter Chinese American classmates had fewer opportunities.

American-born Chinese typically spoke some Chinese, although just as typically they had little more than a child's vocabulary and spoke with a fairly heavy American accent. In each family, the younger children were more functional in English than in Chinese. Until the 1970s at least, Chinese Americans were pretty much limited to the ethnic enclave – Chinatown – for residence and jobs. Chinese Americans were discriminated against and ridiculed by White people in daily life without thought. And they remained forever foreigners in their native land, in the eyes of non-Chinese Americans. There is almost no Chinese American who has not heard, and often, a question sequence like this: "Where are you from?" (Answer: Chicago). "No, where are you really from?" The implication is that they are not Americans but are really from a foreign place they may not ever have seen, based on their appearance and their ancestry.[14]

Second-generation Turkish Germans, too, attend public schools, and the ones they attend frequently do not track them for academic success. Most schools make little or no provision for bridging from Turkish-speaking home environments to the German-speaking school environment. Some dedicated teachers seek out gifted immigrant students, but most track them into *Hauptschule*, or at best *Realschule*, rather than to

Gymnasium, and I have known several teachers who simply could not see academic excellence in a Turkish German face.

Most Turkish Germans have some fluency in Turkish, although the degree varies widely, and younger children in the family usually speak less Turkish than their older siblings. Even those who are relatively fluent often have at most a ten-year-old's vocabulary and speak with a German accent. A lot of Turkish Germans, especially those without university qualifications, find themselves limited to ethnic enclaves like Kreuzberg, Wedding, or Marxloh for residence and economic opportunity. Turkish Germans are routinely discriminated against in daily life without thought. I have encountered not one Turkish German who has not experienced being treated with suspicion by store clerks, and nearly all the young men have been stopped by the police. Like Chinese Americans, Turkish Germans remain foreigners in the land of their birth, at least in the eyes of most other Germans ("Where are you from?" Bremen. "No, where are you really from?").[15]

There is also a parallel between the experiences of these two groups in the way they have been portrayed in the movies. Early depictions of Chinese characters in American movies from the 1930s through the 1970s were pretty much racist nonsense, whether they be of the sinister criminal mastermind Dr. Fu Manchu scheming to destroy civilization; the clever but mysterious detective Charlie Chan sorting out murder and intrigue in Chinatown; or the goodtime girl Suzie Wong, the Asian woman as natural prostitute. Movie depictions only began to look like the actual lives of Chinese Americans in the 1990s, as the American-born generation finally came of age, with films like Wayne Wang's *Joy Luck Club*.[16]

By this measure, film depictions of Turkish Germans still languish in the first phase of sinister and degrading stereotypes. Even the much-praised movies of Fatih Akin, *Auf der Anderen Seite* (2002) and *Gegen die Wand* (2004), depict Turkish Germans and Turkey as exotic, foreign, and dangerous. They are full of crime, drugs, sex, violence, and dysfunction – perhaps because that is the kind of depiction for which Akin can get money to make movies. One hopes it does not take a couple of generations for film portrayals of Turkish Germans to begin to look like actual Turkish German lives. And actual Turkish German lives, it turns out, like actual Chinese American lives, are pretty mundane.

I would like to note one encouraging recent move in fiction and life-writing. In 1950, right at the beginning of the growth of a big American-born Chinese generation, Jade Snow Wong published an autobiography, *Fifth Chinese Daughter*. It was a tale of assimilation and uplift, a young girl growing up in the all-Chinese world of her parents' Chinatown home and going outside, to school and to play, and encountering America. Out of those two worlds – China and America, in Wong's imagination – she fashioned a life and career that became a model of striving and inclusion for Chinese American girls. Actually, the world of Wong's family was more blended than her depiction (her parents had already made several steps into American culture that Wong had a hard time perceiving), but she could not articulate that in-between-ness.[17] A 2009 book by Betül Licht, *In Meiner Not rief ich die Eule,* makes a similar move. Her character is depicted coming of age in a Turkish German world: "Unsere Wohnung war die Türkei – draußen vor der Tür begann Deutschland" (Inside our apartment was Turkey; outside the door lay Germany). Well, no. Inside any Turkish German house one finds not Turkey, but a blended culture of language, foods, objects, values, and manners. But the parallel between Licht's story and Wong's is a hopeful one.[18]

The generation of Chinese Americans that grew up reading *Fifth Chinese Daughter* came of age in the 1980s and 1990s. Two of its number – Gary Locke and Steven Chu – are now members of Barack Obama's Cabinet, the first Chinese Americans to occupy so high a public office. Does this mean that, in a generation perhaps, some younger version of Cem Özdemir may actually become a force in mainstream German political life? Germany, it seems to me, is not at that point yet, partly because the German public has not yet fashioned a language for conceiving of themselves as members of an immigration nation. But profoundly Germany is just that. At present, more than 10 percent of Germany's population are immigrants, and Turks are the largest number. Immigrants and their children together total over 18 percent (the comparable American percentages are 11 and 20 percent, respectively). The task ahead, it seems to me, is for Germany to develop a way of thinking about its manifest, as-yet-unacknowledged, but probably permanent racial and ethnic multiplicity.

NOTES

1. I am grateful for the reactions to my thinking in this paper of several people, among them Semra Sen, Bettina Hoffmann, Sadime Fahin, Annette Kroschewski, Luz Angélica Kirschner, Elisabeth Tuider, Josef Rabb, and Maria Herrera-Sobek. For my views on Chinese American and Mexican American history, see Paul Spickard, *Almost All Aliens: Immigration, Race, and Colonialism in American History and Identity* (New York: Routledge, 2007).

2. See also Thomas Faist, *Social Citizenship for Whom? Young Turks in Germany and Mexican Americans in the United States* (Aldershot, UK: Avebury, 1995).

3. Sources on early Chinese immigration and labor are many; here are a few: Gunther Barth, *Bitter Strength: A History of the Chinese in the United States, 1850–1870* (Cambridge, MA: Harvard University Press, 1964); Susie Lan Cassel, ed., *The Chinese in America: A History from Gold Mountain to the New Millennium* (Walnut Creek, CA: AltaMira Press, 2002); Yong Chen, *Chinese San Francisco, 1850–1943* (Stanford, CA: Stanford University Press, 2000); Mary Roberts Coolidge, *Chinese Immigration* (New York: Henry Holt, 1909; repr. Arno, 1969); Judy Yung, Gordon H. Chang, and Him Mark Lai, eds., *Chinese American Voices: From the Gold Rush to the Present* (Berkeley: University of California Press, 2006); Chris Friday, *Organizing Asian American Labor: The Pacific Coast Canned-Salmon Industry, 1870–1942* (Philadelphia: Temple University Press, 1994).

4. See, for example, Deniz Göktürk, David Gramling, and Anton Kaes, eds., *Germany in Transit: Nation and Migration, 1955–2005* (Berkeley: University of California Press, 2007); Richard Alba, Peter Schmidt, and Martine Wasmer, eds., *Germans or Foreigners? Attitudes toward Ethnic Minorities in Post-reunification Germany* (New York: Palgrave, 2003); Rita Chin, *The Guest Worker Question in Postwar Germany* (New York: Cambridge University Press, 2007); Rita Chin, Heide Feherenbach, Geoff Eley, and Atina Grossman, eds., *After the Nazi Racial State: Difference and Democracy in Germany and Europe* (Ann Arbor: University of Michigan Press, 2009); Betigül Ercan Argun, *Turkey in Germany: The Transnational Sphere of Deutschkei* (New York: Routledge, 2003); David Horrocks and Eva Kolinsky, eds., *Turkish Culture in Germany Today* (Providence, RI: Berghahn, 1996); Ruth Mandel, *Cosmopolitan Anxieties: Turkish Challenges to Citizenship and Belonging in Germany* (Durham, NC: Duke University Press, 2008); Zafer Senocak, *Atlas of a Tropical Germany* (Lincoln: University of Nebraska Press, 2002); Levent Soysal and Ayse Çaglar, eds., *Forty Years of Turkish Migration to Germany: Issues, Reflections, and Futures,* special issue of *New Perspectives on Turkey* 28–29 (Spring-Fall 2003); Klaus Bade, ed., *Auswanderer – Wanderarbeiter – Gastarbeiter: Bevölkerung, Arbeitsmarkt und Wanderung in Deutschland seit dem 19. Jahrhunderts* (Ostfildern: Scripta, 1984); Karl-Heinz Meier-Braun, *Deutschland, Einwanderungsland* (Frankfurt am Main: Suhrkamp, 2002); Karl-Heinz Meier-Braun, *"Gastarbeiter" oder Einwanderer?* (Berlin: Ullstein, 1980); Mark Terkessidis, *Migranten* (Hamburg: Rotbuch, 2000).

5. This has been true for most migration streams, although it runs counter to the myths common in American national memory. See, for example, Theodore Saloutos, *They Remember America: The Story of the Repatriated Greek-Americans* (Berkeley: University of California Press, 1956); Spickard, *Almost All Aliens,* 36–62, 94–106, 173–207.

6. Sucheng Chan, *This Bittersweet Soil: The Chinese in California Agriculture, 1860–1910* (Berkeley: University of California Press, 1986).

7. Matthew Frye Jacobson, *Whiteness of a Different Color: European Immigrants and the Alchemy of Race* (Cambridge, MA: Harvard University Press, 1998); Tomás Almaguer, *Racial Fault Lines: The Historical Origins of White Supremacy in California* (Berkeley: University of California Press, 1994); Paul Spickard, "What's Critical about White Studies," in *Racial Thinking in the United States,* ed. Paul Spickard and G. Reginald Daniel (Notre Dame, IN: University of Notre Dame Press, 2004), 248–74; Tim Wise, *White like Me* (Brooklyn, NY: Soft Skull Press, 2005).

8. Abraham Friesen, *In Defense of Privilege: Russian Mennonites and the State Before and During World War I* (Winnepeg: Kindred Productions, 2006).

9. William A. Barbieri Jr., *Ethics of Citizenship: Immigration Rights and Group Rights in Germany* (Durham, NC: Duke University Press, 1998). My observations about the lack of social acceptance of immigrants and their children in German society are based on thirty-seven interviews I conducted in 2008–2009 in several north German cities with young adults who are children of immigrants; twenty-four of them were with children of immigrants from Turkey.

10. Coolidge, *Chinese Immigration;* Elmer Clarence Sandmeyer, *The Anti-Chinese Movement in California* (Urbana: University of Illinois Press, 1973; orig. 1939); Stuart C. Miller, *The Unwelcome Immigrant: The American Image of the Chinese, 1785–1882* (Berkeley: University of California Press, 1969); Alexander Saxton, *The Indispensable Enemy: Labor and the Anti-Chinese Movement in California* (Berkeley: University of California Press, 1971); Jean Pfaelzer, *Driven Out: The Forgotten War against Chinese Ameri-*cans (New York: Random House, 2007); Charles J. McClain, *In Search of Equality: The Chinese Struggle against Discrimination in Nineteenth-Century America* (Berkeley: University of California Press, 1994). As late as the 1990s, the Chinese American scientist Wen Ho Lee found himself imprisoned and charged with espionage on the flimsiest of grounds, essentially on account of his Chinese ancestry; Wen Ho Lee with Helen Zia, *My Country Versus Me* (New York: Hyperion, 2001).

11. Sources on the anti-Turkish movement in Germany include Göztürk et al., *Germany in Transit;* Uli Bielefeld, *Das Eigene und das Fremde: Neuer Rassismus in der Alten Welt?* (Hamburg: Junius, 1991, 1992, 1998); Manuela Bojadzijev, *Die windige Internationale: Rassismus und Kämpfe der Migration* (Münster: Westfälisches Dampfboot, 2008); Hannes Loh and Murat Güngör, *Fear of a Kanak Planet: Hip Hop zwischen Weltkulturan und Nazi-Rap* (St. Andrä-Wördern: Hannibal, 2002); Christine Morgenstern, *Rassismus: Konturen einer Ideologie: Einwanderung im politischen Diskurs der Bundesrepublik Deutschland* (Hamburg: Argument Verlag, 2002); Jan Werner, *Die Invasion der Armen: Asylanten und illegale Einwanderer* (Mainz: Hase and Koehler, 1992); Günther Lachmann, *Tödliche Toleranz: Die Muslime und unsere offene Gesellschaft* (München: Pieper Verlag, 2006); Stefan Luft, *Abschied von Multikulti: Weg aus der Integrationskrise* (Augsburg: Resch-Verlag, 2006). Even people who are friendly to immigrants sometimes surrender to the anti-Turkish rhetoric in framing their responses; see, for example, Werner Schiffauer, *Parallelgesellschaften* (Bielefeld: transcript, 2008). On the al-Sherbini murder, see "Protestors Accuse Germany of Racism: Egyptian Fury at Dresden Murder," Spiegel Online International, July 7, 2009, http://www.spiegel.de/international/world/egyptian-fury

-at-dresden-murder-protestors-accuse -germany-of-racism-a-634842.html, accessed August 13, 2012.

12. Mildred Crowl Martin, *Chinatown's Angry Angel: The Story of Donaldina Cameron* (Palo Alto, CA: Pacific Books, 1977); Huping Ling, *Surviving on the Gold Mountain: A History of Chinese American Women and Their Lives* (Albany, NY: SUNY Press, 1998); Ruthanne Lum McCunn, *Thousand Pieces of Gold* (San Francisco: Design Enterprises, 1981); George Anthony Peffer, *If They Don't Bring Their Women Here: Chinese Female Immigration Bbefore Exclusion* (Urbana: University of Illinois Press, 1999); Benson Tong, *Unsubmissive Women: Chinese Prostitutes in Nineteenth-Century San Francisco* (Norman: University of Oklahoma Press, 1994); Judy Yung, *Unbound Feet: A Social History of Chinese Women in San Francisco* (Berkeley: University of California Press, 1995).

13. See, for example, Mina Ahadi, *Ich habe abgeschworen: Warum ich für die Freiheit und gegen den Islam kämpfe* (München: Heyne, 2008); Seyran Ates, *Große Reise ins Feuer: Die Geschichte einer deutschen Türken* (Reinbek bei Hamburg: Rowholt Taschenbuch Verlag, 2007); Seyran Ates, *Der Multikulti-Irrtum: Wie wir in Deutschland besser zusammenleben können* (Berlin: Ullstein, 2007); Doris Glück, *Mundtot: Ich war die Frau eines Gotteskriegers* (Berlin: Ullstein Taschenbuch Verlag, 2004); Necla Kelek, *Die Fremde Braut: Ein Bericht aus dem Inneren des türkischen Lebens in Deutschland* (München: Goldmann, 2006). Ayaan Hirsi Ali is not German, but her books are very popular in Germany, including *Mein Leben, meine Freiheit* (München: Piper, 2007) and *Ich klage an: Plädoyer für die Befreiung der muslimischen Frauen* (München: Piper, 2009). Ali is also extremely popular in the United States, where Islam also is racialized. For other, sometimes more muted examples of this genre that have appeared in the United States, see Nujood Ali with

Delphine Minoui, *I am Nujood, Age 10 and Divorced* (New York: Three Rivers Press, 2010); Jillian Lauren, *Some Girls: My Life in a Harem* (New York: Plume, 2010); Asra Q. Nomani, *Standing Alone in Mecca: An American Woman's Struggle for the Soul of Islam* (San Francisco: Harper Collins, 2005); Azadeh Moaveni, *Lipstick Jihad: A Memoir of Growing Up Iranian in America and American in Iran* (New York: Public Affairs Press, 2005); Masuda Sultan, *My War at Home* (New York: Washington Square Press, 2006).

14. Rose Hum Lee, *The Chinese in the United States of America* (Hong Kong: Hong Kong University Press, 1960); Victor G. and Brett deBary Nee, *Longtime Californ': A Documentary Study of an American Chinatown* (New York: Pantheon, 1973); Lin Yutang, *Chinatown Family* (New York: John Day, 1948); Mia Tuan, *Forever Foreigners or Honorary Whites? The Asian Ethnic Experience Today* (New Brunswick, NJ: Rutgers University Press, 1998); Xiaojian Zhao, *Remaking Chinese America: Immigration, Family, and Community, 1940–1965* (New Brunswick, NJ: Rutgers University Press, 2002).

15. H. Julia Eksner, *Ghetto Ideologies, Youth Identities, and Stylized Turkish German: Turkish Youth in Berlin-Kreuzberg* (Berlin: Lit Verlag, 2006); Ruth-Esther Geiger, *Ihr seid Deutschland, wir auch: Junge Migranten erzählen* (Frankfurt am Main: Suhrkamp, 2008); Konstantin Lajios, ed., *Die zweite und dritte Ausländergeneration: Ihre Situation und Zukunft in der Bundesrepublik Deutschland* (n.p.:, 1991); Norbert Gestring, Andrea Janssen, and Ayca Polat, *Prozesse der Integration und Ausgrenzung: Türkische Migranten der zweiten Generation* (Wiesbaden: VS Verlag für Sozialwissenschaften, 2006); Mely Kiyak, *10 für Deutschland: Gespräche mit türkeistämmigen Abgeordneten* (Hamburg: Edition Körber-Stiftung, 2007); Betül Licht, *In meiner Not rief ichy die Eule: Eine*

junge Türkin in Deutschland (Hamburg: Hoffmann und Campe, 2009); Karl Lajos, ed., *Die zweite und tritte Ausländergeneration* (Opladen: Westdeutscher Verlag, 1991); Cem Özdemir, *Ich bin Inländer: Ein anatolischer Schwabe im Bundestag* (München: Deutsche Taschenbuch Verlag, 1997); Katrin Panier, *Zu Hause ist, wo ich verliebt bin: Ausländische Jugendliche in Deutschland erzählen* ([Berlin]: Schwarzkopf und Schwarzkopf, [2004]); Sven Sauter, *Wir sind "Frankfurter Türken": Adolezente Ablösungsprozesse in der deutschen Einwanderungsgesellschaft* (Frankfurt am Main: Brandes und Apsel, 2000); Alois Weidacher, ed., *In Deutschland zu Hause: Politische Orientierungen griechischer, italienischer, türkischer und deutscher junger Erwachsener im Vergleich* (Opladen: Leske und Budrich, 2000); Nilgün Tasman, *Ich träume deutsch . . . und wache Türkisch auf: Eine Kindheit in zwei Welten* (Freiburg: Herder, 2008);

Mark Terkessidis, *Die Banalität des Rassismus: Migranten zweiter Generation entwickeln eine neue Perspektive* (Bielefeld: transcript Verlag, 2004).

16. Matthew Bernstein and Gaylyn Studlar, eds., *Visions of the East: Orientalism in Film* (New Brunswick, NJ: Rutgers University Press, 1997); Peter X. Feng, ed., *Screening Asian Americans* (New Brunswick, NJ: Rutgers University Press, 2002); Darrell Y. Hamamoto, *Monitored Peril: Asian Americans and the Politics of TV Representation* (Minneapolis: University of Minnesota Press, 1994); Robert G. Lee, *Orientals: Asian Americans in Popular Culture* (Philadelphia: Temple University Press, 1999); Jun Xing, *Asian America through the Lens* (Walnut Creek, CA: AltaMira Press, 1998).

17. Jade Snow Wong, *Fifth Chinese Daughter* (New York: Harper, 1950).

18. Licht, *In Meiner Not rief ich die Eule;* see also Tasman, *Ich träme deutsch.*

Bibliography

Ahadi, Mina. *Ich habe abgeschworen: Warum ich für die Freiheit und gegen den Islam kämpfe.* München: Heyne, 2008.

Ahmed, Sara. *Strange Encounters: Embodied Others in Post-Coloniality.* London: Routledge, 2000.

Alba, Richard, and Victor Nee. "Rethinking Assimilation Theory for a New Era of Immigration." *International Migration Review* 31.4 (1997): 826–74.

Alba, Richard, Peter Schmidt, and Martine Wasmer, eds. *Germans or Foreigners? Attitudes toward Ethnic Minorities in Post-reunification Germany.* New York: Palgrave, 2003.

Alcock, John. *The Triumph of Sociobiology.* New York: Oxford, 2003.

Alderson, Priscilla. "Children as Researchers: The Effects of Participation Rights on Research Methodology." In *Research with Children,* edited by Pia Christensen and Allison James, 276–90. London: Palmer Press, 2000.

Ali, Ayaan Hirsi. *The Caged Virgin: An Emancipation Proclamation for Women and Islam.* New York: Free Press, 2006.

———. *Ich klage an: Plädoyer für die Befreiung der muslimischen Frauen* [I Accuse: A Plea for the Emancipation of Muslim Women]. München: Piper, 2009.

———. *Infidel.* New York: Free Press, 2007.

———. *Mein Leben, meine Freiheit* [My Life, My Freedom]. München: Piper, 2007.

Ali, Nujood, with Delphine Minoui. *I am Nujood, Age 10 and Divorced.* New York: Three Rivers Press, 2010.

Alleton, Viviane. *L'écriture chinois.* Paris: Presses universitaires de France, 1984.

Almaguer, Tomás. *Racial Fault Lines: The Historical Origins of White Supremacy in California.* Berkeley: University of California Press, 1994.

Altstein, Howard, and Rita J. Simon. *Transracial Adoptees and Their Families: A Study of Identity and Commitment.* New York: Praeger, 1987.

Ålund, Aleksandra. *Multikultiungdom: Kön, etnicitet, identitet* (Lund: Studentlitteratur, 1997).

Ambjörnsson, Fanny. *I en klass för sig: Genus, klass och sexualitet bland gymnasietjejer.* Stockholm: Ordfront, 2004.

Ambrosini, Maurizio. *La fatica di integrarsi.* Bologna: Il Mulino, 2001.

Anderson, Benedict. *Imagined Communities: Reflections on the Origin and Spread of Nationalism.* London: Verso, 1991.

Andersson, Åsa. *Inte samma lika: Identifikationer hos tonårsflickor i en multietnisk stadsdel.* Eslöv: B. Östlings bokförl. Symposion, 2003.

Ang, Ien. "Can One Say No to Chineseness? Pushing the Limits of the

Diasporic Paradigm." *boundary* 2 25.3 (1998): 223–42.

———. *On Not Speaking Chinese: Living between Asia and the West*. London: Routledge, 2001.

Anthias, Floya. "New Hybridities, Old Concepts: The Limits of 'Culture.'" *Ethnic and Racial Studies* 24.4 (2001): 619–41.

———. "Translocational Belonging, Identity and Generation: Questions and Problems in Migration and Ethnic Studies." *Finnish Journal of Ethnicity and Migration* 4 (April 2009): 6–15.

———. "Where Do I Belong? Narrating Collective Identity and Translocational Positionality." *Ethnicities* 2 (2002): 491–515.

Apo, Satu. "Suomalaisuuden stigmatisoinnin traditio" [The tradition of the stigmatization of Finnishness]. In *Elävänä Euroopassa: Muuttuva suomalainen identiteetti*, edited by Pertti Alasuutari and Petri Ruuska, 83–128. Tampere: Vastapaino, 1998.

Appadurai, Arjun. *Modernity at Large: Cultural Dimension of Globalization*. Minneapolis: University of Minnesota Press, 1996.

Argun, Betigül Ercan. *Turkey in Germany: The Transnational Sphere of Deutschkei*. New York: Routledge, 2003.

Armstrong, Sarah, and Petrina Slaytor. *The Colour of Difference*. Sydney: The Federation Press, 2001.

Aspers, Patrik. *Markets in Fashion: A Phenomenological Approach*. Routledge Studies in Business Organizations and Networks. London: Routledge, 2005.

Ates, Seyran. *Große Reise ins Feuer: Die Geschichte einer deutschen Türken*. Reinbek bei Hamburg: Rowholt Taschenbuch Verlag, 2007.

———. *Der Multikulti-Irrtum: Wie wir in Deutschland besser zusammenleben können*. Berlin: Ullstein, 2007.

Auguin, Estelle, and Florence Lévy. "Langue et vulnérabilité des migrations Chinoises actuelles." *Revue européenne des migrations internationales* 23.3 (2007): 67–84.

Babiński, Grzegorz. "Mniejszości narodowe i etniczne w Polsce w świetle spisu ludności z roku 2002." *Studia Socjologiczn* 1 (January 2004): 139–52.

Bade, Klaus. "Labour, Migration, and the State: Germany from the Late Nineteenth Century to the Onset of the Great Depression." In *Population, Labour, and Migration in Nineteenth and Twentieth Century Germany*, edited by Klaus Bade. New York: St. Martin's, 1987.

———. *Migration in European History*. Oxford: Blackwell, 2003.

———. *Vom Auswanderungsland zum Einwanderungsland? Deutschland 1880–1980* (From a country of emigration to a country of immigration? Germany, 1880–1980). Berlin: Colloquium Verlag, 1983.

———, ed. *Auswanderer – Wanderarbeiter – Gastarbeiter: Bevölkerung, Arbeitsmarkt und Wanderung in Deutschland seit dem 19. Jahrhunderts* [Immigrant – migrant – guest workers: Population, employment, and migration in Germany since the nineteenth century]. Ostfildern: Scripta, 1984.

Bakare-Yusuf, Bibi. "Rethinking Diasporicity: Embodiment, Emotion, and the Displaced Origin." *African and Black Diaspora: An international Journal* 1 (July 2008): 147–58.

Banks, Marcus. *Ethnicity: Anthropological Constructions*. London: Routledge, 1996.

Barbara, Augustin. *Les couples mixtes*. Paris: Bayard, 1993.

Barbieri, William A., Jr. *Ethics of Citizenship: Immigration and Group Rights in Germany*. Durham, NC: Duke University Press, 1998.

Barker, Chris, and Dariusz Galasiński, *Cultural Studies and Discourse Analysis:*

A Dialogue on Language and Identity. Thousand Oaks, CA: Sage, 2001.

Barth, Fredric. "Introduction." In *Ethnic Groups and Boundaries: The Social Organization of Cultural Difference,* edited by Fredric Barth, 9–38. Oslo: Universitetsforlaget, 1969.

Barth, Gunther. *Bitter Strength: A History of the Chinese in the United States, 1850–1870.* Cambridge, MA: Harvard University Press, 1964.

Bashi, Vilna. "Racial Categories Matter because Racial Hierarchies Matter: A Commentary." *Ethnic and Racial Studies* 21 (September 1998): 959–68.

Baum, Bruce. *The Rise and Fall of the Caucasian Race: A Political History of Racial Identity.* New York: NYU Press, 2006.

Baumann, Gerd. *Contesting Culture: Discourses of Identity in Multi-Ethnic London.* Cambridge: Cambridge University Press, 1996.

———. "Dominant and Demotic Discourses of Culture: Their Relevance to Multi-Ethnic-Alliances." In *Debating Cultural Hybridity: Multi-Cultural Identities and the Politics of Anti-Racism,* edited by Pnina Werbner and Tariq Moodood, 209–25. London: Zed Books, 1997.

Bebbington, Anthony, and John Miles. "Background of Children Who Enter Local Authority Care." *British Journal of Social Work* 19.1 (1989): 349–68.

Béja, Jean-Philippe, and Chunguang Want. "Un 'Village du Zhejiang' à Paris?" *Hommes et migrations* 1220 (1999): 61–72.

Bell, David A. *The Cult of the Nation in France: Inventing Nationalism, 1680–1800.* Cambridge, MA: Harvard University Press, 2003.

de Bellaigue, Christopher. *Rebel Land: Unraveling the Riddle of History in a Turkish Town.* New York: Penguin, 2010.

Benton, Gregor, and Frank N. Pieke, eds. *The Chinese in Europe.* London: Macmillan, 1998.

Benz, Wolfgang. "Fremde in der Heimat: Flucht – Vertreibung – Integration" [Foreigners in the homeland: Escape – expulsion – integration]. In *Deutsche im Ausland, Fremde in Deutschland* [Germans abroad, foreigners in Germany), edited by Klaus Bade, 374–86. München: C.H. Beck, 1992.

Bernstein, Matthew, and Gaylyn Studlar, eds. *Visions of the East: Orientalism in Film.* New Brunswick, NJ: Rutgers University Press, 1997.

Bielefeld, Uli. *Das Eigene und das Fremde: Neuer Rassismus in der Alten Welt?* Hamburg: Junius, 1991.

Biernat, Monica, and John F. Dovido. "Stigma and Stereotypes." In *The Social Psychology of Stigma,* edited by Todd F. Heatherton, Robert E. Kleck, Michelle R. Hebl, and Jay G. Hull, 88–124. New York: Guildford Press, 2000.

Birnbaum, Pierre. *The Idea of France.* New York: Hill and Wang, 1998.

Black, Edwin. *War against the Weak: Eugenics and America's Campaign to Create a Master Race.* New York: Four Walls / Eight Windows, 2003.

Bloemraad, Irene. "Who Claims Dual Citizenship? The Limits of Postnationalism, and the Persistence of Traditional Citizenship." *International Migration Review* 38.2 (2004): 389–426.

Blumenfeld, Warren J., Khyati Joshi, and Ellen E. Fairchild, eds. *Investigating Christian Privilege and Religious Oppression in the United States.* Rotterdam: Sense Publishers, 2008.

Bojadzijev, Manuela. *Die windige Internationale: Rassismus und Kämpfe der Migration.* Münster: Westfälisches Dampfboot, 2008.

Bozdogan, Sibel, and Resat Kasaba, eds. *Rethinking Modernity and National Identity in Turkey.* Seattle: University of Washington Press, 2000.

Braudel, Fernand. "L'immigration étrangère: un problème récent." In

L'identité de la France, vol. 2, *Les hommes et les choses*, 185–201. Paris: Arthaud-Flammarion, 1986.

Bredström, Anna. "Gendered Racism and the Production of Cultural Difference: Media Representations and Identity Work among 'Immigrant Youth' in Contemporary Sweden." *Nordic Journal of Women's Studies* 11.2 (2003): 78–88.

Brewer, John, and Frank Trentmann, eds. *Consuming Cultures, Global Perspectives: Historical Trajectories, Transnational Exchanges*. Oxford and New York: Berg, 2006.

Brewer, Marilynn B. "The Social Self: On Being the Same and Different at the Same Time." *Personality and Social Psychology Bulletin* 17 (1991): 475–82.

Bridenthal, Renate. "Germans from Russia: The Political Network of a Double Diaspora." In *The Heimat Abroad: The Boundaries of Germanness*, edited by Krista O'Donnell, Renate Bridenthal, and Nancy Reagin, 187–218. Ann Arbor: University of Michigan Press, 2005.

Britton, Nadia Joanne. "Racialized Identity and the Term 'Black.'" In *Practising Identities: Power and Resistance*, edited by Sasha Roseneil and Julie Seymour, 134–54. London: Macmillan, 1999.

Brubaker, Rogers. *Citizenship and Nationhood in France and Germany*. Cambridge, MA: Harvard University Press, 1992.

———. *Ethnicity without Groups*. Cambridge, MA: Harvard University Press, 2006.

———. "Immigration, Citizenship, and the Nation-State in France and Germany: A Comparative Historical Analysis." *International Sociology* 5.4 (1990): 379–407.

———. "The Return of Assimilation? Changing Perspectives on Immigration and Its Sequels in France, Germany, and the United States." *Ethnic and Racial Studies* 24.4 (2001): 531–48.

Brubaker, Rogers, Mara Loveman, and Peter Stamatov. "Ethnicity as Cognition." *Theory and Society* 33.1 (2004): 31–64.

Brune, Ylva. "Nyheter på gränsen – Tre Studier i journalistik om 'invandrare', flyktingar och rasistiskt våld." PhD diss., Göteborg University, 2004.

Buitelaar, M. W. "Negotiating the Rules of Chaste Behaviour: Re-interpretations of the Symbolic Complex of Virginity by Young Women of Moroccan Descent in The Netherlands." *Ethnic and Racial Studies* 25 (May 2002): 462–89.

Buruma, Ian. *Murder in Amsterdam: Liberal Europe, Islam, and the Limits of Tolerance*. New York: Penguin, 2006.

Butcher, Melissa. "Universal Processes of Cultural Change: Reflections on the Identity Strategies of Indian and Australian Youth." *Journal of Intercultural Studies* 25.3 (2004): 215–31.

Carey, Jane, and Claire McLisky, eds. *Creating White Australia*. Sydney: Sydney University Press, 2009.

Caritas/Migrantes. *Immigrazione. Dossier statistico 2009. XIX Rapporto*. Roma: Idos, 2010.

Cassel, Susie Lan, ed. *The Chinese in America: A History from Gold Mountain to the New Millennium*. Walnut Creek, CA: AltaMira Press, 2002.

Cattelain, Chloé, Marylène Lieber, Clair Saillard, and Sébastian Nguyen. "Les déclassés du nord: Une nouvelle migration chinoise en France." *Revue européennes des migrations internationales* 21.3 (2005): 27–52.

Ceccagno, Antonella. "New Chinese Migrants in Italy." *International Migration* 41.3 (2003): 187–213.

Chan, Sucheng. *This Bittersweet Soil: The Chinese in California Agriculture, 1860–1910*. Berkeley: University of California Press, 1986.

Chapin, Wesley D. *Germany for the Germans? The Political Effects of Interna-*

tional Migration. Westport, CT: Greenwood, 1997.

Chapman, Herrick, and Laura L. Frader,
eds. *Race in France: Interdisciplinary Perspectives on the Politics of Difference.* New
York: Berghahn, 2004.

Chen, Yong. *Chinese San Francisco, 1850–
1943.* Stanford, CA: Stanford University
Press, 2000.

Chin, Rita. *The Guest Worker Question in
Postwar Germany.* Cambridge: Cambridge University Press, 2007.

Chin, Rita, Heide Fehrenbach, Geoff Eley,
and Atina Grossmann, eds. *After the
Nazi Racial State: Difference and Democracy in Germany and Europe.* Ann Arbor:
University of Michigan Press, 2009.

Cini, Michelle, and Angela Bourne, eds.
*Palgrave Advances in European Union
Studies.* London: Palgrave Macmillan,
2006.

Colley, Linda. *Britons: Forging the Nation,
1707–1837,* 2d ed. New Haven, CT: Yale
University Press, 2005.

Colombo, Enzo. "Changing Citizenship:
Everyday Representations of Mem-
bership, Belonging and Identification
among Italian Senior Secondary School
Students." *Italian Journal of Sociology of
Education* 4.1 (2010): 129–53.

———, ed. *Figli di migranti in Italia.* To-
rino: Utet, 2010.

Colombo, Enzo, Lorenzo Domaneschi,
and Chiara Marchetti. "Citizenship and
Multiple Belonging: Representations of
Inclusion, Identification and Participation among Children of Immigrants in
Italy." *Journal of Modern Italian Studies*
16.3 (2011): 334–47.

Colombo, Enzo, Luisa Leonini, and Paola
Rebughini. "Different but Not Stranger:
Everyday Collective Identifications
among Adolescent Children of Im-
migrants in Italy." *Journal of Ethnic and
Migration Studies* 35.1 (2009): 37–59.

Conversi, Daniele. "Mapping the Field:
Theories of Nationalism and Ethnosym-

bolic Approach." In *Nationalism and
Ethnosymbolism: History, Culture and
Ethnicity in the Formation of Nations,*
edited by S. A. Leoussi and S. Grosby,
15–30. Edinburgh: Edinburgh University Press, 2006.

Coolidge, Mary Roberts. *Chinese Immigration.* New York: Henry Holt, 1909; repr.
Arno, 1969.

Crenshaw, Kimberlé W. "Mapping the
Margins: Intersectionality, Identity
Politics, and Violence against Women
of Color." *Stanford Law Review* 43.6
(1991): 1241–99.

Cybulska, Agata. "Das Bild der anderen"
[The picture of others]. In *Standpunkte.
Zum Verständnis deutsch-polnischer
Probleme* [Standpoints: Understanding
the Polish-German problems], edited by
Wolfgang Drost and Marek Jaroszewski,
55–70. Siegen: Akademisches Auslands-
amt der Universität Siegen, 1999.

Daniels, Roger. *Guarding the Golden Door:
American Immigration Policy and Im-
migrants since 1882.* New York: Hill and
Wang, 2004.

Darvishpour, Mehrdad. "'Invandrarflick-
or' som fyrdubbelt förtryckta? En
intersektionell analys av generationskonflikter bland 'invandrarfamiljer'
i Sverige." In *Bortom stereotyperna?
Invandrare och integration i Danmark
och Sverige,* edited by Ulf Hedetoft, Bo
Petterson, and Lina Sturfelt. Göteborg:
Makadam, 2006.

Das Gupta, Tania, et al., eds. *Race and
Racialization: Essential Readings.* Edinburgh: Canongate Books, 2007.

Dave, Bhavna. *Kazakhstan: Ethnicity, Language and Power.* London: Routledge,
2008.

Davies, Peter. *The Extreme Right in France,
1789 to the Present: From de Maistre to Le
Pen.* New York: Routledge, 2002.

De Certeau, Michel. *The Practice of Everyday Life.* Berkeley: University of California Press, 1984.

Dedic, Jasminka, Vlasta Jalusic, and Jelka
Zorn. *The Erased: Organized Innocence
and the Politics of Exclusion.* Ljubliana:
Mirovni Institut, 2003.

de los Reyes, Paulina, and Diana Mulinari.
*Intersektionalitet: Kritiska reflektioner
över (o)jämlikhetens landskap.* Malmö:
Liber, 2005.

De Luca, Rossana, and Maria Rosaria
Panareo. *Storie in transito: Coppie miste
nel Salento.* Milano: Guerini Scientifica,
2006.

Deutschlandstiftung Integration. *Sarrazin: Eine deutsche Debatte.* Munich:
Piper Verlag, 2010.

Dikötter, Frank. *The Discourse of Race in
Modern China.* Stanford, CA: Stanford
University Press, 1992.

———, ed. *The Construction of Racial
Identities in China and Japan.* Honolulu:
University of Hawai'i Press, 1997.

Docker, John, and Gerhard Fischer, eds.
*Race, Colour, and Identity in Australia
and New Zealand.* Sydney: University of
New South Wales Press, 2000.

Dorr, Gregory Michael. *Segregation's Sci-
ence: Eugenics and Society in Virginia.*
Charlottesville: University of Virginia
Press, 2008.

Dosmukhambetova, Galiya. "Yazikovaya politika kak instrument gosudarstvennogo stroitelsva: problemy i
perspektivy" [Language policy as an
instrument of state-building: Problems
and prospects], *Kazakhstan in Global
Processes,* academic edition, 3 (2008):
110–14.

Douglas, Anthony, and Terry Philpot.
*Adoption: Changing Families, Changing
Times.* London: Routledge, 2003.

Dovidio, John F., Brenda Major, and Jennifer Crocker. "Stigma: Introduction
and Overview." In *The Social Psychology
of Stigma* edited by Todd F. Heatherton,
Robert E. Kleck, Michelle R. Hebl, and
Jay G. Hull, 1–28. New York: Guildford
Press, 2000.

Dunn, Kevin M., Natascha Klocker, and
Natanya Salabay. "Contemporary Rac-
ism and Islamophobia in Australia."
Ethnicities 7.4 (2007): 564–89.

Edgar, Adrienne Lynn. *Tribal Nation: The
Making of Soviet Turkmenistan.* Princeton, NJ: Princeton University Press,
2004.

Ehrenreich, Barbara, and Arlie Russell
Hochschild, eds. *Global Woman: Nan-
nies, Maids, and Sex Workers in the New
Economy.* New York: Metropolitan
Books, 2002.

Einbürgerungstest. Wuppertal: Spinbooks,
2008.

Eissenstat, Howard. "Metaphors of Race
and Discourse of Nation: Racial Theory
and State Nationalism in the First
Decades of the Turkish Republic." In
*Race and Nation: Ethnic Systems in the
Modern World,* edited by Paul Spickard,
239–56. New York: Routledge, 2005.

Eksner, H. Julia. *Ghetto Ideologies, Youth
Identities, and Stylized Turkish German:
Turkish Youth in Berlin-Kreuzberg.* Ber-
lin: Lit Verlag, 2006.

Elder, Catriona. *Dreams and Nightmares
of a White Australia: Representing
Aboriginal Assimilation in the Mid-
Twentieth Century.* New York: Peter
Lang, 2009.

Eriksen, Thomas Hylland. *Ethnicity and
Nationalism. Anthropological Perspectives.* 2d ed. London: Pluto Press, 2002.

Eyerman, Ron. *The Assassination of Theo
Van Gogh: From Social Drama to Cultural Trauma.* Durham, NC: Duke University Press, 2008.

Faist, Thomas. *Social Citizenship for
Whom? Young Turks in Germany and
Mexican Americans in the United States.*
Aldershot, U.K.: Avebury, 1995.

———. "The Transnational Turn in Migration Research: Perspectives for the
Study of Politics and Polity." In *Transnational Spaces: Disciplinary Perspectives,* edited by Maja Povrzanovic Fryk-

man, 11–45. Malmo: Malmo University, IMER, 2004.

———. *The Volume and Dynamics of International Migration and Transnational Social Spaces.* Oxford: Oxford University Press, 2000.

Fassmann, Heinz, and Rainer Münz. "European East-West Migration, 1945–1990." *International Migration Review* 28.3 (Fall 1994).

———. "European East-West Migration, 1945–1990." In *The Cambridge Survey of World Migration,* edited by Robin Cohen. Cambridge: Cambridge University Press, 1995.

Favell, Adrian. *Philosophies of Integration: Immigration and the Idea of Citizenship in France and Britain.* 2d ed. New York: Palgrave Macmillan, 2001.

Feldblum, Miriam. *Reconstructing Citizenship: The Politics of Nationality Reform and Immigration in Contemporary France.* Albany, NY: SUNY Press, 1999.

Feng, Peter X., ed. *Screening Asian Americans.* New Brunswick, NJ: Rutgers University Press, 2002.

Fenstermaker, Sarah, and Candace West. *Doing Gender, Doing Difference: Inequality, Power, and Institutional Change.* New York: Routledge, 2002.

Fichte, Johann Gottlieb. *Addresses to the German People,* edited by Gregory Moore. Cambridge: Cambridge University Press, 2009.

Findlay, Carter Vaughn. *Turkey, Islam, Nationalism, and Modernity.* New Haven, CT: Yale University Press, 2010.

Finland's Romani People. Brochures of the Ministry of Social Affairs and Health 2004:2. Helsinki, 2004.

Finzsch, Norbert, and Dietmar Schirmer, eds. *Identity and Intolerance: Nationalism, Racism, and Xenophobia in Germany and the United States.* Cambridge: Cambridge University Press, 1998.

Foley, Pam, Jeremy Roche, and Stan Tucker, eds. *Children in Society: Contemporary Theory, Policy and Practice.* New York: Palgrave, 2001.

Foner, Nancy. "The Immigrant Family: Cultural Legacies and Cultural Changes." *International Migration Review* 31.4 (1997): 961–74.

Fonseca, Isabel. *Bury Me Standing: The Gypsies and Their Journey.* New York: Vintage, 1996.

Forsberg, Margareta. *Brunetter och blondiner: Sex, relationer och tjejer i det mångkulturella Sverige.* Lund: Studentlitteratur, 2007.

Fraser, Angus. *The Gypsies.* 2d ed. Oxford: Wiley-Blackwell, 1995.

Fraser, Steven, ed. *The Bell Curve Wars: Race, Intelligence, and the Future of America.* New York: Basic Books, 1995.

Friday, Chris. *Organizing Asian American Labor: The Pacific Coast Canned-Salmon Industry, 1870–1942.* Phildelphia: Temple University Press, 1994.

Friesen, Abraham. *In Defense of Privilege: Russian Mennonites and the State Before and During World War I.* Winnipeg: Kindred Productions, 2006.

Furri Tedeschi, Valentina. *E se Romeo si chiamasse Alì? Le coppie miste italo-mussulmane.* Civitavecchia: Prospettiva editrice, 2006.

Gabaccia, Donna. *Italy's Many Diasporas.* Seattle: University of Washington Press, 2000.

Galvan, Dennis. *The State Must Be Our Master of Fire: How Peasants Craft Sustainable Development in Senegal.* Berkeley: University of California Press, 2004.

Gans, Herbert J. "Symbolic Ethnicity: The Future of Ethnic Groups and Cultures in America." *Ethnic and Racial Studies* 2.1 (1979): 1–20.

———. "Toward a Reconciliation of 'Assimilation' and 'Pluralism': The Interplay of Acculturation and Ethnic Retention." *International Migration Review* 31.4 (1997): 875–92.

Gao, Yun, Florence Lévy, and Véronique Poisson. "De La Migration Au Travail L'exploitation Extrême Des Chinois-Es À Paris." *Travail, genre et sociétés* 16 (2006): 53–76.

Garrett, Paul Michael, and Jari Sinkkonen. "Putting Children First? A Comparison of Child Adoption Policy and Practice in Britain and Finland." *European Journal of Social Work* 6.1 (2003): 19–32.

Geary, Patrick J. *The Myth of Nations: The Medieval Origins of Europe.* Princeton, NJ: Princeton University Press, 2003.

Geiger, Ruth-Esther. *Ihr seid Deutschland, wir auch: Junge Migranten erzählen* [You are Germany, so are we: Young migrants tell their stories]. Frankfurt am Main: Suhrkamp, 2008.

Gellner, Ernest. *Nations and Nationalism.* Ithaca, NY: Cornell University Press, 1983.

Gestring, Norbert, Andrea Janssen, and Ayca Polat. *Prozesse der Integration und Ausgrenzung: Türkische Migranten der zweiten Generation* [Processes of integration and segregation: Second-generation Turkish immigrants]. Wiesbaden: VS Verlag für Sozialwissenschaften, 2006.

Giddens, Anthony. "The Nation as a Power Container." In *Nationalism,* edited by J. Hutchinson and A. D. Smith, 55–63. Oxford: Oxford University Press, 1994.

Gilroy, Paul. *Against Race: Imagining Political Culture Beyond the Color Line.* Cambridge, MA: Harvard University Press, 2001.

———. "'It ain't where you're from, it's where you're at': The Dialectics of Diasporic Identification." *Third Text* 13 (winter 1991): 3–16.

———. "One Nation under a Groove: The Cultural Politics of 'Race' and Racism in Britain." In *Anatomy of Racism,* edited by David Theo Goldberg, 263–82. Minneapolis: University of Minnesota Press, 1990.

Glück, Doris. *Mundtot: Ich war die Frau eines Gotteskriegers.* Berlin: Ullstein Taschenbuch Verlag, 2004.

Gobineau, Arthur Comte de. *The Inequality of Human Races.* New York: Fertig, 1999; orig. 1853–55.

Göktürk, Deniz, David Gramling, and Anton Kaes, eds. *Germany in Transit: Nation and Migration, 1955–2005.* Berkeley: University of California Press, 2007.

Goldberg, David Theo. "Racial Europeanization." *Ethnic and Racial Studies* 29.2 (2006): 331–64.

Goldschmidt, Henry, and Elizabeth McAlister, eds. *Race, Nation, and Religion in the Americas.* New York: Oxford, 2004.

Gordon, Tuula, and Elina Lahelma. "Kansalaisuus, kansallisuus ja sukupuoli" [Citizenship, nationality and gender]. In *Elävänä Euroopassa: Muuttuva suomalainen identiteetti,* edited by Pertti Alasuutari and Petri Ruuska. Tampere: Vastapaino, 1998.

Gould, Stephen Jay. *The Mismeasure of Man.* Rev. ed. New York: Norton, 1996.

Grant, Madison. *The Passing of the Great Race, or, The Racial Basis of European History.* New York: Scribner's, 1916.

Graves, Joseph L., Jr. *The Emperor's New Clothes: Biological Theories of Race at the Millennium.* New Brunswick, NJ: Rutgers University Press, 2001.

Green, Simon. *The Politics of Exclusion: Institutions and Immigration Policy in Contemporary Germany.* Manchester: Manchester University Press, 2004.

Gregor, Benton, and Frank N. Pieke, eds. *The Chinese in Europe.* London: Macmillan, 1998.

Gullestad, Marianne. "Blind Slaves of our Prejudices: Debating 'Culture' and 'Race' in Norway." *Ethnos* 69 (June 2004): 177–203.

Hall, Catherine. *Civilising Subjects: Metropole and Colony in the English Imagina-*

tion, 1830–1867. Chicago: University of Chicago Press, 2002.

Hall, Stuart. "Minimal Selves." In *Identity: The Real Me*. ICA Documents 6. London: Institute of Contemporary Arts, 1988.

———. "New Ethnicities." In *Stuart Hall: Critical Dialogues in Cultural Studies*, edited by David Morley, Kuan-Hsing Chen, 441–49. London: Routledge, 1996.

———. "The Question of Cultural Identity." In *Modernity and Its Futures*, edited by Stuart Hall, David Held, and Tony McGrew, 273–326. Cambridge: Polity Press and Open University, 1992.

———. "The Spectacle of the 'Other'." In *Representation: Cultural Representations and Signifying Practises*, edited by Stuart Hall, 223–90. London: Sage and Open University, 1997.

———. "Who Needs 'Identity'?" In *Questions of Cultural Identity*, edited by Stuart Hall and Paul du Gay, 1–16. London: Sage, 1996.

Hällgren, Camilla. "'Working Harder to Be the Same': Everyday Racism among Young Men and Women in Sweden." *Race, Ethnicity and Education* 8 (September 2005): 319–42.

Hamamoto, Darrell Y. *Monitored Peril: Asian Americans and the Politics of TV Representation*. Minneapolis: University of Minnesota Press, 1994.

Hancock, Ian. *We Are the Romani People*. Hatfield, UK: University of Hertfordshire Press, 2002.

Harinen, Päivi. *Valmiiseen tulleet: Tutkimus nuoruudesta, kansallisuudesta ja kansalaisuudesta* [Arrivals at the given: A study of youth, nationality and citizenship]. Helsinki: Nuorisotutkimusverkosto, 2000.

Harinen, Päivi, Leena Suurpää, Tommi Hoikkala, Petri Hautaniemi, Sini Perho, Anne-Mari Keskisalo, Tapio Kuure, and Krista Künnapuu. "Membership Contests: Encountering Immigrant Youth in Finland." *Journal of Youth Studies* 8/3 (2005): 281–96.

Haritaworn, Jin. "'Caucasian and Thai Make a Good Mix': Gender, Ambivalence and the 'Mixed-Race' Body." *European Journal of Cultural Studies* 12 (February 2009): 59–78.

Harris, Anita. "Shifting the Boundaries of Cultural Spaces: Young People and Everyday Multiculturalism." *Social Identities* 15.2 (2009): 187–205.

Harris, Perlita. ed. *In Search of Belonging: Reflections by Transracially Adopted People*. London: BAAF (British Association for Adoption and Fostering), 2006.

Heiberg, Marianne. *The Making of the Basque Nation*. Cambridge: Cambridge University Press, 2007.

Herbert, Ulrich. "'Ausländer-Einsatz' in der deutschen Kriegswirtschaft, 1939–1945" [Foreign labor in the German war economy, 1939–1945]. In *Deutsche im Ausland, Fremde in Deutschland* [Germans abroad, foreigners in Germany], edited by Klaus Bade, 354–67. München: C.H. Beck, 1992.

———. *Fremdarbeiter: Politik und Praxis des 'Ausländer-Einsatze' in der Kriegswirtschaft des Dritten Reiches* [Foreign workers: Politics and practice of the foreign labor in the German war economy during the Third Reich]. Bonn, Berlin: Neuauflage, 1980.

Herder, Johann Gottfried von. *J. G. Herder on Social and Political Culture*, edited and translated by F. M. Barnard. London: Cambridge University Press, 1969.

———. *J. G. Herder und die deutsche Volkwerdung* [J. G. Herder and the development of the German people], edited by Kurt Hoffmann. Berlin: Langenscheidt, 1934.

———. *Über den Ursprung der Sprache* [Treatise on the origin of language]. Berlin: Akademie-Verlag, 1959.

————. *Von deutscher Art und Kunst* [Of German character and art]. München: A. Langen, 1940.

Herrnstein, Richard J., and Charles Murray. *The Bell Curve: Intelligence and Class Structure in American Life.* New York: Free Press, 1994.

Hine, Darlene Clark, Trica Danielle Keaton, and Stephen Small, eds. *Black Europe and the African Diaspora.* Urbana: University of Illinois Press, 2009.

Hirschman, Albert O. *Exit, Voice, and Loyalty.* Cambridge, MA: Harvard University Press, 1970.

Hobsbawm, Eric. *On History.* London: Weidenfeld and Nicolson, 1997.

Hobsbawm, E. J. *Nations and Nationalism since 1780.* Cambridge: Cambridge University Press, 1990.

Hoerder, Dirk. *Cultures in Contact: World Migrations in the Second Millennium.* Durham, NC: Duke University Press, 2002.

Honkasalo, Veronika. "Nyt mä oon suomalainen ... varmaan: Nuoret maahanmuuttajat, etnisyys ja rasismi." [Now I am Finnish ... I guess: Young immigrants, ethnicity and racism]. MA thesis, University of Helsinki, 2001.

Horrocks, David, and Eva Kolinsky, eds. *Turkish Culture in Germany Today.* Providence, RI: Berghahn, 1996.

Howe, David. "Modernity, Postmodernity and Social Work." *British Journal of Social Work* 24.5 (1994): 513–32.

Howell, Signe. *The Kinning of Foreigners.* Oxford: Berghahn Books, 2007.

Huh, Nam Soon, and William J. Reid. "Intercountry, Transracial Adoption and Ethnic Identity: A Korean Example." *International Social Work* 43/1 (2000): 75–87.

Hultén, Gunilla. "50 år med främlingen." In *Journalisternas bok: 1901–2001* edited by Agneta Lindblom Hulthén. Stockholm: Svenska Journalistförbundet, 2001.

Huntington, Samuel P. *The Clash of Civilizations and the Remaking of World Order.* New York: Simon and Schuster, 1998.

Ifekwunigwe, Jayne, ed. *'Mixed Race' Studies: A Reader.* London: Routledge, 2004.

Institut für Staatspolitik. *Der Fall Sarrazin.* Albersroda: Rittergut Schnellroda, 2010.

ISTAT. *I matrimoni: Dati relativi agli anni 2004–2008.* April 8, 2010.

————. *Il matrimonio in Italia. Un'istituzione in mutamento. Anni 2004–2005.* February 12, 2007.

Jacobs, Margaret D. *White Mother to a Dark Race: Colonialism, Maternalism, and the Removal of Indigenous Children in the American West and Australia, 1880–1940.* Lincoln: University of Nebraska Press, 2009.

Jacobson, Matthew Frye. *Whiteness of a Different Color: European Immigrants and the Alchemy of Race.* Cambridge, MA: Harvard University Press, 1998.

Jasinskaja-Lahti, Inga, Karmela Liebkind, and Erling Solheim. "To Identify or Not To Identify? National Disidentification as an Alternative Reaction to Perceived Ethnic Discrimination." *Applied Psychology* 58/1 (2009): 105–28.

Jenkins, Richard. *Rethinking Ethnicity: Arguments and Explorations.* London: Sage, 1997.

————. *Social Identity.* London: Routledge, 2004.

Johansson, Johanna. *Learning to Be a Good European: A Critical Analysis of the Official European Union Discourse on European Identity and Higher Education.* Linkoping: Linkopings Universitet, 2007.

Jones, Elizabeth H. *Spaces of Belonging: Home, Culture and Identity in Twentieth-century French Autobiography.* Amsterdam: Rodopi, 2007.

Joshi, Khyati M. *New Roots in America's Sacred Ground: Religion, Race, and*

Ethnicity in Indian America. New Brunswick, NJ: Rutgers University Press, 2006.

Judson, Pieter. "When Is a Diaspora Not a Diaspora? Rethinking Nation-Centered Narratives about Germans in Habsburg East Central Europe." In *The Heimat Abroad: The Boundaries of Germanness*, edited by Krista O'Donnell, Renate Bridenthal, and Nancy Reagin, 219–47. Ann Arbor: University of Michigan Press, 2005.

Jupp, James. *From White Australia to Woomera*. 2d ed. Cambridge: Cambridge University Press, 2007.

Kadyralina, Zhanna. "Evolution of National Idea in Kazakhstan." http://www.ia-centr.ru/expert/1294/, 2007.

Kaluza, Andrzej. "Zuwanderer aus Polen in Deutschland" [Immigrants from Poland in Germany]. *Utopie kreativ* 141/142 (2002).

Al Karadaghi, Mustafa. "The Kurdish Nation Has the Inalienable Right of Self-Determination." *Kurdistan Times* 1.2 (Summer 1992).

Karlsson, Eva. *Att se sig själv: Nio flickors tankar kring massmedias bilder av 'invandrarflickor', samt deras syn på sig själva*. Norsborg: Södertörns högskola, Etnologi, 1999.

Karlsson Minganti, Pia. *Muslima: Islamisk väckelse och unga muslimska kvinnors förhandlingar om genus i det samtida Sverige*. Stockholm: Carlsson, 2007.

Kauanui, J. Kehaulani. *Hawaiian Blood: Colonialism and the Politics of Sovereignty and Indigeneity*. Durham, NC: Duke University Press, 2008.

Keaton, Trica Danielle. *Muslim Girls and the Other France: Race, Identity Politics, and Social Exclusion*. Bloomington: Indiana University Press, 2006.

Kelek, Necla. *Die Fremde Braut: Ein Bericht aus dem Inneren des türkischen Lebens in Deutschland*. München: Goldmann, 2006.

Kertzer, David I., and Dominique Arel, eds. *Census and Identity: The Politics of Race, Ethnicity, and Language in National Censuses*. Cambridge: Cambridge University Press, 2002.

Kevles, Daniel J. *In the Name of Eugenics: Genetics and the Uses of Human Heredity*. Cambridge, MA: Harvard University Press, 1985.

Kingsbury, Damien, and Michael Leach, eds. *East Timor: Beyond Independence*. Clayton, Australia: Monash University Press, 2007.

Kivisto, Peter. "Theorizing Transnational Immigration: A Critical Review of Current Efforts." *Ethnic and Racial Studies* 24.4 (2001): 549–77.

Kiyak, Mely. *10 für Deutschland: Gespräche mit türkeistämmigen Abgeordneten* [Ten for Germany: Conversations with representative people of Turkish origin]. Hamburg: Edition Körber-Stiftung, 2007.

Kleßman, Christoph. *Polnische Bergarbeiter im Ruhrgebiet 1870–1945: Soziale Integration und nationale Subkultur einer ethnischen Minderheit in der deutschen Industriegesellschaft* [Polish miners in the Ruhr Region, 1870–1945: Social integration and national subculture of an ethnic minority in German industrialized society]. Göttingen: Vandenhoeck und Ruprecht, 1978.

Korcelli, Piotr. "Emigration from Poland after 1945." In *European Migration in the Late Twentieth Century: Historical Patterns, Actual Trends, and Social Implications*, edited by Heinz Fassmann and Rainer Münz, 171–85. Brookfield, VT: E. Elgar, 1994.

Krampen, Cornelia. *Zuwanderung aus Polen und die katholische Kirche in Bremen: Migration und Religion in der modernen Gesellschaft* [Immigration from Poland and the Catholic Church in Bremen: Migration and religion in the modern society]. Hamburg: Verlag Dr. Kovac, 2005.

Kuhn, Philip A. *Chinese among Others: Emigration in Modern Times*. Lanham, MD: Rowman and Littlefield, 2008.

Kurczewska, Joanna. "Nationalism in New Poland: Between Culture and Politics." In *Transitional Societies in Comparison: East Central Europe Vs. Taiwan – Conference Prague 1999*, 193–208. Frankfurt am Main: Peter Lang, 1999.

Kurlansky, Mark. *The Basque History of the World: The Story of a Nation*. New York: Penguin, 2001.

Lachmann, Günther. *Tödliche Toleranz: Die Muslime und unsere offene Gesellschaft*. München: Pieper Verlag, 2006.

Lajios, Konstantin, ed. *Die zweite und dritte Ausländergeneration: Ihre Situation und Zukunft in der Bundesrepublik Deutschland* [The second- and third-generation foreigners: Their situation and future in the Federal Republic of Germany]. N.p.: 1991.

Lajos, Karl, ed., *Die zweite und tritte Ausländergeneration* [The second- and third-generation foreigners]. Opladen: Westdeutscher Verlag, 1991.

Lamb, Michael E. *Parenting and Childcare in Non-Traditional Families*. Mahwah, NJ: Lawrence Erlbaum Associates, 1999.

Lamont, Michèle, Ann Morning, and Margarita Mooney. "Particular Universalisms: North African Immigrants Respond to French Racism." *Ethnic and Racial Studies* 25.3 (2002): 390–414.

Larsson, Göran, ed. *Islam in the Nordic and Baltic Countries*. London: Routledge, 2009.

Lauren, Jillian. *Some Girls: My Life in a Harem*. New York: Plume, 2010.

Lee, Robert G. *Orientals: Asian Americans in Popular Culture*. Philadelphia: Temple University Press, 1999.

Lee, Rose Hum. *The Chinese in the United States of America*. Hong Kong: Hong Kong University Press, 1960.

Lee, Wen Ho, with Helen Zia. *My Country versus Me*. New York: Hyperion, 2001.

Lehtonen, Mikko. "Johdanto: Säiliöstä suhdekimppuun" [Introduction: From a container to a bundle of relations]. In *Suomi toisin sanoen*, edited by Mikko Lehtonen, Olli Löytty, and Petri Ruuska. Tampere: Vastapaino, 2004.

———. "Suomi on toistettua maata" [Finland is repeated land]. In *Suomi toisin sanoen*.

Lehtonen, Mikko, and Olli Löytty. "Miksi erilaisuus" [Why Otherness?]. In *Erilaisuus*, edited by Mikko Lehtonen and Olli Löytty. Tampere: Vastapaino, 2003.

Leonini, Luisa, and Paola Rebughini, eds. *Legami di nuova generazione*. Bologna: Il Mulino, 2010.

Levitt, Peggy, and Nina Glick Schiller. "Conceptualizing Simultaneity: A Transnational Social Field Perspective on Society." *International Migration Review* 38.3 (2004): 1002–39.

Levitt, Peggy, and Mary C. Waters. "Introduction." In *The Changing Face of Home: The Transnational Lives of the Second Generation*, edited by Peggy Levitt and Mary C. Waters, 1–30. New York: Russell Sage Foundation, 2002.

Lévy, Florence, and Marylène Lieber. "La Sexualité Comme Ressource Migratoire: Les Chinoises Du Nord À Paris." *Revue française de sociologie* 50.4 (2009): 719–46.

Lewin, Bo. "Sexualities of the World." In *Sexology in Context: A Scientific Anthology*, edited by Bente Træen and Bo Lewin. Oslo: Universitetsforlaget, 2008.

Licht, Betül. *In meiner Not rief ich die Eule: Eine junge Türkin in Deutschland* [In my distress I called the owl: A young Turkish woman in Germany]. Hamburg: Hoffmann und Campe, 2009.

Lie, John. *Multiethnic Japan*. Cambridge, MA: Harvard University Press, 2004.

Lieber, Marylène. "Chinese Migrants in Switzerland: From Mutual Assistance to Promoting Economic Interests." *Journal of Chinese Overseas* 6.1 (2010): 102–18.

———. "'When You Look Chinese, You Have to Speak Chinese': The Valorization of a Shared Unified Culture and Language." Paper presented to International Forum for Contemporary Chinese Studies, Inaugural Conference, "Post-Olympic China: Globalisation and Sustainable Development," Nottingham, 2008.

Lieber, Marylène, and Florence Lévy. "Migrations Chinoise En Suisse: Structures et Dynamiques des Réseaux: Premier Rapport Intermédiare." Neuchâtel: Université de Neuchâtel, 2007.

Lien, Pei-te. "Homeland Origins among Chinese in Southern California." *Ethnic and Racial Studies* 31.8 (2008): 1381–1403.

Ling, Huping. *Surviving on the Gold Mountain: A History of Chinese American Women and Their Lives.* Albany, NY: SUNY Press, 1998.

Łodziński, Sławomir. *Równoś i różnica: Mniejszości narodowe w porządku demokratycznym w Polsce po 1989 roku.* Warszawa: Wydawnictwo Naukowe SCHOLAR, 2005.

Loh, Hannes, and Murat Güngör. *Fear of a Kanak Planet: Hip Hop zwischen Weltkulturan und Nazi-Rap.* St. Andrä-Wördern: Hannibal, 2002.

López, Marta Sofía, ed. *Afroeurope@ns: Cultures and Identities.* Newcastle on Tyne, U.K.: Cambridge Scholars Publishing, 2008.

Lovell, Naida. "Introduction." In *Locality and Belonging,* edited by Nadia Lovell, 1–24. London: Routledge, 1998.

Lovelock, Kirsten. "Intercountry Adoption as a Migratory Practice." *International Migration Review* 34.3 (2000): 907–49.

Löytty, Olli. "Erikoisen tavallinen suomalaiuus" [Especially normal Finnishness]. In *Suomi toisin sanoen,* edited by Mikko Lehtonen, Olli Löytty, and Petri Ruuska. Tampere: Vastapainao, 2004.

———. "Meistä on moneksi" [Diversity is us]. In *Suomi toisin sanoen.*

Luczak, Czeslaw. *Polscy robotnicy przymusowi w Trzeciej Rzeszy podczas II. Wojny Swiatwej* [Polish forced workers in the Third Reich during the Second World War]. Poznan: Wydawn. Poznańskie, 1974.

Luft, Stefan. *Abschied von Multikulti: Weg aus der Integrationskrise* [Farewell to multi-culti: The way out of the integration crisis]. Augsburg: Resch-Verlag, 2006.

Lundström, Catrin. *Svenska latinas: Ras, klass och kön i svenskhetens geografi.* Göteborg: Makadam, 2007.

Lynn, Richard. *Race Differences in Intelligence: An Evolutionary Analysis.* Augusta, GA: Washington Summit Publishers, 2006.

Maira, Sunaina. "Henna and Hip Hop: The Politics of Cultural Production and the Work of Cultural Studies." *Journal of Asian American Studies* 3 (October 2000): 329–69.

Malchow, Barbara, Keyumars Tayebi, and Ulrike Brand. *Die fremden Deutschen: Aussiedler in der Bundesrepublik* [The foreign Germans: Resettlers in the FRG]. Reinbek: Rowohlt, 1990.

Malkki, Liisa. "National Geographic: The Rooting of Peoples and the Territorialization of National Identity among Scholars and Refugees." *Cultural Anthropology* 7 (February 1992): 24–44.

Mandel, Ruth. *Cosmopolitan Anxieties: Turkish Challenges to Citizenship and Belonging in Germany.* Durham, NC: Duke University Press, 2008.

Maniam, Mani, Vijay Patel, Satnam Singh, and Chris Robinson. "Race and Ethnicity." In *Doing Research with Children and Young People,* edited by Sandy Fraser et al., 222–35. London: Sage, 2004.

Mannheim, Karl. *The Problem of Generations.* In *Collected Works of Karl Mannheim.* Vol. 5, 276–320. London: Routledge,

1997; orig. *Das Problem der Generationen,* in *Kölner Vier teljaheres Hefte für Soziologie,* 276–320, 1928.

Marcus, Jonathan. *The National Front and French Politics: The Resistible Rise of Jean-Marie Le Pen.* New York: NYU Press, 1995.

Marshall, Barbara. *Europe in Change: The New Germany and Migration in Europe.* Manchester: Manchester University Press, 2000.

Martin, Mildred Crowl. *Chinatown's Angry Angel: The Story of Donaldina Cameron.* Palo Alto, CA: Pacific Books, 1977.

Martinot, Steve. *The Rule of Racialization: Class, Identity, Governance.* Philadelphia: Temple University Press, 2003.

Maynes, Mary Jo, Jennifer L. Pierce, and Barbara Laslett. *Telling Stories: Use of Personal Narratives in Social Sciences and History.* Ithaca, NY: Cornell University Press, 2007.

McClain, Charles J. *In Search of Equality: The Chinese Struggle against Discrimination in Nineteenth-century America.* Berkeley: University of California Press, 1994.

McCunn, Ruthanne Lum. *Thousand Pieces of Gold.* San Francisco: Design Enterprises, 1981.

McKeown, Adam. *Chinese Migrant Networks and Cultural Change: Peru, Chicago, Hawaii, 1900–1918.* Chicago: University of Chicago Press, 2001.

Meier-Braun, Karl-Heinz. *Deutschland, Einwanderungsland.* Frankfurt am Main: Suhrkamp, 2002.

———. *"Gastarbeiter" oder Einwanderer?* Berlin: Ullstein, 1980.

Melucci, Alberto. *The Playing Self: Person and Meaning in the Planetary Society.* Cambridge: Cambridge University Press, 1996.

Miera, Frauke. "Transnationalisierung sozialer Räume?" [Transnationalism in social spaces?]. In *Die Migration von Polen nach Deutschland,* edited by Chris-

toph Pallaske. Baden-Baden: Nomos Verlagsgesellschaft, 2001.

Miles, Robert. *Racism after 'Race Relations'.* New York: Routledge, 1993.

Miller, Carol T., and Brenda Major. "Coping with Stigma and Prejudice." In *The Social Psychology of Stigma,* edited by Todd F. Heatherton, Robert E. Kleck, Michelle R. Hebl, and Jay G. Hull, 243–60. New York: Guildford Press, 2000.

Miller, David. *Citizenship and National Identity.* Cambridge: Polity Press, 2000.

Miller, Stuart C. *The Unwelcome Immigrant: The American Image of the Chinese, 1785–1882.* Berkeley: University of California Press, 1969.

Misheva, Vessela Ivanova. "Shame and Guilt: Sociology as a Poietic System." Diss., Uppsala University, Department of Sociology, 2000.

Moaveni, Azadeh. *Lipstick Jihad: A Memoir of Growing Up Iranian in America and American in Iran.* New York: Public Affairs Press, 2005.

Modood, Tariq. *Multicultural Politics: Racism, Ethnicity and Muslims in Britain.* Edinburgh: Edinburgh University Press, 2005.

Morgenstern, Christine. *Rassismus: Konturen einer Ideologie: Einwanderung im politischen Diskurs der Bundesrepublik Deutschland.* Hamburg: Argument Verlag, 2002.

Morrison, Toni. "Home." In *The House that Race Built,* edited by Wahneema Lubiano, 3–12. New York: Vintage Books, 1998.

Moustakas, Clark. *Phenomenological Research Methods.* Thousand Oaks, CA: Sage, 1994.

Murphy, Richard. *Gastarbeiter im Deutschen Reich: Polen in Bottrop 1891–1933* [Guest workers in the German Reich: Poles in Bottrop, 1891–1933]. Wuppertal: P. Hammer, 1982.

Muslims in Europe: A Report on 11 EU Cities. New York, London, Budapest: Open Society Institute, 2010.

Nazpary, Joma [Jakob Rigi]. *Post-Soviet Chaos: Violence and Dispossession in Kazakhstan*. Sterling, VA: Pluto Press, 2002.

Nee, Victor G., and Brett deBary. *Longtime Californ': A Documentary Study of an American Chinatown*. New York: Pantheon, 1973.

Nomani, Asra Q. *Standing Alone in Mecca: An American Women's Struggle for the Soul of Islam*. San Francisco: Harper Collins, 2005.

Nugmanova, K. "Yazik i grazhdanskoe samosoznanie v grazhdanskom obshestve" [Language and civil consciousness in civil society]. *Sayasat-Policy* 5 (2003).

Nwankwo, Arthur Agwuncha, and Samuel Udochukwu Ifejika. *Biafra: The Making of a Nation*. New York: Praeger, 1969.

O'Biken, Donaka. *Kazahizatciya i yazikovaya politika v Post-Sovetskom Kazakhstane* [Kazakhization and language politics in post-Soviet Kazakhstan]. 2007.

Obracht-Prondzyński, Cezary. *Kaszubi: Między dyskryminacją a regionalną podmiotowością*. Gdańsk: Instytut Kaszubski w Gdańsku, 2002.

Okitikpi, Toyin. *Working with Children of Mixed Parentage*. Lyme Regis, U.K.: Russell House, 2005.

Olumide, Jill. *Raiding the Gene Pool: The Social Construction of Mixed Race*. London: Pluto Press, 2002.

Omi, Michael, and Howard Winant. *Racial Formation in the United States*. 2d ed. New York: Routledge, 1994.

Ong, Aihwa. *Flexible Citizenship: The Cultural Logics of Transnationality*. Durham, NC: Duke University Press, 1999.

Ordover, Nancy. *American Eugenics: Race, Queer Anatomy, and the Science of Nationalism*. Minneapolis: University of Minnesota Press, 2003.

Owen, Charlie. "'Mixed Race' in Official Statistics." In *Rethinking 'Mixed Race'*, edited by David Parker and Miri Song, 134–153. London: Pluto Press, 2001.

Özdemir, Cem. *Currywurst und Döner: Integration in Deutschland*. Bergisch Gladbach: G. Lübeck, 1999.

———. *Ich bin Inländer: Ein anatolischer Schwabe im Bundestag*. Munich: Deutscher Taschenbuch Verlag, 1997.

Painter, Nell Irvin. *The History of White People*. New York: Norton, 2010.

Pallaske, Christoph, ed. *Die Migration von Polen nach Deutschland: zu Geschichte und Gegenwart eines europaischen Migrationssystems* [Migration from Poland to Germany. A European migration system in past and present]. Baden-Baden: Nomos Verlagsgesellschaft, 2001.

———. *Migrationen aus Polen in die Bundesrepublik Deutschland in den 1980er und 1990er Jahren: Migrationsverläufe und Eingliederungsprozesse in sozialgeschichtlicher Perspektive* [Migration from Poland to FRG during the 1980s and 1990s: Migration characteristics and integration processes from the social-historical perspective]. Münster; New York: Waxmann, 2002.

Pan, Lynn. *Sons of the Yellow Emperor: A History of the Chinese Diaspora*. Tokyo: Kodansha, 1994.

Panier, Katrin. *Zu Hause ist, wo ich verliebt bin: Ausländische Jugendliche in Deutschland erzählen* [Home is where I am loved: Foreign youth in Germany speak]. [Berlin]: Schwarzkopf und Schwarzkopf, [2004].

Papastergiadis, Nikos. *The Turbulence of Migration*. Cambridge: Polity Press, 2000.

Parekh, Bhikhu. *Rethinking Multiculturalism: Cultural Diversity and Political Theory*. London: Palgrave, 2000.

Parreñas, Rhacel Salazar. *Servants of Globalization: Women, Migration, and Domestic Work*. Stanford, CA: Stanford University Press, 2001.

Paul, Kathleen. *Whitewashing Britain: Race and Citizenship in the Postwar Era*. Ithaca, NY: Cornell University Press, 1997.

Peabody, Sue, and Tyler Stovall, eds. *The Color of Liberty: Histories of Race in France*. Durham, NC: Duke University Press, 2003.

Peck, Jeffrey M. "Rac(e)ing the Nation: Is There a German 'Home'?" *New Formations* 17 (1992): 75–84.

Peffer, George Anthony. *If They Don't Bring Their Women Here: Chinese Female Immigration before Exclusion*. Urbana: University of Illinois Press, 1999.

Pellander, Saara. *Aasialainen sukutausta, suomalainen elämä: Naisten kokemuksia ja tulkintoja toiseudesta* [Asian family background, Finnish life: Women's experiences and interpretations of Otherness]. Web Reports Series of the Finnish Institute of Migration, Web Report No. 27 (2007).

———. "Sending and Receiving, Welcoming and Excluding: Developments and Debates in Finland's Migration Policy." In *Debating Migration: Political Discourses on Labour Immigration in Historical Perspective*, edited by Stefanie Mayer and Mikael Spång, 128–36. Innsbruck: StudienVerlag, 2009.

Peltonen, Matti. "Omakuvamme murroskohdat: Maisema ja kieli suomalaisuuskäsitysten perusaineksina" [Turning points of our self-perception: Landscape and language as main elements of concepts of Finnishness]. In *Elävänä Euroopassa. Muuttuva suomalainen identiteetti*, edited by Pertti Alasuutari and Petri Ruuska. Tampere: Vastapaino, 1998.

Perritt, Henry H., Jr. *The Road to Independence for Kosovo*. Cambridge: Cambridge University Press, 2009.

Perry, Pamela. "White Means Never Having to Say You're Ethnic: White Youth and the Construction of 'Cultureless' Identities." *Journal of Contemporary Ethnography* 30.1 (2001): 56–91.

Peruzzi, Gaia. *Amori possibili: Le coppie miste nella provincia italiana*. Milano: FrancoAngeli, 2008.

Pfaelzer, Jean. *Driven Out: The Forgotten War against Chinese Americans*. New York: Random House, 2007.

Pieke, Frank. *Recent Trends in Chinese Migration to Europe: Fujianese Migration in Perspective*. Migration Research Series 6. Geneva: International Organization for Migration, 2002.

Pina-Guerassimoff, Carine. "La Chine et les Nouveaux Migrants Chinois en Europe." *Migrations Société* 15.89 (2003): 21–28.

Piper, Nicola. *Racism, Nationalism, and Citizenship: Ethnic Minorities in Britain and Germany*. Aldershot, U.K.: Ashgate, 1998.

Platt, Lucinda. *Ethnicity and Family. Relationships within and between Groups: An Analysis Using the Labour Force Survey*. Essex: Institute for Social & Economic Research, University of Essex, 2009.

Polikowska, Katarzyna. "Die deutsche Minderheit in Polen, die Polen in Deutschland" [German minority in Poland, Poles in Germany]. In *Standpunkte: Zum Verständnis deutsch-polnischer Probleme* [Standpoints: Understanding the Polish-German problems], edited by Wolfgang Drost and Marek Jaroszewski. Siegen: Universität Siegen, 1999.

Portelli, Alessandro. "The Problem of the Color-Blind: Notes on the Discourse of Race in Italy." In *Race and Nation: Ethnic Systems in the Modern World*, edited by Paul Spickard, 355–63. New York: Routledge, 2005.

Portes, Alejandro. "Immigration Theory for a New Century: Some Problems and Opportunities." *International Migration Review* 31.4 (1997): 799–825.

———, ed. *The New Second Generation*. New York: Russell Sage Fundation, 1996.

Portes, Alejandro, Patricia Fernández-Kelly, and William Haller. "The Adaptation of the Immigrant Second Generation in America: A Theoretical

Overview and Recent Evidence." *Journal of Ethnic and Migration Studies* 35.7 (2009): 1077–1104.

Portes, Alejandro, and Rubén G. Rumbaut. "Introduction: The Second Generation and the Children of Immigrants Longitudinal Study." *Ethnic and Racial Studies* 28.6 (2005): 983–99.

———. *Legacies: The Story of the Immigrant Second Generation.* Berkeley: University of California Press, 2001.

Portes, Alejandro, and Julia Sensenbrenner. "Embeddedness and Immigration: Notes on the Social Determinants of Economic Action." *The American Journal of Sociology* 98.6 (1993): 1320–50.

Prashad, Vijay. *Everybody Was Kung Fu Fighting: Afro-Asian Connections and the Myth of Cultural Purity.* Boston: Beacon, 2002.

Pred, Allan. *Even in Sweden: Racisms, Racialized Spaces, and the Popular Geographical Imagination.* Berkeley: University of California Press, 2000.

Pugliese, Enrico. *L'Italia tra migrazioni internazionali e migrazioni interne.* Bologna: Il Mulino, 2002.

Purkayastha, Bandana. *Negotiating Ethnicity: Second-Generation South Asian Americans Traverse a Transnational World.* New Brunswick, NJ: Rutgers University Press, 2005.

Quiroz, Pamela Anne. "Color-blind Individualism, Intercountry Adoption and Public Policy." *Journal of Sociology and Social Welfare* 34.2 (2007): 57–68.

Raj, Dhooleka Sarhadi. *Where Are You From? Middle-class Migrants in the Modern World.* Berkeley: University of California Press, 2003.

Rastas, Anna. "Am I Still 'White'? Dealing with the Colour Trouble." *Balayi: Culture, Law and Colonialism* 6 (2004): 94–106.

———. "Katseilla merkityt, silminnähden erilaiset: Lasten ja nuorten kokemuksia rodullistavista katseista" [Visibly different, marked by gazes: Children's and young people's experiences of receiving racist stares]. *Nuorisotutkimus* 20/3 (2002): 3–17.

———. "Miksi rasismin kokemuksista on niin vaikea puhua?" [Why young people do not talk about their experiences of racism]. In *Puhua vastaan ja vaieta. Neuvottelu kulttuurisista marginaaleista,* edited by Arja Jokinen, Laura Huttunen, and Anna Kulmala. Helsinki: Gaudeamus, 2004.

———. "Racializing Categorization among Young People in Finland." *Young: Nordic Journal of Youth Research* 13 (May 2005): 147–66.

———. "Racism in the Everyday Life of Finnish Children with Transnational Roots." *Barn* 27 (April 2009): 29–43.

———. "Rasismi lasten ja nuorten arjessa: Transnationaalit juuret ja monikulttuuristuva Suomi" [Racism in the everyday life of children and young people: Transnational roots and multicultural Finland in the making]. PhD diss., University of Tampere, 2007.

———. "Writing Our Future History Together: Applying Participatory Methods in Research on African Diaspora in Finland." In *Afroeurope@n Configurations: Readings and Projects,* edited by Sabrina Brancato, 98–120. Newcastle upon Tyne, U.K.: Cambridge Scholars Publishing, 2011.

Rastas, Anna, Laura Huttunen, and Olli Löytty, eds. *The Finnish Guestbook: How to Deal with Multiculturalism.* Tampere: Vastapaino, 2005.

Reagin, Nancy R. "German *Brigadoon*? Domesticity and Metropolitan Perceptions of *Auslandsdeutschen* in Southwest Africa and Eastern Europe." In *The Heimat Abroad: The Boundaries of Germanness,* edited by Krista O'Donnell, Renate Bridenthal, and Nancy Reagin, 248–66. Ann Arbor: University of Michigan Press, 2005.

Reimers, Eva. "'En av vår tids martyrer':
Fadime Sahindal som mediehändelse."
In *Olikhetens paradigm: Intersektionella
perspektiv på o(jäm)likhetsskapande,*
edited by Paulina de los Reyes and Lena
Martinsson, 141–59. Lund: Studentlitteratur, 2005.

Rocha da Silva, Pascal. "La Population
Chinoise En Suisse Dans L'ère De La
Globalisation." MA thesis, Université
de Genève, 2007.

Romania, Vincenzo. *Farsi passare per
italiani. Strategie di mimetismo sociale.*
Roma: Carocci, 2004.

Root, Maria P. P. "A Bill of Rights for Racially Mixed People." In *Race Critical
Theories,* edited by Philomena Essed
and Theo Goldberg, 355–68. Oxford:
Blackwell, 2002.

———. "Within, between, and beyond
Race." In *Racial Mixed People in Amer-
ica,* edited by Maria P. P. Root, 3–11.
Newbury Park, CA: Sage, 1992.

Rorty, Richard. *Contingency, Irony and
Solidarity.* Cambridge: Cambridge University Press, 1989.

Rushton, J. Philippe. *Race, Evolution, and
Behavior.* New Brunswick, NJ: Transaction Publishers, 1997.

Ruuska, Petri. "Toisen nahoissa ja vähän
sanoissakin" [In the skin and sayings
of the other]. In *Suomi toisin sanoen,*
edited by Mikko Lehtonen, Olli Löytty,
and Petri Ruuska, 208–20. Tampere:
Vastapaino, 2004.

Sackmann, Rosemarie. "Migranten und
Aufnahmegesellschaft" [Migrants and
the receiving society]. In *Zuwanderung
und Städtentwicklung* [Immigration and
urban development], edited by Hartmut Häussermann and Ingrid Oswald,
42–59. Opladen, Wiesbaden: VS Verlag
für Sozialwissenschaften, 1997.

Saloutos, Theodore. *They Remember
America: The Story of the Repatriated
Greek-Americans.* Berkeley: University
of California Press, 1956.

Sandmeyer, Elmer Clarence. *The Anti-
Chinese Movement in California.* Urbana:
University of Illinois Press, 1973; orig.
1939.

Sarrazin, Thilo. *Deutschland schafft sich ab:
Wie wir unser Land auf Spiel setzen.* Berlin: Deutsche Verlags-anstalt, 2010.

Saukkonen, Pasi. "Kansallinen identiteetti" [National identity]. In *Nationalismit,*
edited by Jussi Pakkasvirta and Pasi
Saukkonen. Helsinki: Werner Söderström Osakeyhtiö, 2004.

Sauter, Sven. *Wir sind "Frankfurter
Türken": Adolezente Ablösungsprozesse
in der deutschen Einwanderungsgesellschaft* [We are Frankfurter Turks: Adolescent disconnections in German immigrant society]. Frankfurt am Main:
Brandes und Apsel, 2000.

Sawyer, Lena S. "Black and Swedish: Racialization and the Cultural Politics of
Belonging in Stockholm, Sweden." PhD
diss., University of California, Santa
Cruz, 2000.

Saxton, Alexander. *The Indispensable Enemy: Labor and the Anti-Chinese Movement in California.* Berkeley: University
of California Press, 1971.

Schatz, Edward. *Modern Clan Politics:
The Power of "Blood" in Kazakhstan and
Beyond.* Seattle: University of Wash-
ington Press and Hopkins Fulfillment
Services, 2004.

———. "The Politics of Multiple Identities: Lineage and Ethnicity in Kazakhstan." *Europe-Asia Studies* 52.33 (2000):
489–506.

Schiffauer, Werner. *Parallelgesellschaften.*
Bielefeld: Transcript, 2008.

Scholte, Jan Aart. *Globalization: A Critical
Introduction.* 2d ed. London: Palgrave
Macmillan, 2005.

Schütz, Alfred. *The Phenomenology of the
Social World,* translated by George
Walsh and Fredrick Lehnert. Northwestern University Studies in Phenomenology & Existential Philosophy.

Evanston, IL: Northwestern University Press, 1967.

Selman, Peter. "Intercountry Adoption in the New Millenium: The 'Quiet Migration' Revisited." *Population Research & Policy Review* 21 (2002): 205–25.

Semi, Giovanni, Enzo Colombo, Ilenya Camozzi, Annalisa Frisina. "Practices of Difference: Analysing Multiculturalism in Everyday Life." In *Everyday Multiculturalism*, edited by Amanda Wise and Selvaraj Velayutham, 66–84. London: Palgrave, 2009.

Sen, Faruk, and Hayrettin Aydim. *Islam in Deutschland*. Munich: Beck, 2002.

Sen, Faruk, and Andreas Goldberg. *Türken in Deutschland: Leben zwischen zwei Kulturen*. Munich: Beck, 1994.

Senocak, Zafer. *Atlas of a Tropical Germany*. Lincoln: University of Nebraska Press, 2002.

Shani, Giorgio. *Sikh Nationalism and Identity in a Global Age*. New York: Routledge, 2007.

Shields, J. G. *The Extreme Right in France: From Pétain to Le Pen*. New York: Routledge, 2007.

Siedman, Irving. *Interviewing as Qualitative Research: A Guide for Researchers in Education and the Social Sciences*. 3d ed. New York: Teachers College Press, 2006.

Siikala, Jukka. "The Ethnography of Finland." *Annual Review of Anthropology* 35 (October 2006): 153–170.

Silverstein, Paul A. *Algeria in France: Transpolitics, Race, and Nation*. Bloomington: Indiana University Press, 2004.

Sjögren, Annick. *Här går gränsen: om integritet och kulturella mönster i Sverige och Medelhavsområdet*. 2d ed. Stockholm: Dialogos, 2006.

Skeggs, Beverley. *Formations of Class and Gender: Becoming Respectable*. London: Sage, 1997.

Skeldon, Ronald. *Myths and Realities of Chinese Irregular Migration*. Migration

Research Series 1. Geneva: International Organization for Migration, 2000.

Smith, Anthony D. *The Ethnic Origins of Nations*. Oxford: Blackwell, 1986.

———. "History and National Destiny: Responses and Clarifications." *Nations and Nationalism* 10.1–2 (2004): 195–209.

———. *Nationalism and Modernism*. London: Routledge, 1998.

Sniderman, Paul, and Louk Hagendoorn. *When Ways of Life Collide: Multiculturalism and Its Discontents in the Netherlands*. Princeton, NJ: Princeton University Press, 2007.

Soboczynski, Adam. "Wir Unsichtbaren, Wie funktioniert Integration? Eine ganze Generation polnischer Zuwanderer bemüht sich dabei zu sein, ohne aufzufallen" [We, the invisible. How does integration work? An entire generation of Polish migrants tries to participate without standing out]. *Die Zeit* (August 17, 2006).

Song, Miri. *Choosing Ethnic Identity*. Cambridge: Polity Press, 2003.

Soysal, Levent, and Ayse Çaglar, eds. *Forty Years of Turkish Migration to Germany: Issues, Reflections, and Futures*. Special issue of *New Perspectives on Turkey* 28–29 (Spring–Fall 2003).

Spickard, Paul. *Almost All Aliens: Immigration, Race, and Colonialism in American History and Identity*. New York: Routledge, 2007.

———. "Managing Multiculturalism: America's Identity, Japan's Task?" *Civilizations* 11–12 (2007): 23–32.

———. "What's Critical about White Studies." In *Racial Thinking in the United States*, edited by Paul Spickard and G. Reginald Daniel, 248–74. Notre Dame, IN: University of Notre Dame Press, 2004.

———, ed. *Race and Nation: Ethnic Systems in the Modern World*. New York: Routledge, 2005.

Stankiewicz, Katharina. "Migranten aus Polen – unsichtbar gemacht? Die Folgen der Aussiedlerkategorisierung im Schatten der deutschen Einwanderungs- und Integrationspolitik" [Migrants from Poland – made invisible?] Frankfurt: Diplomarbeit, Europa Universität Viadrina, 2003.

Stainton Rogers, Wendy. "Constructing Childhood, Constructing Child Concern." In *Children in Society*, edited by Pam Foley, Jeremy Roche, and Stan Tucker, 26–33. New York: Palgrave, 2001.

Stern, Alexandra. *Eugenic Nation: Faults and Frontiers of Better Breeding in Modern America*. Berkeley: University of California Press, 2005.

Stoddard, Lothrop. *The Rising Tide of Color against White World-Supremacy*. New York: Scribner's, 1923.

Strand Runsten, Pia. "'Hedersmord,' eurocentrism och etnicitet: Mordet på Fadime – en fallstudie." In *Mediernas Vi Och Dom*, edited by Leonor Camauër and Stig Arne Nohrstedt. Rapport av Utredningen om makt, integration och strukturell diskriminering, SOU 2006:21. Stockholm: Statens Offentliga Utredningar, 2006.

Sultan, Masuda. *My War at Home*. New York: Washington Square Press, 2006.

Synak, Brunon. "The Kashubes Ethnic Identity: Continuity and Change." In *The Ethnic Identities of European Minorities: Theory and Case Studies*, edited by Brunon Synak, 155–166. Gdańsk: Wydawnictwo Uniwersytetu Gdańskiego, 1995.

Szpony, Anna. "Separatyzm czy regionalizm." *Pomerania* 12 (2006).

Sztanke, Michael. "Pékin-Paris: L'étudiant Chinois Est Il Une Marchangise?" *Hommes et migrations* 1254 (2005): 74–81.

Tajfel, Henri. *Human Groups and Social Categories: Studies in Social Psychology*. Cambridge: Cambridge University Press, 1981.

Tasman, Nilgün. *Ich träume deutsch . . . und wache Türkisch auf: Eine Kindheit in zwei Welten* [I dream in German . . . and wake up Turkish: A childhood in two worlds]. Freiburg: Herder, 2008.

Tatla, Darshan. "A Race Apart? The Paradox of Sikh Ethnicity and Nationalism." In *Race and Nation: Ethnic Systems in the Modern World*, edited by Paul Spickard, 299–318. New York: Routledge, 2005.

Tatla, Darshan Singh. *The Sikh Diaspora: The Search for Statehood*. London: UCL Press, 1999.

Tavan, Gwenda. *The Long, Slow Death of White Australia*. Carlton North, AU: Scribe Publications, 2005.

Taylor, Stephanie. *Narratives of Identity and Place*. London: Routledge, 2009.

Terkessidis, Mark. *Die Banalität des Rassismus: Migranten zweiter Generation entwickeln eine neue Perspektive* [The banality of racism: Second-generation migrants develop a new perspective]. Bielefeld: Transcript Verlag, 2004.

———. *Migranten*. Hamburg: Rotbuch, 2000.

Thoburn, June, Liz Norford, and Stephen Parvez Rashid. *Permanent Family Placement for Children of Minority Ethnic Origin*. London: Jessica Kingsley Publishers, 2000.

Thomas, Elaine R. "Keeping Identity at a Distance: Explaining France's New Legal Restrictions on the Islamic Headscarf." *Ethnic and Racial Studies* 29.2 (2006): 237–59.

Tibi, Bassam. *Arab Nationalism: Between Islam and the Nation-State*. 3d ed. New York: Palgrave Macmillan, 1997.

Tong, Benson. *Unsubmissive Women: Chinese Prostitutes in Nineteenth-Century San Francisco*. Norman: University of Oklahoma Press, 1994.

Towns, Ann. "Paradoxes of (in)Equality: Something Is Rotten in the Gender Equal State of Sweden." *Cooperation and Conflict* 37 (2002): 157–79.

Trask, Haunani-Kay. *From a Native Daughter: Colonialism and Sovereignty in Hawai'i.* Monroe, ME: Common Courage Press, 1993.

Triandis, Harry C. *Individualism and Collectivism.* Boulder, CO: Westview Press, 1995.

Tuan, Mia. *Forever Foreigners or Honorary Whites? The Asian Ethnic Experience Today.* New Brunswick, NJ: Rutgers University Press, 1998.

Tucker, William H. *The Science and Politics of Racial Research.* Urbana: University of Illinois Press, 1994.

Umana-Taylor, Adriana, Ruchi Bhanot, and Nana Shin. "Ethnic Identity Formation during Adolescence: The Critical Role of Families." *Journal of Family Issues* 27 (March 2006): 390–414.

Van den Berghe, Pierre L. *The Ethnic Phenomenon.* New York: Elsevier, 1981.

Vertovec, Steven. "Conceiving and Researching Transnationalism." *Ethnic and Racial Studies* 22.2 (1999): 447–62.

———. *Transnationalism.* London: Routledge, 2009.

Virkki, Heidi. "Suomalaisuuden peilissä. Kansainvälisesti adoptoitujen nuorten kokemuksia suomalaisuudesta ja erilaisuudesta" [In the mirror of Finnishness. Experiences of trans-nationally adopted youth on Finnishness and otherness]. MA thesis, University of Tampere, 2006.

Vuorela, Ulla, and Anna Rastas. "With Near and Distant Kin: Growing Up in Transnational Families." Paper presented at the EASA (European Association of Social Anthropologists) Conference, August 26–30, 2008, Ljubljana.

Wang, Hong-zen, and Shu-ming Chang. "The Commodification of International Marriages: Cross-border Marriage Business in Taiwan and Viet Nam." *International Migration* 40.6 (2002): 93–116.

Warmińska, Katarzyna. *Tatarzy polscy: Tożsamość religijna i etniczna.* Kraków: Universitas, 1999.

Webster, Yehudi O. *The Racialization of America.* New York: St. Martin's, 1992.

Weidacher, Alois, ed. *In Deutschland zu Hause: Politische Orientierungen griechischer, italienischer, türkischer und deutswcher junger Erwachsener im Vergleich* [At home in Germany: Comparing the political orientations of Greek, Italian, Turkish, and German youth]. Opladen: Leske und Budrich, 2000.

Weiner, Michael, ed. *Japan's Minorities: The Illusion of Homogeneity.* 2d ed. New York: Routledge, 2008.

Werner, Hans. *Imagined Homes: Soviet Immigrants in Two Cities.* Winnipeg: University of Manitoba Press, 2007.

Werner, Jan. *Die Invasion der Armen: Asylanten und illegale Einwanderer.* Mainz: Hase and Koehler, 1992.

West, Cornel. "The New Cultural Politics of Difference." In *Out There: Marginalization and Contemporary Cultures,* edited by Russell Fergusson, Martha Gever, Trinh Minh-ha, and Cornel West, 19–38. Cambridge, MA: MIT Press, 1992.

Wikan, Unni. *En fråga om heder.* Stockholm: Ordfront, 2004.

Willcox, Walter F., ed. *International Migrations.* 2 vols. New York: Gordon and Breach, 1969.

Wilson, Edward O. *Sociobiology: The New Synthesis.* Cambridge, MA: Harvard University Press, 1975.

Wimmer, Andreas, and Nina Glick Schiller. "Methodological Nationalism and Beyond: Nation-State Building, Migration and the Social Sciences." *Global Networks* 2 (2002): 301–34.

Wise, Amanda, and Selvaraj Velayutham, eds. *Everyday Multiculturalism.* Basingstoke, U.K.: Palgrave Macmillan, 2009.

Wise, Tim. *White like Me: Reflections on Race from a Privileged Son.* Brooklyn, NY: Soft Skull Press, 2005.

Wolff-Poweska, Anna. "Paradigmen der gegenseitigen Wahrnehmung von Deutschen, Russen und Polen" [Paradigms of mutual perception, Germans, Russians, and Poles]. In *Die deutsch-polnischen Beziehungen: Bilanz nach fünf Jahren Nachbarschaft* [German-Polish relations: accounts of five years of neighborship], edited by Claus Montag and Andrzej Sakson, 23–32. Potsdam: Brandenburgische Landeszentrale für Politische Bildung, 1996.

Wong, Jade Snow. *Fifth Chinese Daughter.* New York: Harper, 1950.

Woodward, Kath. "Questions of Identity." In *Questioning Identity: Gender, Class, Ethnicity*, 2d ed., edited by Kath Woodward, 5–42. London: Routledge, 2004.

Xing, Jun. *Asian America through the Lens.* Walnut Creek, CA: AltaMira Press, 1998.

Yang, Wenzhong Eric. "Chinese Language Maintenance: A Study of Chinese-American Parental Perceptions and Activities." *Journal of Chinese Overseas* 3.2 (2007): 220–38.

Yngvesson, Barbara. "Going 'Home': Adoption, Loss of Bearings, and the Mythology of Roots." In *Cultures of Transnational Adoption*, edited by Toby Volkman, 25–48. Durham, NC: Duke University Press, 2005.

Yoors, Jan. *The Gypsies.* New York: Simon and Schuster, 1983; orig. 1967.

Yung, Judy. *Unbound Feet: A Social History of Chinese Women in San Francisco.* Berkeley: University of California Press, 1995.

Yung, Judy, Gordon H. Chang, and Him Mark Lai, eds. *Chinese American Voices: From the Gold Rush to the Present.* Berkeley: University of California Press, 2006.

Yutang, Lin. *Chinatown Family.* New York: John Day, 1948.

Yuval-Davis, Nira. "Intersectionality, Citizenship and Contemporary Politics of Belonging." *Critical Review of International Social and Political Philosophy* 10.4 (2007): 561–74.

Zhang, Guochu. "Migration of Highly Skilled Chinese to Europe: Trends and Perspective." *International Migration* 41.3 (2003): 73–97.

Zhao, Xiaojian. *Remaking Chinese America: Immigration, Family, and Community, 1940–1965.* New Brunswick, NJ: Rutgers University Press, 2002.

Zhou, Min. "Growing Up American: The Challenge Confronting Immigrant Children and Children of Immigrants." *Annual Review of Sociology* 23 (1997): 63–95.

Ziegler, Charles E. "Civil Society, Political Stability and Economic Development in Kazakhstan." Paper presented at the ISA Annual Convention, San Francisco, March 26–29, 2008.

Zurcher, Erik J. *The Young Turk Legacy and Nation Building: From the Ottoman Empire to Ataturk's Turkey.* London: I.B. Tauris, 2010.

Contributors

ENZO COLOMBO is a professor of intercultural relations at the University of Milan. He is currently doing research on youth and children of immigrants in Italy, as well as on racism, social construction of Otherness, and the transformation of citizenship. He is interested in the theoretical definition of everyday multiculturalism. On these topics, he has published *Children of Immigrants in a Globalized World* (Palgrave, 2013, with Paola Rebughini); "Crossing Difference: How Young Children of Immigrants Keep Everyday Multiculturalism Alive," *Journal of Intercultural Studies* 31.5 (2010); and "Changing Citizenship: Everyday Representation of Membership, Belonging and Identification among Italian Senior Secondary School Students," *Italian Journal of Sociology of Education* 4.1 (2010).

MIRA FOSTER received her master's degree in history and social sciences from the University of Bremen, Germany. She has recently received a PhD in public history from the University of California, Santa Barbara. Her research focuses on migration experiences and memories of Polish immigrants to Germany during the second half of the twentieth century.

SERINE GUNNARSSON is a PhD student in sociology at Uppsala University in Sweden. Her interests draw mainly on social identity–related questions, such as ethnic and gender relations, from a social psychological perspective. Her PhD research focuses on social identity processes and lived experiences among young women of Middle Eastern backgrounds in Sweden, based on qualitative interviews conducted with young women either born in Sweden to immigrant parents or immigrants themselves.

After a degree in sinology, FLORENCE LÉVY is now a PhD student in sociology in Ecole des Hautes Etudes en Sciences Sociales (EHESS, Paris, France) and in Neuchatel University (Switzerland). Her PhD thesis analyzes the gender dimensions of contemporary northern Chinese migration to France and the transnational dynamics of its social networks. She uses anthropological methods to collect accounts of migrants and to understand how they experience and give sense to the constant change of their migratory projects. Her fields of expertise are in sinology, gender, and migration studies.

MARYLÈNE LIEBER is an associate professor of sociology at the Institute for Gender Studies of the University of Geneva. After studying Chinese migration in France and Switzerland for several years, she is now working on the making of labor rights in the electronics industry in southern China. She is the author of several articles and coeditor of *Cachez ce travail que je ne saurais voir: Ethnographies du travail du sexe* (2010) and *Chinoises au XXIème siècle. Ruptures et continuités* (2012).

KARINA MUKAZHANOVA has earned MA degrees from Karaganda State University (Kazakhstan) in philosophy and psychology and from University of Oregon (United States) in international studies. She has also studied at Lund University in Sweden. She has published several papers on the phenomenon and philosophy of marginality.

SAARA PELLANDER is a PhD candidate in the Department of Political and Economic Studies, University of Helsinki, Finland. She has studied at the Philipps-Universität Marburg, Germany, and at the University of Turku, Finland, and has been a guest researcher at Stockholm University in Sweden. Her research interests are gender and migration. She is currently working on her PhD thesis on family migration to Finland.

GAIA PERUZZI is a researcher in the sociology of culture and communication at the Faculty of Political Sciences, Sociology, Communication of Sapienza University of Rome. She is currently doing research on young immigrants in Italy and on media and migration. Her publications about immigration include *Amori possibili: Le coppie miste nella provincia italiana* (2008); and "The Adult Youth: Notes for a New Profile of Immigrant Girls in Italy" (2011).

ANNA RASTAS has been working as a researcher, lecturer, and assistant professor of social anthropology at the University of Tampere since 2001. She is currently working as a Research Fellow in the Fluid World Research Development Programme, and her ongoing research projects focus on the ethics and politics of knowledge production in research on minorities. She is also a member of the international Afro-European Cultures and Identities research group (University of León), and her studies on the African diaspora in Finland and in Europe continue her previous ethnographic studies favoring action research approaches. She has published several articles and chapters, both in Finland and internationally, on racism and racialized identities, representations of Africans and the African diaspora in Finland, and ethnographic research methods. She has coedited two books on racism and multiculturalism, and is currently editing a book on literature for children in multiethnic, multicultural societies.

PAOLA REBUGHINI is a professor of sociology and intercultural communication at the University of Milan. She is currently doing research on children of immigrants, as well as on social movements. She is interested in the theoretical definition of identity and subjectivity. On these topics, she has published *Children of Immigrants in a Globalized World* (Palgrave, 2013, with E. Colombo); "Different but Not Stranger: Everyday Collective Identifications among Adolescent Children of Immigrants in Italy," *Journal of Ethnic and Migration Studies* 35.1 (2009) (with E. Colombo and L. Leonini); and "Critique and Social Movements: Looking Beyond Contingency and Normativity," *European Journal of Social Theory* 13.4 (2010).

PAUL SPICKARD is a professor of history and Asian American studies at the University of California, Santa Barbara. He is the author or editor of sixteen other books and seventy-odd articles, including *Mixed Blood: Intermarriage and Ethnic Identity in Twentieth-Century America* (1989), *Pacific Diaspora: Island Peoples in the United States and across the Pacific* (2002), *Racial Thinking in the United States* (2004), *Race and Nation: Ethnic Systems in the Modern World* (2005), and *Almost All Aliens: Immigration, Race, and Colonialism in American History and Identity* (2007).

KATARZYNA WARMIŃSKA is an anthropologist associated with the Department of Sociology at Cracow University of Economics. Her main interests concentrate on ethnic relations in Poland, identity and politics, and anthropology at home. She has conducted fieldwork among Polish Tatars and Kashubians. She has published over forty articles and one book, *Tatarzy polscy: Tożsamość religijna i etniczna* [Polish Tatars: Religious and Ethnic Identity], 1999.

SAIJA WESTERLUND-COOK has studied sociology and policy research at the University of Bristol and is continuing her PhD in Finland.

Index

discrimination: against adoptees, 184; against Arabs, 11; against Blacks, 11; against Muslims, 9, 10, 11; against Roma, 11–12. *See also* racism
Douai, Fouad, 12

Estonia, immigrants in, 5
ethnic group: as basis for the nation, 3, 4–7, 70–71, 117, 148–50; Germans as, 12, 245–46
ethnic homogeneity, 4, 70–71, 189
ethnicity, 14, 22, 41–57, 134–35; Chinese, 134–56; Finnish, 45, 47, 49–50, 57n5, 63–83; German, 12, 245–46; Kashubian, 116–30; and nationalism, 6, 266–68; and racism, 12–13; Swedish, 88–110; tactic, 209–10; Tatar, 116–30
eugenics, 13
Eurasian integration, 276–78
European Union, 10, 29n11, 164

Fichte, J. G., 6
Finland, 4; adoption in, 163–86; immigrants in, 5, 22–23, 24, 41–57, 63–83
foreigners, perpetual, 14, 63, 70–73, 246
Fortuyn, Pym, 17–18
Foster, Mira, 25, 245
France: birth rate, 7; citizenship rules, 11; discrimination against immigrants, 11–12; discrimination against Muslims, 11–12; discrimination against Roma, 11–12; immigrants in, 5, 7, 11–12, 14; nationalism, 6; racism, 11–12
Freedom Party (the Netherlands), 18
Front National (France), 11

Galvan, Dennis, 276
Gastarbeiter (guest workers), 245–46
Gellner, Ernest, 4
gender: and identity, 80–81, 88–110; and immigration, 22–23, 63–83, 88–110; and intermarriage, 213–40
German ethnicity, 12, 245–60
German *Volk*, 5–6, 245
Germany, 4; anti-racism, 12–13; citizenship rules, 10, 16–17; citizenship test,

16–17; immigrants in, 5, 7, 13–14, 26, 245–60, 290–98
Gobineau, Arthur, Comte de, 13
Gordon, Tuula, 66–67
Grant, Madison, 13
Great Britain. *See* United Kingdom
Greece, immigrants in, 5
Gunnarsson, Serine, 23, 88
Gypsy. See *mustalainen;* Roma

Hague Convention for the Rights of the Child, 165
Haider, Jörg, 16
Henry IV, King of France, 6
Herder, J. G., 6
Herrnstein, Richard, 14, 17
Hirsi Ali, Ayaan, 17
Howe, David, 170–71
Hubinette, Tobias, 182
Hungary, immigrants in, 5
Huntington, Samuel, 20

identity: of adoptees, 177–84; Black, 41–43, 52–53, 58n14; among children, 41–57, 177–80, 188–210; Chinese, 23–24, 134–56; and citizenship, 204–208; divided, 259–60; in Finland, 41–57, 63–83; and gender, 80–81; German, 25; in Italy, 24, 188–210; Kashubian, 118–30; in Kazakhstan, 25, 266–69, 278–87; and language, 23–24, 78, 134–56, 278–84, 296–97; of migrants, 21–22; mixed, in Finland, 41–57, 63–83, 177–80; mixed, in Kazakhstan, 266–76, 284–85; mixed, in Sweden, 92, 107–109; mixed, in United Kingdom, 177–80, 181–83; and place, 74–76; in Poland, 114–30; Polish, 23, 25, 114–30; of second generation, 23, 24, 63–83; versus subjectivity, 22, 41–57; in Sweden, 23, 88–110; in Switzerland, 23–24, 134–56; Tatar, 118–30
immigrants: in Australia, 7; in Austria, 5, 16; in Austro-Hungarian Empire, 5; in Canada, 7; in Croatia, 5; in Czech Republic, 5; in Denmark, 15–16; in Es-

www.ingramcontent.com/pod-product-compliance
Lightning Source LLC
Chambersburg PA
CBHW050333270326
41926CB00016B/3437